THE BUSINESS IMPROVEMENT DISTRICT MOVEMENT

This comprehensive book covers the theory and practice of business improvement districts (BIDs)—partnerships between local communities and governments established to revitalize neighborhoods and catalyze economic development in a region. In this book, author Seth A. Grossman demonstrates the ways in which BIDs work, pull stakeholders together, and acquire funds to manage the difficult process of community revitalization especially in urbanized, threatened town centers. BIDs also blur traditional lines between public and private organizations, and their governance raises critical new questions about democratic representation, accountability, transparency, and responsiveness.

As this book illustrates, BID managers act as public entrepreneurs, and management in the public realm requires community development skills (community planning, organization, and leadership) and economic expertise (jobs, business development, housing, and public infrastructure). Through an in-depth examination of BIDs and their managers we begin to see that the future of public administration might no longer be contained behind the walls of formal government, with an increasing number of public administrators defining and creating public solutions to real life commercial problems. This book is essential reading for all practicing urban and regional administrators and government officials, as well as students studying public administration, public management, and urban and regional politics.

Seth A. Grossman is Executive Director of the Ironbound Business Improvement District in Newark, New Jersey and President of Cooperative Professional Services, a consultancy that provides research, planning, and management services to Business Improvement Districts. He designed and directs the Rutgers University National Center of Public Performance Online BID Management certification program as well as the Business Improvement District Program for the State of New Jersey.

THE BUSINESS IMPROVEMENT DISTRICT MOVEMENT

Contributions to Public Administration and Management

Seth A. Grossman

Routledge
Taylor & Francis Group

NEW YORK AND LONDON

First published 2016
by Routledge
711 Third Avenue, New York, NY 10017

and by Routledge
2 Park Square, Milton Park, Abingdon, Oxon OX14 4RN

Routledge is an imprint of the Taylor & Francis Group, an informa business

© 2016 Taylor & Francis

Library of Congress Cataloging in Publication Data
Names: Grossman, Seth A., author.
   Title: The business improvement district movement : contributions to public administration and management / by Seth A. Grossman.
   Description: New York : Routledge, 2016. | Includes bibliographical references and index.
   Identifiers: LCCN 2015046616| ISBN 9781498747721 (cloth : alk. paper) | ISBN 9781138668898 (pbk. : alk. paper) | ISBN 9781315619040 (ebook)
   Subjects: LCSH: Community development, Urban. | Enterprise zones. | Local government. | Public-private sector cooperation.
   Classification: LCC HN49.C6 G76 2016 | DDC 307.1/4068–dc23
LC record available at http://lccn.loc.gov/2015046616

ISBN: 978-1-498-74772-1 (hbk)
ISBN: 978-1-138-66889-8 (pbk)
ISBN: 978-1-315-61904-0 (ebk)

Typeset in Bembo
by Taylor & Francis Books

Printed and bound in the United States of America by Publishers Graphics, LLC on sustainably sourced paper.

CONTENTS

LIST OF ILLUSTRATIONS

Figures

Tables

Box

ACKNOWLEDGMENTS

I thank Rutgers, the State University of New Jersey and The School of Public Affairs & Administration, the numerous BID managers throughout the United States, Australia, Europe, and Canada (and the world) for their support and participation in conducting necessary research. Special thanks to Marc Holzer, the City of Newark (NJ), the Ironbound Business Improvement District (Newark, NJ), the Bergen-Lyons-Clinton Partnership (BID-Newark, NJ), and the Mount Prospect Partnership (BID-Newark, NJ). Special gratitude to: Lawrence Houston, Jr., Göktug Morçöl, Lorlene Hoyt, Jack W. Meek and Ulf Zimmerman, David Feehan and Marvin Feit, Jerry Mitchell, Morton E. and Sarah N. Grossman, Downtown New Jersey, Inc., the New Jersey Managed Districts Association, the International Downtown Association, International Cities, Town Centres and Communities Society, the Association of Town Center Management, and the American Society for Public Administration.

ABOUT THE AUTHOR

Seth A. Grossman (Ph.D., Public Administration, Rutgers University-Newark, NJ) is the Executive Director of the Ironbound Business Improvement District (IBID) in Newark, NJ (United States), and President of Cooperative Professional Services, a consultancy that provides research, planning, and management services to BIDs. He was a senior planner with the City of Trenton, NJ (United States), and was designer and administrator of the Business Improvement District Program for the State of New Jersey (United States). He is co-founder and Past President of the New Jersey Managed Districts Association (NJMDA), an advocacy organization dedicated to the profession of business district management. He designed and directs the Rutgers University-Newark, NJ, National Center of Public Performance's Institute of Business District Management and the online Business Improvement District Executive Management Certification Program. His research is on partnership governance, BIDs, public–private partnerships, entrepreneurship, and the rise of special districts.

PROLOGUE

Business Improvement Districts (BIDs) are units of sub-government based on special assessment forms of public financing that create a formal public–private partnership and a local self-help mechanism to address revitalization and redevelopment needs of a designated business area. Unlike state or county governments, it is difficult to determine the exact number of BIDs because they are established locally with little reporting requirements to state government and they are continually being created. Yet, it is clear BIDs are a dynamic growth field in government. This book examines how BIDs create synergy and a synthesis of traditional public and private capability to unfold a hybrid new capability that borrows from each sector. We cannot ignore that this synthesis is compelling for some and a concern for others, and grappling with its exact governmental nature is ongoing. There is a general consensus that BIDs work and pull stakeholders together, and acquire needed funds and manage the difficult process of community revitalization, especially in urbanized and viable but threatened town centers. Performance data, however, is not succinct, as a thorough public, private, and customer evaluation method has not been developed or vetted. The chapters in this book go beyond descriptions of the promise of BIDs and keenly address the issue of the performance of BIDs, and how it might be applied to these unique organizations. Lloyd and Peel (2008) speak about "a need for a more sensitive performance tool" that addresses the multidimensional public–private processes that BIDs represent.

Of special interest is the BID manager as a public management entrepreneur, representing a pragmatic form of public administration that is well suited to hybrid management techniques necessary for public–private partnerships to succeed. In a democracy, public administration has often evolved when new aspects of private society became the normal practices of government. Often overlooked, this transformation in government can be described as the private sector taking on public sector accountabilities rather than the public sector deferring to private practice. Public–private partnerships (PPPs) at "the edges of government" are traditionally the method of governmental transformation. The most formal and localized PPPs to emerge in the 20th and 21st centuries as a reaction to the social fragmentation caused by suburbanization and the consequent neglect of America's downtowns are BIDs. This book also examines how BIDs impact our understanding of functional governing partnerships.

BIDs continue to be an emerging phenomenon reshaping the nature of public management, its processes and performance. When we examine the current literature on BIDs there is a concern that BIDs, like other forms of PPPs such as transportation, water, and energy districts, simply privatize public space. Evidence reveals that BIDs are quite different and appear designed to make private endeavors public capabilities. Consequently, business district management appears as a form of public administration. Although it is arguable, the management entities of BIDs are persuasively guided by public rules and purpose and they may be appropriately considered to be quasi-governmental agencies. They tend to act as buffers between more formalized government units but, nonetheless, retain governmental characteristics.

The chapters in this book address functional business as well as governmental aspects of managed business districts (MBDs) in general and BIDs specifically, and the community development orientation of this kind of PPP. BIDs, of course, are accepted as forms of governance, therefore, the idea of such concepts as *private government*—lack of transparency and democratic accountability—are not unique, but are measured in the same vein as those understandings that inform us about local government. From this standpoint, we can begin to discern the functionality of MBDs as a form of public management where private and public attributes of society merge with democratic processes. This is most apparent regarding BIDs. MBDs remind us that democracy has transformative origins in which we find purpose and functionality in the public accountability of private interests. In part, BIDs appear to provide a window into the functionality of public and private sector mutuality as it occurs and provides a means of comprehending our sense of community in a quickly changing world (Hoyt, 2006).

Many public administration scholars, rightly so, call for democratic anchorage regarding BIDs and their MBD counterparts, unfortunately with a pervasive limited understanding of how they actually work let alone the nature of governmental responsibility in business development. There has been little examination of how the public nature of economic and business development defines a community in relation to BIDs specifically and managed public business districts in general. An adversarial relationship is often assumed, or worse a sense of separation, without any evidence other than the machinations of naturally occurring democratic processes, which are often muddled at best and fickle. Upon examination there is something quite different. Fayth Ruffin in her 2010 article, *Collaborative Network Management for Urban Revitalization,* regarding the MBD movement, points out that BIDs represent a new paradigm of cooperation, and consequently, network governance. Critics who apply a theory of traditional business/state segregation (let alone agitation) miss the opportunity to apply observations of a business/state partnership. This partnership works without destroying the traditional social constructs of government or free market business characteristics. BIDs appear to provide a synergy that allows for the evolution of freedom within evolving communities, and for that and their emphasis on management, they are the primary focus of this book.

Management in the public realm also requires community development (community planning, organization, and leadership) and economic expertise (jobs, business development, housing, and public infrastructure) and BIDs are no exception. When BID managers are tied to local business oversight and are responsible for producing direct services with market impact, they succeed by applying an array of partnership building skills in both the private and public sector. BIDs represent a decidedly public choice, a choice by private individuals to organize, leverage community assets, and participate in public accountability. When tied to local government contractually through an ordinance, as well as being a direct recipient of public funds, BIDs are neither purely independent nor a privatization of public service. They represent a new manner of providing public services in the form of entrepreneurial public management, translating typically governmentally centralized services to special localized needs and applying business acumen to communal activities. Public entrepreneurship has the element of direct investment at the neighborhood level. This might explain why entities like small businesses with traditional tax aversion subscribe to the creation of BIDs.

The traditional way of addressing community development needs has been by either providing money for a project or identifying some singular need or problem and organizing an effort to meet it or resolve it. This is a fix-it model of community development, well suited when something is actually broken, but poorly suited when the problems in a community have to do with enhancing the systemic organizational networks of the community. Carol Becker in her 2010 article, *Self-Determination, Accountability Mechanisms, and Quasi-Governmental Status,* discusses how PPPs have arisen as another way that strengthens and broadens unity within a community. PPPs develop out of the recognition that there is greater power available in communities through their neighborhood, towns, business organizations, and corporations than the people involved often realize. This collective power resides in the relational purpose—the networks—expressed and acted on as a functioning and real dialogue between community stakeholders.

PPPs are essential mechanisms of governance and as MBDs (specifically BIDs) they act as street level community development networks that unite communities, their sponsors and volunteers around a shared vision of community value and an accepted direction that expresses those values. The special power of partnering provides a significant competitive advantage and breakthrough results. The combination can be nothing less than transformational. Public-oriented partnerships work by bringing people together to solve common problems, develop agreements, and manage those agreements with a commitment over time.

Transformation is a form of performance that stresses outcomes and the sustainability of public process. Public administration and government processes also harness the work and products of transformation by changing private attributes into public accountability, independence into interdependence, commitment into action, and disagreement into agreement. Beyond compromise is the integral promise of multi-sectoral partnerships that break through assumed rational limitations. When this breakthrough occurs and without losing the ability to disagree or complain, communities improve and deliver on their promises. At the crux of this process is the entrepreneurial public administrator, exemplified by the BID manager. The business district manager forges, facilitates, and uses not only new approaches to what is valuable in a community but does this by managing a PPP that unites disparate forces in society.

In determining the success of MBDs, we must measure the quality, accountability, and accessibility of the partnerships they keep. Achieving the ability to be an effective and efficient partner is the result of focusing attention on the community rather than solely on oneself and seeing one's purposes as being enhanced and largely determined by the community(s). Community in this context refers to any political entity, group, organization, family, or society to which one belongs. The process of community building has entrepreneurial roots because it takes courage, action, and creativity to forge new relationships, especially those that are intended to last.

The processes of social capital, not only financial profit or product, identify more clearly the differences between public entrepreneurs and private entrepreneurs. These processes alter, if not transform, the way public values are constructed. This transformation is built on enhancing the definition of what is valuable about the community. It requires the ability to enroll others in the process of change. This transformational process is a networked dialogue resembling public sector activity.

Involving what is typically described as the private sector in PPPs appears as a deliberate means to address this process and to abstract and reassemble community assets necessary to be competitive. It is inescapable, particularly in regards to BIDs, that being competitive in a manner that adds value to the citizen investment has become a public concern. It is competitive by constructing value from devalued or unrecognized community assets and seizing the opportunity to exploit this resource in a manner that positively affects everyone. In other words, through the BID process the community as a whole is seen as being more valuable economically as well as aesthetically. This describes a classic public entrepreneurial skill. Networking seems chiefly to be a process of building and maintaining social capital and establishing a trust environment—one built on shared value constructs, to conduct the business of governance. The public management entrepreneur (that BID managers represent) must master the art of community, the building of dialogues of value that allow each person to act on a value exchange as an opportunity.

In highly competitive arenas—particularly urban areas and old town centers—that have been devalued and are interlocked with established communities, the business market as well as its surrounding community requires a collaborative push that is highly structured. Structures, like BIDs, are well articulated by PPPs. These partnerships are not private ventures but public actions with private participation. They are not privatization schemes. Their interchange redefines, transforms, and re-energizes, through entrepreneurial volition, a community improvement process that is propelled by revitalizing a sense of place that bustles with people-oriented business sensibility.

In the case of BIDs, PPPs, which often are stigmatized as privatization efforts that derail democratic process in favor of purported efficiency, instead seem to act as public orientation devices. An awkward term is publicization, which describes a process of, and movement towards, government. A description of publicization is the democratization of collective market economies. The phenomenon of publicization progressed since the 1970s, as much from the efforts to decentralize government as to develop cooperative business management techniques to compete in every growing, mobile, and local economy that is challenged by globalization. David Listokin and his group, in a 2008 report titled, *The Special Improvement District (SID): A Downtown Revitalization Strategy for Communities in the Meadowlands District*, identified that the lack of organized professional management in downtowns is often overlooked as a significant culprit for the downtown's demise. By using the organized management techniques developed in suburban malls, downtown business communities could also compete in modern economies.

BIDs provide some valuable proof that citizen-driven action is less effective when it is exclusionary, particularly when a vital section of the community, such as the business community, is excluded. The private sector and everyday citizens possess talents and resources that can be accessed to stimulate public processes to tackle the big issues—social and economic equity, economic survival, and innovation in communities—not as offshoots or arm's length transactions, often ascribed to privatization, but as an infusion into real governance.

In this book, we begin to see that the future of public administration might no longer be contained behind the walls of formal government. In the past century, private sector business functions were meritorious in solving the emergence of global impacts. The acceleration of PPPs, like BIDs, is an example of informal government that is more horizontally networked and less vertically controlled. Of course, formal government will not go away and evidence points to an enhancement of civic responsibility, local management capacity, and sustainable planning by these partnerships. Centralized hierarchical government is not the progressive element in society that it once was. Also, private sector technologies (business administration) were and still are necessary in public realms. However, today the technologies of public administration are the skills required for successful private sector operations.

As markets are sustained by civil society, local and global companies must effectively participate in public processes, perceive social impacts, and generate aspects of civil society. The skill set to do this is derived from public administration. It integrates and reinterprets private sector perspectives into the management of public concerns. Consequently, we can expect to find an increasing number of public administrators working in traditional private ventures, defining and creating public solutions to real life commercial impacts. This is not a completely new phenomenon but it is a new requirement for the private sector. In the near future, public managers may need to be trained in capacities that identify a hybrid of public/private technologies that will be desired by formal and informal government as well as private companies furthering a publicization of private sector behaviour. BIDs point to how this can be accomplished. Appendix A is a summary of a 2007 research study on BIDs and the public–private components of the profession of business district management.

References

Becker, C. (2010) Self-determination, accountability mechanisms, and quasi-governmental status. *Public Performance & Management Review*, 33(3), March: 413–435.

Hoyt, L. (2006) Importing ideas: The transnational transfer of urban revitalization policy. *International Journal of Public Administration*, 29(1–3): 221–243.

Listokin, D., Koperweis, S. Z., Grossman, S. A., & Rutgers, The State University of New Jersey (2008) *The Special Improvement District (SID): A downtown revitalization strategy for communities in the meadowlands district.* Lyndhurst, NJ: New Jersey Meadowlands Commission (revised September 2009).

Lloyd, G., & Peel, D. (2008) From town center management to the BID model in Britain: Toward a new contractualism? In G. Morçöl, L. Hoyt, J. W. Meek, & U. Zimmermann (eds), *Business improvement districts: Research, theories and controversies* (pp. 71–94). New York: CRC Press, Taylor & Francis Group.

Ruffin, F. A. (2010) Collaborative network management for urban revitalization. *Public Performance & Management Review*, 33(3), March: 459–487.

INTRODUCTION

Multi-sectoral "special districts" continue to evolve and are known by many names such as: managed business districts (MBDs), business improvement districts (BIDs), business improvement authorities, special improvement districts (SIDs), downtown improvement districts, tourism districts, restaurant districts, entertainment districts, place management districts, neighborhood improvement districts (NIDs), Main Street Programs, enterprise zones, community improvement districts, central improvement districts, special assessment districts (SADs), and others. This book examines managed districts as partnerships between the public and private sectors at the community level and the profession of district management as a form of public administration uniting private–public networks; public entrepreneurship, social capital, and public service; comprehensive community development; asset management; and commercial cooperative management in the development and management of community and economic resources. The profession has been referred to as business district management, place management, downtown revitalization, citizen-driven governance, and public–private partnership (PPP) administration.

This book is dedicated to the theory and practice of PPP administration, MBDs, and special district forms of governance. PPPs represent a contractual agreement between private and public sector actors to accomplish common objectives and purpose to improve economic conditions, develop communities, and improve services. PPPs address the involvement of the private sector in aspects of the provision, maintenance, and sustenance of public utilities and the process of providing private actors with access to public processes and accountability as public representatives. It includes privitization and publicization processes. Public–private partnership administration (PPPA) is a **multi-sectoral expertise that bridges business, government, planning, and community**

development knowledge and skills to solve public problems. The term MBDs refers collectively to variously named, multi-functional, publicly sanctioned entities with self-imposed obligatory or voluntary special public assessments, self-determined public service provision, professional management, and which occupy a legally designated sub-governmental special district. MBDs are an evolving worldwide public administration innovation characterized by their creation under state and local enabling legislation. They are self-governing entities; although, in theory and practice they often blur the traditional distinctions between public and private organizations.

Consequently, governance in a public/private structure raises critical opportunities regarding management that is a hybrid of both public and private technologies, democratic representation, accountability, transparency, and responsiveness. This book describes the emergence of a general profession of PPPA and a specific profession of business district management as forms of public entrepreneurship joined with public service and social capital, and examines how districts, as forms of sub-municipal governance, compel the invention of unique and hybrid forms of public administration. The attributes of entrepreneurship (innovation, leadership, risk taking, and the management of community/collective assets) also characterize the purpose of PPPs. These partnerships tend to have direct social and economic impacts at the local and sub-local government level. Whether legally formed as a municipal commission, quasi-governmental public authority, non-profit, or other entity, the management of a PPP oversees the day-to-day operation of these specially designated districts, formulates their budgets, and determines strategies for their success (Jackson and Vinsom, 2004).

This book is based on the Business District Executive Management Certification Program (BDEMCP) developed at the School of Public Affairs & Administration, Rutgers University–Newark, NJ, by Seth A. Grossman (2006–2014). In almost every organization I have encountered, the managers of business districts, town centers, downtowns, and Main Street Program were considered less important than the subjects and activities surrounding downtown revitalization such as redevelopment, marketing, safety and cleanliness, business recruitment, etc. This is in spite of the fact that without management nothing happens and partnerships disintegrate. And yet, managers are overlooked, neglected, misunderstood, and unsupported as the professionals that they are, and the literature demonstrates this neglect. But, this is an issue throughout public, and to a lesser extent business, administration.

This is partially due to the fact that these managers work in a synthesis of both the public and private sectors and are hard to pin down professionally. But also because there is a general malaise regarding public administration and service; an unfounded and persistent attack on public management that is not only misguided, but irresponsible. Public administration and management is a time-honored profession. Most public managers use technologies from both sectors, particularly managers of PPPs. The difference is that the public side addresses the direct behaviors and motivations of groups and communities, not only individuals; context not only content. The downtown revitalization/partnership governance movement throughout the world has singularly revitalized our cities and town centers. In this book we look at why and how that occurs and work to develop an understanding of how this works in and for society to produce successful communities with a focus on business communities because, as this saying informs us, "as the downtown goes, so goes the town."

The BDEMCP was established in 2006 at Rutgers University's School of Public Affairs & Administration under the supervision of Dean Marc Holzer as the Business District Management Certification Program (BDMCP). It was based on the findings of the doctoral dissertation, *The Role of Entrepreneurship in Public-Private Partnerships: The Case of Business Improvement Districts*, by Seth A. Grossman (2008). The program was a response to discovering in the practice and research of BIDs a new mode of public management, PPA management, and the BID movement. This movement merges the best of the progressive collaborative governance with New Public Management (NPM) and what is being referred to as post–progressive New Public Governance (NPG), or partnership governance (Grossman, 2006–2014, 2016).

In 2010, over 1,000 BIDs were identified (Becker, Grossman, and Dos Santos, 2011). This arena of special district governance continues to grow at approximately 3 percent per year worldwide (IDA, 2011). With average budgets of $350,000 this equates to $350,000,000 of public investment in downtown revitalization by United States BIDs annually. Plus, most BIDs leverage three or more times their base assessment. This capacity was only one aspect of downtown revitalization and MBDs. The profession that involved managing large sectoral partnering was unique. The people who manage the organizations that manage these special districts (and other similar venues) were professionals. But too often, they were professionals without a clearly defined profession. This book and the course it is based on remedy this omission, and focus on the BIDs as excellent examples of public–private management partnerships.

The first part (Part I), Chapters 1, 2, and 3, delves into the theoretical underpinnings of the profession of MBDs as business development PPPs. Although MBDs have been around since the agoras of Babylonia, the general consensus is that formal-modern-government-created BIDs seem to have originated in the Toronto, Canada area during the early 1970s, proliferated first throughout Canada, then moved to the United States where New Orleans is said to have been the first United States BID, and then in the 1990s to other countries primarily due to the work of the International Downtown Association (IDA). These districts continue to evolve and are now known by many names such as: BIDs, SIDs, downtown improvement districts, community improvement districts, central improvement districts. There are other business district-oriented efforts such as the Main Street Programs, economic development corporations, and others. This chapter investigates the operational evolution of MBDs, focusing upon the central role of the professional business district manager in a formal PPP.

This is a comprehensive introduction not just to the theory and practice of MBDs but the profession of district management as an unexplored public administration innovation. MBDs refer collectively to the variously named publicly sanctioned entities with self-imposed obligatory or voluntary special assessments, self-determined public service provision and that occupy a legally designated area. The innovatory characteristics of MBDs arise as state and local legislatively enabled self-governing entities at times blur traditional distinctions between public and private organizations. Consequently, governance raises critical questions of democratic representation, accountability, transparency, and responsiveness. While other chapters investigate these touchstones of public administration in greater detail, this introductory chapter reviews the impact of these standards on MBDs and thereby lays the foundation for the emerging profession of district management. Establishment of that profession compels a combined application of public entrepreneurship and public service together with the recognition, development, and channeling of social capital as a basis of business development.

Whether legally formed as a municipal general purpose government, quasi-governmental (quango), non-profit or other entity, the district management organization, under the leadership of its manager, oversees the day-to-day operation of the designated district, formulates its budget, and strategically plans for its future. The first chapter provides access to the groundwork that fortifies a district manager's ability to engage stakeholders, spearhead strategic planning, collect and interpret citizen-centered data, and employ performance management and evaluative systems as diagnostic tools, all of which are more specifically treated in subsequent chapters.

The first part aims to:

1. define a PPP theory of professional business district management grounded in law, public administration, public entrepreneurship, social capital development, community, PPPs, and business development;
2. provide students with readings, on-line instruction, discussion, and assignments that explore the perspectives, needs, and expectations of business district managers, municipal officials, and other stakeholders;
3. increase knowledge about how contemporary governance leads to public policy implementation through networks or network constellations that emerge from social capital flowing through community and commercial collaborations;
4. re-think public administration standards of accountability, representation, transparency, and responsiveness, and to reflect upon these standards for MBD-specific application in an evolving era of PPP management in public administration;
5. identify the purpose and attributes of formal BIDs.

And examines:

1. organizational design, culture, and identity of the management organization; the interdependence of public entrepreneurship, social capital development, and business development;
2. the interdependence of public entrepreneurship, social capital development, and business development;
3. PPPs;
4. governing network leadership;
5. the professional balance of citizen participation, business management, and public service. In practice, sub-local governance by MBDs creates competing concerns requiring that district managers remain at the helm of the organization yet coalesce divergent stakeholder interests and multi-sector technologies to achieve district goals and objectives. This class presents a less traveled avenue of professional development that insightfully places the respective roles of the district manager, municipal officials, business owners, property owners, citizens, and relevant service providers in context to facilitate efficient community and economic development and to generate effective public service.

Managers must be able to:

1. understand the role and structure of MBDs in general and the unique position and impact of the professional district manager as PPP manager;
2. understand the intention of a jurisdiction's enabling legislation that supports the profession and to apply the MBD formation;
3. articulate the convergence of legal, economic, and administrative structure; and revitalization and community development strategies on district management governance in metropolitan and suburban areas;
4. develop local multi-sectoral strategic partnerships and collaborations and discern the factors at stake in coordinating an organization that emerges from collaborative agreements with, for example, the municipality, economic development corporations, community development corporations and groups, Chambers of Commerce (COCs), and business associations;
5. identify aims of public entrepreneurship and social capital and apply them to co-existing citizen-driven governance and commercial cooperation in the face of a competitive urban (or suburban) political economy.

The second part of this book has two chapters and three instructional appendices.

Chapter 4, Retail/Commercial Cooperative Management and Asset-Based Community Development, discusses the difference and similarities between the key public and private capabilities involved in the implementation and governance of MBDs. In creating a "third door" to public management two key capabilities underscore the managed district PPP: Retail/Commercial Cooperative Management employed most notably by suburban malls, and Comprehensive Community Development, which goes beyond project-oriented activity to managing the assets and value of the district's quality of life. These capabilities fuse private and public sector skills and processes necessary to manage revitalization. This chapter prepares practitioners of MBDs to rise to the challenges and meet the demands looming ahead for PPP development, and dispel the myth that malls and big boxes are the demise of traditional downtowns.

Although rarely explored, MBDs incorporate a presence beyond the physical bounds of the legally prescribed district. Building on Part I, these chapters put the fundamental aspects of Public Entrepreneurship, Social Capital, and Place Management into practice as the implementation domains of the PPP that MBDs represent. Highly overlooked and often inappropriately maligned, as business development entities suburban malls are the precise equivalent to managed districts. The difference is that the former is "a mall with walls," and the later "a mall without walls" requiring MBDs to be a partnership between the public and private sectors of the community. Unlike suburban malls, MBDs do not have lease agreements that determine cooperative arrangements; therefore, an MBD relies on public authority, legitimacy, and processes to determine and sustain agreements, and maintain the financial commitments necessary to support agreements as the organization's services and programs. MBDs exist within complex and comprehensive communities with varieties of mixed uses, opinions, and often contradictory needs. The managers of MBDs must interact with a network of professional skilled contractors, public officials, and citizens who will have a professional influence on the outputs of the MBD.

The chapter explores how the MBD manager can work with the diverse interests of public and private sector actors and technologies by acquiring an intimate understanding of public and private sector organizational cooperation, asset-based business and community development, multi-focused entrepreneurship, destination marketing, and PPP (non-profit) management. The chapter contextually tackles questions of public–private sector merges, applying theories of commercial cooperation and comprehensive community building and goes into the field to examine how the theories work in real practice.

The chapter aims to:

1. identify customer service, community development, and marketing processes of PPP management by familiarizing students with the technologies of Retail/Commercial Cooperative Management and Comprehensive Community Development;
2. develop an understanding of similarities and synergies between suburban malls and managed districts;

3. conceptualize how, as a public servant in the middle of a wheel of private free enterprise and quasi-public authority, a district manager is empowered to:

    a   upgrade services orientation and a community's quality of life as a competitive edge while,
    b   merging private and public collaborative technologies, and
    c   understand the purpose and mechanisms of destination marketing;

4. demonstrate the domain capabilities of a PPP as an integrated "third way" in public management;

5. lead students to rethink collective management technology, community assets, values, and quality of life standards of history, culture, location, potential, accountability, and reinventing these standards for MBD-specific application in the governance and public service of PPP management.

Managers must be able to:

1. understand the role, structure, and technology of suburban malls as it applies and contradicts MBDs;
2. identify, analyze, and critique the service, conservation, and competitive responsibilities of PPPs;
3. demonstrate knowledge of Retail/Commercial Cooperative Management and Comprehensive Asset-Based Community Development;
4. outline the purpose and mechanisms of customer service and destination marketing applications;
5. create a framework for managing business districts that is diverse, cooperative among and responsive to the social and economic aspects of the district.

Chapter 5, Survey Research, Performance Measurement, Budgeting and Evaluation for Management Business Districts, presents an exploration of the linkage between Community/Downtown Revitalization Strategies and Public-Partnership Management and bridging those efforts with methods of financing to implement economic development strategies. This chapter works to identify and understand the different stakeholders and their backgrounds in the governance of MBDs. Formal and informal networks become key to MBD productivity, and a clear understanding of merging the priorities of different interest groups is essential to moving forward the district.

MBDs are first created by, then focus upon and function through, collective action. The business district manager is often faced with the complexity of harnessing and channeling social and economic capital in the best interests of the MBD. He or she must exhibit entrepreneurship characteristics. These characteristics manifest in a myriad of ways for the business district professional: social, political, policy, public, or even economic entrepreneurship. This chapter is concerned with the revitalization strategies that MBDs use to obtain social and economic development results. There are a myriad of strategic approaches from the Main Street Program's Four Points Method, and other variations to Strategic Design Principles that envision and direct an MBD organization to fulfilling on future goals that build the community. Citizen participation in MBD creation and operation is at the crux of building cohesive stable communities. This chapter also investigates role responsibilities of citizen stakeholders, and how district managers can facilitate citizen participation in stakeholder accountability, transparency, and responsiveness.

Revitalization strategies are particularly relevant when it comes time for MBDs to reassess goals, and the means of financing those goals. As special districts, BIDs tend to have special assessments, but can have other forms of financing: fees, loans, grants, etc. In those situations, the MBD must consider financing options that can help realize extensive strategic goals. Moreover, there is a need for a citizen-driven approach to planning the range of services that business management districts offer stakeholders. This chapter explores strategic planning and decision-making methods and the involvement of citizens as a form of social capital mobilized to facilitate action. It also demonstrates the interconnectedness of strategic planning, decision making, responsible risk-taking, and financing. The chapter contextually tackles questions of stakeholder roles, responsibilities, and expectations by examining and developing strategic revitalization plans for their business district.

This chapter provides:

1. demonstration of the factors useful in identifying strategies that target specific goals of the MBD such as planning, clean and safe programs, design/ streetscaping, economic and market development, and business recruitment;
2. demonstration of the mechanics of interorganizational networks that develop among and between individual and group stakeholders fundamentally built upon trust and negotiated terms collectively determined by the participants;
3. a rethink of public administration standards of accountability, representation, transparency, and responsiveness reinventing these standards for MBD-specific application in an emerging era of network governance and public service;
4. understanding of responsible risk-taking and methods for recognizing, analyzing, and developing alternative decisions;
5. development of a set of tools for gaining community and board support for such goals as service provision, event planning, public relations, market research and development, and other goals;
6. demonstration of the link between environmental complexities and economic/ community development; and
7. application of action steps for developing a performance budget and implementing a strategic plan for the development of your MBD and the financing of that plan.

Managers are expected to be able to:

1. understand how to match a district's revitalization objectives and capabilities with the anticipated demands of the environment so as to produce a plan of action;
2. appreciate the importance of involving in the strategic planning and decision-making process individuals affected by changes that will result from those plans and decisions;
3. identify and apply performance budgeting to the various conceptual frameworks actually or potentially used by stakeholders as planning tools in assessing the future actions of the managed district;
4. outline pertinent provisions of collaborative agreements to engage stakeholders that include elements of accountability, transparency, and conflict resolution;
5. identify financing options to enable implementation of strategic plan proposals.

The first part of this chapter examines Performance Measurement and Evaluation and presents an opportunity to identify, develop, and apply methods of collecting data, particularly for surveys, as well as interpreting and presenting that data to stakeholders of the MBD to assess and guide success.

This applies measurement and evaluation to performance management. Surveys and focus groups are data collection tools that are used to collect information and provide feedback and evaluation about organizations. Surveys are becoming especially important and commonplace in many jurisdictions as they attempt to gauge stakeholder expectations. Focus groups allow verbal collective feedback often engaging divergent viewpoints that are instrumental in data analysis and presentation. This section explores performance management and measures, evaluation techniques and strategies, and survey construction, identifies important aspects of focus groups, and adds to the transformation process of making use of information collected. That is, students see how to convert raw numbers and statistics into graphics that are informative, to the point, and that keep the audience engaged.

This part provides:

1. increased knowledge about performance management, evaluation strategies, and surveys of:

   a business and property owners in the MBD;
   b residents in the MBD;
   c consumers and visitors of the MBD;

2. discussion on how to design an effective instrument and how to develop a good research plan;
3. discussion on how to reach citizens and to increase response rates;
4. understanding of how a focus group operates as well as the nature of information that it can deliver;

5. review of public and private sector processes and current practices of collecting and reporting data by a variety of methods;
6. familiarity with how to make sense of data collected and how to communicate it to district management, business and property owners, and municipal authorities and to the general citizenry.

Managers are expected to be able to:

1. understand the importance of stakeholder surveys in measuring and evaluating performance;
2. comprehend the systemic factors that influence the effectiveness and utility of stakeholder surveys as well as other methods of data collection;
3. understand the complexities of focus groups and use of focus groups;
4. appreciate the visual potential of data presentation as an audience-specific technique in the professionalism of business district management;
5. discover international trends of MBDs and the customizing of sub-local managing and governing accomplishments.

The second part of this chapter looks at Planning and Implementing a BID. The goal of BIDs is to enhance local management capacity by permitting a municipality's economic generators (downtowns, neighborhoods, and commercial/industrial areas) to compete more effectively and efficiently with existing retail/commercial markets such as shopping malls and other business areas. By implementing structures for the professional organization and management of downtown business services, districts develop management strategies for competitive business development utilizing private/public partnerships. They begin with the understanding that customer service is a requirement for business development and excellent service is a competitive advantage. The goal of a BID is to serve the customer by adding value to the customer's experience of the community.

The Profession of Business District Management offers an exploration into the theories and practices that identify the multi-sectoral profession of business district management as a form of PPP. Business district management is a unique form of public management that unites a community's public and private capabilities to address legal structures and working models, to examine revitalization, business, and community development technologies applicable to managed district PPPs, to highlight the working relationships between numerous stakeholders, and to sharpen the data collection and evaluation techniques of participants. (Lynn, 1996). When we address business district management as a profession, we must address legal structures and working models, to examine revitalization performance, business, and community development technologies applicable to managed district PPPs, to highlight public responsibilities, and to sharpen the performance and evaluation techniques of the profession.

Appendix A is a summary of Seth A. Grossman's 2007 research study on BIDs and the role of public entrepreneurship in PPPs. This United States, nationwide quantitative study of over 650 BIDs examines entrepreneurship as a public process as it is a private attribute, and its role in PPPs (3Ps) works to transform private sector ambitions into public accountabilities. In general, it is its public nature that appears to tell us a great deal about the role of entrepreneurship as it is strongly correlated with social capital. A PPP, especially the BID model, is highly entrepreneurial, but with a public twist that is synergistic with social capital and the networks that produce it. BIDs are units of sub-government based on special assessment forms of public financing that create a formal PPP and a local self-help mechanism to address revitalization and redevelopment needs of a designated business area (Mitchell, 1999; Hoyt, 2001; Stokes, 2002; Justice, 2003; Morçöl and Zimmerman, 2006).

Appendix B is the 2005 Final Report and Proposal for a BID in the North Ward of Newark, NJ, on Mount Prospect Avenue and is a study of how BID and legal action formation occurs. The BID Planning Committee met on Tuesday evenings from March 23, 2005, to June 21, 2005, and met thereafter to complete the BID planning process. The Committee's tasks were to:

1. determine the applicability of a BID according to New Jersey statute for Mount Prospect Avenue, North Ward, Newark, NJ;
2. conduct a discussion and study of business community needs; and
3. present a final report of its findings and recommendations to the Newark Municipal Council.

Appendix C is the 2015 Annual Report of the Ironbound Business Improvement District, Newark, NJ. This is an example of what MBDs, and specifically BIDs, actually do. BIDs are generally required to produce formal annual reports of their activities and plans as part of their annual budget request. The Ironbound Business Improvement District (IBID) is a certified SID established in December 2000 by local ordinance. As stated above, first and foremost, the IBID is a unique PPP between the Ferry Street business community, the municipal government, and the neighborhood. The IBID works with the City to improve business and community development services, rebuild our infrastructure, and market the Ironbound as a reliable and exciting destination.

References

Becker, C., Grossman, S. A., & Dos Santos, B. (2011) *Business improvement districts: Census and national survey*. Washington, DC: International Downtown Association.

Grossman, S. A. (2006–2014) The Business District Executive Management Certification Program. Newark, NJ: Rutgers, The State University of New Jersey, School of Public Affairs & Administration.

Grossman, S. A. (2008) (2007 research). *The role of entrepreneurship in public-private partnerships: The case of business improvement districts*, Doctoral Dissertation. Newark, NJ: Rutgers, The State University of New Jersey, School of Public Affairs & Administration.

Grossman, S. A. (2016) *Partnership governance*. London: Routledge.

Hoyt, L. (2001) *Business improvement districts: Untold stories and substantiated impacts*, Doctoral Dissertation, University of Pennsylvania. Dissertation Abstracts International, 62: 3961–4221.

Jackson, E. L., & Vinsom, C. (2004) *Public authorities and public corporations*. Athens, GA: Institute of Government, University of Georgia, University of Georgia Press.

Justice, J. B. (2003) *Business improvement districts, reasoning, and results: Collective action and downtown revitalization*, Doctoral Dissertation. Newark, NJ: Rutgers University.

Lynn, L. E., Jr. (1996) *Public management as art, science and profession*. Chatham, NJ: Chatham House Publishers.

Mitchell, J. (1999) *Business improvement districts and innovative service delivery* (Grant report). Arlington, VA: PricewaterhouseCoopers Endowment for the Business of Government.

Morçöl, G., & Zimmerman, U. (2006) Metropolitan governance and business improvement districts. *International Journal of Public Administration*, 29: 1–29.

Stokes, R. J. (2002) *Business improvement districts: Their political, economic and quality of life impacts*. New Brunswick, NJ: Rutgers University.

PART I

1

FOUNDATIONS OF THE PROFESSION OF BUSINESS DISTRICT MANAGEMENT

Public–Private Partnerships and Public Management

Participating, caring for, and being committed to our communities are time-honored concerns, and this certainly includes business communities (Berk, 1976). More and more communities are looking for and finding ways to build successful organized approaches to development, revitalization, and improvements by creating special (business) improvement districts (SIDs). But, do they work? Do they accomplish the intention of enabling legislation? Does this intention, and BIDs specifically, foster public management entrepreneurship? Do BIDs present an effective model for functions of social capital and the practice of public management entrepreneurship (Harvey, 1989)? Do BIDs prove Charles Tiebout's theory that people are exceedingly concerned about their primary home-based investments (such as home and business), and choose governance programs and services that help manage these investments most effectively (Tiebout, 1956) by voting with their feet; that is, moving to places where their investments have a better chance of succeeding? In the case of BIDs, this concern is an extended reinterpretation of local governance apparently chosen, designed, and implemented by the entrepreneurial citizen as a collective response to asset management. Do BIDs sustain better business investment opportunities? As we delve into these questions, we look at the essential structure and purpose of BIDs, their public and private nature, and the impact of the management of collective and common interests that BIDs represent.

Without reliable resources and strong administrative support, volunteer efforts often are limited inadequate legal structures that do not sustain hard-earned plans. To address this, government often will attempt to work with communities to build lasting capability, but often is held responsible for economic trends it cannot control, services that are poorly designed, and service delivery systems that do not meet the day-to-day requirements of dynamic and changing environments. SIDs/BIDs are designed to remedy this problem, particularly in, but not limited to, business areas commonly known as downtowns or shopping corridors.

BIDs and SIDs are similar terms used for a type of public authority allowable in 49 states and many countries. State statutes regarding BIDs give authority to municipalities to create special BIDs to strengthen business in communities through PPPs, where in most cases the local private sector business community has significant authority to manage the district. Legislation establishing SIDs/BIDs throughout the world provide statutory authority to local governments to create tax-supported BIDs. The districts provides services to encourage and support retail/commercial economic activity, community development, and to utilize cooperative technologies similar to shopping malls.

These BIDs are designed to provide local governments with the ability to focus, elevate, and manage services specifically designed to enhance the economic viability of business areas and downtown business centers. The services that are provided are specific and unique to each business district, but tend to involve overall management, environmental clean-up and safety, streetscape redesign and upgrades, marketing and promotions, business development services and advocacy, and redevelopment.

The clear purpose of BIDs is to promote economic growth and employment, encourage self-help and self-financed business districts, designate professional management of the districts, and develop PPPs that implement self-help programs consistent with local needs, goals, and objectives. When a BID is enacted it empowers a District Management Corporation (a non-governmental organization (NGO) or municipal commission) to provide all variety of business management and economic development activities including administering district affairs (adopt by-laws), purchasing and managing property, and managing the provision of specific services and standards (design, promotions, marketing, rehabilitation, clean-up, security).

BIDs are usually private sector organizational entities, not-for-profit (NGO) corporations, possessing real public authority by offering a public–private partnership. Often credited with being the primary revitalization factor in towns where they are established, they are key partners with other economic development agencies and programs (e.g. enterprise zones, economic development corporations business and community development associations, and Chambers of Commerce (COCs)).

BIDs also often act as community development organizations and delivery systems that interface directly with business concerns at the point of direct customer interaction. Statewide businesses, commercial entities, non-profits, churches, and residences are also known to contribute to BIDs, and serve as a vital tool in negotiating private–public partnerships that facilitate the investment of social capital, provide targeted customer service programming, and essential capital and business development strategies.

In the late 1990s and early 21st century, academia became more and more interested in the phenomena of BIDs and a number of excellent studies were conducted chiefly in the field of public administration. I reviewed two of these doctoral dissertations (Justice, 2003; Stokes, 2002) that illustrate a contextual anxiety regarding public sector vs private sector partnering that seems to pervade the field of public administration. BIDs are looked at with suspicion or awe.

In this light, it is noteworthy that the Stokes (2002) dissertation is a result of the Urban Policy and Planning Development Program—Rutgers University–New Brunswick, NJ, and the Justice (2003) dissertation is a result of the Public Administration Program—Rutgers University–Newark, NJ. The approach and tone differences may be indicative of the academic intentions of these institutions. The Urban Policy and Planning Program approach in the Stokes dissertation seemed to be focused more on the success of privatization and equity and accountability issues from a public policy perspective. However, an anti-decentralization tone was present towards BIDs. The author, falling back on an unsubstantiated concern of public and private sector cooperation, projects BIDs as an anomaly rather than a reasonable evolution of governance.

The public administration approach in the Justice dissertation focused on collective action and decentralization issues of public process evolution, democratization, and community development functions from a social investment and participation perspective. Both approaches eventually focused on the concept of defining "place" (definable geography, market, and sense of community) as significant, and indeed, BID technology incorporates a field known as "place management." However, neither addressed the role of BID management, therefore, professionalism at the BID level. This was true of virtually almost all research on BIDs until 2008. This was chiefly due to the fact that few researchers had any practical knowledge or prior experience of BIDs.

Justice does address normative and cognitive aspects of BID success and points to the pragmatic sensibility of BIDs as collective action and decentralization/privatization, which points to policy as well as management. Stokes helps clarify the purpose of BIDs and this lends itself to a clarification of BID management stating that, "the key to BID success has not been that they are private organizations per se; instead, it is that they endeavor to improve long-neglected areas with courteous, professional, and civic-minded staff" (Stokes, 2002, p. 235). Jerry Mitchell (1999), Loylene Hoyt (2001), and G. Morçöl and Ulf Zimmerman (2006) saw the impact of BIDs worldwide and attempted to describe what they were noting, that governance concepts and policies seemed to be changing from traditional top-down control government to non-traditional cooperative governance. Some were concerned about an erosion of democratic capacity; others considered it a remarkable expansion of public action. More in-depth examination of the role of the BID manager, the planning of BIDs, governmental interactional administration of BIDs, or the unique role of the BID Board of Directors came later (Grossman, 2008; Mitchell, 2008). This began to fill a fairly large hole in the discussion of PPPs considering the private/public dilemma posed. Both dissertations agreed that BIDs have unique public and private aspects impacting public administration and governance. Public entrepreneurship and entrepreneurship in general were not highly considered in favor of trying to discern the collection issues of BIDs, but entrepreneurship studies later became a key theme in pursuing how BIDs worked.

The reason for this may lie in the substantial community building aspects of BIDs, and the economic aspects of PPPs, particularly from a process and governance perspective. Most researchers, at the time, acknowledge that hard data about BIDs was hard to find. But, there is little inquiry into why this might be so. The point may be that both researchers were not considering economics or management, therefore found it less important to study. They were looking at what BIDs were (whether they were a good or bad thing), not how they functioned. Almost all missed the management dilemma of multi-sector partnering. They were interested in how BIDs functioned as governmental units. Certainly, market researchers and business development specialists who work for BIDs and provide this information might have better data and technical ability to analyze community economics. And, contributing to the confusion were the BIDs themselves that had little governmental guidance and relied on private consultants whose interests were not community benefit or descriptive accuracy. BIDs struggled with an identity crisis; were they public or private, or both? The answer to the economic success of BIDs lies in the difficulty of assessing economic data in the aggregate and applying it accurately to a community as a whole; that is, are we defining and managing our markets and the well-being of our communities? Public administration researchers tend not to ask those questions, even if it is the crux of the object to be studied, such as BIDs, unless they have an economic development background. A quest for appropriate data about BIDs might begin by asking related economic questions such as: How much accurate economic data is available for malls, shopping centers, industrial parks, or similar economic generators like BIDs?; or, How accurate are the other economic analysis models such as the GNP, property values, or employment data, in determining true economic success?; or, Who or what determines what signifies success? However, economic data will not always provide accurate community and quality of life data, or community organization, management, and participation, which also define BIDs.

From my experience, it appears more a matter of perspective, an individual assessment, particularly in the idiosyncratic world of the independent entrepreneur. General sensibility regarding BID success appears in both dissertations to be linked more to quality of life and community-identity improvements than economics. "Overall, the success of BIDs … in producing positive quality of life results maybe … most generalizable" (Stokes, 2002, p. 228). This makes sense as BIDs are essentially and specifically community focused rather than individual business or regional economic focused. BIDs may take an entrepreneurial approach to public policy and we might expect that economic indicators would be the key measurement of success, but success was articulated in terms of the health and vitality of the community. This provides us with a public perspective on entrepreneurship.

Stokes looks for economic explanations without economic tools of inquiry and falls back on notions of privatization and equity anxieties to voice critical analysis. He is in each final analysis drawn again and again to the insight that BIDs, "restore a level of community faith in collective efforts ..." (Stokes, 2002, p. 234). This is where Justice begins his research by looking at the individual motivations within a social realist model and community causations within the social constructionist model of human motivation in collective action. Indeed, this explains well the roots of the PPP anxiety that pits individual vs community needs: the social realist perspective of individual motivation and rights, and the social constructionist perspective of contextual causation and communal authority. Stokes seems to lament the erosion of the social realist perspective in the BID process, but is eventually drawn to the potential of community (collective) action to extract investment, particularly social investment.

This PPP dilemma is also at the heart of emerging public administration practices, which is, I believe, initially based on a post-Enlightenment sensibility that there is a dignity of collective occurrence that informs the role of individuals, and may supersede the individual thereby providing the rights of individuality by context rather than by content. In this way, it may not be the content of our character, but the context of our character that provides a workable reality, one that sustains our investments, and provides measurable benchmarks of success based as much on quality of life indicators as on economic indicators. Economic quantifiable analysis of cooperative business models may indicate relative success if all indicators are equal, but tend not to indicate precisely a sense of community success or opportunities for collective action potential that individuals can act on with confidence. An individual's access to community success appears to require an understanding of contextual evolution in defining collective social formations. This realm of understanding is a strong investigative goal of today's public administration professional.

A second component of public administration as it emerges into the 21st century is new forms of social entrepreneurialism. The value of investing one's time, skill, and passion into community endeavors can be primary to capital investment and often precedes it when public–private partnering occurs in the development of communities. Justice noted that, "self-governing BIDs proved more effective in mobilizing and coordinating a variety of resources ..." (Justice, 2003, p. 348). Self-governing BIDs tend to provide more transferred public authority to self-determining community-based BIDs. This may be due to "the recognition by property owners that the value of their asset (i.e., their property) depends to a significant extent on the surrounding environment" (Houstoun, 2003, p. 6—report of North American BIDs by researchers from the London School of Economics), including the physical, social, and economic environment.

Both dissertations had to identify and tract the decentralization movement that BIDs represent. It appears that the further the decentralization evolves and the greater the polycentric movement is captured in community agreements (law), then the more successful the endeavor is. The caveat is that decentralization must attend to normative governmental elements if it intends to succeed, and this means that structured democratic methods must be employed as part of, but separate from, governmental structures. Democratic methods employ citizen participation formalities: participation that is reconstituted as collective action and communal authority. Externally controlled BIDs merely are extensions of existing government; but self-governed BIDs, which represent the large majority of BIDs, are additions to the governance process. Apparently, they tend to tap new fields of democratic initiative. In these new fields:

> economic and social variables might not be the most appropriate place to look. Instead, an examination of how BIDs contribute to the less concrete variables such as community spirit and citizen involvement as well as increasing usage of public areas might prove more telling.
>
> *(Stokes, 2002, p. 70)*

The BID model is essentially based on the private sector providing funds and technical expertise, and the public sector providing political legitimization and taxing powers; essentially a classic PPP. However, as in all PPPs, these roles can be exchanged. The BID avoids the problem of free riders, addresses upkeep of common areas, and provides place management by being formal special districts created by law. They are not associations or clubs; membership is mandatory not optional. In this way, "BIDs formalize the interests of the local community" (Stokes, 2002, p. 228). At the level of governance, BIDs represent two forces that could define benchmarks of success: citizen participation and professional management. If we accept as a definition that citizen participation is "the role of self-governance in promoting institutional legitimacy, the formation of common understandings between public and private participants" (Justice, 2003, p. 4), we can see the role BIDs might play in furthering participation by citizens. Institutional legitimacy is a hollow reward if it lies fallow.

This, however, also requires professional management, to allow for the "facilitation of agreement" (Justice, 2003, p. 6). BIDs are an addition to democratic governance and without a doubt are at the defining point of a private/public social and economic dichotomy that defines the term "community" in our society. Access to the processes of community definition appears to elicit perceptions of success based initially on a sense that one's quality of life is improved, and this seems to be tied to the ability to invest personal time and energy into the development of the community and to participate collectively in the activities that make a community viable. A BID apparently "restores a level of community faith in collective processes …" (Stokes, 2002, p. 234). Is it possible that BIDs may be the means to restore trust in government as well?

Questions that BIDs Pose as Multi-Sectoral Organizations

- What special motivations have people that establish BIDs?
- Are BIDs effective?
- If so, how are they effective? If not, why?
- How do BIDs help us differentiate between private and public entrepreneurship?
- What is the role of social capital in entrepreneurship models like BIDs?

The analysis examines the original intent of BIDs and follows this intention to the actual planning and implementation of BIDs by addressing how:

1. the intended outcomes of BID legislation addresses Kenneth Shepsle's premise that effective institutional models deliver individual and community commitments;
2. the establishment of BIDs at the municipal level achieves outcomes by applying an Agreement-Management-Commitment model;
3. BIDs implement planning and management practices to achieve successful outcomes; and
4. BIDs create a public entrepreneurship model by addressing William A. Fishel's homevoter hypothesis that hypothesis is tuned to the business and commercial aspects of a community.

Although there are numerous how-to programs and what-are publications on downtown revitalization practices, there is little research as to how BIDs successfully address the intent of their enabling legislations, further effective government, or help communities to succeed. The following questions remain:

1. Do BIDs foster a beneficial form of decentralized local government built on establishing effective community partnerships, or are BIDs a privatization of public services?
2. Do BIDs resolve business sector disenfranchisement in municipal political processes, or do they inhibit due process and citizen participation?
3. Does the Agreements, Management, Commitment, and Accountability model describe the community-based process of BIDs?

We begin by examining both the idea and practices of entrepreneurism in the public realm as well as areas of social capital that threaten to redefine economic theories based simply on individual consumeristic rational approaches. We enter the discussion of transrational/collective action in a market setting.

The Emergence of Public Management Entrepreneurship

The BID Movement and Its Antecedents

In the later part of the 20th century into the beginning of the 21st century, public administration has been engaged in a struggle between process-driven bureaucracy, managing a top-down hierarchical model of governance, and entrepreneurial forces of revitalization and renewal that emphasize a bottom-up model. This struggle has traditional roots present in the early formation of the country. The Hamiltonian tradition favored a top-down (centralized) administrative model. The Jeffersonian tradition advocated a bottom-up (decentralized) model. The decentralization emphasis in American governance began with the emergence of the nation.

In the 1700s, and for almost two more centuries, the agrarian rural economy was equal to, if not more significant than, urban life in dictating economic system norms. The country was built on its agricultural prowess and potential, and to a large degree this remains true. What has changed is the technological needs of the populace (more and better things to improve living conditions), and the mechanization of labor (more things for everyone with less effort). Agriculture will always be the backbone of a civilization, but today it is not the management concern it once was, therefore does not dictate social norms. However, it still supports, and by tradition determines, economic norms. People may toil in conceptually different fields, less agricultural and more industrial and informational, but they still toil in the fields of human endeavor and this requires teamwork, cooperation, and coordination (Axelrod, 1984).

In many ways, BIDs are direct descendants of early American agrarian economic life. Acting as economic cooperation organizations, both BIDs and early forms of agriculture communities share many attributes. The key distinction is that BIDs are democratic (more than one owner) and resemble modern agriculture co-ops; whereas suburban malls are autocratic (one owner) and resemble traditional "plantation-style" organization. The agrarian life is by necessity decentralized and spread out, establishing networks that are unique to its purpose. In early America, agrarian life was organized as economic generators, which spurred specific social norms. In this report, the economic mechanism is examined.

The concept of growth and development that the agrarian lifestyle supports is essentially entrepreneurial and cooperative. It takes initiative and teamwork. American entrepreneurialism is cast in this light and speaks to the ability to be practical and creative at the same time. Practical in its output-driven and results-oriented technology, and creative in operating complex organizational (communal) behaviors both with the goals of improving quality of life and, in all senses, profit. The agrarian model of mutual cooperative effort is the American entrepreneurial model. The differences are noted by whether the co-op is democratically or autocratically governed.

Autocratic economic co-ops (Figure 1.1) tend to be private sector corporate structures that have a direct link to the tradition of early American agrarian co-ops (plantations) and operate accordingly, making slight adjustments to meet modern social requirements. Democratically governed economic co-ops tend to be PPPs, and act as an extension of local government (Figure 1.2). Herbert Kaufman concluded that there are three primary factors that give rise to American public administration: *representativeness*, which dominated governmental thinking until The Pendleton Act of 1883, ushered in a sensibility of *neutral competence*, which later under The Brownlow Commission in 1933 gave way to *executive leadership* as the dominant focus of public administration. In the 21st century, we might add a fourth value to Kaufman's three preceding values, and that is *entrepreneurship*, which has currency in the lexicon of governance banter even if it is unrecognized as such by the same practitioners. "As a result, the language of public administration is likely to become increasingly strategic and tactical in tone rather than scientific" (Kaufman, 1956, p. 1072).

Downtowns and their modern antecedents, corporations (in retail: suburban malls), are essentially cooperatives. The height of the agrarian-co-op prior to the 1900s was the plantation, today it is agribusiness. This is not pejorative from a collective and entrepreneurial standpoint, although it does connote a fixed social-work system rather than an evolving community-based economic system. However, if indeed the agrarian model of entrepreneurialism is at the heart of our internal economic system, efforts to bring back elements of society that have strayed away from this system would be viewed as positive.

To the extent that the agrarian-co-op model of cooperative, interdependent social-economic structures are created and maintained, we might determine that economic and social success have been achieved. Consequently, the business

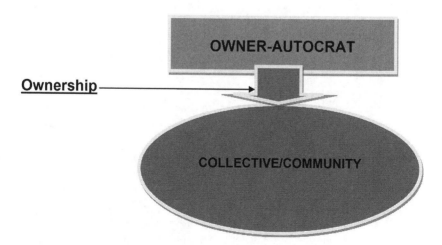

FIGURE 1.1 Agrarian–Autocratic-Co-op Model, i.e. suburban malls

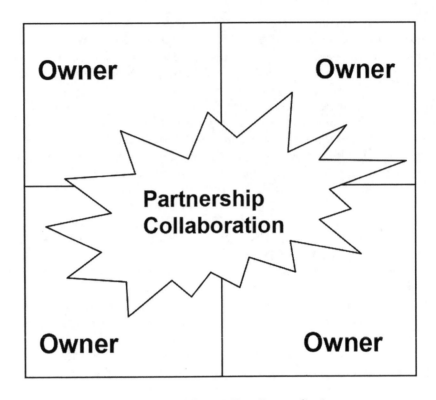

FIGURE 1.2 Democratic Co-op Model, i.e. BIDs—Decentralization

professional is also traditionally tied to the agrarian-co-op model, and is not professional simply by expertise in product development, but as a manager of community action, as a public manager.

Decentralization tends to expand public management towards the private sector not unlike the agrarian drive to harness the land (Fischel, 2001). Centralization gathers and focuses public management to harness the people (Figure 1.3). These two elements are at play in our concepts of community, and consequently lend definition to the role of management. In our society, both centralizing and decentralizing forces are constantly at work garnering and exploring social and economic possibilities. Management is a centralizing conservation effort even in the act of exploration.

The professional manager, both private and public, is expected to have the tools to garner and sustain collective action to produce real outcomes. At the extremes, private management sustains an external thrust to explore, define, and refine potential (expectation), and public management sustains an internal assumption to deliver agreed upon potential (expectations). When public management moves towards private management the community-based public entrepreneur is created (Lynn, 1996). This is the BID manager. BIDs, like

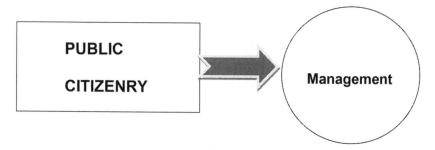

FIGURE 1.3 Urban—Centralization

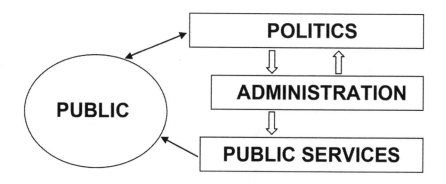

FIGURE 1.4 Bureaucratic Public Administration

suburban malls, are successful because they incorporate a communal function akin to an agrarian-co-op. We can hearken back to governmental structures that have evolved to accommodate this.

Woodrow Wilson is credited with initiating public administration professionalism by installing the concept of the expert and a hierarchical structured organization leaning towards Hamilton (Figure 1.4).

This led to modern bureaucracies and a socialization of the public professional. It did not encourage, nor desire, entrepreneurialism in the public sector as this was seen as private sector opportunism, and autocratic behavior. This system practically invented the concept of the public servant as publicly motivated rather than privately motivated (which was the norm, and still is in almost every corruption case).

In the beginning of the 21st century, we seem to be embracing a more Jeffersonian model, which might be called the Reagan/Clinton tradition of decentralized community-based management, which is akin to the agrarian-co-op-democratic model (Figure 1.4). Modern American public administration, a Wilsonian model, built on hierarchy and authority in practice actually works less hierarchically. This may be a result of an increasingly urbanized middle class that exploded in the

20th century, causing communal action, higher standards, and with it an eruption of public interest; both horizontal expansions of community consciousness. When Kettl expresses that "public administration is out of sync with the way we practice it" (Kettl, 2002, p. xi), he is referring to a sense that centralization is not a core value of agrarian-co-op entrepreneurship. To many, including Kettl, the idea that public administration is becoming more public (and pragmatic) is remedial.

Public administrationists cannot escape the pragmatic call to connect theory to action. The public demands participation, input, and the opportunity to craft public policy. The struggle between bureaucratic (theory) and entrepreneurial public management (action) is a traditional struggle of personal expression being tested perhaps in no more dynamic a place than at the local level in BIDs. Known as BIDs, SIDs, neighborhood improvement districts (NIDs), or special assessment districts (SADs), restructuring of local government is occurring in these decentralized, community-driven development organizations that blend private sector investment, community organization, and localized governance redefining the public realm. BID managers are responsible actors in the definition, maintenance, and marketing of community assets and represent governance for the public interest. By necessity they are on the cutting edge of public administration and management. "BIDs are the essence of innovative thinking" (Mitchell, 1999, p. 201), and they are placed in the role of political and entrepreneurial activist.

Public administration has struggled throughout the 20th century to define its professional role as government began to provide programs that were designed to be implemented by state, local, and private contractors; a role that increasingly became tied to professional management. Professionalism in public administration today tends to be management focused, often crossing the lines between private and public administration and blending techniques into one virtual technology that leans towards entrepreneurialism and pragmatism (Figure 1.5). Entrepreneurship signals an economic immediacy in governance.

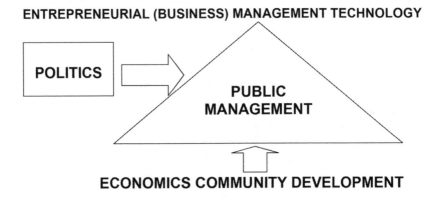

FIGURE 1.5 Entrepreneurial Public Management

As a public force, public entrepreneurship dabbles in material and non-material capital. It assumes that society itself has economic value and that the co-joining of material and social wealth aspiration requires a proficiency in the management of collective as well as individual potential with the latter a subset of the former. Additionally, the public management entrepreneur is expected to be an active partner in community and economic development at every level of society. This begins the era at the local level, which now includes the federal government, of PPPA. Government is no longer here to simply help, but to be part of social/economic endeavors.

This is because the management sphere is the domain where service delivery and democratic action function, and the terms efficiency and effectiveness can be measured. Also, when a community reaches into the private sector to establish public order rather than assuming an established public order, we can expect private sector influence in public processes. Management in the public realm also requires community development (community planning, organization, and leadership) and economic expertise (jobs, business development, housing, and public infrastructure).

When tied to local business oversight and being responsible for producing direct services with market impact, BID managers succeed by applying skilled partnership building with both the private and public sectors. BIDs represent an ultimate public choice, a choice by private individuals to organize, leverage community assets, and participate in public accountability. When tied to local government through ordinance and a direct recipient of public funds, BIDs are neither purely independent nor a privatization of public service. They represent a new form of public service in the form of entrepreneurial public management translating centralized service to special needs and reciprocating by applying business acumen to communal activities.

Democracy is local, most people's lives occur locally, and the practice of democracy is experienced in the ever-evolving nature of community. A key democratic tenet is that each individual is responsible for creating, participating, and managing the communities they live in (by choice: participation or neglect, representation, active or complacent). Decentralization is an avenue reinforcing public choice because its quest can only go away from the governing towards the people. The trajectory of decentralization naturally travels from the state to the county to the municipality, and from there, to newly emerging quasi-governmental authorities that define local perceptions of what constitutes the sense of community or neighborhood. Decentralization in a democracy is a process of bringing government closer to the people, and BIDs are common decentralization practices. The administrative politics that permit such a process require a resolution of the conflict between control vs cooperative political and public administration structures.

BIDs represent this resolution as they require an orderly transfer of power; real political power, the power to govern oneself, and the power to emerge from autocratic centralized models to democratic partnership/entrepreneurial models that emphasize a process of agreement construction; pragmatic management professionalism; and direct financial commitment. The democratic partnership/ entrepreneurial model is a bottom-up or community-based model and it announces a collaborative approach to governance.

This movement assumes a professional premise that managers know how to do their jobs and elected officials and appointees ought to get out of their way and let them perform. The bottom-up model, in the modern era, which predated the reinvention of the government movement, is a direct result of the emergence of the 20th century American middle class, which emphasized education and expertise, and expresses an urge to act responsibly and participate. It also signals a need for innovation to revitalize communities.

It hearkens back to early American agrarian management technology, which acted as decentralized and managed cooperatives. A key tenet of this capacity is that it assumes competence and requires the facilitating of assets, particularly social assets such as education and expertise. Management of cooperatives relies on managing assets. Downtown revitalization is based in traditional progressive early agrarianism. It caused economic success by unique effort. That unique effort is the ability to create new communities, establish leadership that works, and succeed in collective effort. The emerging entrepreneurial and competitive collective set the format for similar ventures.

The new frontier of civilization and the American experiment is no longer rural, but urban. It is often disguised by the fact that a once thriving community existed, roads and buildings are already there, as well as government. The urban frontier results from an undefined, altered, deteriorated, or non-existent traditional sense of collective action: community. Urban areas and town centers are the new frontiers of opportunity. Again, one successful method is the BID known in Pennsylvania as the NID, because all BIDs possess a sense of neighborliness and of concern for others that seems to underwrite successful collective action and the onset of a functional sense of community; one that embraces a merging of public and private capacities.

"As American governments pursued more public policy through nongovernmental partners, public policy increasingly became entangled in private goals and norms" (Kettl, 2002, p. 143). In the process of decentralization that BIDs represent, it is inevitable that public interest becomes private practice and vice versa. The lines that separate public and private administration blur. With prescience, Luther Gulick observed that public administration and private administration are part of a unified science of administration (Gulick, 1937). Gulick could have been announcing the arrival of BIDs. The emergence of BIDs in the late 1970s followed the general tenets of the New Public Management (NPM) movement: privatization of public services, decentralization, citizen participation, and customer orientation, but in each of these areas BIDs represent something a bit different; a partnership with traditional public administration rather than a departure. However, where government administration may be seen as bureaucratic and process oriented (Gingrich, 2005), BIDs are seen as entrepreneurial, management focused, and innovative (Osbourne and Gabler, 1992). BIDs walk a fine line between traditional public administration and entrepreneurial public management: "the historic boundary between those things public and those things private is no longer as meaningful as it once was" (Menzel, 2000, p. 11).

On August 1, 2005, I sent an informal email questionnaire to 20 New Jersey BID managers and received seven responses (one was in person), which represents approximately 10 percent of all BID managers in New Jersey. The following question was asked: "When you hear the term Public Administration Entrepreneur, what does it mean to you?" (a) it describes a BID/SID manager; (b) it's a contradictory statement; and (c) it's an interesting term. Seventy-one percent said it described a BID/SID manager; 28 percent said it was a contradictory term; and 1 percent said it was an interesting concept. Although this is not intended to be conclusive, the answer seems to point to an intellectual dilemma in the public administration field that has not resolved private and public sector interchanges, and indicates that Gulick's statement has not been realized. We may be in less of a politics/administration dichotomy and more in a public vs private sector management dichotomy, which seems equally superficial.

I also asked the following question: "Do you consider yourself a professional?", and received a 100 percent affirmative answer. The public sector tends to regard professionalism as enhanced technology, therefore technology transfers from the private sector to the public sector infer expertise. Expertise is often confused with professionalism. Expertism is an aspect of professionalism, but the difference lies in individual vs communal reference. Expertism is an individual achievement and accomplished by action, and professionalism is accountability to the community and accomplished by acknowledged behavior. We find a similar confusion regarding privatization. Strictly speaking, privatization refers to public services provided by the private sector: what once was public is now private. Public contracts to private firms for public services are not essentially privatization, but outsourcing where the product remains a public service. The service remains a public (communal) controlled interest. This confusion is exacerbated when private firms operating under purely public law provide a public service such as charter schools, or motor vehicle services. The private/public sector dichotomy causes confusion when they overlap, since they are not mutually exclusive.

Professionalism, particularly management, tends to be commonly viewed as sourced from the private sector and grafted to public endeavors. This is understandable from an agrarian-co-op model. Frederick W. Taylor's scientific management system may have re-initiated this notion by mechanizing this model for industry, but his system drew from autocratic models. Those that adopted it interjected a tried and true private sector productivity model into the practice of public management. In many cases this distorts the communal purposes of both public and private sector management by assuming that private productivity gains are somehow equivalent to or greater than the public gain. The self-serving rational actor is an elitist in the context of an industrial opportunist, but a poor fit to emerging a new context of public service, i.e. community development. Elitism doesn't fit democracy well, and is the rebellious cause of democratic initiative, but as it infers leadership, it can appear apt in the absence of true leadership. The rational actor is a contextual being, responsive not causal and a poor substitute for an adult. The communal Logos is causal and each of us contributes to its purpose. Human beings are more than rational actors because human beings have a greater potential and are not relegated to being childlike as Herbert Simon (1997, p. ii) tells us:

> Economist (and others) argue that human behavior in organizations, like all other human behavior, is driven by self-interest, and hence appropriate mechanisms are required to link that self interest, expressed in the profit motive, to broader social goals and needs. The only effective mechanism for achieving this linkage, their argument continues, are economic markets, Adam Smith's "invisible hand" ... I find this argument badly flawed ... its major motivational premise is simply false. Human beings make most decisions, not in terms of individual self-interest, but in terms of the perceived interest of the groups, families, organizations, ethnic groups, and national states with which they identify and to whom they are loyal.

What we see when we look at BIDs is that, at the heart of a BID is the management of a new sense of community. One that builds on its assets, sustains its values, and provides a place that people literally get their lives out of participating in. The professionalism of BID management is a pragmatic tale of emerging and evolving community spirit, and this seems to be what Herbert Simon was pointing at. What are at stake are the decisions (or choices) we make about the kind of communities we create and operate. But, if we assume a static community structure, which orthodox public administration did, we have no choice except that structure. After the 1950s, the New Public Administration movement attempted to remove all assumptions because the public order had in fact changed, and the assumed structure simply didn't fit in a world where the "fields" of endeavor changed. Although agricultural and industrial economies exist and thrive, the new 20th century middle class had succeeded in creating its own economies based not on products produced, but services provided; services that sustain a high quality of living.

Using the agrarian-co-op model principles of collective action and professional management and applying it to democratic effort, a BID is a legal structure to organize collective action in a new field of endeavor. BIDs upgrade business opportunity, provide higher levels of customer satisfaction, and can be effective in the delivery of real services. But, their best success is the success of the agrarian-co-op; a sense of community pride and purpose.

Starting with the traditional power and success of the agrarian-co-op model, and later the adapted scientific management as an import from a 19th century private sector industrial business archetype, government and public administration have consequently tended to be viewed as a subsidiary to private (business) administration. But, this can hardly be controversial, even if misguided, when so much of American social development relies on the economic success of the free market system. On the other hand, citizen participation and consensus building, hallmarks of modern public administration and applied democracy, do not initially yield substantive quantifiable profit, but are equal if not more highly prized goals.

There is a clear difference of purpose between public and private. That is, until the 19th century, the industrial economy was replaced by 20th century service and information economies, which require flexibility, integration, and adaptable external exchange. Service economies, both private and public, have similarities. Areas that adapted did well, those that didn't decayed. This is well illustrated in traditional urban areas with central business districts (economic generators) that deteriorated rapidly when they did not adjust to entrepreneurial and customer-oriented development models. Those that did succeed redefined their areas. The key to these models is "place management": a term that denotes community as a real place to live and work (in the modern world suburban locations may only be a place to live, urban places only a place to work; this constitutes a function not a place). Customer orientation is the new twist on the agrarian-co-op model. The most replicated public management model that incorporates place management with customer satisfaction is the BID or NID (Figure 1.6). "They blend public management expertise with business acumen into a unique administrative form." (Mitchell, 1999, p. 203).

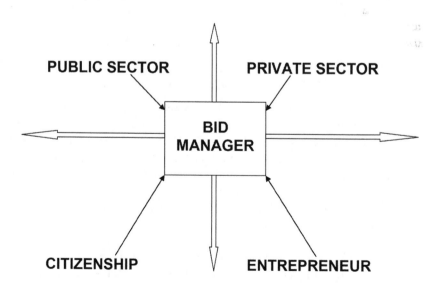

FIGURE 1.6 BID Management

At the edge of public administration, where the public sector meets the private, where free enterprise meets social capital, we can expect to find a no man's land of public policy that is often dysfunctional. At this point there is a struggle in terms of allegiance to a private/public sector dichotomy. BIDs operate in this "no man's land" using both entrepreneurial and public management models. As entrepreneurial models, BIDs are expected to "channel private-sector energy towards the solution of public problems" (MacDonald, 1996, p. 42).

At the same time, to achieve functionality in the governance system and lead the community out of chaos, they also employ a public management model to provide public sector legitimacy towards the recognition of everyday communal needs. The gray area, the "no man's land," between the private and public sector operates at the local level, and is dysfunctional when it exists in a pre-20th century forum dominated by centralized urban markets. The public order has shifted from urban to suburban, international, transnational, to global.

Today, these older urban markets must compete within their regional area, which do not automatically sustain and manage mutual interests. BIDs re-examine the localization of mutual interests and adopt retail commercial cooperative technology utilized by suburban malls to establish self-reliant service-sector economic generators. Service-sector economies are based on convenience, and area malls excel at this in a mobile society. However, convenience and ease can become monotonous. Suburban malls tend to excel in standardization and are consequently monotonous. Traditional downtowns tend to excel at diversity and niche opportunities, but suffer when poorly managed and appear inaccessible. Both suburban and urban areas share quality of life issues to define success. Standards of safety, cleanliness, accessibility, and design tend to be foundation requirements of both suburban and urban areas, with suburban areas setting the standard.

A Discussion of Entrepreneurship in BID Management

The "epoch" (Jones, Baumgartner, and True, 1998), beginning around 1956 and seemingly cumulating shortly after the 2000 Presidential election, encompasses the initiation of the home-based entrepreneur. The basis of capital for this newly minted entrepreneur is the family home and the zoned small business and commercial property, which are intractably linked by property investment, local zoning laws, and customer relations. Many small business people, and most people, "do not really own much else" (Fischel, 2001, p. 4) than their home, business, or business property. The home-based entrepreneur is Fischel's homevoter, and in the case of the small business person, the commercial voter.

The homevoter is linked to the small business commercial voter by the amount of personal investment in a single property and with a chief interest in "managing assets well" (Fischel, 2001, p. 64). Both are also linked by their voting behavior, which is aimed to maximize their primary property asset. If this asset is exceedingly compromised they will both "vote with their feet" and purchase in a better managed community (Tiebout, 1956). The home-based entrepreneur seeks governance that is accessible and directed towards maximizing their primary property asset. The enticement of real governance authority is a chief cause of SIDs, which represent a reaction to centralization and perceived government inaccessibility and indifference to economic maximization of property assets. SIDs that focus on business communities work to equalize the relationship between the homevoter and the small business voter by emphasizing linked entrepreneurial interests. This is accomplished by extending authorities of the municipal corporation to the business sector, defining a district community, and requiring stockholder participation both financially and managerially.

The recognition that within municipalities exist not only neighborhoods, but systems of communal interaction based on a variety of social and economic interdependencies that define the context of private investment is at the heart of the SID concept. In this way, SIDs fundamentally reinforce practices that support successful community development and provide the public sector with asset management structure necessary to define and implement property investment maximization strategies. The SID concept is first and foremost a community building movement, and relies on community definition and implementation practices.

In this way, the home/commercial voter can be characterized as the community-based entrepreneurial voter. The entrepreneurial voter clearly apprehends the value of their personal property as a chief asset, but must soon come to appreciate the impact of common property on this private asset. Addressing and managing common property as a linked asset to private property is less determinable unless a consistent and formalized structure, effective in identifying agreed upon mutual assets and managing these assets, is determined. Managing the aspects of private property is often less complicated because it is often not a democratic, but autocratic process. Managing common community assets tends to be more complicated particularly in a democratic process. In both private and public situations without a management structure, investment potential is compromised. This requires additional attention at the public level. The successful entrepreneur pays attention to the internal private risks of an investment, and equally important, the impact of external public risks. In the case of the community-based entrepreneur, without a public asset management structure, the risk factor in managing the public impact of private investment may be too great, and eventually would be relinquished to the few that are heavily capitalized by privilege or demeanor; essentially a feudal system.

Management of assets, both private and public, is the key to success for the entrepreneur. The preferred method of management at the level of homeowner/ small business appears to be the localized municipal corporation and its antecedent, SADs (Houstoun, 2003). Small business entrepreneurs and "homeowners will, at the local level, want to adopt the mix of policies that maximizes the value of their primary asset" (Fischel, 2001, p. 6). Successful management is asset-driven and maintains a close proximity to its charge. As private independent investments grew in the middle class following WWII, so did local government which aimed at managing these investments.

In this way the homevoter is partnered with the commercial voter sharing a symbiotic entrepreneurial link with both behaving as entrepreneurial voters. Personal property assets at the scale of the modern homeowner or small business person function by the contextual framework of the community they are in. The explosion in personal property ownership caused a fragmentation of community assets. This fragmentation causes a disturbance in the value of community assets because the level of small scale private investment potentially interrupts communal identity disrupting interdependent alliances through overemphasized independent alignments. "Once you've made the purchase, your only protection against community decline is watchfulness and activism" (Fischel, 2001, p. 75) alludes to the purpose of municipal corporate strategies. The framework of the municipal corporation is to harness the exogenous assets that comprise the sense of contextual value thus permitting fragmentation to sustain a rational purpose.

Zoning and other land use designs are none other than the conceptual framework of asset valuation in the face of community fragmentation/individualized disturbance. A disturbance having no contextual relation withers away to meaninglessness, which is another way of saying it erodes contextual value. This is witnessed in situations of urban blight as well as rural devaluation. However, a community fragmentation disturbance, if managed, can increase the overall value of the community by accentuating its constituent parts.

Modern local government efforts are designed to identify and manage asset impactors (fragmentation disturbances) as they evolve in the successful development of real neighborhoods and extended communities. This sustains the value of contextual assets, which the personal (privatized) asset is a part of. The entrepreneurial voter will "vote with their feet" when contextual (community) assets are poorly managed and undefined. Community-based entrepreneurs and other localized investors tolerate property taxes (and special assessments) only when the public services financed by them are capitalized in their property values.

Because a home or small business property may in fact be most people's primary investment, this implies that the home-based entrepreneur is very local. The investment is a locally generated motivator. Different than tribalism, which is inclusive, the fragmentation of common goods in itself is disruptive to managing contextual assets. To counter this, "homeowners were becoming conscious that the attractiveness of the entire community, not just their own structure and those of their neighbors, made a difference in the value of their homes" (Fischel, 2001, p. 216), and the same is true of the small business investor. The local municipal corporation balances the fragmentation disruption by effectively managing common assets and continuously interpreting their value over time.

The risk facing the modern civic entrepreneur is that the independent entrepreneur tends towards an irrational abuse of the commons (Ostrom, 1990; Elliot,

1997), which can disrupt the value of private investment by eliminating or reducing its contextual linkages. A rational response might be to establish management structures that sustain contextual assets while private property assets are recognized through community fragmentation. This response recognizes that when the contextual asset is eroded, the value of the private asset is corroded and will also degenerate. Then only attuned and sustained efforts to redefine and manage contextual assets will permit revitalization and investment maximization. Fragmentation is most effective when contextual assets are valued at a premium. No fragment of a community can be a premium asset unto itself. If a trend towards primary fragmentation occurs, making a fragment of a community the premium contextual value, then each adjoining parcel value is at risk of degradation equal to the value of the primary fragment. This means that an entire community is at risk of being sufficiently devalued by the reliance on one or more fragments of the community achieving the full asset value of the community. Company towns throughout the country are testament to this axiom. When the company is successful everyone wins, when it isn't everyone loses.

Municipal corporations are similar to private corporations, however, "different than private corporations because of the localized economic interests of the shareholders" (Fischel, 2001, p. 30). Local municipal governments work to maximize stockholder assets just like a private corporation. "Sub-municipal" business and NIDs are extensions of this effort with often an even more articulated economic goal. It seems inevitable that decentralization will continue as long as homeownership is permitted because it empowers residents and local businesses to manage their chief assets. Again, the "homevoter hypothesis" is more accurately an entrepreneurial voter hypothesis that matches a fundamental model utilized by BIDs to determine and maximize contextual assets: *Agreements, Management, Commitments, and Accountability*. Although the entrepreneurial voter is initially motivated by the preservation of a private property asset, what has emerged by way of the municipal corporation is a clear understanding of the importance of contextual community assets arrived at by applying the BID model: **Agreements** efficiently resolve the fragmentation problem when the "fragmentation of local government causes property owners, who are mainly homeowners, to see a mix of local services that maximizes the value of their holdings" (Fischel, 2001, p. 223); **Management** resolves the erosion of achieved agreements by sustaining clear direction and recognizing that "the financing of local services from the property tax is a key element of this efficiency seeking activity" (Fischel, 2001, p. 223); and **Commitment** is the resolution of fragmentation irrationality, the result of a process where business support and "homevoters will vote for property tax increases if the expenditures they finance will increase their home values" (Fischel, 2001, p. 223).

Accountability resolves the distortion of trust and problems of misdirection, miscommunication, and miscue. It asserts management and is the completion of a promise and performance process where performance is based on articulated and

TABLE 1.1 Agreement–Management–Commitment–Accountability Trust Matrix

	Trust	
	Low	High
Agreement	Instant Gratification	Real Change
	Output-only orientation	Outcome Orientation
	Adversarial. Dichotomous	Partnership
Management	Ad hoc/Proxy	Professionalism
	Manipulative	Transparent
	Exclusive	Inclusive
	Miscommunication	Communication
Commitment	Deception	Commitment
	Compromise	Collaboration
	Incompletion	Action
	Short-lived	Longevity
Accountability	Disagreement	Promises
	Confusion	Clarity
	Low performance	High performance
	No measurement	Balanced measurement

established promises (Grossman, 2016). This model defines the entrepreneurial advantage by equalizing public and private investment impactors, sharing common exogenous risk factors, and managing contextual community assets.

BID management begins in traditional commercial areas (downtowns, neighborhoods, city centers, industrial areas, etc.) that have not adapted to current competitive trends. These trends are consumer and employment standards: cleanliness, pedestrian accessibility, signage, modern store display, advertising, dining, entertainment, automobile safety, operable public leisure space, definable destination. Each business area is distinct and BID management must be innovative. Innovation as the cutting edge of governance often embodies the blending of private and public sector practices; entrepreneurial with public choice; market-driven with accountability; and self-interest with public good. In 2001, Jerry Mitchell describes three BID management approaches that blend (to one degree or another):

a an entrepreneurial approach focused on independent decision making and creative thinking;

b a public service approach centered on the development of political relationships and the need to work with alternative stakeholders to advance particular objectives; and,

c a supervisory approach concerned with efficient management of day-to-day activities.

(Mitchell, 2001, p. 206)

Entrepreneur, public servant, and supervisor address the themes of the BID manager. The BID manager is a different kind of animal in the public management field. For decades many have attempted to define the profession. It is not one that can easily be pigeonholed into a simple discipline. It requires not only public administration and organizational skills, but business economic and development, public relations and marketing, personnel and project management, finance and budgeting, and political skills. The fact is that BID managers must adapt and use all of the three management aspects Mitchell describes above because BID management is as much a venture in building community management capacity as it is in delivering services. The competencies of a BID management expert (also from the August 1, 2005 questionnaire) are:

- business retail development and marketing;
- public policy development, community development, and organization;
- personnel and group management;
- not-for-profit financing and budgeting;
- multi-task project management;
- public relations and communications; and
- urban planning and development.

Mitchell ranks nine knowledge and skill requirements for the management of BIDs based on a questionnaire mailed to 404 BIDs nationwide in June 1999 (Mitchell, 2001, p. 213):

- speaking effectively to audiences;
- financial analysis and budgeting;
- planning for and designing projects;
- situation and political analysis;
- bargaining and negotiating methods;
- writing policy statements and reports;
- impact analysis and evaluation;
- research methods and data analysis; and
- job analysis and performance evaluation.

In short, a BID manager is a blended public administrator with an economic development focus "combining practical business skills with community knowledge and consciousness" (Stanford Graduate School of Business, 2005). However, at the risk of obscuring these competencies, the BID manager must be looked at first and foremost as a change agent; a facilitator of public processes that engage individuals in developing and sustaining community competencies and competitive practices that draw out real potentials and refine assets. "Public managers need to rely more on interpersonal and interorganizational processes as complements – sometimes as substitutes for – authority" (Kettl, 2002, p. 169). This is why BID managers, as public managers, transcend strict expertism even while accomplishing necessary competencies. The chief expert capability of a BID manager is a fundamental pursuit of interdependent-co-operative functionality. This does not rely on the interest of individual actors, but on the sensibility of aggregate determination. The competency missing in the above charts is that of the transrational actor, one whose self-interest is communally based.

The BID movement is a transformational governance axiom that reinvents and redefines the functionality of our communities, which derive economic relevance through the investment of social capital. In many urban and transitional communities, economic relevance is marginalized in large part to a process of disinvestment in social norms and shifting global relationships. Communities must be reinvented by the citizenry and the expressed agreements managed effectively to avoid erosion. This shifts government to more localized formats such as BIDs. BIDs operate in a context of emerging governance. BIDs are decentralized government structures; however, decentralization does not only depart from centralized structures, but also works back to formalized government and is most successful when that is accomplished. BIDs are generally designed as legal PPPs. These partnerships predict not only required BID management competencies, but also dictate an essential accountability to provide legitimate financial and organizational capability to emerging communities. In this way, the BID model is adaptable to many public forums.

Teamwork, cooperation, and coordination allow the entrepreneurial spirit to evolve. Entrepreneurialism is not an individual occurrence; even if its benefits tend to inure to the risk-taker, it is a potential available through collective assignment. Because it is the potential of the land, the greater substance, which provides opportunity, an individual cannot be entrepreneurial if the society they exist in is not. An individual can only be an opportunist if the rewards derive from the community. A hypothetical equation for this transaction: potential (assets) plus value infused by agreement equals values; values are that which is valuable. Obtaining that which is determined valuable by the community is rewarding to the individual. Profit is a matter of sustainable exchange within a value system. Value is a result of discovered and agreed upon community assets. That agreement is communal, a dialogue not an individual monologue. A monologue has no value unless it is in the context of a dialogue.

The public management entrepreneur must master the art of community; the building of dialogues of value that allow each person to act on a value exchange as an opportunity. If we look at this practically, we can see that in deteriorated communities there is (virtually) little or no conversations of value. There is only a chaos of competing monologues, which by their nature have no value. The result is slum and blight. The great role of public administration and management beyond maintaining a community's value is to create it by reinventing a sense of collective action where it is lost or assumed.

In almost every study of BIDs, there is a lament that there are no useful comparative studies to determine whether or not BIDs work: "both the critics and the defenders of BIDs make their assertions without a fig leaf of useful comparative research to cover them" (Houstoun, 2003, p. 144). The odd thing here is that Houstoun's entire book is a series of reports feigning comparisons. The reason there aren't comparisons is that this kind of quantitative analysis seems to tell someone something about what they can see simply by walking down the street: a successful or failed economy, a store open or closed. The greatest benefit in BIDs, as opposed to a suburban type mall, is that the community is more viable, enjoyable, and functioning. The cause is difficult to measure because an exact sense of community success is difficult to measure. Like pornography, you know it when you see it, but it's hard to define exactly what it is that differentiates it from other human and nonhuman behaviors (*Jacobellis v. Ohio*, 1964).

In their business plans, malls may not state or care what their general impact is on the greater community. They are concerned about the impact the community has on them. BIDs have an opposite perspective and are obsessed with their impact on the community because BIDs are the community. They are comprised of not only invested businesses but residences; invested people. An improvement in the BID is an improvement to the community. This cannot be wholly said for a suburban mall. It can't even be said for government institutions. (Not that malls and government institutions do not contribute to the welfare of a community, and one might expect government to benefit the community over elite politics.) However, in both cases improvements are not direct benefits to the community at large and often amiss. The same can be said regarding "big boxes" such as Wal-mart who have great community impact, but often little interest in that impact. Therefore, the impact can be, but often is not, beneficial to the host community.

Most people's lives (that is, the actual life of a person) are local. Decentralization efforts, such as BIDs, address the erosion of specific locality. This means the erosion of our very specific lives. In the face of economic circumstances larger than ourselves and our neighborhoods, efforts to restore reasonable determination and the ability to make decisions and choices must be reconstituted by extending governance authority to the disenfranchised. This is exactly what BIDs accomplish, and why the BID manager is chiefly a professional public administrator and government operative with an entrepreneurial bent. In almost every aspect of the literature this is overlooked.

A public administrator may be inclined to be bureaucratic or entrepreneurial. Both aspects are two faces of one system that pull public management from centralization to decentralization and back again; from unified benefit to fields of endeavor that need to be tilled; from conservation to risk taking. The BID movement is a practice of pragmatic citizenship based in the traditions of early American agrarian entrepreneurship. The creation of community, its spirit, values, and direction on the frontiers of social and economic change call forth a unique element in public administration. This element is a compulsion to transform a cadre of competing individuals (monologues) into a team (a dialogue); a functioning, organized, and recognizable entity that manages its assets effectively:

The world has changed and public management is not an exception. Using resources in the most efficient way in order to satisfy citizens' demands and take advantage of the opportunities of a competitive and globalised world, for getting societies more in agreement with collective wishes, all this requires changes, imagination and innovation.

(Janeiro, 2003)

This type of public administrator manages the human process of agreement; a process that "brings people together to solve common problems, develop agreements, and manage those agreements with commitment over time" (Grossman, 1998). Agreement requires partnership, which implies cooperation, direction, and communication. Partnership development is the cornerstone of community development. The BID manager is a public administrator in its essential form: an expert practitioner of economic and social community processes that maximize the potential of opportunity.

Towards a Theory of Partnership Rationalization

Two Hypotheses—Two Conversations

1. A Hypothesis of the Art of Community: Managing Context; Partnerships

This section explores fundamental differences in management that BIDs pose. BIDs lead us towards the possibility of management *in partnership* (transrational/ collective) rather than from principal to agent (rational/individualistic). It presupposes a New Public Governance (NPG—a 21st century concept following the New Public Management (NPM) of the 1990s; a return to democratic governing processes and functions) that is based on the need for collaboration and the skills of partnering to accomplish public goals. BIDs clearly work in this realm and seem to have anticipated and applied NPM and NPG requirements (Chandler, 1996). Bringing market and private practices into public administration has been fruitful, but also anemic when it cannot forge lasting and productive collaboration. How do we know collaboration is occurring, when we observe partnerships being built and/or sustained? Rational theories are useful in predicting the functional behaviors of individuals. However, they are limited in describing sociability and the behavior of groups, partners, and collectives, especially when that is not only the driving force but the intended outcome. This is a discursive exploration into collaborative phenomena within management applicable to business district and partnership management in public administration. What are the possible context, conversations, and beliefs in this system?

Questions arise as to the normative concept of the rational actor in public decision-making processes. Is the action of each person an event of uniquely individual effort (the rational actor), or is it an interpretation of a communal event (contextual performance)? Bryan D. Jones, in describing policy punctuations, alludes to this question: "Expanding our gaze to cover a greater range of observations creates a more difficult modeling task, but offers a possibility for a more accurate theory of political change" (Jones et al., 1998, p. 26). In either case, in what way does human expression contribute to our contextual understandings when at the same time contextual events are reinforced by individual action? This proposal looks at the theory of contextual motivation; that individuals are an expression of existing or potential communal understandings. Individual choice occurs once a contextual event has been articulated.

A theory of contextual motivation begins with the following hypothesis: If we say there is a way we are as individuals *that is an event*, that when distinguished has us understand our impact in the world, then the actions of the individual are contingent on the event they participate in. The rational actor may perform without this contextual aspect distinguished. If how we describe our lives creates our entire lived reality and possibly the reality *we* attract, then if distinguished, it is alterable, thereby altering reality and (literally) existence as we know it. Consequently, we could change or transform the events (context) that occur for us by our ability to express something new. Additionally, what happens to us and around us is then caused by the contextual event that we and others describe. If the action of each person is not simply an event of uniquely individual effort (bounded rationality), and it can be described as an interpretation of a communal event (contextual performance), then the attention to the contextual performance will alter all interpretations of individual events instantaneously.

A contextual event is the sum of conversations of both "institutional and brute facts" (Searle, 1995) and intuition that we have mastered and traffic into which we express our humanity. It is our culture and it looks like the communities we live in. The sum of conversations is our *sense of community*. Our sense of community is the *contextual event* that our individual (singular) event expresses. In this way, each person and each community is a network of conversations (context). The rational actor then only speaks the context available to them at any given time. In this way, the sum of all conversations, the human discourse, and the greater network of all human conversations give us the context of our humanity. Discourse analysis is an awareness of the network of conversations that motivate social interaction and enable us to solve concrete problems—not by providing unequivocal answers, but by asking ontological and epistemological questions.

The first question is: Where do conversations come from? The second question is: How do they stay around when once spoken they appear to disappear instantly? The third question is: How are they managed? The first question's answer is obvious; they come from each of us. The second question's answer is not so obvious, but appears to be that somehow conversations are managed so that they do not disappear. The third question is answered by noticing that conversations are managed by dialogue and discourse occurring in the representational and structural environment of human beings. This appears to be the nature of language expression, i.e. conversations that are managed so that they do not disappear. And, the network of conversations gives us our reality. This is the purpose of discourse.

A "contextual event" is the sum of conversations (Foucault, 1972) and the discourses we have mastered and traffic into which we express our humanity, our reality. It is the holistic expression (both potential and kinetic) of ourselves that we have learned to express. What occurs in the field of this expression is an "Event of Being"; a contextual event, which permits social interaction. Both by context and singularity we are an expression of this event. In other words, an individual and a collection of individuals is an expression of a context; of a community. Individual expression refers to contextual understandings, and each expression expresses an aspect of the community necessary for the community to exist. And, this seems undistinguished for most people. For most, individual expression is only the motivations of the rational actor. They express the individual in juxtaposition to other individuals or collections of individuals. In this theory, individual expression is a result of a community's understanding or agreement as to what is possible. They express the growth and development of the community.

A singular event occurs wholly within a greater event. Each part is a whole within something that is a greater whole and complete event (Wilber, 2000). There is no event that is isolated. All occurrences are contextual as all events are events within other events. A greater event housed within a lesser event will give rise to a background discourse of scarcity and limitations if it does not perceive itself as part of a greater event. This is experienced as failure to be, and results in efforts to protect one's sense of being. This is considered the norm. When a lesser event perceives itself as a part of a greater event, essential to the expression of the greater event, the background discourse of scarcity is transformed into one of potential and evolution.

Who we are then is not a failure to be. This appears to be a trick of singularity; however, it is a conversation in the world. The failure is not personal, but a failure to distinguish the whole self in its eventuality, and to distinguish the event-context that each event or each of us occur in. The individual (singularity) cannot by seeking its independence (monologue) perceive the contextual-event (dialogue), and cannot alone see the horizon of its own event. This is distinguished only by placing oneself within a greater context, which operates in dialogue. Successful community development efforts seem to break down monologues and encourage dialogue that distinguishes context.

Distinguishing "our event" (singularity) accomplishes at least two practical things. **One**, it reveals the event (singularity) we cause thereby giving us access to alter it. **Two**, it reveals the event-context that causes us, thereby giving us freedom to be altered. An undistinguished event (of any kind) by its nature causes a static at the (last) event horizon perceived. Growth and development occur when the event horizon is perceived. And, it is perceived in the moment the event-context (community) is distinguished.

Each event-singularity (individual expression) is also an integral event. What is an "event-context"? It is a constructed integral event, a whole entity (Wilber, 2000), which for human beings tells us who we are contextually; it is the source of our social concepts of humanity and presupposes partnership. This is supported by a strict social constructionist who expresses that "there is no objective reality but only the construction itself" (Schneider and Ingram, 1993, p. 335; Spector and Kitsuse, 1987). Similarly, the event-context is what it is to be a human being that is not depleting or a response to a failure to be. It is the sum total of what it is to be … human. And, these conversations are sourced by each person distinguished by what they say. It leads to a pragmatic question of what dignity is. Dignity could be said to be the graceful aware-ness, acceptance, and acknowledgment of each person's event as a contributing expression of the event-context. Dignity is an articulation of one's purpose in a community.

The study of human action, decision making, and choice is derived from a closer examination of how each individual (event-singularity) is an expression of the larger context of the human community (event-context). It is a study of human dignity. Language and the conversations that arise from language are specifically human (Stubbs, 1983). Human beings can be said to be language inventors, and live in a world of language. What is known is that which is *languaged*. Therefore, to understand human behavior we must listen and understand the language expressed (Foucault, 1972). This language is chiefly expressed representationally through the spoken and written word, and structurally through created and per-ceived objects. This language tells us what reality is or is not, and it is always evolving. Language evolves. It is plastic, malleable, describing what we can con-ceive, and how we process the noetic experience. Human beings live in an ocean of language of which the greatest amount appear undistinguished as conversations because they are enormous and long lasting discourses, both cultural and global.

Questions evoked are: "What practice reveals communal context? What model would unconceal it?"

The role of government in this analysis is perceived as a mechanism to manage the discourses that constitute our communities (the contextual culture). John Heritage (1997) argues:

> the assumption is that it is fundamentally through interaction that context is built, invoked and managed and that it is through interaction that institu-tional imperatives originating from outside the interaction are evidenced and are made real and enforceable for the participants.
>
> *(Heritage, 1997, p. 163)*

The role of public administrator may be somewhat different: as a manager of change rather than a protector of the status quo, "managers play a major role in interpreting critical contingencies" (Miller, Justice, and Illiash, 2002, p. 97). At stake are the decisions (or choices) we make about the kind of communities we create and operate (Frohmann, 1992).

Public administration itself may or may not be a profession, but its practices, both in and out of government, certainly are. This is because it describes more than it prescribes a sense of humanity, of human behavior, than a set of real outcomes that are achieved by good management practices. Public administration is an outcome of a desire for collective action and communal identity that seems ontological and naturally evolving. The outcomes of public administration derive from this desire, and the actions necessary to translate desire into real things.

"Creating reality in which resources are contingent and in which finance is the critical agency for commanding resources and wisely allocating them among uses, the [public] ... manager provides many institutional facts in public organizations" (Miller, Justice, and Illiash, 2002, p. 97). Professional aspects, alive within the realm of public administration, have two components described above and are separated by the need and role of management, which implies that there is a business of government. The business of government, as opposed to the private sector, trades in the realm of public values, ethics, and interest that are simply not measurable by market forces. They cope with the interdependencies of society rather than independent aspirations of the individual. Although leadership and political identity may promote one individual over another, it is not simply personal interest, but the public trust that advises government.

The public sector professional is the focused aspirant of the community, representing core values and managing those values as assets to produce a healthy economic state. Communal values are derived by a pursuit of that which promotes growth and development ... for all; essentially, an entrepreneurial drive. The paradox in public administration professionalism is the balancing of one's personal values with that of the community. An assumption that they are aligned can result in inequity. The professional public administrator's task then is to eliminate assumptive values and work to discover, reveal, and sustain agreements. The questions are: Where do we draw the line of community? What establishes context? How do we determine agreements? The nature of agreements may lead us to answer these questions and provide a better science of administration. "Part of the work of implementation analysts, then, maybe to construct these texts ..." (Yanow, 1993, p. 43).

The public administration professional practices the art of community; of directing his or her intention to the public good. A public administration professional might not ignore, but promote what is valuable about a community. In the same analysis, Dwight Waldo pointed out that logical positivism tended to simply ignore the importance of values (Waldo, 1954, p. 86), "it is not sufficient to treat values as mere data in causal theory or simply present them to others under the guise of an academic division of labor" (Fry and Nigro, 1997, p. 1190). It would seem that public administration is as much an art as a science. Yet, if there is an art to public administration it would be the art of community; the creation and occurrence of not only the sense, but the practice of community that sustains the community. If there is an "art of community" then this is a strong direction for public administration research. This may help distinguish the practice of public administration as less a political science and more a mastery of the art of community development. Today the public manager steps onto the cutting edge of public administration as a revitalizationalist; a facilitator of value-based community identity and the management of the agreements that eventually sustain that identity. This describes a process of transformation from individual, rational actor, to interdependent transrational activist.

2. A Hypothesis of Community Development Management

There is the traditional way of either providing money for a project when requested or identifying some singular need or problem and organizing an effort to meet it or resolve it. These are ways to fix things. However, there is another way that strengthens and broadens that approach: *Partnerships*. There is greater power available in communities, i.e. neighborhoods, towns, organizations, or corporations, than the people involved often realize. Partnership is the mechanism that unites communities, their sponsors and volunteers around a shared vision. The special power of "partnering" provides a significant competitive advantage and is the way to achieve breakthrough results. Partnerships are a direct result of: *Bringing people together to solve common problems, developing agreements, and managing those agreements with a commitment over time* (Grossman, 2000–2005).

Successful communities might be identified by the quality, accountability, and accessibility of the partnerships they keep. Achieving the ability to be an excellent partner is the result of focusing our attention on the community rather than solely on ourselves, and to see ourselves as being that community, literally (the term community used here means any group, organization, family, or society we belong to or are engaged in). Trust is referred to as the ability to empower others and be empowered by others (see Table 1.1).

What the public manager chooses depends on the amount of agreement about goals and about the technology most reasonably suited to achieve agreed upon goals. Communities that aren't moving ahead often have a lot of conversations about what to do, but not much actually happens. If something does happen, it is disjointed, out of step, or inadequate. People wonder how they are ever going to have their communities step up to the plate and take real initiative in making things better.

When the energy to move ahead is lost in a community, it often turns out that the community's attitude is one of managing its disagreements rather than its agreements. The community may have no idea what to agree about let alone what agreements to commit themselves to. On the other hand, communities that put their plans into action and achieve results seem to have discovered something important. They have learned how to discover their agreements, and to manage their agreements with a *commitment* over time. A commitment may be credible not because contemporary politicians are themselves motivated to keep it, but because institutional or structural arrangements compel their compliance (Shepsle, 1991).

Where we put our attention not only has a lot to do with our attitude, but also extends to our ability to get something accomplished. When we put our attention on "disagreements" what occurs are exclusionary experiences that often result in a compromised effort rather than progress towards true and needed goals. The "attention" of disagreements is on the individual, or better said on "me."

Agreements are quite different. "There are portions of the real world, objective facts in the world that are only facts by human agreement" (Searle, 1995, pp. 1–2). If our attention is focused on community agreements—the community in which all the individuals or subgroups participate—then an inclusionary experience occurs. Disagreements tend to only be concerned with an individual's, or a single group's, idea of itself. "The more humans agree, the more institutional facts they accept, and, therefore, the more reality humans perceive" (Miller et al., 2002, p. 95; Searle, 1995). Agreements have a broader concern about how the entire community envisions itself. This vision is not arrived at by compromise, as compromise implies contraction or lessening. It is arrived at through consensus, as consensus implies expansion and embracing or growing capability.

However, disagreements as well as agreements are not accidental. They are maintained. To endure over time, each has to be maintained by a "structure" in the community that manages them. A structure is necessary. Sometimes the structures are apparent and institutionalized, and sometimes they are less visible. Nonetheless, it is not just the matter of agreeing or disagreeing, or only the focus of our attitudes or attention, that makes things happen or not happen. What matters is that there is a "structure" that manages what we experience. Language, culture, rules, law, institutions, organizations (such as government, corporations, or community agencies), politics, or family can define this *management* structure.

All this still doesn't completely explain why something progresses; why something is accomplished or effective over time. You can have agreement and management, but there is one other ingredient that is necessary to get things done. That ingredient is *commitment*. Many people would say, "it's money." And they are actually correct. That is because money and commitment are inseparable concepts in our culture. Therefore, where we put our money is directly linked to the commitment we have to make things happen.

And finally, there is the question of *accountability* for actual real outcomes. How do we know that our agreements are fulfilled? What measurements account for a reasonable understanding that something real occurred according to what we agreed upon? Essentially, we encounter a trust issue regarding who we are and what we can be counted on for. To ascertain this we need to balance our evaluations according to the essential aspects of our partnership. In the case of

BIDs, as PPPs, we must look at three components of the partnership: public, private, and the partnership as a whole.

Partnership theory does not base its assumptions on the same level of restrictions as does normative budget theory because it encompasses more social values interpreted as capital. Scarcity is a problem to be solved by the partnership, not an absolute condition. The prevalent assumption in budgeting theory is that "scarcity of resources in relation to demands confronts us at every level of public budgeting" (Lewis, 1952, p. 43). This is not a solitary lament, but often stated as fact exhibited most clearly in Garrett Hardin's metaphorical "tragedy of the commons" in which we are told to expect eventual ruin if we leave things up to the polite but selfish entrepreneurial commoner. Running with this assumption, the best and highest uses are argued in terms of (Brubaker, 1997):

a   relative value compared to competing needs and desires;
b   an investment that creates a "profit" in terms of the ability to encourage more resource investment;
c   a moral exercise that sustains equal advantages and avoids ruin for all; or
d   an admission that "so far we have not indicated how this question can be answered".

(Lewis, 1952, p. 44)

Assumptions of scarcity provoke financial illusion and incremental changes; collective satisfaction provides financial reality and comprehensive change. This proposal does not suppose that scarcity in the short term is not valid, but that it is a theoretical tool for determining human behavior rather than the eleventh commandment. It is a good tool, but it can be perceived of in more than one way although it usually acts as dogma rather than opinion. Scarcity conversations and the subsequent logic seem to be designed to pervert the evolutionary theory of survival of the fittest by assuming that such a quest (survival) is based on limitations rather than on expansion of potential. Scarcity assumes a static reality rather than a true evolutionary possibility of synergistic growth and development. When did evolution take on the meaning of dominance? Is it possible that the "fittest" refers simply to that which fits where the winner is the entity that fits best the circumstances of an evolving universe rather than dominating it.

Evolution may not be a function of becoming the best, but fitting the circumstances appropriately. If we look at budget theory in this light, we can imagine that budgets are not a matter of extracting an advantage, but ascertaining the correct potential of any known situation and attempting to achieve that potential. In this way, budgeting may be an asset management tool rather than simply a survival tool. Scarcity may then be considered a term for what is (at any given moment), and then it might beg the question: "What is possible?" As it is, scarcity is a term that describes impossibilities and impotencies. Budgets developed under this terminology are pos-mortems reflecting society's efforts to cling to a life preserver as the perceived commons, in a raging sea of uncertainty. Rather we might imagine budgets as the occurring collective voice of exploration steering the direction we are going as a people; as a society.

The inquiry, "What is possible?" could be the background discourse to Key's question, "On what basis shall it be decided to allocate **x** dollars to activity A instead of Activity B?" (Key, 1940, p. 1137) if we look at budgeting from an asset management perspective. The basis upon which one might choose budget allocations asking the question, "What is possible?" might be that which builds on community assets and expands human potential rather than simply avoiding contraction. A best capability might expand community assets and human potential. At worst we would avoid contraction of assets and the expression of potential because an expansion redefines the commons and seems to unconceal new opportunities (Ostrom, 1990). To understand how scarcity as possibility differs from scarcity as protectionism, we need only look at the discoveries of new resources that have propelled mankind such as: fire, wind power, fossil fuels, electricity, atomic energy, aerodynamics, and information technology. Each of these "discoveries" reshaped our notion of the "commons" which in turn reshaped our notions of what constitutes a citizen of the commons, and the benefits thereof.

It would seem a mistake to budget solely on past performance when it is clear that new phenomena, materials, and energy are discovered in the commons on a regular basis and reshape not only the potential of the commons, but of the life of the commoner. In this way, we might see that government budgeting is a process of discovery instituting the realization of an acquired or perceived potential. That potential is available to everyone potentially. If it were not, there would be no commons and all arguments would be moot.

This argument does not preclude conservation, nor should it be taken as a denial of the individual, and the profound persuasion of idealized individual limitations. However, it is this limitation hoisted on its own petard as fact that is tragic. The tragedy of the commons (Garret Hardin) is a resultant disaster of the Enlightenment notion of primacy of the individual, when that notion supersedes the evident collective potential of society. This potential has historically been honored, and is missing in the metaphor of the tragedy of the commons, which assumes that the commons existed without supervision. Truthfully, in the old world, "commons" situations were not left to whimsy, but in fact where regulated and in some instances privatized. The commons were not managed by the wind, but by institutions of communal agreements and authority. The reason for management may be easily explained as a method of communal survival, but may also be understood to be the manner of cherishing the expression of human potential, thereby allowing for the enjoyment of less material interests.

We put our money where our commitments are. This brings us to the next step after Key's question, "On what basis shall it be decided to allocate **x** dollars to activity A instead of Activity B?". That next step is: What are we committed to?

Last is the accountability aspect of collaboration that is necessary for partnerships. They are measures of "reality" based on stated promises. Accountability in this way tells us that there is no discernible performance, that is, one we can measure and know, without a promise to tell us what we were intending to do. Accountability tells us who we are, what we can be counted on for, and manages reality; the conversations of our realities. This model will be discussed and represented throughout this book as a model of partnerships.

Agreement–Management–Commitment–Accountability

1. **AGREEMENTS**—Successful communities work on agreements not disagreements. (These agreements become the services the community provides.)
2. **MANAGEMENT**—Agreements like conversations must be managed in order to be sustained, therefore, management is the key to successfully maintaining and implementing our agreements.
3. **COMMITMENT**—Success is achieved when communities are committed to accomplishing their agreements. Commitment is when everyone in the community contributes equitably to sustaining agreements. This enables accountability (Grossman, 2000–2005).
4. **ACCOUNTABILITY**—Success is evaluated by examining an organization's promises (agreements) against specific measurable results.

Conclusion

The idea of professionalism in public administration has its controversies, starting with the appropriate question of accountability to democratic processes. This controversy extends to all forms of public administration, and is less an issue when the task being assigned is strictly technical such as: building inspector, postal clerk, soldier, garbage collector, police, firefighter, economic development, etc. These task positions are aptly described as being "professionals in government," and those that provide the task of managing government services are "professionals of government" (Gargan, 1998, p. 1092).

In either case the term "professional" not only describes a recognized mastery of a particular and useful skill or technology, but ascribes to itself a sense of mission and purpose. Both derive from the establishment of collective order and purposeful public action: government. Public administration itself may still be arguing for its profession, but its practices both, in and of government, certainly are. This is because it describes and prescribes collective human transorganizational behavior and a set of appropriate management practices, ethics, and skills. Public administration is an outcome of a desire for collective action and communal identity that seems ontological and naturally evolving. The outcomes of public administration derive from this (communal) desire, and the actions necessary to translate desire into real things.

Professional aspects, alive within the realm of public administration, have two components described above and are separated by the need and role of management, which implies that there is a business of government. The business of government, as opposed to the private sector, trades in realms of public values, ethics, and interest that are simply not measurable by market forces. They cope with the interdependencies of society rather than only the independent aspirations of the individual. Although leadership and political identity may promote one individual over another, it is the public trust that advises the government, not simply personal interest.

The public sector professional is the focused aspirant of the community representing core values and managing those values as assets to produce a healthy economic state. Communal values are derived by a pursuit of that which promotes growth and development ... for all; essentially, an entrepreneurial drive. The paradox in public administration professionalism is the public balancing of one's personal values with that of the community. An assumption that they are aligned will result in inequity. The professional public administrator's task then is to eliminate assumptive values and work to discover, reveal, and sustain agreements. The questions are: Where do we draw the line of community? What establishes context? How do we determine agreements? The nature of agreements may lead us to answer these questions and provide a better science of administration in general. All these attributes including private sector aspirations are encompassed in the BID management professional. In public administration, we notice the BID manager is an excellent example of NPM values. But, there is something different in the merger of public and private capacities and processes that shows us something new in the importance of a range of distinct skills attributed to multi-sectoral partnership development necessary in the emergence of a new 21st century state rediscovering its collective capacity to succeed. Here, an exclusive NPM gives way to an inclusive NPG as a foundation of public management.

References

Axelrod, R. (1984) *The evolution of cooperation*. New York: Basic Books.

Berk, E. (1976) *Downtown improvement manual*. Chicago, IL: The ASPO Press.

Brubaker, E. R. (1997) The tragedy of the public budgetary commons. *The Independent Review*, 1(3): 353–370.

Chandler, J. (1996) *The new public management and local governance*. Sheffield: Sheffield Hallam University.

Elliot, H. (1997) *A general statement of the tragedy of the commons* (pp. 1–12). Gainesville, FL: University of Florida.

Fischel, W. A. (2001) *The homevoter hypothesis*. Cambridge, MA: Harvard University Press.

Foucault, M. (1972) *The archaeology of knowledge*. New York: Routledge.

Frohmann, B. (1992) The power of images: A discourse analysis of the cognitive viewpoint. *Journal of Documentation*, 48(4): 365–386.

Fry, B. R. & Nigro, L. G. (1997) Five great issues in the professionalism of public administration. In J. M. Shafritz & A. C. Hyde (eds), *Classics of public administration* (4th edn). Fort Worth, TX: Harcourt Brace College Publishers.

Gargan, J. J. (1998) The public administration community and the search for professionalism. In RHM (eds), *Handbook of public administration* (2nd edn) (pp. 1089–1163). New York: Marcel Dekker.

Gingrich, N. (2005) *Entrepreneurial public management as a replacement for bureaucratic public administration: Getting government to move at the speed of the information age.* Washington, DC: Gingrich Communications.

Grossman, S. A. (1998) *Business improvement district information guide and handbook.* Working paper. Newark, NJ: Cooperative Professional Services.

Grossman, S. A. (2000–2005) *Business improvement district information guide.* Newark, NJ: Cooperative Professional Services.

Grossman, S. A. (2008) *The role of entrepreneurship in public-private partnerships: The case of business improvement districts,* Doctoral Dissertation. Newark, NJ: Rutgers, The State University of New Jersey, School of Public Affairs & Administration.

Grossman, S. A. (2016) *Partnership governance.* London: Routledge.

Gulick, L. (1937) Notes on the theory of organization. In J. M. Shafritz & A. C. Hyde, *Classics of public administration* (4th edn) (pp. 90–98). Fort Worth, TX: Harcourt Brace College Publishers. Cited in: L. Gulick and L. Urwick (eds) (1997). *Papers on the science of administration* (pp. 3–13). New York Institute of Public Administration.

Harvey, D. (1989) From managerialism to entrepreneurialism: The transformation of urban governance in late capitalism. *Geografiska Annaler,* 71(B1): 3–17.

Heritage, J. (1997) Conversation analysis and institutional talk: Analyzing data. In D. Silverman (ed.), *Qualitative research: Theory, method and practice* (pp. 161–182). London: Sage.

Houstoun, L., Jr. (2003) *Business improvement districts.* Washington, DC: Urban Land Institute.

Hoyt, L. (2001) *Business improvement districts: Untold stories and substantiated impacts,* Doctoral Dissertation, University of Pennsylvania. Dissertation Abstracts International, 62, 3961–4221.

Jacobellis v. Ohio (1964) Washington, DC, Stuart, Potter, Supreme Court Justice.

Janeiro, D. B. (2003) Training of senior managers. Conference: Public Administration: Challenges of Inequality and Exclusion, International School of Administration, Galician School of Public Administration, September.

Jones, B. D., Baumgartner, F. R., & True, J. L. (1998, February). Policy punctuations: U.S. budget authority, 1947–1995. *The Journal of Politics,* 60(1): 1–33.

Justice, J. B. (2003) *Business improvement districts, reasoning, and results: Collective action and downtown revitalization,* Doctoral Dissertation. Newark, NJ: Rutgers University.

Kaufman, H. (1956) Emerging conflicts in the doctrines of public administration. *American Political Science Review,* 50(4): 1057–1073.

Kettl, D. F. (2002) *The transformation of governance.* Baltimore, MD: Johns Hopkins University Press.

Key, V. O. (1940) The lack of budgetary theory. *American Political Science Review,* 34, December: 1137–1140.

Lewis, V. (1952) Toward a theory of budgeting. *Public Administration Review,* 12: 43–54.

Lynn, L. E., Jr. (1996) *Public management as art, science and profession.* Chatham, NJ: Chatham House Publishers.

MacDonald, H. (1996) BIDs really work. *City Journal,* 6, Spring: 29–42.

Menzel, D. C. (2000) *Privatization and managerial ethics in the information age.* Abstract, University of South Florida.

Miller, G., Justice, J., & Illiash, I. (2002) Practice as interpretation. In A. Kahn & W. Hildreth (eds), *Budget theory* (pp. 89–114). Newark, NJ: Rutgers University.

Mitchell, J. (1999) *Business improvement districts and innovative service delivery* (Grant report). Arlington, VA: PricewaterhouseCoopers Endowment for the Business of Government.

Mitchell, J. (2001) Business improvement districts and innovative service delivery. *American Review of Public Administration*, 31(2), June: 201–217.

Mitchell, J. (2008) *Business improvement districts and the shape of American cities*. Albany, NY: State University of New York Press.

Morçöl, G., & Zimmerman, U. (2006) Metropolitan governance and business improvement districts. *International Journal of Public Administration*, 29: 1–29.

Osbourne, D., & Gabler, T. (1992) *Reinventing government*. Reading, MA: Addison-Wesley Publishing Co.

Ostrom, E. (1990) *Governing the commons: The evolution of institutions for collective action*. Cambridge, MA: Cambridge University Press.

Schneider, A., & Ingram, H. (1993) Social construction of target populations. *American Political Science Review*, 87: 334–347.

Searle, J. R. (1995) *The construction of social reality*. New York: Free Press.

Shepsle, K. A. (1991) Discretion, institutions, and the problem of government commitment. In P. Bordieu & J. Coleman (eds), *Social theory for a changing society* (pp. 245–263). New York: Russell Sage.

Simon, H. A. (1997) *Administrative behaviour* (4th edn). New York: Free Press.

Spector, M., & Kitsuse, J. (1987) *Constructing social problems*. New Brunswick, NJ: Transaction Publishers.

Stanford Graduate School of Business (2005) Public Management Program: Public Management Initiative, "1996–1997 Public Management Initiative Social Entrepreneurship," Stanford University, CA.

Stokes, R. J. (2002) *Business improvement districts: Their political, economic and quality of life impacts*. New Brunswick, NJ: Rutgers University.

Stubbs, M. (1983) *Discourse analysis: The sociolinguistic analysis of natural language*. Chicago, IL: University of Chicago Press.

Tiebout, C. M. (1956) A pure theory of local expenditures. *The Journal of Political Economy*, 64(5), October: 416–424.

Waldo, D. (1954) Administrative theory in the United States. *Political Science*, 3: 86.

Wilber, K. (2000) *Integral psychology*. Boston, MA: Shambhala Publications.

Yanow, D. (1993, March). The communication of policy meanings: Implementation as interpretation and text. *Policy Sciences*, 2(1): 41–61.

2

FOUNDATIONS OF THE PROFESSION OF BUSINESS DISTRICT MANAGEMENT

Entrepreneurship, Social Capital, and Multi-Sectoral Partnerships

Entrepreneurship is as much a public process as it is a private attribute and its role in PPPs works to transform private sector ambitions into public accountabilities (National Commission on Entrepreneurship, 2001). In general, public nature appears to tell us a great deal about the role of entrepreneurship because it is strongly correlated with social capital. A PPP, especially the BID model, is highly entrepreneurial but with a public twist that is synergistic with social capital and the networks that produce it. BIDs are units of sub-government based on special assessment forms of public financing that create a formal PPP and a local self-help mechanism to address revitalization and redevelopment needs of a designated business area (Mitchell, 1999; Hoyt, 2001; Stokes, 2002; Justice, 2003; Morçöl, 2006). "BIDs have been given the financial and managerial capacity to make a difference" (Mitchell, 2008, p. 38). "Business Improvement Districts are self-assessment districts that are initiated and governed by property or business owners and authorized by governments to operate in designated urban and suburban geographic areas" (Morçöl, Hoyt, Meek, and Zimmerman, 2008, p. xv). The BID manager is strongly identified as a public management entrepreneur, representing a pragmatic form of public administration that is well suited to hybrid management techniques necessary for PPPs to succeed. "BID organizations act as an 'entrepreneurial holding company' … a means of governing the center of communities through a partnership involving public, private and civic actors" (Segal, 1998, p. 1). However, entrepreneurial activity, as progressive as it may be, does not come without concerns regarding public accountability, gentrification, conflicts with residential advocates, service provision, and policy influences (Hoyt, 2001; Stokes, 2002; Justice, 2003). There was virtually no evidence that BIDs were exceptional in these ways. "The caricatures of BIDs – that they are too consumption-oriented, undemocratic, and unaccountable – are likewise criticisms of city administration in many policy areas" (Mitchell, 2008, p. 14). BIDs may get involved in local political controversies but seem to act as vehicles for accelerated citizen involvement and dialogue. Unlike purely economic agencies, BIDs are so localized that they become extensions of the community and their true nature is community development. Their positive impact on quality of life issues that affect everyone in the community may be the reason for their popularity and persistence.

In a democracy, public administration often evolved when new aspects of private society became the normal practices of government. This transformation in government was best described as the private sector taking on public sector accountabilities rather than the public sector deferring to private practices (Bozeman, 1987). PPPs at "the edges of government" (Becker, 2007) were traditionally the method of governmental transformation. The most formal and localized PPPs to emerge as a reaction to the social fragmentation caused by suburbanization and the consequent neglect of America's downtowns were BIDs (Berk, 1976; Mitchell, 1999; Hoyt, 2001; Stokes, 2002; Houstoun, 2003; Morçöl, 2006). BIDs infuse community development processes with a new entrepreneurship based on community ownership of the process.

The sub-governmental special BID movement formalized this partnership (Houstoun, 2003) and since the 1970s, BIDs emerged to challenge the private/public dichotomy. As public entities, BIDs take on what has been assumed to be much of the private sector function of community-based entrepreneurship. As private entities, BIDs have public authority and accountability for community development. But the emerging result is not just a quasi-governmental form of governance but a public organization that utilizes entrepreneurial capability with a distinctly social aim. Consequently, traditional public administration must assimilate the concrete functions of interdisciplinary public managers that embrace entrepreneurship.

This research examined the role of entrepreneurship in formal PPPs. The specific form that these PPPs took were BIDs, in that they were established by law and were formal governmental institutions, while, nevertheless, managed by predominately private interests. The research used a mixed methods approach. Initial interviews were conducted with nine BID managers: three in New Jersey and six others throughout the United States. A pilot test, including 15 people, was conducted with the proposed email survey. The final email survey of known BID managers in the United States, based on available data, numbered 650. It should be noted that BIDs are allowed in 49 states, excluding Wyoming, and established in 48 states; South Dakota had not yet created a BID (Mitchell, 2008). However, formal reporting requirements and centralized data collection were largely non-existent and certainly not routine. Identifying BIDs was an exploratory process based on looking into non-standardized state programs, advocacy agencies, such as the International Downtown Association (IDA), and similar networks that were not necessarily focused on BIDs. Prior to the research conducted in 2007, only 574 BIDs had been verified, chiefly by Becker (2007). During this research, beginning in January 2008, an additional 76 were identified. After the research was completed in March 2008, it was speculated that an additional 100 BIDs might exist in the United States, although this was not confirmed. At the time of this research, the known number of BIDs in the United States was surveyed with 275 (42 percent) responding. Later, in 2010, Grossman and Becker conducted a United States BID census and the number of BIDs counted was 1,002.

Efforts to understand the merger of public and private sector management behavior in business and community development appeared to be a challenge to both normative public and business administration practices (Hoyt, 2001, Justice, 2003; Morçöl, 2006; Jeong, 2007). Both sectors express independence but often act interdependently. A problem in determining the capacity of public management arises when public administration exists within a PPP. There is natural confusion regarding which sector the partnership is chiefly aligned with. This confusion extends to the professionals who manage these partnerships.

The research question for this study examined the role of entrepreneurship in these partnerships and sought understanding of how the management of a PPP in the context of government might be determined without diminishing either sector. Since the 1980s or before, entrepreneurship was vigorously attributed to public sector behavior. Definitions of entrepreneurship universally disavowed a strict profit motive and supported a definition that spoke of exploration, creativity, and the ability to organize others around new notions of what was valuable (Schumpeter, 1947; Lewis, 1984; McClelland, 1987; Thornton, 1999; Newbert, 2003). Entrepreneurs were notable because they identified and exploited opportunities that others did not act on or observe. Contrary to the common assumption, entrepreneurship seemed to stem from as much a social as an economic interest (Ashoka, 2007; Wiklund, Davidsson, and Delmar, 2003) and that interest could bridge public and private domains.

The attributes of entrepreneurship (innovation, leadership, and the reconfiguring of community/collective assets) also characterize the purpose of PPPs. These partnerships tend to have direct social and economic impacts at the local and sub-local government level. Public aspects of entrepreneurship appear well suited to describe the components of the management environment of this partnership as they address the relevant terminology of both private and public concerns. Entrepreneurship, both theoretically and practically, suggests a synergy between the traditional management purposes and practices attributed to both the public and private sectors. Recently, entrepreneurship has been used to examine the role of public management. Consequently, prefixes to entrepreneurship (e.g. social, public, policy, political, etc.) were added to describe its social and public potential. This study examined entrepreneurship and its implications for public administration.

Although the term *public entrepreneurship* is widely used, in this chapter it denoted that the indication from the data that social capital and networking that supported social capital were highly correlated to entrepreneurship in PPPs. This was not unexpected, but had rarely been documented. It altered the study to include social capital and networking as additional independent variables and prompted the hypotheses. The dependent variable in this study was PPPs and the independent variable was entrepreneurship (Figure 2.1).

Hypotheses

- HO1: If PPPs are strongly identified, then entrepreneurship will be strongly identified.
- HO2: If entrepreneurship is strong, then PPP managers will identify themselves strongly as change agents.
- HO3: If public entrepreneurship is strongly identified with PPPs, then social capital will be strong.
- HO4: If social capital is strongly identified with public entrepreneurship, then networks will be important.

It should be noted that there was an ongoing debate regarding the public and private nature of PPPs and the management of these partnerships. The significance of a finding that entrepreneurship was strongly associated with PPPs would suggest that PPPs acted as change agents in normal government processes. This further suggested that, as the public sector created participation opportunities for traditionally private sector actors and private sector technologies were utilized in the public realm, private sector roles became infused with public behavior to the extent that their interaction resulted in public behaviors. The significance of finding that social capital was associated with entrepreneurship in PPPs suggested that there was a social aspect of entrepreneurship applicable to public administration.

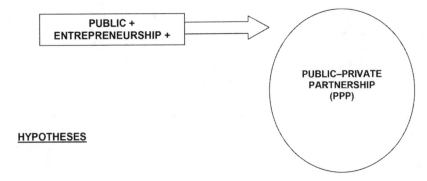

FIGURE 2.1 Research Question: What is the Role of Entrepreneurship in PPPs?

Definitions

Public–Private Partnership (PPP)—A contractual agreement between private and public sector actors to accomplish common objectives and purposes (Grossman, 2007b). "The involvement of the private sector in aspects of the provision, maintenance and sustenance of public ... utilities" (Somorin, 2008).

Public–Private Partnership (PPP) Management—A multi-sectoral expertise that bridges business, government, planning, and community development knowledge and skills to solve public problems (Stokes, 2002; Justice, 2003; Grossman, 2007b).

Entrepreneurship—A strategic process of organization and leadership that identifies and exploits previously unexploited opportunities (Hitt, Ireland, Camp, and Sexton, 2001); the strategic development of innovative value constructs (Schumpeter, 1934; Thornton, 1999).

Public Entrepreneur—"[A] person who creates or profoundly elaborates a public organization" (Lewis, 1984, p. 9); "individuals who generate, design, and implement innovative ideas in the public domain" (Roberts, 1992, p. 56).

Social Capital—"[T]he invisible lever through which citizens collectively influence the quality of their shared public life – the shared resource produced by trust in others, which in turn enables individuals to participate in organized networks" (Pierce, Lovrich, and Moon, 2002, p. 381; Putnam, 1993); trust, a vexing but certainly not important aspect of social capital (Fukuyama, 1995), is both functional and phenomenological rather than a product (Bhattacharya, Devinney, and Pillutla, 1998; Bigley and Pearce, 1998; Mayer, Davis, and Schoorman, 1995; Hosner, 1995; Abramson and Finifter, 1981; Larzelere and Huston, 1980) and defined as the *social glue* between relationships (Coleman, 1998; Fukuyama, 1995; Putnam, 1993; 2000), or a "moral glue that makes it possible for people to live together in communities of shared meaning" (Wolfe, 1999, p. 42).

Approach

Research on entrepreneurship is not a wicked problem but it can be tricky because it describes a human behavior and not a technique (see Appendix A). Although there is a generally accepted understanding of what characterizes the entrepreneur, a uniform definition does not exist and, perhaps, should not. It is a term that is applicable to virtually every human endeavor and, when discussed, must take on the inferences of that endeavor. The more one explores entrepreneurship, the more it appears not as a function but as human potential. For this study, entrepreneurship provided an explanatory variable as an inquiry into the nature of PPPs as vehicles of public service and citizen participation. Immediately, it became obvious that these partnerships could be viewed as a continuum of public to private. For this chapter, the examination was at the public end of the spectrum and although there are other types of PPPs, this research focused on

BIDs. The findings suggested that BIDs were considered as bona fide PPPs by their practitioners.

During the initial interviews to pilot test the survey, an effect was noted but not unanticipated. It was clear through the interviews that social capital, especially aspects of organization, networking, and trust, played a part in explaining the role of entrepreneurship in the PPPs that BIDs represented; consequently, that fact needed to be incorporated into the survey. This expanded the scope of the chapter from considering entrepreneurship generally to public entrepreneurship, specifically.

The objectives of this exploratory study were to analyze if and how entrepreneurship influenced the manner in which BIDs operated by surveying the known population of its practitioners. To accomplish these objectives, a mixed method (quantitative and qualitative) research design collected data from primary and secondary sources. Primary data was collected using a 32-question, 13-page electronic survey of the population as well as semi-structured telephone interviews with nine BID managers. Secondary sources included examination of BID statutes, scholarly papers, newspaper articles, trade magazines, and educational and conference materials.

The research was initiated by conducting nine telephone interviews with BID managers in the United States (three interviews in New Jersey and six throughout other areas of the United States, including California, North Carolina, Nebraska, New York, Pennsylvania, and Wisconsin; see Appendix A). The interviews explored the general themes of PPA, entrepreneurship, social capital, trust, and networking and helped establish the questions for the electronic survey. Email addresses were obtained from a 2007 email list compiled by Jerry Mitchell and Carol Becker to survey BIDs in the United States, from personal research and from the International Downtown Association (2007) utilizing a definitive email database of the known BIDs and MBDs. This research surveyed the known "universe" of United States BIDs. The survey contained dummy and multiple choice formats using a Likert-type scale with no open-ended questions; the survey featured descriptive indicators of entrepreneurship found in the literature, the General Social Survey's widely used trust measurements, attendance in meetings of clubs, and participation in organizations as indicators of social capital. The survey was applied using SurveyMonkey.com. The survey produced 275 responses, a 42 percent response rate.

In the initial phase, interviewees were contacted by email or telephone to arrange a time for the interview. The average interview was 75 minutes and recorded using a digital recorder attached to the telephone receiver. The interviews totaled 11.5 hours and spanned a three-week period. Participants did not receive a copy of the interview questions in advance. Telephone interviews seemed to facilitate the interview process.

Prior to sending out the official survey, a beta test was conducted with 15 people, ten of whom were BID managers throughout the United States. Survey emails were reduced in number when a test revealed that addresses were invalid.

The functioning emails totaled 650. The survey was opened at 12 a.m. on February 27, 2008, closed at 9 p.m. on March 12, 2008, and was initiated with an email message, which was followed up with nine reminders during the survey's availability. Although the survey instrument excluded those who had previously responded, ten respondents, or 1.5 percent, conveyed their annoyance at the number of reminders they received. However, each reminder did result in a significant increase in email responses within a two-hour period that far surpassed responses in a 48-hour period without reminders. Approximately 50 respondents, or 7.6 percent, emailed to ask questions, support the survey, or indicate that they were pleased to be reminded. Results of the survey were emailed to all 650 of the survey population at the conclusion of the survey.

Review of PPPs

PPPs are a growth field in government, for both project-specific public service contracts and the establishment of ongoing and increased public management capacity. The partnerships represent a continuum from almost purely public to almost purely private. In this dynamic arena, private investment and technology is transformed into public accountability. The private sector may look at these partnerships from the private end of the spectrum; however, public need and public actions bring forth and control the partnership and its methods of management, service delivery, accountancy and finance structures:

> The social entrepreneurship buzz phrase refers to the involvement of the private sector in aspects of the provision, maintenance and sustenance of public or what should ordinarily be public owned utilities: transportation, water, electricity, health, information, sport, telecommunications and other infrastructural assets. Most often these could be new or existing infrastructure services that have traditionally been provided by the government.
>
> *(Somorin, 2008)*

This chapter examines the purpose and function of PPPs.

There was once a clear difference of purpose between the public and private sectors (Schumpeter, 1947; Moe, 1984; Kettl, 1993, Schaeffer and Loveridge, 2002; Morçöl and Zimmerman, 2006) and, for most, it followed that there was a difference between public and private sector management. Yet, no one could escape a sense of unease that the differences were porous and becoming more so, the knowledge and experience of governance and business less reliable, and the mystery of what is private and the sanctity of that which is public was eroding. Virtually worldwide, the love affair between the public and private sectors was heating up, eroding traditional epistemology of what was what and who was whom and merging, mutating, and evolving public management into something completely new.

Since the progressive era and the business applications of Frederick Taylor (1911), this distinction displayed advanced signs of slippage, or "mission creep" (Hoagland, 1993) if one were a strict public–private sector segregationalist of either persuasion. Despite the arguments of proponents of social equity on the one hand, and the concerns of market efficiency proponents on the other hand, a curious blur was settling over the public landscape. Private actors were becoming publicly active and accountable. In many respects, the dichotomous private vs public sector discourse threatened to become a distinction without a difference. This was approved by some (Osborne and Gaebler, 1992) and created dismay for others (Denhardt and Denhardt, 2000). The modern era in human commerce is notable due, partially, to an astounding private/public integration that seems to have spirited away most reliable distinctions. This has furthered an ongoing fusion, particularly of the role of the public manager. But, since the 1970s, there emerged the business district manager who lurked in the murky and growing world of special districts designed to revitalize neglected urban America and improve business conditions at the local level. Driven perhaps more by a growing private consultancy, the public nature of this process was neglected or obscured. By muddling through (Lindblom, 1988), this downtown revitalization movement merged, blurred, fused, and redefined the role of public manager and, suddenly and appropriately, public administration became interested.

If "the market is a way of managing scarcity" (Kettl, 1993, p. 206), the public arena conversely might be a way to manage human potential, which was not unlimited but certainly abundant, growing, and not scarce. The private sector tends to attribute value from an individualistic perspective, engages personal interest and competing market forces, and exhibits limitations that are somehow overcome by the magic of an omniscient market administrator and the threat of a zero-sum game. The latter is evident but the former, as witnessed by the recent economic collapse of financial markets (2007–2008), requires a leap of faith not seen since the conversion of St. Peter.

The public sector attributes value from a communal perspective that causes the emergence and sustainability of responsive civil society and engages our collective interests. In order for this perspective to be realized requires pragmatism (James, 1909; Dewey, 1925), not prayer. The curiosity of what or which comes first, the individual or the society, is the crux of much modern argument. This divided the intellectual world into two camps: social realists that held the individual as dear and marched the dignity of the Enlightenment (Newland, 1997) to the point of disaster; and the social constructionists who stressed that humanity's social nature was its most unique invention (Berger and Luckmann, 1966; Searle, 1995). In the midst of this debate, a new phenomenon emerged on the public administration scene: the business (improvement) district (BID) manager. Having done little to ease the private vs public debate, this new character appeared to be a bona fide hybrid of both the public and private sector: an entrepreneur in a public no man's land as well as a pragmatic manager of communal intent.

The dichotomy between the public and private aspects of society enjoyed vigorous debate in the American intellectual tradition. That is, until the 19th century industrial economy was replaced by 20th century service and information economies, which required flexibility, integration, and adaptable external exchange. Service economies, both private and public, have similarities, most prominently because both serve rather than exploit. Necessity and interdependence blurred the boundaries between the public and private sectors (Kettl, 1993; Briffault, 1999). Areas of the economy that adapted to this interplay seemed to do well; those that did not, decayed. This was well illustrated in traditional urban areas with central business districts (economic generators) that deteriorated rapidly when they did not adjust to entrepreneurial and customer-oriented development models and held onto industrial models. Those that adapted or built on existing service models enjoyed better success. For government, "the BID phenomenon forces us to rethink our dichotomous conceptual foundation of public versus private on which traditional public administration is built" (Morçöl and Zimmerman, 2006, p. 22).

The key to understanding BID-oriented PPPs was "place management" (Berk, 1976; Mant, 2007); a term that denoted or revitalized community as an outcome of a real place to live and work. In the modern world, suburban locations might only be a place to live and urban sites, only a place to work. This would constitute a function, not a place. Customer orientation became the new twist on the service model. The articulation of "live" and "work" merged public and private concerns. The BID model formalized a concern that once might have been taken for granted. The most replicated public management model that incorporated place management ideas with customer satisfaction appeared to be the BID or NID. "They blend public management expertise with business acumen into a unique administrative form" (Mitchell, 2001, p. 203), and "are rooted in the long privatist tradition of urban governance and politics in the United States" (Morçöl and Zimmerman, 2006, p. 6).

At the edge of public administration, where the public sector meets the private and where free enterprise meets social capital, there is found a no man's land of public policy that is often dysfunctional. This may be due to an allegiance to a private/public sector dichotomy. "As American governments pursued more public policy through nongovernmental partners, public policy increasingly became entangled in private goals and norms" (Kettl, 2002, p. 143). BIDs operate in this no man's land, using both private entrepreneurial and community development approaches, synergistically. As entrepreneurial models, the PPPs that BIDs represent were expected to "channel private-sector energy towards the solution of public problems" (MacDonald, 1996, p. 42). Where government administration might be seen as bureaucratic and process-oriented (Gingrich, 2005), BIDs were viewed as entrepreneurial, management focused, and innovative. BIDS walked a fine line between traditional public administration and entrepreneurial public management making; "the historic boundary between those things public and those things private is no longer as meaningful as it once was" (Menzel, 2000, p. 23).

Not unlike other formal PPPs, often established as special districts, the BID model was frequently seen as the private sector providing funds and technical expertise and the public sector providing political legitimization and taxing powers. By working as a unit of sub-government with assessment powers, BIDs avoided the problem of free riders associated with volunteerism, addressed upkeep of common areas, and provided place management (Berk, 1976; Houstoun, 2003; Justice and Goldsmith, 2006). "BIDs formalize the interests of the local community" (Stokes, 2002, p. 3). At the neighborhood level of governance represented by BIDs, two forces could define benchmarks of success: citizen participation and professional management. If the definition of citizen participation was accepted, the role of self-governance in promoting institutional legitimacy, the formation of common understandings between public and private participants (Justice, 2003), and the role BIDs might play in furthering participation by citizens became evident.

BIDs also required professional management to allow for the "facilitation of agreement" (Justice, 2003) around compatible goals and committed resources (Schaeffer and Loveridge, 2002). BIDs were a form of managed cooperation and an addition to democratic governance that operated at the defining nexus (Figure 2.2) of a private/public–social/economic dichotomy that defined and often transformed the term *community* in society. Stokes stated in his 2002 dissertation that a BID "restores a level of community faith in collective processes" (p. 10).

Bozeman's 1987 diagram (Figure 2.3) depicted a multidimensional theory of the impact of publicness on organizational behavior. It described PPPs and clearly illustrated the unifying role of organizations like BIDs as a "focal organization" (Bozeman, 1987, p. 91). Access to the processes of community definition appeared to elicit perceptions of success, based initially on a sense that one's quality of life was improved, which seemed to be tied to the ability to invest personal time and energy into the development of the organization. Multidimensional theory could be successfully relabeled PPP theory. Figure 2.3 depicts the entrepreneurial aspects of economic authority and the constraints that bind innovation and sustain its benefits through institutional structures and sustained agreements. BIDs are unique because they possess both economic and political legitimacy. It is clear from the design that the feedback loop caused by the focal organization, the BID, worked to impact both public and private processes so that political and economic authority was altered. The buffers represent the factual conditions that public and private forces must contend with to achieve the competency to operate. Figure 2.3 must be read so that all the buffers have both public and private attributes and the buffers act as equalizers to keep one sector from displacing another and eroding the partnership.

Buffers also act to protect each sector from itself or from excessive intrusions that would destabilize the partnership. In this way, buffers are the foundations of network capacity and act as confidence and trust builders by allowing the correct interpretation of each sector's assets. Improper or inadequate judgment of valued

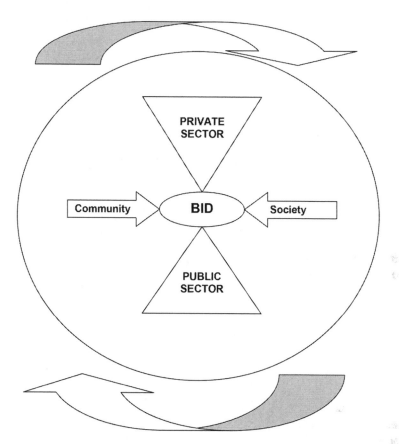

FIGURE 2.2 PPP: BID Nexus

assets of one sector on another corrupts the rational process by attributing weakness or strength ineffectually. It creates a false animosity and a foolish adversity that promotes the idea that one sector is a problem, rather than an opportunity for the other. The buffers, in effect, reduce political adversity, an attribute necessary for functional partnering. For example, resources are both public and private; boundary spanning denotes not only markets but political jurisdiction; technology must respect strengths and weaknesses of each sector; and mediating authority refers to constitutional law and, in the case of BIDs, the state enabling legislation. The focal organization acts as the fulcrum of the PPP conferring the legitimacy of each sector.

Entrepreneurship

This chapter is about the human behavior of entrepreneurship that combines personality traits with skill. Co-opted by the business community, entrepreneurship

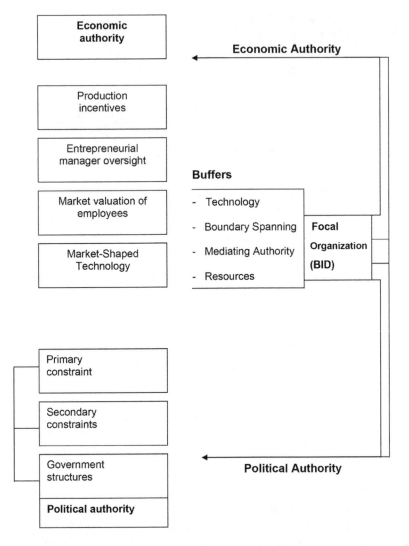

FIGURE 2.3 Multidimensional Theory of the Impact of Publicness on Organizational
Behavior
Source: Bozeman, 1987.

was not meant to define business prowess only, but the ability to identify new
things and enroll others in making something new, something real. In the arena
of PPPs, both public and private aspects of entrepreneurship converge to present
a hybrid capacity that may be necessary for successful community development to
occur. Until recently, the field of entrepreneurship has been dominated by
positivist/functionalism (Filion, 1997; Pittaway, 2003) and yet all definitions

acknowledged that organization and contextual occurrences (Weber, 1946; Pittaway, 2003), culture (Goetz and Freshwater, 2001), and climate (Goetz and Freshwater, 2001) were necessary for the entrepreneur to thrive. Since the 1990s, the study of entrepreneurship exploded into almost every field (Filion, 1997) of social, economic, and political studies. Due to this or the complexity of human nature (Schumpeter, 1947; Pittaway, 2003), there was a great deal of confusion regarding a definition of entrepreneurship (Filion, 1997; Pittaway, 2003; Kruger, 2004). Yet, there were two key aspects to which virtually every definition alluded: innovation and creativity. Entrepreneurship tumbled into the study of the business-oriented entrepreneur, which assumed a profit-motivated rationalist. But this assumption is changing as entrepreneurship becomes understood as more an aspect of human behavior rather than solely a management orientation. Both Max Weber (1904), by addressing the cultural value system behind entrepreneurship, and Joseph Schumpeter (1947), who launched the field of entrepreneurship and associating it with innovation, made seminal contributions to economic and sociologic theory.

From an individual point of view, entrepreneurialism appeared to be based on two factors: (1) human beings are the products of their environments; and (2) people become entrepreneurs when they act: "entrepreneurs do not just plan. They act" (Carton, Hofer, and Meeks, 1998, p. 5). A person becomes an entrepreneur only by carrying out a new contribution accomplished by establishing an organizational planning and implementation structure (Carton, Hofer, and Meeks, 1998). The entrepreneurial process began and ended with the observation, capturing, and implementation of the innovative enterprise. It disappeared in the maintenance stage (Schumpeter, 1934), when the enterprise is no longer new and when creativity solidified opportunity and produced real product or capability. When this occurred, it created a management/functional stage that was no longer entrepreneurial. This was why an entrepreneur and a small business person were not mutually inclusive. An entrepreneur might set up a business but once it was established and operating, it became a regular business (see Figure 2.4).

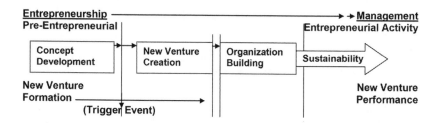

FIGURE 2.4 The Entrepreneurship Paradigm
Source: Carton, Hofer, and Meeks, 1998.

The missing piece in Figure 2.4 is that the process of Venture Formation up to Venture Performance, which is the entrepreneurial effort, has an intermediary step: Venture Strategy. In this way, entrepreneurship and business acumen were not the same thing because entrepreneurship expressed a human potential to develop opportunity rather than an economic technique to maximize production, which formalizes the "Trigger Event" and directs entrepreneurial action. Management begins a production maintenance function (sustainability) that is not entrepreneurial unless a new venture is created.

Entrepreneurship did not exist as an outside element only, but could occur in organizations because it was not a function but a process of human potential. The internal development of the entrepreneurial process, and often a term to describe entrepreneurship in public organizations, was *Intrapreneurship* (Carton, Hofer, and Meeks, 1998; Kruger, 2004). The Intrapreneur represents a strategic form of corporate entrepreneurial activity and new venture creation within an organization (Guth and Ginsberg, 1990); therefore, it appealed to the corporate/bureaucratic nature of government where the public sector was urged to be more creative. Essentially, the entrepreneur is one who has direct ownership of an enterprise, while an Intrapreneur does not have direct ownership. In this way, the term Intrapreneur applies well to representative democratic systems.

The term Intrapreneur was devised initially as a way to encourage and reward competition within corporations. It pitted departments against each other as a way of developing product. Today, the initial practice might apply but its chief aim was to encourage entrepreneurial behavior within organizations. Nonetheless, the essential aspect of an Intrapreneur was developing entrepreneurship. The term Intrapreneur added to the confusion in defining entrepreneurship because it diluted, by euphemistic tactics, an evolving understanding of entrepreneurship as "the pursuit of a discontinuous opportunity involving the creation of an organization (or sub organization) with the expectation of value creation to the participants" (Carton, Hofer, and Meeks, 1998, p. 1) and the entrepreneur as the "individual (or team) that identifies the opportunity, gathers the necessary resources, creates and is ultimately responsible for the performance of the organization" (ibid.).

Public Entrepreneurship

A uniform definition of public entrepreneurship was not established, but some aspects differentiated public from private entrepreneurship, as follows:

a   Public vs private information (Lewis, 1984; Schneider and Teske, 1992). The public entrepreneur must not only share (disclose) more information but should pursue information dissemination that was inclusive, while the private entrepreneur was more secretive and exclusive about information.

b   There was a "centrality of the social mission" (Mort, Weerawardena, and Carnegie, 2002, p. 86) in public entrepreneurship, and public entrepreneurs could be called "collection action problem entrepreneurs" (Schneider and Teske, 1992, p. 737) motivated by a collectionist sentiment to maximize collective value. The private sector entrepreneur sought to maximize financial profit and was motivated by rational choice theory (Lewis, 1984) that inured profit to specific investors.

c Public entrepreneurship worked to create public value (Moore, 1995), while private entrepreneurship worked to create private profit (Weber, 1904).

d Private entrepreneurship was influenced primarily by the supply-side of goods, while public entrepreneurship was influenced primarily by the demand-side for goods (Thornton, 1999).

The differences are intellectually stimulating but it is the similarities of entrepreneurship across all fields of human endeavor that are intriguing and most compelling. There was little substantial difference in character, competence, and behavior between the private and public entrepreneur because entrepreneurship appeared to be a unique human behavior that worked to allow change, value reorientation, community building, and discovery (Thornton, 1999). These attributes could be applied to every field of human endeavor and aptly functioned when ascribed to normative understandings of private and public sectors. The difference between the entrepreneur and the regular citizen was that the entrepreneur was on a mission to solve an identified social or economic problem, the solving of which created new products, affiliations, and value possibilities as well as the organizational constructs to maintain them (Carland, Hoy, Boulton, and Carland, 1984). The simplest definition of entrepreneurship was the strategic development of innovative value constructs (Schumpeter, 1934; Thornton, 1999). Throughout the literature in both private and public sectors, entrepreneurship shared the distinctions of:

- innovation;
- transformation;
- risk taking;
- trust (Stephens, 2001);
- value creation;
- organization and collective action;
- strategic manipulation; and
- leadership.

These distinctions identified the entrepreneur, both public and private (Weber, 1904; Schumpeter, 1934; Carland, Hoy, Boulton, and Carland, 1984; Lewis, 1984; McClelland, 1987; Baumol, 1990; Thomas and Mueller, 2000; Mort, Weerawardena, and Carnegie, 2002). Human behavior that worked to transform old concepts, values, and performance into new ones seemed to be the telltale sign of entrepreneurial activity (Schumpeter, 1934; Guth and Ginsberg, 1990; Schneider and Teske, 1992). The ideas of transformation were identical to the understandings of entrepreneurship. Entrepreneurship is a pragmatic transformation. Where there is the smoke of entrepreneurship, there may be the fire of transformation. This is applicable to every field of endeavor, not only financial or product-oriented business transactions. The NPM significantly contributed to this understanding about entrepreneurship and, consequently, non-business descriptions of entrepreneurship entered the everyday lexicon to the extent that entrepreneurship was beginning to have a public hue as it applied to business.

At its core, the concept of entrepreneurship was value generation (Weber, 1904), whether it was financial, social, or political. It was particularly human to attribute exchangeable and sustainable value to real objects and occurrences (James, 1909). Value generation was a pragmatic and creative act elicited by inducing innovation and action, both individual and communal, that solved the ever-evolving question of what was valuable. Entrepreneurship flourished when a society was stable enough to allow for innovation (Schumpeter, 1934). This innovation appeared to the beholder as an individual who changed (Lewis, 1984) the direction and flow of an entire community by:

- defining a vision of value;
- enrolling others in that vision;
- organizing a strategic vision quest; and
- developing a structure to manage the value obtained over time.

Public entrepreneurship began to take on pragmatic application in the 1990s with the NPM movement. At the same time, BIDs began to flourish at an exceedingly rapid rate and built international policy bridges. The term public entrepreneurship had been around since at least 1984 when Lewis published *Public Entrepreneurship: Toward a Theory of Bureaucratic Political Power*. Lewis defined public entrepreneurship by concentrating on the public entrepreneur "as a person who creates or profoundly elaborates a public organization so as to alter greatly the existing pattern of allocation of scarce public resources" (Lewis, 1984, p. 9).

One again, a dichotomy in the term lies in its economic origins that assume that entrepreneurship is an individualist endeavor rather than (also) a public activity. Entrepreneurship was not confined to the rational choice model but also applied to collaborative network (Lowndes and Skelcher, 1998) and cultural models (Ozminkowski, 2003). These models were transrational. Roberts (1992) defined public entrepreneurship as "the generation of a novel or innovative idea and the design and implementation of the innovative idea into public sector practice" (p. 56). She also names public entrepreneurs as "individuals who generate, design, and implement innovative ideas in the public domain" (p. 56). This was echoed by Ozminkowski (2003) who described entrepreneurship as the ability "to find opportunities and to create opportunities" (p. 27), to facilitate the "entrepreneurial environment" (p. 24) and to function as "agents of change" (p. 28). Roberts (1992) insinuated a link between social capital and public entrepreneurship by indicating that what enabled the public entrepreneur was the involvement of others in the policy process. This required participation and trust. Ozminkowski identified two key ideas that linked social capital and public entrepreneurship to public administration, furthering the cooperative aspects of public entrepreneurship as opposed to concepts of individual entrepreneurship:

1. that the public realm, i.e., culture, matters, and
2. aspects of social capital are present in public entrepreneurship, such as: trust, open mindedness, uncertainty avoidance, and public achievement.

(Ozminkowski, 2003, p. 59)

Due to its contextual nature, entrepreneurship could be a driving force of political/economic change in society as it harnessed the charismatic aspects of strategic leadership (Mort, Weerawardena, and Carnegie, 2002) in divulging human potential. Mort et al.'s description of leadership defined the individual *and* group entrepreneur and appeared reliant on the opportunities society presented in the pursuit of collective opportunity growth and value development. In this way, entrepreneurship is distinguished by its transformational directionality that points to efforts that pursue a new future rather than reconciling the past.

As community-based organizations with quasi-governmental functions and authority, BIDs operated in the public entrepreneurship realm, emphasizing economic development, decentralization, leadership, and cultural values (Justice, 2003). Without argument, the general purpose of a BID is economic success; success that must be measured not only on the individual level but especially on the community level as improvements in the quality of life for the community at large, not just the community of the BID. As a public force, public entrepreneurship dabbles in material and non-material capital. It assumes that society has economic value and that the co-joining of material and social wealth aspirations require a proficiency in the management of collective as well as individual potential with the latter a subset of the former. Additionally, the public management entrepreneur is expected to be an active partner in community and economic development at every level of society. This describes the governance concerns of PPP administration. Government is no longer here simply to help but to be part of social/economic endeavors.

BIDs operate on the local level of governance, acting as a link between the public and private sectors and a broker of municipal services; as a result, they become a potential technology and knowledge transfer mechanism with the aim of improving both sectors. The public administration argument, it seems, is that public entrepreneurship (as exhibited by BIDs) takes on a somewhat different perspective when examined from a public or cultural standpoint, rather than from a private or individualistic standpoint. Therefore, in determining the effect of entrepreneurship on the management of BIDs, the literature suggested that one should examine its public, rather than private, expressions.

The term social entrepreneur is almost the same as public entrepreneur. The distinction is that social entrepreneurs do not necessarily address change in government. Social entrepreneurship provides commercial entrepreneurs with the advantage of going public without being public, apparently an important nuance for those that have an aversion to governance and faithfully connote the superiority of the market. Bornstein (2007) described social entrepreneurs as "people who solve social problems" (p. 1). The Ashoka website (2007) defined social entrepreneurs as "individuals with innovative solutions to societies' pressing social problems." Although virtually all definitions of entrepreneurship addressed correlations between environment, creativity, visioning, leadership, strategy, risk taking, proactiveness, innovation, organization building, resource and asset realignment, sustained focus and problem solving (Schumpeter, 1934; Miller, 1983; Osborne and Gaebler, 1992; Hitt, Ireland, Camp, and Sexton, 2001; Bornstein, 2007), there appeared to be a clear distinction between social entrepreneurship and public entrepreneurship. The former addressed specific social problems and social change; whereas the latter encompassed the field of public administration and governmental processes. The literature noted that social entrepreneurship was not solely a public sector endeavor and was largely viewed as an alternative private sector movement, even though many social entrepreneurs seemed to behave in political arenas (Ashoka, 2007; Bornstein, 2007).

Emerging strongly in the late 20th century, entrepreneurship in the 21st century was equated with productivity and performance and public entrepreneurship, with obtaining solutions to public problems. This may be because entrepreneurship is a pragmatic process. However, most of the descriptions are managerial and not specifically entrepreneurial. The distinction between the two is important but it does raise the issue of noticing the managerial necessity in evaluating the success of an entrepreneurial endeavor. Entrepreneurship has been considered both positively and negatively but, generally speaking, entrepreneurship is considered important, which might explain its co-optation by the public realm. Its importance is due not only to its ability to tap into human potential but also because it opens up managerial opportunity.

At its core, entrepreneurship is value generation in both the public and private sectors. Value generation is a pragmatic and creative act that is elicited by inducing action, both individual and communal, and answers the question of what is valuable. Entrepreneurs are doers, not dreamers (Nolan Bushnell, founder of Atari and Chuck E. Cheese). Entrepreneurship flourished when a society was stable enough to allow for innovation (Schumpeter, 1934; Maslow, 1943) and appeared to correlate with specific encouraging environmental factors. However, an entrepreneurial innovator appeared to the beholder as an individual who changed the direction and flow of a community (Lewis, 1984; Ashoka, 2007) by:

- defining a new synergistic vision of what is valuable;
- enrolling others in that vision;

- organizing others to develop and implement a strategic plan to build the potential of the vision and garner resources to support the plan; and
- developing an organization structured to manage the value obtained over time.

Definitions of the public entrepreneur were well suited to entrepreneurship in general. A public entrepreneur was "a person who creates or profoundly elaborates a public organization" (Lewis, 1984, p. 11) and social entrepreneurs acted as the "change agents for society" (Ashoka, 2007). There was an overlap between public entrepreneurship and social entrepreneurship emphasized by "the fusion of public service with the private sector and civil society" (*CSIS-GSI online blog*, 2008). This requires the compliance, if not intention, of the community at large. Social entrepreneurship is a function of groups inclined to or desirous of change and new value creation. The social entrepreneur, due to circumstance and traits and well documented by entrepreneurial research, becomes the leader of the change action in a community.

Due to its contextual nature, entrepreneurship was a driving force of social/ economic change in society as it harnessed the charismatic aspects of strategic leadership (Mort, Weerawardena, and Carnegie, 2002) in divulging human potential. This leadership, more than any other trait, defined the individual and group entrepreneur and appeared reliant on the opportunities society presented in the pursuit of collective opportunity, growth, and value development.

Entrepreneurship is distinguished by its direction. It points to future potential rather than reconciling deficiencies of the past. The entrepreneur, as leader, is forward thinking, where change creates a new construct rather than an incremental refinement. Entrepreneurship is the practice of transformation, in which new elements of social action are created and sustained to achieve positive social and/or economic change.

Fundamentally and seemingly contrary to the hero worship that characterizes much of the economic literature, entrepreneurs consistently operate in a social milieu and are the catalysts of socially desired change. The distinction appears whether or not one is a *social entrepreneur*, as all entrepreneurs are publicly motivated. The distinction is whether one is a private entrepreneur, which may be simply another term for capitalist that does not diminish the entrepreneurial intention but only points to its limitations. The private sector enunciates property wealth (capital) and the public sector enhances this opportunity because of the collective value (wealth) of society. Public entrepreneurship announced the role of leadership in society with a deterministic impact on both social and economic situations as having distinctly mixed motives (Bozeman, 1987); whereas, business entrepreneurship described change and leadership in commerce with social impact poorly analyzed and adhered to a bottom line.

Entrepreneurship is now an expansive term that illuminates the possibilities of other viable and fundamental sources of capital other than financial, such as:

social, political, knowledge, information, culture, and spiritual. It is difficult to find a definition of entrepreneurship that does not have the social implications of leadership and organization as mutually inclusive and virtually synonymous, particularly when viewed through the lens of society. Social entrepreneurship is distinct in that it elicits a sense of adventure and competence in the pursuit of new definitions and abilities of society as well as new opportunities for each member of that society to express himself or herself in a community building function. Entrepreneurship appears not as an exclusive activity but as a causal factor in society. In this way, social/public entrepreneurship is understood to grapple with the problems of man's inhumanity to man by redefining purposeful inclusiveness in emerging and evolving cultures.

Entrepreneurship is not a business, economic, or strictly personality trait. It expresses the human potential of exploration, curiosity, and organization. Fundamentally, it speaks to the ability to synthesize independent variables in the environment into something newly identified, enroll others to see this new potential, and have others commit to developing this potential in an organized manner. Communal potential is the dependent variable in entrepreneurship. Entrepreneurship produces a process of inquiry into human development and the potential of social capacity. If entrepreneurs were the explorers of human potential, then social entrepreneurs are the architects of society's promises.

Public entrepreneurship, which impacts governance systems, includes social, cultural, and other forms of human capital. Research on public entrepreneurship was sparse at best, often because the questions defining its purpose were difficult to measure. The growing world of social/public entrepreneurs attests to the pervasiveness of social and governmental consciousness in entrepreneurial phenomena. Its encompassing and essential nature speaks pragmatically to the art of being a good citizen, an honest person, and an adult. Nonetheless, it is clear that entrepreneurship in social and organizational concerns is a growing phenomenon associated with those with the means or manner to provoke new solutions to stubborn social norms. The study of social and public entrepreneurship is not experimental, but functional, and requires catching practitioners in the field. Public entrepreneurship is a driven human behavior, planned and executed in action. Its gestation is ordinary but its evolution is extraordinary, an extraordinary feat of locution and locomotion. The entrepreneur simply did not stand still for observation but must be captured in flight and this seemed even more apt to entrepreneurs of the social persuasion.

The Ashoka Foundation, founded in 1980 by Bill Drayton in Washington, DC, is not only the world's leading proponent of social entrepreneurship but also its keenest observer. Its premise was that social change was best promoted by investing in social entrepreneurs and built its premise on a platform of nonviolence, a perspective associated strongly with Quakers. Its laboratory was one of action, integrating social activism with social innovation. Although social entrepreneurs exist at various levels of society, the prominence of named and known social entrepreneurs creates the who's who of human leadership. Ashoka promoted the concept of a profession of *social* entrepreneurship that identified leaders of social change by their social impact on the improvement of definable citizenship and enhanced societal inclusivity. It follows that public entrepreneurship identifies leaders of public/governmental change by their impact on public process, civil society, and governance.

Around the world, universities are beginning to study public entrepreneurship including the Social Entrepreneurship Monitor, a project of the London Business School. However, a consensus of what determines and defines social entrepreneurship has not been reached and faulty normative understandings associated with profit making have obscured the research. Schumpeter (1947), the father of modern entrepreneurship, concluded that profit was not a chief motivator of entrepreneurship but "simply the doing of new things or the doing of things that are already done in a new way (innovation)" (p. 151). In this statement, the themes of organization, leadership, risk taking, and innovation are clearly expressed and must not be supposed as purely economic. The role of entrepreneur as a change agent in society seems well established.

There is a strong consensus that entrepreneurship was a predictive factor in organizational effectiveness (Louis, Blumenthal, Gluck, and Soto, 1989). In a 1989 two-survey study on academic entrepreneurship by Louis et al. at the University of Minnesota, it was found that there was "no evidence that a new kind of entrepreneurial scholar" has taken over most universities (p. 127). This indicated that entrepreneurship was a unique expression as only a small percentage of people in society characterized themselves as entrepreneurs. Additionally, the study suggested "that individual characteristics provide weak and unsystematic predications of entrepreneurship" (p. 128), indicating that entrepreneurship might have strong social, cultural, and organizational correlates, which supported the socialization of entrepreneurship.

The lack of extensive research on public entrepreneurship was countered by a significant amount of research on entrepreneurship in general. However, most of this research assumed that the entrepreneur was chiefly an economic actor. Social and public entrepreneurship research noted that entrepreneurship was not chiefly a social function, rather a fundamental, albeit advanced, facet of human potential. Entrepreneurship expresses the human traits of leadership, collective functionality, and curiosity. The entrepreneur flourishes, not in isolation but in fellowship. The social entrepreneur delves into the causes and purposes of human expression in what may be best described as the ability to value the unheard and to know what importance lies therein.

BIDs, as formal PPPs, arguably operate in the realm of public entrepreneurship, emphasizing economic development, decentralization, leadership, and cultural values. The goal of BIDs was economic success measured not only on the individual level but also on the community level (Stokes, 2002). BIDs, on the local level of governance, link the public and private sector and, as a result, become a potential technology and knowledge transfer mechanism with the aim of improving both sectors. The public administration argument is that social capital and public entrepreneurship (as exhibited by BIDs) take on a somewhat different perspective when examined from a public or cultural standpoint, rather than from a private or individualistic standpoint. In determining community needs, success of a BID must also be measured by determining its public manifestations as improvements to the quality of life.

BIDs are fascinating because they exemplify a new pragmatism in public management, working to unite the best functioning practices of public and private business. This pragmatism begins with a few intended promises of BIDs that are associated with creating formalized PPPs, determining self-help approaches and establishing a citizen-driven government forum. These promises examine and explore trust within the community: between people and groups; between government administration and the common man; and between what has been and what can be. At its heart is the examination of the importance of *professional* management by acknowledging its absence at the stages and local applications that are most crucial in maintaining agreement of direction, purpose, and value. Prior to a promise unfolding (performance), a mechanism to manage the promise is required; the operation of managing a promise is evidenced through the performance(s) it generates. The quality of the performance may then be tied to the precision and public nature of the promise. The intended promises of a BID appear to cause sustained collective action to maintain and improve community assets.

Social Capital and Entrepreneurship

Social capital was defined as an interactional process of networks and inter-relationships (Nahapiet and Ghoshal, 1998); as "a negotiated action taking place among individuals whose identities and decisions are shaped by their social roles" (Dubnick, 2005, p. 388) in the process of account giving; as "dyadic sensegiving exchanges" (Maitlis, 2005, p. 47); as "the invisible lever through which citizens collectively influence the quality of their shared public life … the shared resource produced by trust in others, which in turn enables individuals to participate in organized networks" (Pierce, Lovrich, and Moon, 2002, p. 381; Putnam, 1993); as "a collective dimension of society external to the individual" (Lochner, Kawachi, and Kennedy, 1999, p. 260); as "a variety of entities with two elements in common: They consist of some aspect of social structures, and they facilitate certain actions of actors – whether persons or corporate actors" (Coleman, 1998, p. 98); and as "a resource that actors derive from specific social structures and then use to pursue their interest; it is created by the changes in the relationship among actors" (Baker, 1990, p. 619). Each definition struggled with the chicken or egg axiom. Which came first, the individual or the community? Pierce and Putnam recognized the contextual imperative of social capital, while Coleman, Lochner, and Baker dismissed it.

The concept of social capital was both compelling and enigmatic (Portes, 1998; Onyx and Bullen, 2000; Adler and Kwon, 2002; Smith and Kulynych, 2002; Sabatini, 2005). Every discipline and author offered a new description (Adler and Kwon, 2002), and attempts to measure it were sparse and unsatisfying. This proposal deconstructs the notions and expressions of social capital as a term and proposes its operations at the heart of a new communitarianism (Onyx and Bullen, 2000), which stated that "community is essential" (Etzioni, 1968). From a public communitarian perspective, there was no such physical thing as social capital (DeFilippis, 2001; Smith and Kulynych, 2002) as a normative element. It was descriptive and acted as a metaphor for social processes rather than as a product or a stock, which could be traded (Smith and Huntsman, 1997). Yet, research indicated that it almost certainly influenced productivity (Holzer and Zhang, 2004). Nonetheless, a strong argument that social capital might, indeed, be a form of capital was made in the sense that it was an appropriable and convertible asset, even though it acted like a "collective good" (Coleman, 1998) rather than private property. It seemed that "no one player has exclusive ownership rights" of social capital (Burt, 1993, p. 58).

Social capital pointed to a capacity for exchange (Sabatini, 2005) within a field of relationships where the sense of value for a community arose (Bourdieu, 1985; Putnam, 1993; Coleman, 1998). Since that exchange was essentially a conscious act, it was often associated with organic social qualities like trust and reality building. As Fukuyama (1995) defined it, trust was a qualifying condition of social capital, not because it could be measured accurately but because it evoked an essential purpose of sociability. If trust were the lubricant of social exchange, then reality building was the glue. Both were socially constructed human phenomena (Berger and Luckmann, 1966). This dual aspect of social capital appears fundamental to the understanding of the term. Economic perspectives of social capital emphasize and value trust; whereas, social perspectives of social capital tend to value reality. This proposal unites these often-dichotomous perspectives by discussing the limits of the monological perspective and delving into a definition of social capital based on the collective nature of mankind. To this extent, it is considered that it is the community that defines the individual, not the individual that defines the community, and that individual expression is an expression of the community, both micro and macro, to which the individual belongs.

Social capital is a packaged paradox because its existence is causal rather than instrumental. Social capital is, like all forms of capital, descriptive of something of value. Social capital specifically refers to the value of sociability and infers its exchangeability as fundamental to all other forms of capital. Simply put, social capital infers that sociability is valuable. If this were true, the question becomes: how valuable is sociability? Social/public entrepreneurship suggests it is pervasive in every notion of humanity as it defines who we are as human beings. It gives a sense of identity, both singularly and commonly, because it is a context-determining device.

Public administration is at a point of reckoning regarding its co-optation to business administration, which has persuaded society that public administration is somehow inferior in theory and practice to business administration. The NPM, in reinvigorating commercial fiscal and human resources efficiencies to public management, was at the point of completing this co-optation of the profession of public service and flattening it into a simple commodity exchange system (Denhardt and Denhardt, 2000). At the heart of public service is accountability for progressive growth and development geared to maximize human potential through structural agreements, which translate into a civil society. When NPM builds its actions on the management of these agreements and their processes, a truer public administration paradigm is achieved. However, when governance is solely a broker of short-term cost–benefit ratio exchanges and the neglect of value determinations in the commons, public administration is simply a facet of business administration.

Because the concerns for democratic accountability remain unabated with regard to NPM, clearly something has been missing from NPM. DiIulio (1994) indicated that what was missing was a "moral factor" (Barnard, 1938) as NPM relied on rational choice theory that ignored collective moralism. NPM's chief architects do tend to rely on business metaphor and theory to justify what appears to be a privatization of public service, rather than simply employing good business management practices and recognizing the need for citizen participatory processes. Ignoring these processes erodes one of the key premises of democratic societal public administration, which is, above all, to foster the progress of those very societal values. Assuming that market forces are correlated to democratic values appears to be NPM's clear, but unacknowledged, weakness.

Government services, NPM advocates say, will be better if allowed to function with market forces, a metaphor for individual, not communal, profit seeking. This sounds naïve but the reason why it is not is that NPM asserts that public processes are a function of politics, not management, and that politics is market-driven in the same simplistic way that product development is driven. However, it is not (DiIulio, 1994; Derthick, 1990). NPM continues to ignore, or take for granted, the legal basis of a democratic society based on law, due process, and citizen participation. But this is exactly what public servants do not do. Yet, there was something to be said for the professional aspects of public administration vs the effect of elected and appointed politicians in government who attempted to be public managers and "leap into the dark" (Heclo, 1977, p. 1) of public bureaucracies. Support of public sector professionalism may be NPM's strong card. The bottom line is, as professionals, public managers perform well and have their communities perform in a manner that even private sector market-driven analysts might admire. NPM can be too one-sided in its admiration for the private sector. Private sector admiration for the craft of management must be joined with public sector admiration in order to instill public trust.

It is within this dilemma that the arguments about social capital occur. This may determine that social capital is the battleground, which may determine the fate of public administration. Today, the term *social capital* often acts as a private sector Trojan horse penetrating the realm of public administration. It belongs to the field of economics, while coveting a public source of power and production. By attempting to co-opt the epistemology of social capital, its purpose is reduced to a functional commodity exchange. This takes the social out of the equation and, consequently, removes social processes that are the impetus of public action. Because of the social nature of social capital, it cannot truly be co-opted and may cause a reverse co-optation, which works to define values and the processes of human sociability essential to human action. In the final analysis, no other value system can exist without it, just as no system can function without the structures of governance.

Social capital, therefore, was not simply a function but a foundation of sociability (Portes, 1998; Putnam, 2000). It supersedes and encompasses all human social endeavor and production. In its unique convoluted way of mixing public and private sector metaphors, the concept of social capital is an attempt to define the process of social consciousness and the actions of human relationships at all levels, degrees, and functions. In this way, social capital is a modern term that places public processes at the source of human endeavor; therefore, its administration is the appropriate setting for other aspects of human expression, including business, culture, knowledge, technology, and, of course, government. Social capital may rightly be called community capital. Both refer to a source of exchange, not a commodity. Attempts to harness social capital are attempts to manipulate the exchange of value at its source. Paradoxically, this source appears as both singular and communal but as the term (social capital) implies, the paradox is resolved by addressing its communal origins. In this way, an individual's capability in the social realm increases by an accountability to greater communal expressions. This accountability may point towards more appropriate measures of social capital.

The term social capital evoked an air of mystery because it appeared to be "a feature of the social structure not of individual actors within the structure; it is an ecologic characteristic" (Lochner, Kawachi, and Kennedy, 1999, p. 260), entirely interdependent and defining the mechanisms of human relations and the practice of humanity. At first glance, it makes sense but often reveals more about what it is not than what it may be. It cannot be seen or held but it is everywhere. "Social capital is a slippery but nonetheless important concept: slippery because it has been poorly defined, important because it refers to the basic raw material of civil society" (Onyx and Bullen, 2000, p. 24). It cannot be bought or sold but its transactions increase value in many domains of capital exchange and describe social cohesion and community competence. It cannot be manufactured but it can be discovered and encouraged and its accumulation enhances lives as a heuristic rather than rote phenomenon. Social capital was not a separate form of capital or commerce but a transformational mechanism of social context (Dubnick, 2005).

The slipperiness of the term social capital lies in the word *capital*, which portrays a sense of individual propriety. The paradox that engenders this slippery metaphorical slope is that the words "social" and "capital" pull at opposite ends of the human condition. The term capital refers to a physical exchange mechanism, which can be possessed by anyone, but it may also point to a transformational process. In this way, "community characteristics ought to be distinguished from individual characteristics, and measured at the community level" (Lochner, Kawachi, and Kennedy, 1999, p. 267). This is more difficult to do than it may seem because we live in a world with very little agreement or language regarding the nature of a human being from a community perspective. This means that whenever something is defined from a community perspective, it will necessitate using the language of individualism. That is the paradox of social capital that causes confusion and misguidance in its measurement.

Social capital is contextual. In line with Bourdieu (1985), social capital was defined as the actualized context of all values that comprise the potential of the common good, which might be "different at various levels of aggregation" (Lochner, Kawachi, and Kennedy, 1999, p. 269). Therein lays the sticky-wicket because human potential is understood differently by different societies and certainly not understood entirely by any. Separate, independent, or individual valuations occur within the value-making concept of social capital. Yet, one clear outcome of social capital—its discovery, applications, and investments—is the creation of community. This is another way of saying the creation of context. Social capital is, clearly, socially constructed. However, that construction involves real investments of time, trust, and determination in the process of relationship and network building.

Bourdieu (1985), who provided the first modern systematic analysis of social capital, defined the concept of social capital as "the aggregate of the actual or potential resources which are linked to possession of a durable network of more or less institutionalized relationships of mutual acquaintance or recognition" (Bourdieu, 1985, p. 248). This outcome was not simply a matter of counting component outputs of social action but understanding that aggregate; consequently, Bourdieu (1985) did not propose investigating social capital using economic methodology. Social capital "is not simply a moderator ... but also appears to have its own direct influence on both incremental and radical innovative capabilities of organizations [and] appears to be the bedrock of innovate capabilities" (Subramaniam and Youndt, 2005, pp. 457, 459). Social capital, like the community outcomes derived from its exchange mechanisms, would aptly be the foundation of all commerce and the equity that arose in a field of social desire, impetus, and action.

Social capital was probably best viewed as a value-laden discourse (Coleman, 1998; Fukuyama, 1995; Morrow, 1999; Putnam, 2000) and its performance, the result of the potential of these discourses that defined humanity within any community (Foucault, 1972). Social capital was not difficult to perceive if experienced as the transformation of human capital into a functioning society (Coleman, 1998).

According to Adler and Kwon (2002), the concept of social capital had become increasingly popular in a wide range of social science disciplines. Up against the long-standing theory of individualism as the rational social force, social capital peered into the "primordial feature of social life" (p. 17), our ties to one another and transcendence to a transrational force. Not unlike a fish in water, which does not perceive itself as being wet, human beings do not perceive they are aspects of communities and their sociability is latently valuable. We cannot live without it. This is illustrated by noticing that human capital represents individual knowledge, which, by definition, is limited. Social capital represents community knowledge, which may or may not be limited and certainly is less limited than individual knowledge, while allowing for individual knowledge. Individual knowledge requires a community referent and does not exist without it. This referent is a result of the exchange mechanism of social capital. When society is structured, social and community capital are released. What we perceive is the social referent that gives meaning to all other forms of capital. In this way, we understand social/community capital not as a product but as an ongoing process that produces social referents through social networks.

Social capital, as community capital, is available not as a personal commodity but as the matrix of human endeavor thats presence allows for a relationship of exchanges to make all other forms of capital express value. Social capital acts as accountability between different groups. Social capital can be measured by this transformation process and the outcome of social networks that manage the meaning, metaphor, and myths of human exchange. Separately, this can be described as forms of exchangeable or investable capital. Social capital, in describing general reciprocity, may be an "umbrella concept" (Adler and Kwon, 2002, p. 18) of which social attributes, such as organization, trust, culture, social support, social assets, relationships, and networks naturally occur. In this way, each form of capital, at its core, has the traits of social value and meaning. Social capital provided the exchange mechanism as a "negotiated action taking place among individuals whose identities and decisions are shaped by their social roles" (Dubnick, 2005, p. 388). For instance, one might say the umbrella exchange mechanism in social capital humanizes economic processes, i.e. financial capital exchanges commitment and trust; physical capital exchanges power and performance; cultural capital exchanges self-expression and affinity; intellectual and knowledge capitals exchange contribution and curiosity; and human and organizational capitals exchange trust and security. Social capital embraces all of these forms of human exchange, each of which clearly is available at different levels of effectiveness and efficiency.

Social capital is different from the normal concept of "capital" because it does not solely transact information from one to another; it transforms concepts of human interaction into social phenomena. "An inherent characteristic of knowledge associated with social capital is its evolution" (Subramaniam and Youndt, 2005, p. 452). Social capital does not inform as much as it transforms. What it transforms is the potential each individual has to construct social reality with others. Consequently, it transforms each individual's conception of what is possible for humanity. Measures of social capital are congregate and holistic, rather than linear or fixed. These measures have qualitative results with quantitative symptoms.

Social capital, and its chief variable trust (Fukuyama, 1995) in governance processes, may be at an all time low while lamentations of its importance may be at an all time high. Concerns regarding public trust certainly appear to be persistent over time (Putnam, 2000; Holzer and Zhang, 2004) as evidenced by Woodrow Wilson's (1887) concern about management ethics in an ideological politics/administration dichotomy; the Brownlow Commission's (1939) concern about financial accountability and executive management; Sen. William Proxmire's Golden Fleece Awards, highlighting a war on waste (1976–1982); Ronald Reagan's neo-liberal rhetoric "government is the problem" (1980–1988); and, most recently, with Vice President Cheney's (2007) interpretations of the constitutional role of the office of Vice President and his concern for secrecy and close ties to private corporations. Clearly in government, there is a problem with sabotaging public trust that looks more like congenital distrust.

Public trust, its processes and impacts on public performance may be the truest measure of a successful democracy but too often appears to be in peril. Does this mean that government is not performing well? Is the trust/distrust agenda a systemic and evolving aspect of the organic nature of a democracy? Perhaps Woodrow Wilson was implying that a more accurate dichotomy for understanding how public administration functions was not simply politics/administration but trust/distrust.

Economic, rational actor theories, which go as far back as Adam Smith (1776), noted that individual profit maximization, in both public and private interests, was the key motivator of human behavior. A motivation to promote a quality community, or contextual community environment, in which a "tragedy of the commons" (Hardin, 1968, p. 1243; Elliot, 1997, p. 1) did not occur, is not a persuasive or reliable indicator of human transactions. Yet, there is no evidence that business is more ethical, less political, or a better performer than government, particularly as measured against social impacts. Nonetheless, business management theory has pervaded public administration and organization theory since its modern conception.

Today, public administration cannot be separated from its business-oriented adaptations. In many respects, this has proven to be positive, chiefly in the areas of financial accountability but muddled regarding accountability for policy development and implementation. Nor have business perambulations into the public sector achieved Woodrow Wilson's pursuit of democratic governance, a truer politics/administration dichotomy. One might safely say that since this dichotomous pursuit began, almost immediately the desired segregation backfired and forged a politicization of administration that inculcated a modern entrepreneurial-professional-political public servant. Furthermore, pushing past the anarchism that modern bureaucracy is a fourth branch of government (rather than the anchorage of government), a fifth branch of government may have emerged in the form of the private-sector-public-service provider also known as *privatization* but, in the case of BIDs, seems more a matter of publicization. This phenomenon appears not to disturb either liberal or conservative political ideologies, even though it is more constitutionally vague than proper public administration.

It is difficult to characterize the rational actor (business) model as a trust model of governance. This is the limitation of the model as it veers towards disregard of democratic accountabilities at times to such an extent that it nullifies any true sense of public responsibility. Odd as it may first appear, this may be a limitation imposed by representative democracy that may, at extremes (benevolent/malevolent), accept any form of representation as having more importance than the rights of the citizens on which it is based. Public potential can, indeed, be characterized as stemming from an essential trust in which not only relationships, networks, and the whole community are of primary importance but this contextual adherence causes the very individuality that business admires.

Adam Smith (1776), by invoking a virtually mystical concept of the "invisible hand" of socialization, inferred a transrational importance that overshadowed rational determination when he wrote about the individual in society, as follows:

> he intends only his own security; and by directing that industry in such a manner as its produce may be of the greatest value, he intends only his own gain, and he is in this, as in many other cases, led by an invisible hand to promote an end which was no part of his intention. Nor is it always the worse for the society that it was no part of it. By pursuing his own interest he frequently promotes that of the society more effectually than when he really intends to promote it.
>
> *(p. 1.1)*

The inquiry this statement endorses and the trust we are to assume are misconstrued by the eternally positivist. The rational actor-business model, often labeled as positivist and scientific management, may explain immature individualism but cannot explain with much confidence the concept, implication, and practice of the more developed skills of trust. Without distorting its explanation towards distrust and its inherent limitations, it is anemic in explaining the most pressing concerns of governance: citizen-driven participation, citizenship, and community development. Midway through the 20th century, Dwight Waldo (1954), H. A. Simon (1967), the Minnowbrook Conference of 1968 and George Fredrickson (1971) and, in the 21st century, Denhardt and Denhardt (2000) and others worked to correct this imbalance by addressing the social equity, citizenship, organizational behaviour, and community development concerns of public service.

Business continues, by tradition and determination, to influence public opinion regarding the public sector and its practices. This may be due to the fewer constraints of the private sector in exploring new social and economic realms in globalizing humanity as well as impacting socio-economic changes at the most local levels as evidenced in America's downtowns. Business is imbued with novel tendencies generally unaffordable to the public sector. This may explain why downtown revitalization, with its economic aspects merging private and public sector actors, is a chief motivator of community development. At the heart of the downtown revitalization movement are business interests, organized formally as improvement districts (Houston, 2003), which bravely tangle with the merger of public and private sectors into workable community governance partnerships.

Although normally business-motivated, BIDs exist as a form of public authority with quasi-governmental purposes. When the concept of trust is applied to the performance of BIDs, it shifts the entrepreneurial aspects of the BID. Its management interests describe less the profit maximization impulses of a private investor (Carton, Hofer, and Meeks, 1998) and more the motivations of the public entrepreneur (Lewis, 1984). The public entrepreneur manages the organization of people and resources in obtaining an agreed upon community vision or promise of what the community can be, i.e. community development as a maximization of communal assets.

Much has been said about the public entrepreneur by focusing on the individual who advances policy or programmatic solutions and takes advantage of political opportunity. However, little was said about public entrepreneurship (Lewis, 1984; Schneider and Teske, 1992; Kingdon, 2003) as it defined the processes of public trust and the impact of these processes on performance. The term *entrepreneur* suggests personal motivation and investment, while entrepreneurship expresses a human potential to organize, develop opportunity, and address asset and values enhancement. Public entrepreneurship invokes a Gulickian transcendence of public and private motivations.

BIDs, and other types of MBDs, appear to endorse a form of pragmatic democratic accountability that decentralizes public authority towards a citizen-driven format. In a free enterprise economy, this alone might encourage entrepreneurship in the resolution of public problems. It emphasizes a classic trust dilemma between the private sector (business and private property owners) and the public sector (government and community values). BIDs, when they survive, thrive in this dilemma. How they do it may lie in the construction and reconstruction of private and public sector values and definitions and in the importance of social networks over strict performance. Being able to recognize and bridge vertical and horizontal relationships enables a BID manager to manage stakeholders in a supportive network that encourages self-reinforcing and cumulative increases in social capital using trust, norms, and networks. A BID manager could steer perceptions into recognition of collective achievement arising from stakeholder engagement (Justice and Goldsmith, 2006).

One of the more important problems in contemporary society was the confusion most of the citizenry had in defining exactly what the government does and how well it was performing (Holzer and Zhang, 2004; Light, 1997; Pressman and Wildavsky, 1973). "At the core of this confusion is trust" (Light, 1997, p. 44). The topic of trust has received increased interest in public administration and organizational studies as a significant key to policy and performance at a time when trust in government appears to be at an all time low. The impact of trust has been cited in public processes and performance (Pressman and Wildavsky, 1973; Cummings, 1983; Lung-Teng, 2002; Holzer and Zhang, 2004). "That trust enhances the value of a relationship is unanimously agreed among trust theorists" (Hwang and Burgers, 1999, p. 118). According to Ouchi (1981), "productivity and trust go hand-in-hand" (p. 5), while Jefferies and Reed (2000) asserted that management research on organizational trust was largely in agreement that "organizational trust is beneficial for performance" (p. 873). In addition, "The relationship between public trust in government and government performance is a two-way track. These two factors interact with each other, especially in the long term" (Holzer and Zhang, 2004, p. 226). The confusion regarding definitions of trust was due to the peculiar mixture of its cognitive and collective aspects. Trust feels personal but acts social. In this way, one may see trust as access to social sensibility and, consequently, examine how this sensibility is constructed, exchanged, and maintained.

Trust can be examined in BID organizations as prevalent throughout the policy and performance process and from a social constructionist perspective, keenly noticeable in the processes of public policy and management. Many concepts of the policy stages have been put forth from problem definition to agenda setting to implementation or as Planning-Programming-Budgeting-Systems (PPBSs). Trust could be examined by its social meaning and it appeared to be instrumental in causing "the social meaning upon which political discourses turn ... derived from moral and ideological positions that establish and govern competing views of the good society" (Fischer, 2003, p. 56).

A definitive operationalization of trust is hard to come by but a pragmatic attempt may reveal its everyday function. A resolution to this question relies on how trust is defined. The short answer is sociability or the inclination to be social measured by the number of organizations to which a person belongs, which explains, in large part, the linking of trust with social capital (Fukuyama, 1995). Both production and trust address social operations between people as either producers and consumers or part and partner. There was general agreement that trust was a peculiar social discourse (Foucault, 1972) that was both functional and phenomenological and not a product (Larzelere and Huston, 1980; Abramson and Finifter, 1981; Hosner, 1995; Mayer, Davis, and Schoorman, 1995; Bhattacharya, Devinney, and Pillutla, 1998; Bigley and Pearce, 1998). Trust is not a product but it is essential to implementation and production, which may simply be a result of our human agency to be social rather than solitary creatures. In order to be social, the cogent barriers inherent in perceived and actual physical separateness must be dissolved in a manner that reconstitutes a greater advantage. This process of dissolution and reconstitution might be called trust as it was arrived at through argumentation (Fischer and Forester, 1993). In many ways, trust is so ordinary that it is often unobserved. But, more epistemologically, it was a form of learning with its stops and starts, trials and errors, struggles and breakthroughs mimicking disjointed incrementalism (Simon, 1955) or Etzioni's (1968) mixed scanning.

Reflecting on the intellectual history of public administration, trust breaks down the simplicity of positivism, "the demystification of technocratic expertise" (Fischer and Forester, 1993, p. 37), and scientific management without reducing the cleverness of the observations. This may also be due to the pervasiveness of trust (or its noticeable lack) in virtually all human social endeavors. Trust builds and diminishes, gives more or less grist for the mill, and is one of the few seemingly inexhaustible (albeit less utilized) resources known to humankind.

Not unlike concepts of truth, trust was a human agency that disrupted dichotomous concepts, acted as a door to human potential, and functioned as the *social glue* between relationships (Coleman, 1998; Putnam, 1993; Fukuyama, 1995; Putnam, 2000). Or a "moral glue that makes it possible for people to live together in communities of shared meaning" (Wolfe, 1999, p. 42). There are many definitions of trust; all require some form of dialogue between two or more people. Due to the dialectic nature of trust, trust might be best described as being socially constructed as its outcomes were attempts to find agreement on what was true (Berger and Luckmann, 1966; Dahl, 1989; Lindblom, 1990; Searle, 1995; Fernandez-Armesto, 1997; Habermas, 2000); therefore it required skill, which implied that it could be learned. If trust, like truth, were a social phenomenon, as a monologue, it would appear vacant because the "possibility of individualism is directly linked to the possibility of unsuccessful socialization" (Berger and Luckmann, 1966, p. 171).

Trust can be ascribed to any human relationship as fundamental to the function or dysfunction of that relationship. "Much of the economic backwardness in the world can be explained by the lack of mutual confidence" (Galston, 1996, p. 129); conversely, much of economic achievement might be a result of the function of trust in social exchanges, both dyadic and social (Larzelere and Huston, 1980). If this were true, one should expect to find social capital as a strong determinant of public entrepreneurship.

The function of trust, of which distrust was a subset (distrust as a loosening, not an elimination of trust), appeared to be the production of reasonable stability and reduced uncertainty: the reduction of complexity (Lewis and Weigert, 1985) in social constructs; trust can reduce anxiety (Goffman, 1971; Zucker, 1986; Bhattacharya, Devinney, and Pillutla, 1998) and risk; and increase relative predictability and the framing of outcomes (Parks and Hulbert, 1995). "Thus trust, is an orientation towards others that is beyond rationality" (Jefferies and Reed, 2000, p. 873).

Deconstruction occurs when a social reality does not function according to its intention (Derrida, 1973), which further explains distrust as the non-functioning of trust, rather than an absence of trust.

The functionality of trust also supports the learned aspects of trust. If trust were thought of in this way, distrust can be observed as a matter of the lesser, or poorly acquired, skills of trust rather than as a social malady or a rationalist's inevitable limitation. If trust is a necessary component of public processes, poor outcomes can be expected if trust is operating poorly. Public decision making and the policy process are also likely a matter of skill. This social skill may begin with trust and should be an important element of entrepreneurship.

The extraordinary expressions of reality engendered by trust are powerful enough to propel us into a sociability that creates an environment that can be accountable. A trust environment, therefore, refers to a field of accountability responses; reciprocity in which we can be counted on by others and we can count on them. The reference for the social premise is a declarative, functional, illocutionary expression, and act, in other words, a promise. A promise was defined as "a declaration or assurance that something will or will not happen, be done, etc." (Random House College Dictionary, 1983, p. 1059). The intention of a promise is foremost one of trust, relationship building and the competency gained from that endeavor. A promise requires sociability, a promise, and a pro-misor, and exhibits the necessary aspects of social construction, dialogue, and argument. Trust functions in the social discourse of promises made, maintained, broken, restated, or destroyed. The social premises that trust acts on are main-tained through expressed promises. Clearly stated promises, agreements, and contracts can be expected if trust is present.

This social premise is operationalized as a *public* promise: the shared formal/ spoken/written agreement between one or more people that cites a desired outcome. "Promises also have the world-to-word fit, because part of the point of the promise is to try to make the world change to match the words" (Searle, 1995, p. 217) of the promise. It is social because a promise is most pow-erful when it is a shared language between two or more people that establishes a known desired mutual reality. This implies that a promise invents or constructs a unique language transaction that intends a social functionality. Clearly stated promises become real agreements and contracts if (public) entrepreneurship is present.

Trust, like entrepreneurship, appeared to be the process of transforming "value designated outcomes [of individuals] to support the collective goals/vision" (Jung and Avolio, 2000, p. 950) of social ability, e.g. partnerships, organizations, and communities. If this were true, it might establish a mechanism for public (com-munal/organizational) trust vs private (affected/interpersonal) trust. Trust as social capital, by its nature, transforms the personal into the public. This might explain the statement attributed to Tip O'Neill, "politics is local" (Thomas Phillip "Tip" O'Neill, Jr., 1977–1987, Speaker of the U.S. House of Representatives) because trust was always perceived of as personally local, regardless of how public it might actually be. Trust could be described as the personal experience of being public.

Trust is a deliberative hermeneutic process. Trust builds social competence and proceeds with the intention to maximize human potential through collaboration, requiring a transrational breakthrough that moves individuals into and through social relationships as they grow and develop. Trust is the set of conversations that purposely limits (or contains) the reality we share with others as we attempt to ground visions of our maximum potential from moment to moment. The purpose is to produce an intended reality outcome based on the potential identified. This outcome is dependent on the articulation of the trust motive over time. Trust can be understood as the binding mechanism in bounded rationality (Simon, 1997). Hosner (1995) summed up a definition of trust that pulled together the elements of collaboration, maximization of potential, and the self-centered to social-centered breakthrough:

> Trust is the reliance by one person, group, or firm upon a voluntarily accepted duty on the part of another person, group, or firm to recognize and protect the rights and interests *of all others* [emphasis added] engaged in a joint endeavor or economic exchange.
>
> *(p. 393)*

A "joint endeavor" leads us to an operationalization of trust as intrinsic with partnership management, i.e. the ability to integrate, organize, and sustain a joint venture. This joint venture is a fundamental social dialectic that describes partnering, which is identified as a trust system. Conversations about trust must be managed, spanning rational interests. This *spanning* is transrational in which the greater need is sustaining the dialogue that maintains a working relationship that intends not only to better each person but also the whole relationship. Essentially, the betterment of the whole causes the betterment of each person. This rational motivation is a transrational acknowledgment that two heads are better than one. Trust and good management may operate at higher levels of social competency. Trust operates at a higher level of social discourse furthering the dialogues of social competence. This is chiefly a management skill.

Scarcity models (the market model, essentially a distrust model) (Howlett and Ramesh, 2003) assumed that there was not enough space, place, or time for everything to show up 100 percent all the time or at the same time. Distrust put its faith "in compliance and the capacity to create and enforce deterrence" (Light, 1997, p. 77). This was a normative conversation in which distrust conversely assumed that trust reduced risk by exploiting what did show up (Bigley and Pearce, 1998). Distrust is based on an assumption that we live in a finite quantum universe that has limited capacity. Scarcity may well be true for human beings as individuals. An individual may clearly have limitations but it is far from known whether a group of individuals, let alone all of humanity, has similar limitations.

As an example, one can take a good look at termites, one of the few creatures that can digest wood (cellulose), allowing forests to recycle as an example of the logic of collective action (Olson, 1971). Termites make us reconsider our standard notions of individuality. This is not about the fact that single termites die when away from the rest of their colony. This is about the insides of the termite. The termite cannot digest cellulose. Rather, it is inhabited by smaller creatures that can. A termite's intestinal tract is full of organisms (separate organisms with their own DNA), without which a termite would starve no matter how much wood it had in its gut. These smaller organisms live in the termite's innards, move around with hair-like projections and break down the cellulose. In addition, the hair-like projections are themselves unique separate organisms that are somewhat like galley slaves. But each cooperates in order to partake of the sustenance that results from breaking down the cellulose.

As individuals, we might be literally "bounded" by our individuality (Simon, 1997). Our maximum potential may be unavailable to us except in relationships. As individuals, we may be limited but that limitation can be reengineered by effective sociability. Our limits are fairly obvious. Mechanically, we cannot physically see ourselves completely without aids and we cannot hear or feel ourselves as the environment does or as the environment perceives us without a response from the environment. Therefore, we must trust the ability to perceive ourselves fully and express ourselves for the generosity of others. It is very possible that there is a *quid pro quo* in generosity but it is clearly necessary and organic, which places many egoistic motivations into the realm of myth (Brubaker, 1997).

Trust must be able to function independently of a market theory of supply and demand since the demand for trust is persistent and the supply inexhaustible. Trust is a form of human attention. Because we rely on each other for our identity and sense of purpose, trust is an acknowledgment of the gift another has to support, by attentive listening, the potential of another. This is the definition of how social capital functions. Social capital can be expressed as the power inherent in us all to transform our motives to survive the individual moment for the prospect of a social reality that allows growth and development of humanity and expands the horizons of human potential. Within social potential rests the realization of our individual potential. "When trust and social capital are destroyed, democracy becomes difficult or impossible" (Putnam, 1993, p. 35). Trust functions in the public realm as the result of the ability to accept social interaction as an opportunity to be accountable for another. Therefore, trust can be operationalized as accountability for others and we can find this accountability by looking for formal promises and promise making. If one were seeking social capitalists and the entrepreneurship that turns that capital into things of value, the search would be for people who were strongly involved in social organizations and networks.

BIDs

A Distinctly Formal PPP

Normative conversations about PPPs were skewed towards ideas and practices of privatization and the privatizing of public interests (Kettl, 1993). Little was said or observed about the publicization (Bozeman, 1987) of private interests, even though it is one of the growth areas in government and community development, particularly with the advancement of special districts like BIDs. Examining *publicness* receives little more than a passing glance. Privateness does have influence on public processes but publicness also has considerable influence. BIDs have been identified as PPPs (Meek and Hubler, 2006; Justice and Goldsmith, 2006).

One would think upon reading most of the literature on the PPPs that they are created solely as a means of enticing private investors to invest in public projects like hospitals, transportation, and large-scale development. Success of such PPPs is often measured by the project investment and the capital raised for that project. Success is rarely looked at in terms of joint management opportunity. At the end of the project, the partnership fades and the participants return to their respective public or private corners. The partnership is project-oriented and short-lived. This is not true of BIDs and sub-unit public authorities that undertake projects as an outgrowth of community development. Another implication was that PPPs leveraged efficiency because private sector shareholders were more attentive to financial success than were public stakeholders (Ostrom and Ostrom, 1977; Osborne and Gaebler, 1992). This is not a proven fact. Private investors in the public and private realms, when permitted, run up the costs of public services for some of the same reasons that the government does. Often, in public processes, there is an uncertainty of outcomes tied to the peculiar processes of determining a consensus of the value of an outcome. Often, a stated preliminary and planned outcome, as it is pursued, later sheds light on the full needs and designs of the project and these adjustments usually mean new and higher costs to achieve the adjustment. Costs that reflect greater quality of life standards, like safety, convenience, social connection, and, yes, beauty, that are not fully understood at the beginning of a project become insistent as the end approaches. This is not a private sector or public sector disposition but a human faculty desirous of growth and development. One aspect of a PPP may be to encourage private investment but the other is certainly to encourage public participation. The latter institutionalizes the outcomes of intermingling and the former infuses the process of institutionalization with innovation, ideas, performance, and entrepreneurship. The interest in entrepreneurship seems a higher motivator than conditional efficiency.

PPPs work to engage the private sector in not only investing in the public welfare but also in enhancing public services for niche markets. This is and always has been obvious; however, what is not so obvious is the extent to which private actors not only become public players but also expand our understanding of public authority. The sword, it seems, cuts both ways and it is arguable that it cuts subtly, but also substantially, in the public direction. Public interests and services might take on private aspects; private process not only took on public aspects but also became public (governmental/political) entities and assumed *public dimensions* (Bozeman, 1987). This observation is operative in BIDs. Bozeman stated that hybrids like BIDs caused a conceptual ambiguity regarding the nature of publicness but it might be that the specific hybrid nature of such units of sub-government broke down the public–private dichotomy, opening a third door to citizen governance.

BIDs represent interdependence in social and economic markets. Managing publicness, therefore, is managing interdependence. The straddling of traditional public and private sectors provides insight into the nature of hybrid public processes, like BIDs, and substantiates not only the private nature but also the public nature of such endeavors. The BID organization, and specifically its management, represents the same hybrid characteristics as the public entrepreneur, social capitalist, and cooperative economist. The approach is intended to take nothing away from either sector, while adding the best from each to form an alternative that builds local public management capacity. When publicness is a critical determinate, it suggests a dynamic that recognizes the synergy of public/private balances by trading off weaknesses and strengths as they occur.

Business Development PPP Management is Business District Management

Business communities and the municipalities where they were located seek and find ways to build successful organized approaches to development, revitalization, and improvements by creating Special (Business) Improvement Districts (SIDs/BIDs) that forged a unique public–private community-based partnership (MacDonald, 1996; Mitchell, 1999; Briffault, 1999; Hoyt, 2001; Stokes, 2002; Justice, 2003; Morçöl and Zimmerman, 2006; Hoyt, 2006). Most studies of BIDs focus on the concept of defining *place* (definable geography, market, and sense of community) and the legal structure of the BID. However, the role of BID management and the professional aspects of the managers of BIDs are virtually ignored.

The idea of professionalism in public administration has its controversies, starting with the nagging question of accountability to democratic processes. This controversy extends to all forms of public administration and is less an issue when the task being assigned is strictly technical, such as: building inspector, postal clerk, soldier, garbage collector, police, firefighter, economic development, etc. These task positions were aptly described as being "professionals in government," while those that provided the task of managing government services were "professionals of government" (Gargan, 1998, p. 1092).

In either case, the term *professional* not only describes a recognized mastery of a particular and useful skill or technology but also ascribes to itself a sense of mission and purpose. Both derive from the establishment of collective order and purposeful public action: government. Public administration may or may not be a profession but the practices, both in and of government, certainly are. It describes more than it prescribes a sense of humanity, of human behavior, than a set of real outcomes achieved by good management practices. Public administration is an outcome of a desire for collective action and communal identity that seems ontological and naturally evolving. The outcomes of public administration derive from this (communal) desire and the actions necessary to translate desire into real things.

Professional aspects, alive within the realm of public administration, have those two components and are separated by the need and role of management, which implies that there is a business of government. The business of government, as opposed to the private sector, trades in the realm of public values, ethics, and interests that are simply not measurable by market forces. They "focus on interdependence" (Bozeman, 1987, p. 149) created by political authority rather than on the independent aspirations of the individual. Although leadership and political identity may promote one individual over another, it is the public trust, not only personal interest, which advises the government.

The public sector professional is the focused aspirant of the community, representing core values and managing those values as assets to produce a healthy economic state. Communal values are derived by a pursuit of that which promotes growth and development for all, essentially, an entrepreneurial drive. The paradox in public administration professionalism is the balancing of one's personal values with that of the community. An assumption that they are aligned will result in inequity. The professional public administrator's task then is to eliminate assumptive values and work to discover, reveal, and sustain agreements. The questions are: (1) Where do we draw the line of community? (2) What establishes context? and (3) How do we determine agreements? The nature of agreements may lead to the answer and provide a better science of administration.

BIDs; Formal Management Business Districts: Premise, Purpose, and Position

Participating in, caring for, and being committed to our communities are time-honored concerns and this certainly includes business communities. More communities are looking for and finding ways to build successful organized approaches to development, revitalization, and improvements by creating SIDs/BIDs. BIDs began in Toronto, Ontario, Canada, in the 1960s, and in New Orleans, Louisiana, in the United States in the 1970s. However, it was not until the late 1980s and early 1990s when BID creation accelerated and in the mid-1990s when BIDs began to be exported around the world at the same time as the NPM was gaining global acceptance. In 2007, there was an estimated 650-plus BIDs in the United

States and by 2010 there were 1,002, 400-plus in Canada, 1,000 plus BIDs in North America, 350-plus in Europe, and over 60 BIDs in the United Kingdom. BIDs are the growth field in government in South Africa (50), Japan (290), Australia (200), New Zealand (180), France, Belgium, and Germany (International Downtown Association, 2007).

The premise for BIDs is based on the observation that, without reliable resources and strong administrative support, volunteer efforts are limited. Simply being a non-profit community organization or an NGO is not enough to sustain long-term revitalization. Inadequate legal structures do not sustain hard-earned plans. Government needs to work with communities to build lasting local management capability but it is often held responsible for economic trends it cannot control, services that are poorly designed, and service delivery systems that do not meet the day-to-day requirements of dynamic and changing environments. BIDs are designed to remedy this problem, particularly in traditional downtown business areas, although this is not the only application of the model.

BIDs are a common decentralization practice, which merges the political will of a municipality with a commitment to participate by its business community. Decentralization is a unique and formative aspect of American democracy, beginning with strong state rights and, thereby, creating an institutionalized movement of government away from a centralized federal core (federalism) and, at the same time, defining over time the need for such a core. "Institutions consist of cognitive, normative, and regulative structures that provide stability and meaning to social behavior [through] multiple levels of jurisdiction" (Scott, 1995, p. 33). Decentralization is not an end in itself but an intention to put the reach and practice of government in the hands of the citizens through sustained action and agreement. Decentralization leads to legal PPPs.

Decentralization in the form of BIDs has fomented (over time) a true (and necessary) profession of public administration that, in practice, tends to dissolve the private/public (politics/administration) dichotomy and is applicable universally. Decentralization is a process of bringing government closer to the people to the extent that BIDs can properly be labeled as citizen-driven sub-governments (McCool, 1990). The administrative politics that permit such a process requires a resolution of the conflict between traditional principal/agent vs network political structures. BIDs represent this resolution because they require an orderly transfer of political power and the legitimate power to emerge from a centralized model to a partnership model.

BIDs are acknowledged as a creative, pragmatic, and effective mechanism for solving intractable problems of community revitalization in threatened, but viable, areas. Much of this success is due to formalization of a PPP between the local citizenry, business, and the local government (Morçöl, Hoyt, Meek, and Zimmerman, 2008). BIDs, as a new form of governance, do face concerns regarding public accountability (Ross and Levine, 2001; Hoyt, 2008); community participation and representation; and accountability to local government

(Briffault, 1999). It must be noted that criticisms are not generalized, but always are in reference to a specific incident in a specific BID. The importance of context is necessary when determining local issues regarding BIDs (Gross, 2005). The concerns raised above are symptomatic of government in general. Accountability controls are readily available to government in regard to BID. Much of the problems faced in understanding and formulating BIDs is in the evolution of the contractual arrangement of the PPP. It is often the inexperience of the government partner that creates political and managerial issues that could have been avoided had the planning and ordinance process contributed to better arrangements. There is a learning curve regarding the function and authority of a BID that seems to be resolved in mature BIDs as evidenced in *2nd Roc-Jersey Associates, et al. v. Town of Morristown, et al.* (1999) in which the state had to reaffirm that the public financing mechanism for BIDs was an assessment not a tax. This would seem obvious, but these misunderstandings contribute to early confusions regarding the function of BIDs nationwide.

BID is the generic term used for a type of public authority allowable in 48 states and Washington, DC in the United States (excluding New Mexico) by state statute that gives authority to municipalities to create BIDs to strengthen business in local communities. BID-enabling legislations provide statutory authority for municipalities to create tax-supported BIDs. The districts provide services to encourage and support retail/commercial economic activity similar to shopping malls. The BID legislation is designed to provide municipalities with the ability to focus, elevate, and manage services specifically designed to enhance the economic viability of business areas and downtown business centers. The services that are provided by a BID are specific and unique to that business district. Districts are managed as public agencies utilizing cooperative retail/commercial management technologies similar to shopping malls.

The purposes of the state BID legislation is to promote economic growth and employment, encourage self-financed business districts, designate the professional management of those districts, and develop PPPs that implement supplemental self-help programs consistent with local needs, goals, and objectives. BIDs are distinct because they are special districts that utilize special assessment forms of financing (Justice and Goldsmith, 2006). In the Kessler case (*Kessler v. Grand Central District Management Association*, 1998), the New York court decided (and most jurisdictions agree), that the Grand Central District (and by extension, other BIDs) is a limited purpose institutional design because its services are: (1) supplemental and secondary to municipal services; (2) quantitatively dwarfed by those of the City; and (3) qualitatively different from core municipal functions.

All existing state BID legislation empowers a District Management Corporation (DMC) to provide business management and economic development activities, including administering district affairs (adopting by-laws), purchasing and managing property, and managing the provision of specific services and standards (design, promotions, marketing, rehabilitation, clean-up, security).

BIDs were defined as SADs (Morçöl and Zimmerman, 2006; Justice and Goldsmith, 2006) enabled by state legislation, approved by the local government by an ordinance, and initiated by property and business owners. They deliver public services but are managed by private interests and, often, by private management corporations. Today, BIDs are not targeted solely for downtown revitalization efforts but extend into multi-use districts, industrial and purely residential neighborhoods, which shifts the definition towards broader community revitalization. For example, the Pennsylvania BID statute (2000) describes the districts as "neighborhood improvement districts" (NIDs), which includes every form of neighborhood from industrial to commercial to multi-use to residential, urban to suburban and, potentially, rural.

"BIDs are an evolving phenomenon" (Morçöl and Zimmerman, 2006, p. 8). The first BID was established in Toronto, Canada, in 1970 (Houstoun, 2003). The first bona fide BID in the United States with a special assessment form of financing was the Downtown Development District in New Orleans, established by the state legislature in 1974. This format for a BID has essentially remained intact and the numbers of BIDs (also called SIDS, SADs, and NIDS) have increased from approximately 800 in the 1990s to over 1,500 in the 2000s. Morçöl and colleagues argue that BIDs have become like general-purpose governments. BIDs, they argue, challenge the sovereignty of governments in urban/metropolitan areas and force us to rethink the traditional distinctions between public and private realms (Morçöl, Hoyt, Meek, and Zimmerman, 2008). Justice and Goldsmith (2006) and Hoyt (2008) note the precocious policy transfer that is occurring with BIDs as they become a community development method of choice internationally. This is chiefly seen as a reaction to the problems of suburbanization (Morçöl and Zimmerman, 2006) and an increased interest in smart growth strategies that emphasize urban development around existing mass transit hubs.

In New Jersey, the average growth of BIDs was approximately 3 percent per year (Grossman, 2007b), a trend that appeared to be similar nationwide. There were a number of explanations as to why BIDs began to take off as a substantive form of community development. Much was attributed to the privatization movement in response to the Reagan administration's privatization policies and political rhetoric (Briffault, 1999). Certainly, the upsurge of public choice arguments during the 1970s–1990s supported this claim. But other key motivations can also be found in the serious deterioration of urban retail and commercial economic generators (downtowns) and, with it, an important tax base. Downtowns once represented the mainstay of American retail commerce as well as its social life. Yet, by the 1950s, downtowns were seriously losing their prominence, a condition that might have contributed to Robert Putnam's lament (Putnam, 2000, *Bowling Alone*). This decay extended beyond urban areas to small towns. The zeitgeist of the traditional socio-economic milieu was eroding. No one was immune to the erosion of the downtown.

The culprit, besides the usual one, the television, was clear to see: the suburban mall. The suburban mall summarized the conflicts between urban and suburban, social rest and unrest, political fight and flight, middle class and lower class, and modernity and the mundane. The first attempt to design a BID was to emulate the physical structure of suburban malls and many BIDs were extensions of state statutes that permitted what were called *pedestrian malls*, in which the heart of the downtown area was cordoned off and paved like a piazza, emulating European and South American town center plazas. Today, BIDs are still explained as malls without walls. The pedestrian mall concept did have long lasting value as a reinforcement of the social scale, at ground level, of the created urban space as a sense of a real, rather than forced, community that a suburban mall tended to represent.

However, almost all pedestrian mall projects failed for two fundamental reasons: (1) the town they were in was never designed to block traffic at such a strategic location, therefore, the mall was poorly engineered to support the community's real needs; and (2) the benefits of an enclosed environment of a suburban mall were never realized, thereby letting in and not preventing urban transgressions (safety and cleanliness problems). As the urge to emulate the successful suburban mall proved less than successful, what did prove successful was the organizing of the business and property owning community around common issues. As the false specter of competition from the suburban mall muddled urban revitalization planning, competition continued to increase from other sources with the advent of big boxes—the store as mall (Walmart, Home Depot, etc.) and by the Internet and online purchasing (such as Ebay), signaling forms of competition unheard of half a generation (or less) earlier.

This indicated that downtown decline was not specifically suburban mall induced but caused by other even greater social and economic factors. Downtowns went from virtually no competition to global economic warfare. The simple rule for BIDs was not to engage in direct competition with suburban malls (a classic miscalculation) but to offer better customer service, organization, and niche marketing. Downtowns, through their BIDs, began to address the special retail and social-entertainment aspects of their immediate markets. This was, and remains, a transformation of the existence of downtown from being the only game in town to being a professionally managed economic generator that addressed the cooperative needs of customers and consumers as a value enhancement for the entire town.

BIDs emphasized collaboration-management similar to Stone and Sanders' (1987) urban regime theory with heavy social capital attributes plus innovation planning similar to Molotch's (1976) growth machine theory with even heavier entrepreneurship attributes. Both theories emphasized organization, either through formal institutional coalitions of the like-minded (Molotch, 1976) or local economic desire and the informal acquiescence of neighborhood interests to elite economic agents, which Stone and Sanders (1987) referred to as *urban regimes*; whereas, traditionally, only one of these aspects would further a community development effort. These two elements were synergistic within BIDs and drove the BID movement, while "embracing a vision of community governance" (Lowndes and Skelcher, 1998, p. 316). Placed in the role of political and entrepreneurial activists, "BIDs are the essence of innovative thinking" (Mitchell, 2001, p. 201).

For public administration and political science, BIDs also represent a political shift. With the advent of suburbanization and, later, globalization, communities, which traditionally had a politically active business community centered in its downtown, noted the trend of business and commercial property owners no longer living in the towns in which their business was located (Hunter, 1953). The bottom line was that they could no longer vote in the towns that held their commercial investment. This caused a tremendous (and poorly recorded) political power shift from commerce to residential concerns, particularly in urban and small town areas. Consequently, following the suburbanization of the 1950s and the social unrest of the 1960s, more mayors and legislative members of local government seemed to have a social agenda, rather than a traditional business agenda. Additionally, business faced the status of taxation with no representation, which exacerbated a fundamentally adverse relationship between business and the community at large.

The business community lost its essential voting power because its members resided outside the urban and business municipality and lived in suburban "bedroom" communities. This was certainly less politically effective regarding their business interests. For the same reasons, Kiwanis, Rotary, Lions clubs, and even COCs began to lose political power, which was previously quite substantial. Additionally, the business community could not field political candidates to advance their concerns. Robert Putnam and others seem to have missed this essential political phenomenon of declining social capital caused by the loss of political capability within the business community in traditional economic generators. Although this is not the thrust of this report, BIDs restore the social capital that formal and informal political effectiveness engenders, that which was lost to suburbanization. BIDs may be successful because they recreate formally, by ordinance and the logic of collective action (Olson, 1971), the special interest of business, thereby, not only giving them a political forum but the means to manage it. In this way, we see an injection (or transmission) of suburban political power into the urban and downtown realm.

BIDs are created formally by municipal ordinance, which is the chief aspect of what makes BIDs different from other economic and community development efforts. No other effort, whether it is a business association, economic development corporation, redevelopment authority, or civic association, is created to extend the capability of government in such a manner, gives private sector control to legitimate public sector processes, and extends the public trust to the business and investment community with the ability to self-finance through public assessment in quite the manner that BIDs enjoy. In the 2nd Roc-Jersey

Associates case, the New Jersey court found that assessments did not amount to a "taking without just compensation [because] the SID provides sufficiently identifiable benefits to the subject properties, and ... that the special assessments are measured reasonably and fairly in proportion to the benefits conferred" (*2nd Roc-Jersey Associates, et al. v. Town of Morristown, et al.*, 1999).

Due to their formal nature, BIDs are a function of government at the level of the neighborhood, affecting an immediate form of civic engagement aimed at community improvement. "BIDS have the additional advantage of being an institutional design that explicitly binds the local government into the groups of collective actors we know well, by involving it in revenue collection" (Justice, 2003). The BID functions as both a collective unit of sub-governance and an economic collective. Additionally, BIDs are true PPPs in which the contract is defined in the enabling ordinance. The partnership can be initially sought by either the public or private sector but retains its public persona and extends public authority to traditional private interests.

The BID represents an invitation by the public sector to act in partnership, not in a solely advisory or diplomatic capacity, but as an exchange of public authority for economic technology without reducing the effectiveness of either party. In other words, the private sector assumes a public trust, which extends to the entire community and the public sector defers some of its authority to the economic interests of the neighborhood.

Although mandatory financing does eliminate free riders as it establishes fiscal equity in the BID, the method of financing a BID does not seem to determine if a BID is a BID. A mandatory tax or special assessment seems more precise, equitable, and requires the sort of direct commitment that legitimates a partnership. It is important to note that BID property owners and business owners are not taxed, but assessed. A special assessment was defined as a form of public financing that provided "a combination of services and improvements that are intended and designed to benefit particular properties and demonstrably enhance the value and/or the use of function of the properties that are subject to the special assessments" (*2nd Roc-Jersey Associates, et al. v. Town of Morristown, et al.*, 1999). Since BIDs generally utilize assessment forms of public financing and not taxes, BID residents and any other defined entity can be exempt from assessments (Justice and Goldsmith, 2006; Ruffin, 2008). However, the type of financing appears to be more of a nuance than a determining factor.

Simply put, if a BID is a BID by law, then it is a BID. The financing formula does not alter the legal status of a BID. Incidentally, there appears to be nothing in BID statutes that requires a BID to have an assessment or a budget, although some would argue the practicality of a BID that has no public assessment. This indicates that BIDs have public authority and that authority and how it is organized and managed is what indicates if a BID is present. Additionally, a BID could get financing from alternative private or public sponsors or have a unique fundraising scheme that would satisfy its financial needs. Both of those alternatives do not require mandatory public financing but could finance a BID.

Although public and private funding have different regulatory concerns, what determines the legal status of a BID is not so much the funding, or whether it utilizes public or private management, but how the BID is created and for what public purpose. If it were created by ordinance that passes enumerated powers of the state to a new public entity and it is called a BID (or something equal), we are compelled to identify it as a BID.

This indicates that what fundamentally makes a BID a BID is that it is a unit of government. One that offers the private sector a reasonable entrée into government processes. This is accomplished through the ordinance. In this way, BIDs are PPPs in name and practice because they openly fuse distinct and descriptive public and private societal constructs.

But it is arguable that these are invented distinctions and not organic agents. Examining the way in which these distinctions are constructed in a democracy, one can say that essentially all societal agents are intended to be public to one degree or another. Privateness is not considered a separate aspect of human behavior; it is derivative of publicness (Bozeman, 1987). In other words, privateness is the degree of removal one has from public accountability, a deviation ascribed to cultural nuance, not an innate characteristic. Absolute removal or pure privateness is unachievable, although there is a possible absolute public responsibility. This is because all citizens are potentially 100 percent sovereigns even if their motives are less communal. This sovereignty cannot be denied in a democracy even if it is ignored. It is prudent that we are primarily public people with public responsibilities and our private aspects are negotiated after the public welfare is determined, not before. Privateness is a deviation ascribed to cultural nuance. The intersection of private property law and eminent domain are a good example of this process.

Regarding BIDs, the management entity (private or public) is not the BID. The BID is a public trust (owned by the people). The authorized agents of that trust, municipal legislatures, determine by decree the management entity, contractually, through the local ordinance and sometimes through other attached contractual devices. Additionally, the financing of the BID always requires municipal legislative oversight, whether direct financing (assessments) or indirect tax increment financing (TIF) are employed. Unless a management entity is specifically designated in the enabling local ordinance, it is not authorized to use its budget for BID supplemental services *per se* unless it is approved by the municipal legislature. The municipally approved budget is an approved spending plan for the BID public trust. This further emphasizes the public nature of the BID and this designation is what distinguishes BIDs from other revitalization efforts, like the COCs (private advocacy group) and Main Street Program (a private consulting service of the National Trust for Historic Preservation).

Again, the financing of a BID is not what makes a BID a BID, although public financing does indicate public authority. It is the act of creating a sub-unit of government, citizen-driven to one degree or another. The peculiarities of the citizens anointed to *drive* the district may be aligned with the type of financing along philosophical lines that flirt with the notion of taxation with representation but it is rarely required. A BID, and its cousins, is a BID because of its public, not private, nature.

What occurs in a BID is not privatization but *publicization*. The public purpose does not become more private. The private becomes more public even if normative private sector attributes like entrepreneurship are driving forces. Those aspects also become public as in public entrepreneurship. But this should not be a surprise as in democracy, as stated above, the social imperative is to be more public. This is more often than not overlooked in BID research and generally misunderstood by BID practitioners. The PPP that a BID represents is another name for the localizing process of democratic government. The intention is to enhance citizen investment.

Entrepreneurship and the Performance Paradox of BIDs

BIDs throughout the world were reshaping the nature of public administration, its processes, and performance (MacDonald, 1996; Stokes, 2002; Justice, 2003; Morçöl and Zimmerman, 2006; Hoyt, 2008) at the most local of government levels, the neighborhood. The key to this metamorphosis was not only the PPP but the merging of public and private management technologies in such a way as to forge a distinctive branch of public management: business district management, an expertise within public administration that required a manager to bring together business, government, planning, and community development knowledge and skills pragmatically to achieve citizen-driven governance (Grossman, 2007b).

The *epoch* (Jones, Baumgartner, and True, 1998), beginning around 1956 and seemingly cumulating shortly after the 2000 Presidential election, encompassed the initiation of the home-based entrepreneur. The basis of capital for this newly minted entrepreneur was the family home or the zoned small business and commercial property, which were intractably linked by property investment, local zoning laws, and customer relations. Many small business people and most people "do not really own much else" (Fishel, 2001, p. 4) than their home, business, or business property. The small business person became Fishel's homevoter and, in the case of the small business person, the commercial voter.

The homevoter was linked to the small business commercial voter by the amount of personal investment in a single property and with a chief interest in "managing assets well" (Fishel, 2001, p. 64). Both were also linked by their voting behavior, which aimed to maximize their primary property asset. If this asset were exceedingly compromised, they would both *vote with their feet* and purchase property in a better managed community (Tiebout, 1956).

The home-based entrepreneur seeks governance that is accessible and directed towards maximizing their primary property asset. The enticement of real governance authority is a chief cause of SIDs, which represent a reaction to centralization and perceived government inaccessibility and indifference to economic maximization of property assets. BIDs that focus on business communities work to equalize the relationship between the homevoter and the small business voter by emphasizing linked entrepreneurial interests. This is accomplished by extending the authorities of the municipal corporation to the business sector, defining a district community, and requiring stakeholder participation, both financially and managerially.

The recognition that, within municipalities, there exist not only neighborhoods but also systems of communal interaction based on a variety of social and economic interdependencies that define the context of private investment is at the heart of the BID concept. In this way, BIDs fundamentally reinforce practices that support successful community development and provide the public sector asset management structure necessary to define and implement property investment maximization strategies. The BID concept is primarily a community building movement and relies on community definition and implementation practices.

In this way, the home/commercial voter can be characterized as the community-based entrepreneurial voter. The entrepreneurial voter clearly comprehends the value of their personal property as a chief asset but must soon come to appreciate the impact of common property on this private asset. Addressing and managing common property as a linked asset to private property is less determinable unless a consistent and formalized structure, effective in identifying agreed upon mutual assets and managing these assets, is determined. Managing the aspects of private property is often less complicated because it is frequently not democratic, but autocratic. Managing common community assets tends to be more complicated, particularly in a democratic process. In both private and public situations, without a management structure, investment potential is compromised. This requires additional attention at the public level. The successful entrepreneur pays attention to the internal private risks of an investment and, equally important, the impact of external public risks. In the case of the community-based entrepreneur, without a public asset management structure, the risk factor in managing the public impact of private investment may be too great and, eventually, would be relinquished to the few that are heavily capitalized by privilege or demeanor, essentially a feudal system. This issue may propel many of the criticisms of BIDs (Briffault, 1999; Ross and Levine, 2001).

Management of assets, both private and public, is the key to success for the entrepreneur. The preferred method of management at the level of homeowner/ small business was the localized municipal corporation and its antecedent, SADs (Houstoun, 2003). Small business entrepreneurs and "homeowners will, at the local level, want to adopt the mix of policies that maximizes the value of their primary asset" (Fishel, 2001, p. 6). Successful management is asset-driven and maintains a close proximity to its charge. As private independent investment grew in the middle class following WWII, so did local government, which aimed at managing those investments.

In this way, the homevoter is partnered with the commercial voter, sharing a symbiotic entrepreneurial link and both behaving as entrepreneurial voters. Personal property assets at the scale of the modern homeowner or small business person function by the contextual framework of the community in which they are. The explosion in personal property ownership caused a fragmentation of community assets. This fragmentation created a disturbance in the value of community assets because the level of small-scale private investment potentially interrupted communal identity, disrupting interdependent alliances through overemphasized independent alignments. "Once you've made the purchase, your only protection against community decline is watchfulness and activism" (Fishel, 2001, p. 75), alluding to the purpose of municipal corporate strategies. The framework of the municipal corporation is to harness the exogenous assets that comprise the sense of contextual value, thus, permitting fragmentation to sustain a rational purpose.

Zoning and other regulated land use designs are none other than the conceptual framework of asset valuation in the face of community fragmentation/individualized disturbance. A disturbance having no contextual relation withers away to meaninglessness, which is another way of saying it erodes contextual value. This is witnessed in situations of urban blight as well as in rural devaluation. However, a community fragmentation disturbance, if managed, can increase the overall value of the community by accentuating its constituent parts.

Modern local government efforts are designed to identify and manage asset impactors (fragmentation disturbances) as they evolve in the successful development of real neighborhoods and extended communities. This sustains the value of contextual assets, of which the personal (privatized) asset is a part. The entrepreneurial voters will vote with their feet when contextual (community) assets are poorly managed and undefined. Community-based entrepreneurs and other localized investors tolerate property taxes (and special assessments) only when the public services financed by them are capitalized in their property values.

Because a home or small business property may, in fact, be most people's primary investment, this implies that the home-based entrepreneur is local. The investment is a locally generated motivator. Different from tribalism, the fragmentation of common goods in itself is disruptive to managing contextual assets. To counter this, "homeowners were becoming conscious that the attractiveness of the entire community, not just their own structure and those of their neighbors, made a difference in the value of their homes" (Fishel, 2001, p. 216) and the same was true of the small business investor. The local municipal corporation balances the fragmentation disruption by effectively managing common assets and continuously interpreting their value over time.

The risk facing the modern civic (interdependent) entrepreneur was that the independent entrepreneur tended to an irrational abuse of the commons (Elliot, 1997), which could disrupt the value of private investment by eliminating or reducing its contextual linkages. A rational response might be to establish management structures that sustained contextual assets, while recognizing private property assets through community fragmentation. This response notes that, when the contextual asset is eroded, the value of the private asset is corroded and will degenerate. Then, only attuned and sustained efforts to redefine and manage contextual assets will permit revitalization and investment maximization. Fragmentation is most effective when contextual assets are valued at a premium. No fragment of a community can be a premium asset unto itself. If a trend towards primary fragmentation occurs, making a fragment of a community the premium contextual value, then each adjoining parcel value is at risk of degradation equal to the value of the primary fragment. This means that an entire community is at risk of being sufficiently devalued by the reliance on one or more fragments of the community achieving the full asset value of the community. Company towns throughout the country are a testament to this axiom. When the company is successful, everyone wins; when it is not, everyone loses.

Municipal corporations are similar to private corporations, however, "different than private corporations because of the localized economic interests of the shareholders" (Fishel, 2001, p. 30). Local municipal governments work to maximize stockholder assets just like private corporations. *Sub-municipal* BIDs and NIDs are extensions of this effort with often an even more articulated economic goal. It seems inevitable that decentralization will continue as long as private property is permitted because it empowers residents and local businesses to manage their chief assets. Again, the homevoter hypothesis can also be described as an entrepreneurial voter hypothesis that matches a fundamental model utilized by BIDs to determine and maximize contextual assets: Agreements, Management, Commitments, and Accountability. Although the entrepreneurial voter is initially motivated by the preservation of a private property asset, what has emerged by way of the municipal corporation is a clear understanding of the importance of contextual community assets arrived at by applying the BID model. **Agreements** efficiently resolve the fragmentation problem when the "fragmentation of local government causes property owners, who are mainly homeowners, to see a mix of local services that maximizes the value of their holdings" (Fishel, 2001, p. 223). **Management** resolve the erosion of achieved agreements by sustaining clear direction and recognizing that "the financing of local services from the property tax is a key element of this efficiency seeking activity" (Fishel, 2001, p. 223). **Commitment** resolve fragmentation irrationality, the result of a process where business support and "homevoters will vote for property tax increases if the expenditures they finance will increase their home values" (Fishel, 2001, p. 223). **Accountability** resolves performance confusion and asserts value equilibrium. This model defines the entrepreneurial advantage by equalizing public and private investment impactors, sharing common exogenous risk factors, and managing contextual community assets (Grossman and Holzer, 2016).

As stated above, this model also defines the entrepreneurial advantage by equalizing public and private investment impactors, sharing common exogenous risk factors, and managing contextual community assets. The Agreement–Management–Commitment–Accountability-Partnership Model describes the collaboration process that causes partnerships (Figure 2.5).

At stake in this process are the antecedent notions of democracy-in-action and its standard limitations: information asymmetry, particularism and exclusivity, and xenophobia of every hue that triggers a world economy based on distrust, disagreement, and conditional acceptance assumed as a broad and invisible discourse. The western arena of public service and its varied management apparatuses toil to extract the promise of democracy while human potential cowers to the mean of economic efficiency, clientelism, and, more disastrously, economic tactics often misinterpreted as entrepreneurship.

There often seems to be a sequacious attitude about public performance and productivity that alienates the various public administration camps: management, policy, fiduciary, and political. It is a performance assumption in which the components of human endeavor, let alone public human endeavor, are compartmentalized and examined as self-fulfilling and functioning. In other words, it is as if an individual part of the performance creation and performing process is unique and set aside as a function of the entirety of accomplishment by itself.

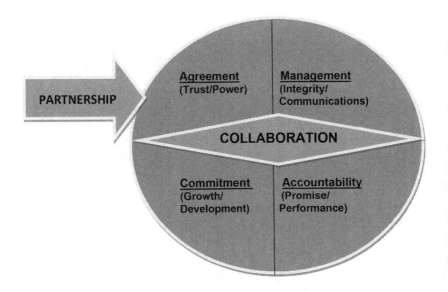

FIGURE 2.5 Partnership Develops and Enhances Collaboration

This has worked to erode the purpose of public management, which may recognize aspects of its mission but is a functioning whole. As a whole, outcome measures tuned to the frequency of quality of life actualities are often more accurate measurements of public performance, which does not diminish, but rather places outputs in the supportive capacity they represent in the process of accomplishment (Figure 2.6).

Performance management and its measures begin with data collection but, ultimately, end with how that data is presented and used. In order to measure and monitor performance-based outputs and outcomes, a baseline data record must be established and a reasonable strategic goal stated. These two objectives (outputs and outcomes) offer primary assessment-driven choice (Wang, 2002). However, in the public sphere, measuring outputs leans towards control, tactical production, and content orientation where the goal is to function efficiently while the citizen remains purely advisory rather than managerial. Outcomes take us in the direction of public entrepreneurship (Wang and Berman, 2000), in which strategic education/decision making and performance are the goal of transforming community capability and encouraging the citizen as a management participant.

When we speak about public performance, we are speaking fundamentally (and ongoing) about how the promise of democracy affects the performance of tasks that are generated by public organizations (both informally and formally, although, in regard to BIDs, we are restricted to the latter): the planning process, the execution of projects and plans, the implementation of policy and the

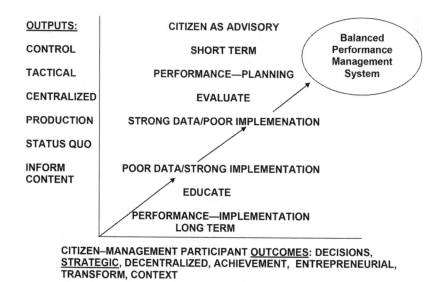

FIGURE 2.6 Performance Measurement—Function vs Transforming

evaluation of the endeavor. In every performance there resides a promise, or a set of promises, that guides the human endeavor and this is true in both private and public environments. When we speak about performance in general, we are speaking fundamentally about measuring outputs and outcomes against inputs and implementation; therefore, we are assessing management processes. This process is the managing and evaluation of the inherent promise(s) in every performance. The chief differences between private and public sector management are the degree of inclusion and the fulfillment of outcomes, i.e. the promised levels of inclusion and envisioned contextual goal. If we are on the high end of either of these, we can safely presume that we are operating in a more public environment. If we are on the lesser end, then we are most likely operating in a private environment. The importance of this distinction is twofold:

1.   inclusion underwrites democratic functions and tends to diminish autocratic functions; and
2.   the often greater depth and breadth of the promises between people is imperative in public environments, due to:

   a   the extent of partnering needs, which places outputs as parts of outcomes;
   b   the performance process is non-linear so that input "A" may not directly impose upon or predict the output or outcome "B"; and
   c   the timeline for expected results to occur and retain impact is expanded; it is long term (even short-term events often have lasting public effect).

Private promises usually point in the opposite direction of these distinctions. The bottom line for the BID manager begins with an assessment of the inclusive, promise/performance process. To the extent that private management dabbles in the public trust (a perquisite in every case, but to varying degrees), it is not immune to public accountability and attempts such at its peril (not unlike dismissing the importance of a traffic signal). However, the very promise of inclusion faced with results-oriented timetables obfuscates both the promise and the performance. The paradox lies in emphasizing one or the other; promise or performance, which negates either or both. In everyday terms, the paradox causes an incessant performance anxiety, which results in poorer perceived performance. Since the paradox exists in normative democratic practices, on evaluation we might notice an ongoing performance anxiety in democratic processes and undue attention to this anxiety. It is the illocutionary act, interdependency, and symbiosis of public and private that provides the DNA of the promise–performance paradox. The paradox pits the individual against the collective performance, the communitarian against the libertarian. and the rational against the transrational. Promises lean towards public behavior, while performance tends to adopt private practices.

One might say that the promise of democracy is not so great, thus, permitting an interceding appropriation by economic mediums to quantify efficiency over effectiveness. This intercession may be the default of the democratic promise and we can expect to find a culture that exalts the individual and shifts public accountability from participation (citizens) to enlightenment (individuals). Democracy tells us that the mean of individual pursuits is apparently the efficiency of the majority. In a democracy, one cannot expect consensus, only a constructed majority. Here, we can expect to find definitions of the majority to be extremely conditional and in many cases statistically unreliable. Practical democratic effectiveness must rely on recognition if not on reasonable inclusion of a minority but only one(s) that mathematically deduces the majority or creates a cooperative political majority necessary to govern legitimately. Majority rule does not fully accommodate collective performance except by a subtraction or the tendency to marginalize the minority and ignore the silent. Concurrently and correspondingly, it must be remembered that, regardless of personal charisma, "individual abilities do not automatically translate into collective performance" (Allison and Nicolaïdis, 1997, p. 39). This, of course, points to the intellectual collision of individualism vs community that forms the promise–performance paradox of democracy and is possibly the paradox of modernity. This offers a third option, a *third door*, rather than an either/or resolution of the paradox in which the resultant outcome is greater than the sum of its parts.

The gap between public promise and performance is infused with the jujitsu of public and private partnerships. This is what BIDs seem to step into with aplomb, or as some say, abandon (Houstoun, 2003; Grossman, 2007b). This has led BIDs to suffer the slings and arrows of political misfortune from both/ many/all sides of the economic aisle. Public advocates get frothy about the seemingly demonic aspects of private government and the private advocates get apoplectic about the thought of public businessmanship and governmental (public) entrepreneurship. Either obiter dictum is a wholly unproven malady. This argument provides us with a (possible) great promise of democracy: tossing out notions of culturally defined public/private sector dualism and replacing it with the British and New Zealand approach of private, quasi-private (quango) quasi-government (quago) and government/public. In this great democratic promise, every citizen, regardless of persuasion and creed, may practice governance with their fellow citizen as it occurs to that person. But this would require the elimination of the cults of particularness, exclusion, and the system of closed privilege, which ravage, contort, and betray even the basic justifications of democratic capability.

BIDs exemplify a new pragmatism in public management, working to unite the best functioning practices of public and private business. This pragmatism begins with a few base promises of BIDs associated with creating formalized PPPs, determining self-help approaches, and establishing a citizen-driven government forum. The promise system allows network actors to examine and explore trust within the community, between people and groups, between government administration and the common person, and between what has been and what can be.

At its heart is the examination of the importance of "professional" management by acknowledging its absence at the level, stages, and local applications that are most crucial in maintaining agreement of direction, purpose, and value. Required prior to a promise unfolding is a mechanism to manage that promise. We experience the operation of managing a promise by the performance(s) it generates. The quality of the performance is tied to the precision and public nature of the promise.

The intended promise of a BID is to cause sustained collective action to maintain and improve community assets (Stokes, 2002; Justice, 2003). BIDs addressed four fundamental themes (Mitchell, 1999; Stokes, 2002; Justice, 2003; Houstoun, 2003; Morçöl, 2006; Grossman, 2007b):

1. **Public Entrepreneurship:**

    - builds upon the assets of the community;
    - emphasizes organization and management to achieve a strategic vision;
    - utilizes business development technologies;
    - builds on comprehensive community development strategies; and
    - unites public and private sector stakeholders.

2. **Social Capital:**

    - a value derived from the social, cultural, and expressive assets of the community;
    - is attained through an organized social network that achieves community goals and maintains community assets;
    - a system that manages the articulation and fulfillment of community agreements, promises, and commitments for improvement;
    - is the primacy of goodwill, trust, and the strength of social accountability networks; and
    - a network governance that builds upon stakeholder engagement and applies strategic planning and decision making.

3. **Comprehensive Asset-Based Community Development:**

    - unites organization, planning, economic and social development;
    - citizen driven and managed;
    - is revitalization oriented;
    - quality of life issues address community assets; and
    - strategic and integrative planning.

4. **Retail Commercial Cooperative Management:**

    - management addresses common/collective concerns;
    - management is formalized in contracts;

- attention to design;
- customer service oriented—value added policy;
- place management; and
- political aggregate.

When accurately assessing and evaluating the performance of BIDs, we must do so by measuring within the contexts of these four constructs, referring to the pragmatic purpose of BIDs.

BID Manager as Public Administrator

The idea of professionalism in public administration has its controversies, starting with the reasonable question of accountability to democratic processes (Behn, 2001). It's noted that this question extends to all forms of public/private administration, including BIDs, but is less an issue when the task being assigned is strictly technical or a vertical part of government itself, such as: building inspector, postal clerk, soldier, garbage collector, police, firefighter, economic development, etc. These task positions were aptly described as being professionals in government, and those that provide the task of managing government services are professionals of government (Gargan, 1998).

In either case, the term professional not only describes a recognized mastery of a particular and useful skill or technology but ascribes unto itself a sense of mission and purpose. Both derive from the establishment of collective order and purposeful public action: government. Public administration may not be a profession but its practices, both in and of government, certainly are. This is because it describes more than it prescribes a sense of humanity, of human behavior, than a set of real outcomes that are achieved by good management practices. Public administration was a result of the need for collective action and communal identity (Axelrod, 1984). The professional outcomes of public administration derive from this communal desire and the actions necessary to translate this desire into real things.

Alive within the realm of public administration, professional aspects have two components and are separated by the need and role of management, which implies that there is a business of government. The business of government, as opposed to the private sector, trades in the realm of public values, ethics, and interests that are simply not limited to market forces. They cope with the interdependencies of society rather than independent aspirations of the individual. Although leadership and political identity may promote one individual over another, it is the public trust that is embodied in government, not simply personal interest.

The public sector professional aspires to represent the community's core values, and to manage those values as assets to produce a healthy economic society. Communal values are derived from a pursuit of that which promotes communal growth and development for all, essentially an entrepreneurial activity. The challenge in public administration professionalism is the balancing of one's personal values with that of the community. However, an assumption that they are aligned results in inequities. The professional public administrator's task, then, is to eliminate assumptive values and work to discover, reveal, and sustain agreements that are or can be commonly shared. The nature of agreements leads us to answer questions of their context and, in so doing, we can provide a better science of administration.

The BID manager is an entrepreneurial public administrator whose profession arose when "private market solutions are inadequate or infeasible and collective public action is required" (Gargan, 1998, p. 1135). In almost every case, BIDs are created by choice through community-based planning processes. They start at the bottom, the common ground, and work upward and outward. The determining choice of a community is to take collective action and this, inevitably, moves towards other established forms of collective action so that a PPP is brokered. The desire to sustain this partnership defines the BID management professional through the provision of business development services. These services reflect a public choice to be decentralized, participatory, pluralist, and inclusive, while managing that choice effectively. BID managers step onto the cutting edge of new public administration as revitalizationalists—facilitators of value-based community identity and the management of the agreements that eventually sustain that identity. This describes a process of transformation from an individual, rational actor, to an interdependent transrational activist. The profession of BID management, therefore, steps beyond and above technical aspects of community development, such as clean and safe public places, promotions, design, and business recruitment and retention, to the practice of the purely public administration task of governance.

However, what is equally important in measuring community improvement are: social investment, upgraded infrastructure, support from the community, effective PPPs, residential investment, a sense of identity and purpose, established functioning community organizations, diversity, political activity, and a sense of being safe and protected, in other words, all the elements of social or community capital. The concern about quality of life, as a community standard that is inclusive and acts as a dialogue of the value of each individual as part of a community, is what seems to differentiate private administration from public administration. The differentiation is not the desire for quality of life but the intention directed to the individual or the community. When this concern is directed to the individual, we sense the profit maximizer (Ostrom, 1999). When it is directed to the community, we sense social and public entrepreneurship (Roberts, 1992; Schneider and Teske, 1992; Mort, Weerawardena, and Carnegie, 2002). The deeper truth might dictate that we are all public beings and that "all organizations are public" (Bozeman, 1987) and yet we operate as individuals, which skews our perspectives because neither is perceptibly more effective.

The public administration professional, as BID manager, practices the art of community and of directing his or her intention to the public good. Profit making does not appear to be a singular goal. Discovering, articulating, and institutionalizing community values (Justice and Goldsmith, 2006) is the motivation for the public administration professional because there is a sense that everyone is improved, including the professional actor. This suggests that BID managers, as public administration professionals, ignore what is valuable in a community at their professional risk and appear instead to promote these values as community assets. In the same analysis, Waldo (1954) pointed out that logical positivists tend to ignore the importance of values. Fry and Nigro (1998) added, "it is not sufficient to treat values as mere data in causal theory or simply present them to others under the guise of an academic division of labor" (p. 1190). Public administration is as much an art as a science. It may be derived as much from the public sector as from the private through public entrepreneurial behavior, which does not have personal profit as its chief goal. It would suggest that most BID managers attest to this sentiment as they attempt to garner cooperation from the Boards of Directors of the PPPs they manage.

BID Management: Public–Private Cooperation in Community Revitalization

In the midst of this debate, spurred on by the redefining factor of a growing middle class, a new creature on the public administration scene has emerged, the BID manager. Having done little to ease the private vs public debate, nonetheless, this new creature appears to be a true hybrid of both public and private sector impulses, an entrepreneur in a public no man's land and a pragmatic manager of communal intent. Is community revitalization reliant upon this newly found cooperation between the private and public sectors?

This dichotomy between the public and private aspects of society has enjoyed reasonable separation in the American intellectual tradition. That is, until the 19th century industrial economy was replaced by the 20th century service and information economies, which require flexibility, integration, and adaptable external exchange. Service economies, both private and public, do have similarities, the most prominent of which is that they serve rather than exploit, which, as modernity proceeds, may be becoming a disintegrating distinction. Interdependence blurred the boundaries between the public and private sectors (Kettl, 1993; Briffault, 1999). Areas of the economy that adapt seem to do well, those that do not decay. This is well illustrated in traditional urban areas with central business districts (economic generators) that deteriorated rapidly when they did not adjust to entrepreneurial and customer-oriented development models and held onto industrial models. Those that adapted or built on existing service models (such as New York City's financial markets or cities that house government) have enjoyed better success.

The key to the success of the BID model is *place management* (Berk, 1976; Mant, 2007): a term that denotes or revitalizes community as an outcome of a real place to live and work (in the modern world, suburban locations may only be a place to live and urban areas only a place to work, which constitutes a function not a place). Customer orientation is the new twist on the BID service model. The articulation of *live* and *work* merge public and private concerns. The BID model formalizes a concern that once might have been taken for granted. The most replicated public management model that incorporates place management ideas with customer satisfaction appears to be the BID or NID (Figure 2.7). "They blend public management expertise with business acumen into a unique administrative form" (Mitchell, 2001, p. 203) and "are rooted in the long privatist tradition of urban governance and politics in the United States" (Morçöl and Zimmerman, 2006, p. 6).

At the edge of public administration, where the public sector meets the private and where free enterprise meets social capital, we can expect to find a no man's land of public policy that is often dysfunctional. At this point, there seems to be a struggle in terms of allegiance to a private/public sector dichotomy. BIDs tend to operate in a professional no man's land, using both private entrepreneurial and public management models that are both altruistic and self-interested. As entrepreneurial models, BIDs are expected to "channel private-sector energy towards the solution of public problems" (MacDonald, 1996, p. 42). Where government administration may be seen as bureaucratic and process-oriented (Gingrich, 2005), BIDs are seen as entrepreneurial, management focused, and innovative. BIDS walk a fine line between traditional public administration and entrepreneurial public management.

The BID model, essentially, has the private sector providing funds and technical expertise and the public sector providing political legitimization and taxing powers. The BID avoided the problem of free riders associated with volunteerism, addressed upkeep of common areas, and provided place management (Berk, 1976; Houstoun, 2003). "BIDs formalize the interests of the local community" (Stokes, 2002, p. 3). At the level of governance that BIDs represent, two forces could define benchmarks of success: citizen participation and professional

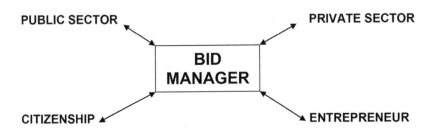

FIGURE 2.7 BID Management Network

management. If we accept the definition that citizen participation was "the role of self-governance in promoting institutional legitimacy, the formation of common understandings between public and private participants" (Justice, 2003, p. 4), we could see the role BIDs might play in furthering participation by citizens.

BIDs also require professional management to allow for the "facilitation of agreement" (Justice, 2003, p. 16). BIDs are an addition to democratic governance and tend to be at the defining point of a private/public social and economic dichotomy that defines and often transforms the term *community* in society. Access to the processes of community definition appears to elicit perceptions of success, based initially on a sense that one's quality of life is improved, and this seems to be tied to the ability to invest personal time and energy into the development of the community and to participate collectively in the activities that make a community viable. Stokes (2002, p. 17) stated in his dissertation that a BID "restores a level of community faith in collective processes."

Today, older urban markets must compete within their regional areas, which do not automatically sustain and manage mutual interests. BIDs re-examine the localization of mutual interests and adopt retail commercial cooperative technology utilized by suburban malls to establish self-reliant service-sector economic generators. Service-sector economies are based on convenience and area malls excel at this in a mobile society. However, convenience and ease can become monotonous. Suburban malls tend to excel in standardization and are, consequently, monotonous. Traditional downtowns tend to excel in diversity and niche opportunities but suffer when poorly managed or appear inaccessible. Both suburban and urban areas share quality of life issues to define success. Standards of safety, cleanliness, accessibility, and design are foundation requirements of both suburban and urban areas, with suburban areas setting the standard.

BIDs are governmental but are not government programs. They represent a unique community development strategy determined by the business community. BIDs convey a partnership between the municipal government and a local business community and its citizens and require the desire to work cooperatively, share responsibilities, and communicate effectively across private/public, residential/business, government/commerce sectors.

At the heart of a BID is management of a PPP that builds on the assets of the community, encourages entrepreneurship, efficiently utilizes resources, and sustains a compelling commitment to public accountability and service. When the business community is truly committed to cooperation and the municipality has the will to provide appropriate authority to the business community, a BID thrives and so does the rest of the town. The challenge before those looking at managing a BID is whether to look forward with commitment or remain looking backwards with unresolved complaints. A BID is a structure to manage agreements and commitments about future possibilities, legally and effectively. It requires a highly institutionalized level of commitment, responsibility, and accountability for the community. BID planning processes (developmentally, organizationally, and economically) explore and define the structure and agreements of the PPP.

A BID creates a third form of management. A hybrid form of public administration in which entrepreneurship is supported, both publicly and privately, and the BID successfully manages the institutionalized PPP. To achieve this success, the partnership must be well defined, informed, and committed to a positive future that is understandable to everyone.

In terms of its function in government, the BID is a unit of sub (local) government but, throughout the world, legislation allows it to be, and it usually is, managed by private stakeholders in a local community development process. The private sector stakeholders must accept and understand necessary public processes, while the public sector must support entrepreneurship and the leadership associated with this human ability. In this way, the BID is a valued partner of government, entrusted to manage its processes, plans, services, and capabilities. Conversely, the BID understands that its legitimization derives from its governmental role, its responsibility to the greater citizenry, and its partnership with the governing body that provides appropriate underwriting, oversight, guidance, and authority. BID management has a specific job to achieve agreement between the public and private sectors, to remain non-political but politically astute, and to keep all stakeholders motivated and engaged in a process of change that may take many years and requires vigilance. In almost every case, the deterioration of not only physical but also social infrastructure requires a BID to plan for and rebuild the infrastructure to sustain future potential. This is a public process that can create great private success.

BIDs, as PPPs, are established due to a breakthrough in public and private sector behavior. The breakthrough is a movement past a traditional adversarial relationship often experienced between government and business and the beginning of a true partnership that utilizes the strengths and offsets the weaknesses of each sector. This allows the public sector to enjoy more vigorous entrepreneurship and allows the private sector to utilize public authority and processes to achieve economic revitalization. The public sector takes on private aspects and the private takes on public responsibility. The increased knowledge of social, political, and economic processes benefits each sector but will confront established systems that have not achieved an institutional understanding of this unique partnership. The common discourse on PPPs focuses on the privatization aspects of the partnership in which public services become privatized. BIDs represent a *publicization* process in which private sector actors take on public accountabilities and begin to dissolve the public–private dichotomy to create a new hybrid capacity for community and business development. This new capacity acts as a *third door* to economic and social stability and success.

BID Management Primer

BID management begins in traditional commercial areas (downtowns, neighborhoods, city centers, industrial areas, etc.) that have not adapted to current competitive trends. These trends are consumer and employment standards: cleanliness, pedestrian accessibility, signage, modern store display, advertising, dining, entertainment, automobile safety, operable public leisure space, and definable destination. Each business area is distinct and BID management must be innovative. Innovation, as the cutting edge of governance, often embodies: the blending of private and public sector practices, arriving at a hybrid or third option; being entrepreneurial and market-driven, combined with public accountability; and blending self-interest with the public good. Appendix B summarizes the final report and proposal for the City of Newark, New Jersey–Mt. Prospect BID as an example of how BIDs are planned and determined.

Falconer (2007) of the Maplewood Village BID in New Jersey stated: "I see the role of the BID manager in meeting the maximum potential of a BID to be a cross between an entrepreneur and a coach" (from interview). Three BID management aspects blend (to one degree or another) Falconer's observation:

a   an entrepreneurial approach focused on organizing, enrollment, and creative thinking;

b   a public service approach centered on the development of political relationships and the need to work with alternative stakeholders to advance particular objectives; and

c   a supervisory approach concerned with the efficient management of day-to-day activities. Entrepreneurship, public service, sociability, networking, and supervision address the themes of the BID manager.

The BID manager is clearly a different kind of animal in the public management field. For decades, many have attempted to define the profession. It is not one that can easily be pigeonholed into a simple discipline. It requires not only public administration and organizational skills but also business economic and development, public relations and marketing, personnel and project management, finance and budgeting, and political skills. BID managers must adapt and use all of these skills because BID management is as much a venture into community development as it is in delivering services.

In short, a BID manager is a public administrator of a PPP with an entrepreneurial focus, combining practical business skills with the knowledge of community and economic development. However, at the risk of obscuring these competencies, the BID manager must be looked at primarily as a change agent and a facilitator of public processes that engage district stakeholders in developing and sustaining community competencies and competitive practices that draw out real potentials and refine assets. "Public managers need to rely more on interpersonal and interorganizational networks as complements – sometimes as substitutes for–authority" (Kettl, 2002, p. 168). That is why BID managers, as public managers, transcend strict expertism even though accomplishing necessary competencies. The chief expert capability of a BID manager, therefore, is a fundamental pursuit of interdependent-co-operation (networking and partnering), i.e. the management of the PPP, which is strongly entrepreneurial. This does not rely on the interest of individual actors but on the sensibility of the community aggregate.

Efforts to understand the merger of public and private sector management behavior in business and community development challenge both normal public and business administration practices. Both sectors express independence but often act interdependently. This presents a challenge in determining the exact capacity of BID management as public administration responsibilities arise within the PPP. Determining to which sector the partnership is chiefly aligned is a challenge that can often confuse a BID organization. This confusion can extend to the professionals who manage these partnerships.

There is an ongoing debate regarding the public and private nature of BIDs as PPPs and the management of those partnerships. The significance of entrepreneurship is strongly associated with PPPs (Grossman, 2008) and suggests that PPPs act as change agents in normal government processes. This further suggests that, as the public sector creates participation opportunities for traditionally private sector actors and private sector technologies are utilized in the public realm, private sector roles become infused with public behavior. This is not an accident but is fully intended by the state, enabling legislation that allows BIDs. BIDs, on the local level of governance, act as a link between the public and private sector and, as a result, become a potential technology and knowledge transfer mechanism with the aim of improving both sectors.

The profession of BID management steps beyond the obvious technical aspects of community development, such as clean and safe programs, promotions, design and business recruitment and retention, to the practice of governance, which is public administration. D. Durband, Executive Director of the Tucson Arizona Downtown Alliance, expressed the public–private debate regarding whether BIDs were quasi-governmental or fully governmental by stating:

> You have no direct peers when you are the head of the downtown organization in your city. There is no set of similar professionals in your city that your citizens know and can compare you to, as they can with attorneys, doctors, and other professionals. In your own city, you are an anomaly. An identity confusion results from the very nature of the complex private–public partnership that is a BID organization.
>
> *(interview carried out in 2007)*

Few seem opposed to the quasi-government description but BIDs as government raises provocative questions that cannot be ignored as the BID movement grows.

There is no consensus or full understanding of this phenomenon. The BID functions as both a collective unit of sub-governance and an economic collective. Additionally, BIDs are true PPPs in which the contract is defined in the enabling ordinance. The partnership is initially sought by the public sector, retains its public persona, and extends public authority to traditional private interests. The BID represents an invitation by the public sector to act in partnership, not solely as advisory or diplomatic, and is an exchange of public authority for economic technology without reducing the effectiveness of either party. In other words, the private sector assumes a public trust, which extends to the entire community, and the municipal government defers some of its authority to the economic interests of the neighborhood.

Entrepreneurship and the Strategic Purpose of the BID

"The promising outlook for BIDs is that more of them will be created and existing BIDs will grow larger and learn how to do a better job" (Mitchell, 2008, p. 119). Business Improvement District Management Corporations and Commissions are designated in the local enabling ordinances necessary to establish a BID. BID statutes allow the BID to be managed by either a government commission or a non-profit corporation. Overwhelmingly, BIDs tend to be managed by non-profit corporations. This may be due to a need to balance perceived public–private roles in achieving a more even partnership. It is not hard to imagine that the private sector is less adept at managing in the public sphere and needs encouragement. Nonetheless, this management capacity is established due to a breakthrough in public and private sector behavior. The breakthrough moves past the traditional adversarial relationships, often experienced between government and business, and institutes the beginning of a true partnership that utilizes the strengths and offsets the weaknesses of each sector.

This allows the public sector to enjoy more vigorous entrepreneurship, while the private sector can utilize public authority and public processes to achieve economic revitalization. Mitchell (2008) observed that, "BIDs are linked to the economic development policy mania in American cities and to the conviction that the public interest is best served through the entrepreneurial activities of public-private partnerships" (p. 39). However, Mitchell correctly noted that the public sector assumed private aspects but failed to observe that the private sector took on public responsibilities. Nonetheless, it was clear from Mitchell's statement that entrepreneurship appropriates an important role. The increased knowledge of social, political, and economic processes benefits each sector but confronts established systems that have not achieved an institutional understanding of that unique partnership. BID management is unique because it encompasses a PPP. Functional knowledge of how the partnership effects, changes, and reconstitutes each sector as well as redefining the roles of each organization stakeholder is addressed by examining the intention and performance of the BID management organization.

The BID organization, not unlike any business venture, generally must achieve a level of organizational competency based on the cooperation and commitment that established the BID's sense of revitalization. What is also required is a pragmatic evaluation of performance, the thorough knowledge of the nature of the PPP as it is intended to function, and the impetus to move forward built on a professional and detailed seven–ten-year *business-style* plan. This formal plan was often addressed after the BID had been established for three–five years (Houstoun, 2003; Grossman, 2007a). This plan becomes the road map to true redevelopment, community building, and business development that details the community's assets, markets, and potential and how the BID will utilize them to achieve successful results. The plan establishes promises and activities that unfold a strategic vision of the future (Allison and Nicolaïdis, 1997). It is a document of change in order to meet an identified potential. A plan should consist of the following steps of inquiry: (1) Where are we? (Situation Analysis); (2) Where do we want to go? (Goals); (3) How do we get there? (Strategy); and (4) How do we know we made it? (Implementation and Evaluation).

Partnerships require accurate knowledge of each partner's skills and resources, mutual respect for this knowledge, articulated promises of real performance, the understanding that success is built on the willingness to fail, and the sense to reflect on successes and failures as well as strengths and weaknesses, while being fully committed to the vision and, ultimately, to the promise of the BID.

References

Abramson, P. R., & Finifter, A. W. (1981) One meaning of political trust: New evidence from items introduced in 1978. *American Journal of Political Studies*, 25(2), May: 297–307.

Adler, P. S., & Kwon, S.-W. (2002) Social capital: Prospects for a new concept. *Academy of Management Review*, 27(1): 17–40.

Allison, G. T., & Nicolaïdis, K. (1997) *The Greek paradox: Promise vs. performance*. Cambridge, MA: The Center for Science and International Affairs, John F. Kennedy School of Government, Harvard University.

Ashoka. (2007) Summary of results. Retrieved 2008 from www.ashoka.org/files/2006_Summary_of_Results.

Axelrod, R. (1984) *The evolution of cooperation*. New York: Basic Books.

Baker, W. E. (1990) Market networks and corporate behavior. *American Journal of Sociology*, 96: 589–625.

Barnard, C. (1938) *Functions of the executive*. Cambridge, MA: Harvard University Press.

Baumol, W. J. (1990, October). Entrepreneurship: Productive, unproductive, and destructive. *The Journal of Political Economy*, 98(5): 893–921.

Becker, C. (2007) Is public administration dead? *Public Administration Times*. Washington, DC: ASPA.

Becker, C., Grossman, S. A., & Dos Santos, B. (2011) *Business improvement districts: Census and national survey*. Washington, DC: International Downtown Association.

Behn, R. D. (2001) *Rethinking democratic accountability*. Washington, DC: Brookings Institution Press.

Berger, P. L., & Luckmann, T. (1966) *The social construction of reality: A treatise in the sociology of knowledge.* New York: Anchor Books.

Berk, E. (1976) *Downtown improvement manual.* Chicago, IL: The ASPO Press.

Bhattacharya, R., Devinney, T. M., & Pillutla, M. M. (1998) A formal model of trust based outcomes. *The Academy of Management Review,* 23(3), July: 459–472.

Bigley, G. A., & Pearce, J. L. (1998) Straining for shared meaning in organization science: Problems of trust and distrust. *The Academy of Management Review,* 23(3), July: 405–421.

Bornstein, D. (2007) *How to change the world: Social entrepreneurs and the power of ideas.* New York: Oxford University Press.

Bourdieu, P. (1985) *The forms of capital: Handbook of theory and research for the sociology of education.* Westport, CT: Greenwood.

Bozeman, B. (1987) *All organizations are public: Comparing public and private organizations.* San Francisco, CA: Jossey-Bass.

Briffault, R. A. (1999) A government for our time: Business improvement districts and urban governance. *Columbia Law Review,* 99(2): 365–477.

Brubaker, E. R. (1997) The tragedy of the public budgetary commons. *The Independent Review,* 1(3): 353–370.

Burt, R. S. (1993) *Structural holes: The social structure of competition.* Cambridge, MA: Harvard University Press.

Carland, J. W., Hoy, F., Boulton, W. R., & Carland, J. A. C. (1984) Differentiating entrepreneurs from small business owners. *The Academy of Management Review,* 9(2), April: 354–359.

Carton, R. B., Hofer, C. W., & Meeks, M. D. (1998) *The entrepreneur and entrepreneurship: Operational definitions of their role in society.* Athens: University of Georgia, Terry School of Business.

Coleman, J. S. (1998) Social capital in the creation of human capital. *American Journal of Sociology,* 94: 95–120.

CSIS-GSI online blog. (2008) *The Global Strategy Institute, Center for Strategic & International Studies,* March 20. Message posted to http://forums.csis.org/gsi/index.php?page_id=89. Access date: November 2008.

Cummings, L. L. (1983) Performance evaluation systems in context of individual trust and commitment. In F. J. Landy, S. Zedrick, & J. Cleveland (eds), *Performance measurement and theory* (pp. 89–93). Hillside, NJ: Earlbaum.

Dahl, R. A. (1989) *Democracy and its critics.* New Haven, CT: Yale University Press.

Denhardt, R., & Denhardt, J. V. (2000) The new public service: Serving rather than steering. *Public Administration Review,* 60(6), July/August: 549–559.

DeFilippis, J. (2001) The myth of social capital in community development. *Housing Policy Development,* 12(4): 781–806.

Derrida, J. (1973) *Speech and phenomena.* Chicago, IL: Northwestern University Press.

Derthick, M. (1990) *Agency under stress.* Washington, DC: Brookings Institution Press.

Dewey, J. (1925) *Experience and nature.* Chicago, IL: Open Court Publishing.

DiIulio, J. D., Jr. (1994) Principled agents: The cultural basis of behavior in a federal government bureaucracy. *Journal of Public Administration Research & Theory,* 4(3), July: 277–318.

Dubnick, M. (2005) Accountability and the promise of performance. *Public Performance & Management Review,* 28(3), March: 376–417.

Elliot, H. (1997) *A general statement of the tragedy of the commons.* Gainesville, FL: University of Florida.

Etzioni, A. (1968) *The active society.* New York: Free Press.

Falconer, V. (2007) Email communication, Executive Director, Maplewood Village Alliance, Maplewood, NJ.

Fernadez-Armesto, F. (1997) *Truth.* New York: St. Martin's Press.

Filion, L. J. (1997) *From entrepreneurship to entreprenology.* Montreal, Canada: The University of Montreal Business School.

Fischer, F. (2003) *Reframing public policy: Discursive politics and deliberative practices.* New York: Oxford University Press.

Fischer, F., & Forester, J. (1993) *The argumentative turn in policy analysis and planning.* Durham, NC: Duke University Press.

Fishel, W. A. (2001) *The homevoter hypothesis.* Cambridge, MA: Harvard University Press.

Foucault, M. (1972) *The archaeology of knowledge.* New York: Routledge.

Fredrickson, H. G. (1971) Toward a new public administration. In F. Marini (ed.), *Toward a new public administration* (pp. 309–331). San Francisco, CA: Chandler.

Fry, B. R., & Nigro, L. G. (1998) Five great issues in the professionalism of public administration. In RHM (eds), *Handbook of public administration* (2nd edn) (pp. 1163–1208). New York: Marcel Dekker.

Fukuyama, F. (1995) *Trust: The social virtues and the creation of prosperity.* New York: Free Press.

Galston, W. A. (1996) Trust – but quantify. *Public Interest,* Winter. Washington, DC: National Affairs Inc.

Gargan, J. J. (1997) The public administration community and the search for professionalism. In J. M. Shafritz and A. C. Hyde, *Classics of public administration* (4th edn). Fort Worth, TX: Harcourt Brace College Publishers.

Gargan, J. J. (1998) Five great issues in the professionalism of public administration. RHM (eds), *Handbook of public administration* (2nd edn) (pp. 1089–1163). New York: Marcel Dekker.

Gingrich, N. (2005) *Entrepreneurial public management as a replacement for bureaucratic public administration: Getting government to move at the speed of the information age.* Washington, DC: Gingrich Communications.

Goetz, S. J., & Freshwater, D. (2001) State-level determinants of entrepreneurship and preliminary measure of entrepreneurial climate. *Economic Development Quarterly,* 15(1): 58–70.

Goffman, E. (1971) *Relations in public.* New York: Basic Books.

Gross, J. S. (2008) Business improvement districts in New York City's low- and high-income neighborhoods. In G. Morçöl, L. Hoyt, J. W. Meek, & U. Zimmermann (eds), *Business improvement districts: Research, theories and controversies* (pp. 221–248). New York: CRC Press, Taylor & Francis Group.

Grossman, Seth A. (2007a). *New Jersey Managed Districts Association (NJMDA) handbook.* Retrieved April 2008 from NJMDA.com.

Grossman, Seth A. (2007b). *Business district management certification program.* National Center for Public Performance. Newark, NJ: Rutgers University.

Grossman, Seth A. (2008) *The role of entrepreneurship in public-private partnerships: The case of business improvement districts,* Doctoral Dissertation. Newark, NJ: Rutgers, The State University of New Jersey, School of Public Affairs & Administration.

Grossman, Seth A., & Holzer, M. (2016) *Partnership governance in public management.* New York: Routledge.

Guth, W. D., & Ginsberg, A. (1990) Corporate entrepreneurship. *Strategic Management Journal,* 11: 5–15.

Habermas, J. (1973) *Legitimation crisis* (T. McCarthy, Trans.). Boston, MA: Beacon Press.

Hardin, G. (1968, December 13). The tragedy of the commons. *Science*, 162(3859), 1243–1248.

Heclo, H. (1977) *A government of strangers: Executive politics in Washington.* Washington, DC: Brookings Institution Press.

Hitt, M. A., Ireland, R. D., Camp, S. M., & Sexton, D. L. (2001) Strategic entrepreneurship: Entrepreneurial strategies for wealth creation. *Strategic Management Journal*, 22: 479–491.

Hoagland, J. (1993) Prepared for non-combat, April 15, and Beware "mission creep" in Somalia, July 20, *Washington Post*, Washington, DC.

Holzer, M., & Zhang, M. (2004) Trust, performance, and the pressures for productivity in the public sector. In M. Holzer and S.-H. Lee (eds), *Public productivity handbook* (2nd edn) (pp. 215–229). New York: Marcel Dekker.

Hosner, L. T. (1995) Trust: The connecting link between organizational theory and philosophical ethics. *The Academy of Management Review*, 20(2), April: 379–403.

Houstoun, L., Jr. (2003) *Business improvement districts.* Washington, DC: Urban Land Institute.

Howlett, M., & Ramesh, M. (2003) *Studying public policy: Policy cycles and policy subsystems.* Ontario, CA: Oxford University Press.

Hoyt, L. (2001) *Business improvement districts: Untold stories and substantiated impacts*, Doctoral dissertation, University of Pennsylvania. Dissertation Abstracts International, 62: 3961–4221.

Hoyt, L. (2006) Importing ideas: The transnational transfer of urban revitalization policy. *International Journal of Public Administration*, 29(1–3): 221–243.

Hoyt, L. (2008) From North America to Africa: The BID Model and the role of policy entrepreneurs. In G. Morçöl, L. Hoyt, J. W. Meek, & U. Zimmermann (eds), *Business improvement districts: Research, theories and controversies* (pp. 111–138). New York: CRC Press, Taylor & Francis Group.

Hunter, F. (1953) *Community power structure: A study of decision makers.* Chapel Hill, NC: University of North Carolina Press.

Hwang, P., & Burgers, W. P. (1999). Apprehension and temptation: The forces against cooperation. *Journal of Conflict Resolution*, 43(1), February: 117–130.

International Downtown Association (2007) *Conference handbook, summary of results.* Washington, DC: IDA.

James, W. (1909) *The meaning of truth: A sequel to "Pragmatism."* Amherst, NY: Prometheus Books.

Jefferies, F. L., & Reed, R. (2000) Trust and adaptation in relational contracting. *Academy of Management Review*, 25(4): 873–882.

Jeong, M.-G. (2007) Public/private joint service delivery in American counties: Institutional theory of local governance and government capacity. *World Political Science Review*, 3(4): 1–16.

Jones, B. D., Baumgartner, F. R., & True, J. L. (1998) Policy punctuations: U.S. budget authority, 1047–1995. *The Journal of Politics*, 60, February: 1–33.

Jung, D. I., & Avolio, B. J. (2000). Opening the black box: An experimental investigation of the mediating effects of trust and value congruence on transformational and transactional leadership. *Journal of Organizational Behavior*, 21(8), December: 949–964.

Justice, J. B. (2003) *Business improvement districts, reasoning, and results: Collective action and downtown revitalization*, Doctoral Dissertation. Newark, NJ: Rutgers University.

Justice, J., & Goldsmith, R. (2006) Private governments or public policy tools? The law and public policy of New Jersey's special improvement districts. *International Journal of Public Administration*, 29(1–3): 107–136.

Kessler v. Grand Central District Management Association (1998) 158 F.3d 92, 132 (2nd Circuit).

Kettl, D. (1993) *Sharing power: Public governance and private markets.* Washington, DC: Brookings Institution Press.

Kettl, D. F. (2002) *The transformation of governance.* Baltimore, MD: Johns Hopkins University Press.

Kingdon, J. W. (2003) *Agendas, alternatives and public policies.* Upper Saddle River, NJ: Addison-Wesley Educational Publishers, Inc.

Kruger, M. E. (2004) *Entrepreneurship theory & creativity: Chapter two.* Pretoria, South Africa: University of Pretoria.

Larzelere, R. E., & Huston, T. L. (1980) The Dyadic Trust Scale: Toward understanding interpersonal trust in close relationships. *Journal of Marriage and the Family*, 42(3), August: 595–604.

Lewis, E. (1984). *Public entrepreneurship: Toward a theory of bureaucratic political power.* Bloomington, IN: Indiana University Press.

Lewis, J. D., & Wiegert, A. (1985). Trust as a social reality. *Social Forces*, 63(4), June: 967–985.

Light, P. C. (1997) *The tides of reform: Making government work, 1945–1995.* New Haven, CT: Yale University Press.

Lindblom, C. E. (1988) The science of muddling through. In J. Rabin (ed.), *Handbook of Public Administration* (5th edn) (pp. 177–187). Belmont, CA: Thomson-Wadsworth.

Lindblom, C. E. (1990) *Inquiry and change: The troubles to attempt to understand and shape society.* New Haven, CT: Yale University Press.

Lochner, K., Kawachi, I., & Kennedy, B. P. (1999) Social capital: A guide to its measurement. *Health and Place*, 5: 259–270.

Louis, K. S., Blumenthal, D., Gluck, M. E., & Soto, M. A. (1989, March). Entrepreneurs in academe: An exploration of behaviors among life scientists. *Administrative Science Quarterly*, 34(1): 110–131.

Lowndes, V., & Skelcher, C. (1998, Summer). The dynamics of multi-organizational partnerships: An analysis of changing modes of governance. *Public Administration*, 76: 313–333.

Lung-Teng, H. (2002) *Proposal for a public trust in government.* Newark, NJ: Rutgers University.

McClelland, D. C. (1987) Characteristics of successful entrepreneurs. *Journal of Creative Behavior*, 21: 219–233.

McCool, D. (1990) Subgovernments as determinants of political viability. *Political Science Quarterly*, 105(2), Summer: 269–293.

MacDonald, H. (1996) BIDs really work. *City Journal*, 6, Spring: 29–42.

Maitlis, S. (2005) The social processes of organizational sensemaking. *Academy of Management Journal*, 48(1): 21–49.

Mant, J. (2007) *Place management: Why it works and how to do it.* (Sydney Vision, UTS Papers in Planning No 13). Sydney, Australia: Faculty of Design, Architecture and Building, University of Technology.

Maslow, A. (1943) A theory of human motivation. *Psychological Review*, 50: 370–396.

Mayer, R. C., Davis, J. H., & Schoorman, F. D. (1995) An integrative model of organizational trust. *The Academy of Management Review*, 20(3), July: 709–734.

Meek, J. W., & Hubler, P. (2006) Business improvement districts in Southern California: Implications for local governance. *International Journal of Public Administration*, 29: 31–52.

Menzel, D. C. (2000) *Privatization and managerial ethics in the information age.* Abstract, University of South Florida.

Miller, D. (1983, July). The correlates of entrepreneurship in three types of firms. *Management Science*, 29(7): 770–791.

Mitchell, J. (1999) *Business improvement districts and innovative service delivery* (Grant report). Arlington, VA: PricewaterhouseCoopers Endowment for the Business of Government.

Mitchell, J. (2001) Business improvement districts and innovative service delivery. *American Review of Public Administration*, 31(2), June: 201–217.

Mitchell, J. (2008) *Business improvement districts and the shape of American cities*. Albany, NY: State University of New York Press.

Moe, T. (1984) The new economics of organization. *American Journal of Political Science*, 28, November: 739–777.

Molotch, H. (1976) The city as growth machine. *American Journal of Sociology*, 82, 309–355.

Moore, Mark H. (1995) *Creating public value: Strategic management in government*. Cambridge, MA: Harvard University Press.

Morçöl, G. (2006) Business improvement districts: A new organizational form in metropolitan governance. *International Journal of Public Administration*, 29(1–3): 1–4.

Morçöl, G., & Zimmerman, U. (2006) Metropolitan governance and business improvement districts. *International Journal of Public Administration*, 29: 1–29.

Morçöl, G., Hoyt, L., Meek, J. W., & Zimmerman, U. (eds) (2008) *Business improvement districts: Research, theories and controversies* (pp. xv–xviii). New York: CRC Press, Taylor & Francis Group.

Morrow, V. (1999) Conceptualizing social capital in relation to well-being of children and young people: A critical review. *The Sociological Review*, 47(4), November: 744–765.

Mort, G. S., Weerawardena, J., & Carnegie, K. (2002) Social entrepreneurship: Towards conceptualization. *International Journal of Nonprofit and Voluntary Sector Marketing*, 8(1), July: 76–88.

Nahapiet, J., & Ghoshal, S. (1998) Social capital, intellectual capital, and the organizational advantage. *The Academy of Management Review*, 23(2), April: 242–266.

National Commission on Entrepreneurship. (2001) What does public policy have to do with entrepreneurial growth? In *Five myths about entrepreneurs: Part three* (Vol. 31, pp. 201–217), March. Washington, DC: National Commission on Entrepreneurship.

Newbert, S. L. (2003) Realizing the spirit and impact of Adam Smith's capitalism through entrepreneurship. *Journal of Business Ethics*, 46: 251–261.

Newland, C. A. (1997) Realism and public administration. *Public Administration Review*, 57(2), March/April: ii–iii.

Olson, M. (1971) *The logic of collective action: Public goods and the theory of groups*. Cambridge, MA: Harvard University Press.

O'Neill, Thomas (Tip) (1977–1987) Speaker of the U.S. House of Representatives.

Onyx, J., & Bullen, P. (2000) Measuring social capital in five communities. *The Journal of Applied Behavioral Science*, 36(1), March: 23–42.

Osborne, D., & Gaebler, T. (1992) *Reinventing government*. Upper Saddle River, NJ: Addison-Wesley Publishing.

Ostrom, E. (1999) Institutional rational choice: An assessment of the institutional analysis and development framework. In P. A. Sabatier (ed.), *Theories of the policy process* (pp. 35–71). Boulder, CO: Westview Press.

Ostrom, V., & Ostrom, E. (1977) Public goods and public choices. In E. S. Savas (ed.), *Alternatives for delivering public services: Toward improved performance* (pp. 7–49). Boulder, CO: Westview Press.

Ouchi, W. G. (1981) *Theory Z: How American business can meet the Japanese challenge*. Reading, MA: Addison–Wesley.

Ozminkowski, M. (2003) *Culture matters: Culture, political and economic influences on the formation of public entrepreneurship*. New York: iUniverse, Inc.

Parks, C. D., & Hulbert, L. G. (1995) High and low trusters' responses to fear in a payoff matrix. *The Journal of Conflict Resolution*, 39(4), December: 718–730.

Pierce, J. C., Lovrich, N. P., & Moon, C. D. (2002) Social capital and government performance: An analysis of twenty American cities. *Public Performance and Management Review*, 25, June: 381–397.

Pittaway, L. (2003) *Paradigms as heuristics: A review of the philosophies underpinning economic studies in entrepreneurship*. Lancaster: Lancaster University School of Management.

Portes, A. (1998) Social capital: Its origins and applications in modern sociology. *Annual Review of Sociology*, 24: 1–24.

Pressman, J. L., & Wildavsky, A. (1973) *Implementation*. Berkeley, CA: University of California Press.

Putnam, R. D. (1993) The prosperous community: Social capital and public life. *America Prospect*, 13: 35–42.

Putnam, R. D. (2000) *Bowling alone: The collapse and revival of the American community*. New York: Simon & Schuster.

Random House College Dictionary (1983) *Promise*. New York: Random House.

Roberts, N. C. (1992) Public entrepreneurship and innovation. *Policy Studies Review*, 11(1): 55–74.

Ross, B. H., & Levine, M. A. (2001) *Urban politics: Power in metropolitan America* (6th edn). Itasca, IL: F. E. Peacock Publishers.

Ruffin, F. (2008) *Business district management certification program*. Newark, NJ: Rutgers University, School of Public Affairs & Administration.

Sabatini, F. (2005) *The role of social capital in economic development. Investigating the causal nexus through structural equations models*. University of Rome La Sapienza, Department of Public Economics, mimeo.

Schaeffer, P., & Loveridge, S. (2002) Toward an understanding of public-private cooperation. *Public Performance & Management Review*, 26(2), December: 169–189.

Schneider, M., & Teske, P. (1992) Toward a theory of the political entrepreneur: Evidence from local government. *The American Political Science Review*, 86(3), September: 737–747.

Schumpeter, J. A. (1934) *The theory of economic development*. Cambridge, MA: Harvard Press.

Schumpeter, J. A. (1947) The creative response in economic history. *The Journal of Economic History*, 7(2), November: 149–159.

Scott, W. R. (1995) *Institutions and organizations*. Thousand Oaks, CA: Sage Publications.

Searle, J. R. (1995) *The construction of social reality*. New York: Free Press.

2nd Roc-Jersey Associates, et al. v. Town of Morristown, et al. (1999) 545 NJ, Supreme Court.

Segal, M. B. (1998) *A new generation of downtown management organizations*, April. Washington, DC: Urban Land Institute.

Simon, H. A. (1955) A behavioral model of rational choice. *Quarterly Journal of Economics*, 69, February: 99–118.

Simon, H. A. (1967) The changing theory of and changing practice of public administration. In I. Pool (ed.), *Contemporary political science* (pp. 86–120). New York: McGraw-Hill.

Simon, H. A. (1997) *Administrative behavior* (4th edn). New York: Free Press.

Smith, A. (1776) *An inquiry into the nature and causes of the wealth of nations*. London, England.

Smith, G. E., & Huntsman, C. A. (1997) Reframing metaphor of the citizen-government relationship: A value centered perspective. *Public Administration Review*, 57(4): 309–318.

Smith, S. S., & Kulynych, J. (2002) It may be social, but why is it capital?: The social construction of social capital and the politics of language. *Politics and Society*, 30(1): 149–186.

Somorin, K. (Retrieved 2008) Demystifying public-private partnership, *Leadership Nigeria*, April 29, 2008, Abuja, Nigeria (Internet Posting). http://allafrica.com/stories/200804290704.html

Stephens, C. U. (2001) The ontology of trust and the transformation of capitalism in a knowledge economy. *Organizational Science*, 12(2): 238–240.

Stokes, R. J. (2002) *Business improvement districts: Their political, economic and quality of life impacts*. New Brunswick, NJ: Rutgers University.

Stone, C., & Sanders, H. T. (eds). (1987) *The politics of urban development*. Lawrence, KS: University Press of Kansas.

Subramaniam, M., & Youndt, M. A. (2005) The influence of intellectual capital on the types of innovative capabilities. *Academy of Management Journal*, 48(3): 450–463.

Taylor, F. (1911) *The principles of scientific management*. New York: Norton.

Thomas, A. S., & Mueller, S. L. (2000) A case of comparative entrepreneurship: Assessing the relevance of culture. *Journal of International Business Studies*, 31(2): 287–301.

Thornton, P. H. (1999) The sociology of entrepreneurship. *Annual Review of Sociology*, 25: 19–46.

Tiebout, C. M. (1956) A pure theory of local expenditures. *The Journal of Political Economy*, 64(5), October: 416–424.

Waldo, D. (1954) *The administrative state: The study of the political theory of American public administration*. Transaction Publishers; New edn (revised December 1, 2006).

Wang, X. H. (2002) Perception and reality in developing an outcome performance measurement system. *International Journal of Public Administration*, 25(6): 805–829.

Wang, X. H., & Berman, E. (2000) Hypotheses about performance measurement in counties: Findings from a survey. *Journal of Public Administration Research and Theory*, 11(3): 403–428.

Weber, M. (1904) The objectivity of the sociological and social-political knowledge, *Archiv für Sozialwissenschaft und Sozialpolitik*, 19. Bd., Heft 1, S. 22–87.

Weber, M. (1946) Selected works. In H. H. Gerth & C. Wright Mills (eds), *From Max Weber: Essays in sociology*. New York: Oxford University Press.

Wiklund, J., Davidsson, P., & Delmar, F. (2003) What do they think and feel about growth?: An expectancy-value approach to small business managers, attitudes towards growth. *Entrepreneurship Theory & Practice*, 27(3): 247–270.

Wolfe, A. (1999) A necessary good. *The New Republic*, November 1, pp. 37–42.

Zucker, L. G. (1986) Production of trust: Institutional sources of economic structure. In B. M. Staw, & L. L. Cummings (eds), *Research in organizational behavior* (pp. 53–111). Greenwich, CT: JAI Press.

3

BUSINESS IMPROVEMENT DISTRICTS

Public–Private Cooperation in Community Revitalization*

BIDs are distinctive, formalized partnerships between the public and private sectors operating as units of sub-government at the local level. Controversies surrounding BIDs range from public manipulation to private governing, all submitted by people who have rarely if ever participated in the establishment of a BID or manage one. BIDs are arguably one the most democratic of processes bringing private citizens into a public governing process. But, this is often the height of muddling through, and that lets us know democracy is present even if convoluted and, at times, intemperate. All BIDs, formally—that is as part of government—are special districts designed to bring together public, private, and civic actors to achieve comprehensive community revitalization, economic development, and quality of life improvements in primary business and mixed use areas. Therefore, the study and practice of BIDs requires the study of special district governance. These governing structures far outnumber all other forms of government. Such entities tend to develop recognizable partnerships that allow the public sector to enjoy more vigorous entrepreneurship, while allowing the private sector to utilize public authority and public processes to achieve economic and community revitalization.

BIDs are unique because they are ultimately authorized by local ordinance, local processes, and legislation, but tend to be managed by private and non-profit entities that function as publicly oriented PPPs. BIDs dissolve and resolve public–private dichotomies to create new hybrid capacities for mutually beneficial community and business development; a noticeable entrepreneurial attribute. Performance concerns arise as BID managers employ bridging forms of public management that explores, identifies, and crafts market as well as collective community values to revitalize a sense of destination and place in traditional and non-traditional business districts and/or downtowns; the most public of places where we meet and greet and come to engage, partake, and observe each other. The BID movement provides new tools for describing public entrepreneurship in public administration necessary to bridge special interests and formulate sustainable social and economic networks. In this way, the BID movement speaks directly to a clearly evolving policy of NPG based on partnership building and learning network across sectors and interests to sustain mutual advantage.

BIDs are special districts established at the local level of government to bring together public, private, and civic actors to address necessary revitalization, economic development, and quality of life improvements in a designated business area. BIDs are unique because they are established by local ordinance, usually managed and overseen by private as well as public agents, and funded through a special assessment. They offer an avenue of public impact, participation, and organization for invested private actors.

The BID partnership represents a movement past a traditional adversarial relationship often experienced between government and business, and the beginning of a legal partnership that utilizes the strengths and offsets the weaknesses of each sector. Such partnerships allow the public sector to enjoy more vigorous entrepreneurship while allowing the private sector to utilize public authority and processes to achieve economic and community revitalization. The public sector takes on private aspects and the private sector takes on a measure of public responsibility.

The emergent phenomena of BIDs is a process in which private sector actors take on public accountabilities and begin to dissolve the public–private dichotomy to create a new hybrid capacity for mutually beneficial community and business development. This new capacity is notably entrepreneurial and acts as a functional third option for achieving economic and social stability and success.

BIDs represent a worldwide evolution in the capacities of government to develop and transform local communities and their cooperative economies. BIDs represent a relatively new form of sub-governance that relies on a functioning partnership between the public and private sectors at the neighborhood level. BIDs appear to extend functional aspects of democracy that invite and permit traditionally business and private citizens into the formal processes of community development and governance. At the heart of a BID is its partnership between the community and the local government (Grossman, 2008). This PPP is determined by state statute and the consequent passing of local laws that enable and describe the partnership. The controversies that surround BIDs tend to travel along the continuum of the partnership. There are those who are unsure of the privatized conveniences of profit seekers at the private end, and the usury proclivities of government at the public end. BIDs are not strict forms of privatization and may be better understood as preliminary, albeit primitive, forms of democratic process that call the private citizenry to become publicly involved and accountable as well as creative in solving immediate social and economic problems. PPPs are poorly evaluated when the aim is to diminish either party in the partnership. It would be expected that the specter of diminishing attributes contributes to diminishing results, and the practice of mutually expanding attributes in such partnerships are not only intended, but functional.

BIDs tend to be pragmatic rather than ideological. BIDs are evaluated on their ability to translate municipal to neighborhood capacity. In this way, BIDs translate general public capability into specific public practice. The practice usually has very specific and measurable determinants of success: Is the community's quality of life improved and are businesses thriving? These questions derived from a melding of local-GDP (Gross Domestic Product) and GDH (Gross Domestic Happiness) index provide a straightforward measurement by community members: Is our community better off today than it was yesterday? Because BIDs are usually small business oriented, the horizon of this measurement is within days or weeks rather than months or years. On a daily basis, these questions tend to define the conversations about the BID between BID partners, Board of Directors, and communications between the BID management entity and the local government. BIDs are oriented towards public response and, therefore, are responsive to public measurements even as businesses reconcile daily cash receipts. At the end of the day, bills must be paid, but in order to live another day the customer must be happy.

Often in comparison to surrounding communities and after years of planning in the form of soul searching, BIDS are eventually built on the premise that the community needs improving. Facing great anticipation by a community that has seen the light, the BID management entity (assuming the mantle of "the BID") is faced with the job of interpreting and implementing comprehensive strategies that satisfy political, economic, and social concerns that help the community understand and feel articulate about its specific identity and purpose within its regional markets. The BID is generally successful if it can be trusted to deliver the economic and social promises of the community without promising too much. Therefore, BIDs must be political about expectations and even more practical about the promises the community makes based on its inherent assets, political will, and competitive nature. The assets are economic, cultural, physical, and social. Concisely understood, "the BID's" job is to best understand these assets and develop them competitively. Community development in BIDs attends not only to quality of life improvements, but also to how quality of life improvements uniquely generate the economy of the community.

The premise for BIDs seems based on the observation that without reliable resources and strong administrative support, volunteer efforts are limited. Simply being a non-profit community organization, or an NGO, is not enough to sustain long-term revitalization. Inadequate legal structures do not sustain hard-earned plans. Government needs to work with communities to build lasting local management capability, but is often held responsible for economic trends it cannot control, services that are poorly designed, and service delivery systems that do not meet the day-to-day requirements of dynamic and changing environments. Special (Business) Improvement Districts (SIDs/BIDs) are designed to remedy this problem, particularly in traditional downtown business areas, although this is not the only application of this model.

BIDs are a common decentralization practice, which merges the political will of a municipality with a commitment to participate by its business community. Decentralization is a unique and formative aspect of American democracy beginning with strong state rights thereby creating an institutionalized movement of government away from a centralized federal core (federalism), and at the same time defining overtime the need for such a core. "Institutions consist of cognitive, normative, and regulative structures that provide stability and meaning to social behavior," through "multiple levels of jurisdiction" (Scott, 1995, p. 33). Decentralization is not an end in itself, but an intention to put the reach and practice of government in the hands of the citizens through sustained action and agreement. Decentralization leads to legal PPPs.

BIDS and the PPP Dilemma

There used to be clear difference of purpose between the public and private sectors (Schumpeter, 1947; Moe, 1984; Kettl, 1993, Schaeffer and Loveridge, 2002; Morçöl, 2006), and to most of us it follows that there is a difference between public and private sector management. Yet, no one can escape a sense of unease that this certainty is porous and becoming more so, the knowledge and experience of governance and business less reliable, and the mystery of that which is private and the sanctity of that which is public is eroding like the Jersey shore. It is an inconvenient truth that virtually worldwide the love affair between the public and private sectors is heating up, eroding our traditional noesis of what is what and who is who, and merging, possibly mutating, possibly evolving, into something completely new.

Since the progressive era and the business applications of Frederick Taylor (1911), this distinction is displaying more and more advanced signs of slippage, or "mission creep" (Hoagland, 1993). Despite the rhetoric of the progressive social equity crowd on one hand, and the rants of the market efficiency lobby on the other, a curious blur is settling over the public landscape as well as private domains. In many respects, the private vs public sector discourse is threatening to become a distinction without a difference—bringing joy to some (Osborne and Gaebler, 1992) and dismay to others (Denhardt and Denhardt, 2000). The modern era in human commerce is notable due partially to an astounding private/public purpose mélange that seems to have spirited away any reliable distinction furthering an ongoing fusion, particularly of the role of the public manager, and in further particularity, the urban public manager. This bibliographic study describes the emergence (out of the fog) of the BDI manager who lurks in the murky and growing world of special districts designed to improve business conditions at the local level. It is an examination of how by "muddling through" (Lindblom, 1959), the downtown revitalization movement has merged, blurred, fused, and redefined the role of public manager pointing to a change in the role of the urban public administrator.

If "the market is a way of managing scarcity" (Kettl, 1993, p. 206), then the public arena conversely may be a way to manage human potential; this may not be unlimited, but is certainly abundant and apparently growing. This may not be a distinction, but it is a description. The private sector tends to attribute value from an individualist perspective, engages personal interest and competing market forces. The public sector tends to attribute value from a communal perspective that causes the emergence and sustainability of responsive civil society and engages our collective interests. The curiosity of what, or which, comes first, the individual or the society, is the crux of much modern argumentation dividing the intellectual world into two generally identified camps: social realists that march the dignity of the Enlightenment (Newland, 1997), and all that holds the individual as dear, even if necessary, to the point of disaster; and the social constructionists who point out, in the face of little agreement, a new Enlightenment to the bored and fatigued, that humanity's social nature appears to be its most unique attribute (Berger and Luckman, 1966; Searle, 1995). This while lamenting that the tragedy of the commons (Elliott, 1997) is that the commons is considered so contrived. In the midst of this debate, spurred on by the redefining factor of the pandemic of a growing middle class, has emerged a new creature on the public administration scene; the BID manager. Having done little to ease the private vs public debate, nonetheless this new creature appears to be a true hybrid of both public and private sector impulses; an entrepreneur in a public no man's land; a pragmatic manager of communal intent. What forms this man and how would we know him if we saw him? Is community revitalization reliant upon this new found cooperation between the private and public sectors?

This dichotomy between the public and private aspects of society has enjoyed reasonable separation in the American intellectual tradition. That is, until the 19th century industrial economy was replaced by 20th century service and information economies, which require flexibility, integration, and adaptable external exchange. Service economies, both private and public, do have similarities most prominently in that they serve rather than exploit, which, as modernity proceeds, may be becoming a disintegrating distinction. Interdependence blurs the boundaries between the public and private sectors (Kettl, 1993; Briffault, 1999). Areas of the economy that adapt seem to do well, those that don't decay. This is well illustrated in traditional urban areas with central business districts (economic generators) that deteriorated rapidly when they did not adjust to entrepreneurial and customer-oriented development models and held onto industrial models. Those that adapted or built on existing service models (such as New York City's financial markets or cities that house government) have enjoyed better success.

The key to the success of the BID model is "place management" (Berk, 1976; Mant, 2007): a term that denotes or revitalizes community as an outcome of a real place to live and work (in the modern world suburban locations may only be a place to live, urban places only a place to work; this constitutes a function not a place). Customer orientation is the new twist on the BID service model. The articulation of "live" and "work" merge public and private concerns. The BID model formalizes a concern that once may have been taken for granted. The most replicated public management model that incorporates place management ideas with customer satisfaction appears to be the BID or NID (Figure 3.1). "They blend public management expertise with business acumen into a unique administrative form" (Mitchell, 2001, p. 203) and "are rooted in the long privatist tradition of urban governance and politics in the United States" (Morçöl and Zimmerman, 2006, p. 6).

At the edge of public administration, where the public sector meets the private, where free enterprise meets social capital, we can expect to find a no man's land of public policy that is often dysfunctional. At this point there seems to be a struggle in terms of allegiance to a private/public sector dichotomy. "As American governments pursued more public policy through nongovernmental partners, public policy increasingly became entangled in private goals and norms" (Kettl, 2002, p. 143). BIDs tend to operate in a professional "no man's land" using both private entrepreneurial and public management models. As entrepreneurial models, BIDs are expected to "channel private-sector energy towards the solution of public problems" (MacDonald, 1996, p. 42). Where government administration may be seen as bureaucratic and process oriented (Gingrich, 2005), BIDs are seen as entrepreneurial, management focused, and innovative. BIDS walk a fine line between traditional public administration and entrepreneurial public management as the historic boundary between those things public and those things private is no longer as meaningful as it once was.

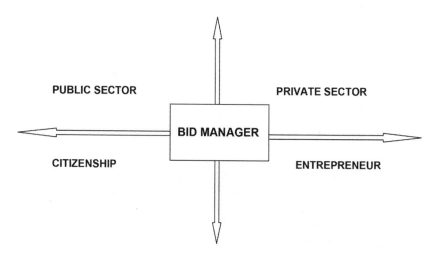

FIGURE 3.1 BID Management

The BID model essentially has the private sector providing funds and technical expertise, and the public sector providing political legitimization and taxing powers. The BID avoids the problem of free riders associated with volunteerism, addresses upkeep of common areas, and provides place management (Berk, 1976; Houstoun, 2003). At the level of governance that BIDs represent, there are two forces that could define benchmarks of success: citizen participation and professional management. If we accept as a definition that citizen participation is "the role of self-governance in promoting institutional legitimacy, the formation of common understandings between public and private participants" (Justice, 2003, p. 4), we can see the role BIDs might play in furthering participation by citizens.

BIDs also require professional management to allow for the "facilitation of agreement" (Justice, 2003, p. 16). BIDs are an addition to democratic governance and tend to be at the defining point of a private/public social and economic dichotomy that defines and often transforms the term "community" in society. Access to the processes of community definition appears to elicit perceptions of success based initially on a sense that one's quality of life is improved, and this seems to be tied to the ability to invest personal time and energy into the development of the community and to participate collectively in the activities that make a community viable. R Stokes stated in his 2002 dissertation that a BID "restores a level of community faith in collective processes ..." (Stokes, 2002).

Today, older urban markets must compete within their regional area, which do not automatically sustain and manage mutual interests. BIDs re-examine the localization of mutual interests and adopt retail commercial cooperative technology utilized by suburban malls to establish self-reliant service-sector economic generators. Service-sector economies are based on convenience, and area malls excel at this in a mobile society. However, convenience and ease can become monotonous. Suburban malls tend to excel in standardization and are consequently monotonous. Traditional downtowns tend to excel at diversity and niche opportunities, but suffer when poorly managed and appear inaccessible. Both suburban and urban areas share quality of life issues to define success. Standards of safety, cleanliness, accessibility, and design tend to be foundation requirements of both suburban and urban areas, with suburban areas setting the standard.

BID Management: The BID Manager

BID management is initially found in traditional commercial areas (downtowns, neighborhoods, city centers, industrial areas, etc.) that have not adapted to current competitive trends. These trends are consumer and employment standards: cleanliness, pedestrian accessibility, signage, modern store display, advertising, dining, entertainment, automobile safety, operable public leisure space, and definable destination (Brodeur, 2003). Each business area is distinct and BID management must be innovative. Innovation as the cutting edge of governance often embodies the blending of private and public sector practices;

entrepreneurial with public choice; market-driven with accountability; and self-interest with public good. Jerry Mitchell (2001) describes three BID management aspects that blend (to one degree or another):

> **a)** an entrepreneurial approach focused on independent decision making and creative thinking; **b)** a public service approach centered on the development of political relationships and the need to work with alternative stakeholders to advance particular objectives; and **c)** a supervisor approach concerned with "efficient management of day-to-day activities."
>
> *(p. 206)*

Entrepreneur, public servant, and supervisor address the themes of the BID manager. In this vein, the BID manager is a different kind of animal in the public management field. For decades many have attempted to define the profession. It is not one that can easily be pigeonholed into a simple discipline. It requires not only public administration and organizational skills, but business economic and development, public relations and marketing, personnel and project management, finance and budgeting, and political skills. BID managers must adapt and use all of the three management aspects Mitchell describes because BID management is as much a venture in building community management capacity as it is in delivering services. The competencies of a BID management expert are generally agreed to be:

* business retail development and marketing;
* public policy development, community development, and organization;
* personnel and group management;
* not-for-profit financing and budgeting;
* multi-task project management;
* public relations and communications; and
* urban planning and development.

Mitchell ranks nine knowledge and skill requirements for the management of BIDs based on a questionnaire mailed to 404 BIDs nationwide in June 1999:

* speaking effectively to audiences;
* financial analysis and budgeting;
* planning for and designing projects;
* situation and political analysis;
* bargaining and negotiating methods;
* writing policy statements and reports;
* impact analysis and evaluation;
* research methods and data analysis; and
* job analysis and performance evaluation.

(Mitchell, 2001, p. 213)

In short a BID manager is a blended public administrator with an economic development focus "combining practical business skills with community knowledge and consciousness" (Stanford Graduate School of Business, 2005). However, at the risk of obscuring these competencies, the BID manager must be looked at first and foremost as a change agent; a facilitator of public processes that engage individuals in developing and sustaining community competencies and competitive practices that draw out real potentials and refine assets. "Public managers need to rely more on interpersonal and interorganizational processes as complements – sometimes as substitutes for–authority" (Kettl, 2002, p. 169). This is why BID managers, as public managers, transcend strict expertism even while accomplishing necessary competencies, which define a key aspect of the public entrepreneur (Lewis, 1984). The chief expert capability of a BID manager is a fundamental pursuit of interdependent-co-operative functionality. This does not rely on the interest of individual actors, but on the sensibility of aggregate determination. The competency missing in the above charts is that of the transrational actor, one whose self-interest is communally based.

The BID movement is a new governance axiom (Osborne and Gaebler, 1992) that reinvents and redefines the functionality of our communities, which derive economic relevance through social investment. In many urban and transitional communities, economic relevance seems marginalized in large part to a process of disinvestment in social norms and shifting global relationships. Communities must be reinvented by the citizenry and the expressed agreements managed effectively to avoid social erosion, blight, or economic decline. This shifts government to more localized formats such as BIDs. BIDs operate in a context of emerging governance. BIDs are decentralized government structures; however, decentralization does not only depart from centralized structures, but also works back to formalized government and is most successful when that is accomplished. BIDs are generally designed as legal PPPs (Houstoun, 2003). These partnerships predict not only required BID management competencies, but also dictate an essential accountability to provide legitimate financial and organizational capability to emerging communities. In this way, the BID model is adaptable to many public forums.

Teamwork, collaboration, and coordination allow the entrepreneurial spirit to evolve (Schumpeter, 1947). Entrepreneurialism is not an individual occurrence; even if its benefits tend to inure to the risk-taker, it is a potential available through collective assignment and active organization (Schumpeter, 1947). Because it is the potential of the land, the greater substance, which provides opportunity, an individual cannot be entrepreneurial if the society they exist in is not. Without a society an individual can only be an opportunist as the rewards of an entrepreneur derive from the community. Profit defined in a social context is a matter of sustainable exchange within a value system. Value is a result of discovered and agreed upon community assets. That agreement is communal, and exists as a dialogue not an individual monologue. Therefore, a monologue has little value unless it is in the context of a dialogue.

The NPM entrepreneur must master the art of community and the building of dialogues of value that allow each person to act on a value exchange, an opportunity. If we take a windshield survey of deteriorated or threatened communities, we can see that in deteriorated communities there are virtually no overt conversations of value. There is generally a chaos of monologues, which by their nature have little value. The result is slum and blight. The great role of public administration and management beyond maintaining value is to create it by reinventing a sense of collective action where it is lost or assumed.

In almost every study of BIDs, there is a concern that there are no useful comparative studies to determine whether or not BIDs work. Lawrence Houstoun asserted that "both the critics and the defenders of BIDs make their assertions without a fig leaf of useful comparative research to cover them" (Houstoun, 2003, p. 144). This was and is simply not true and ignored a pervasive interest in BIDs by academic researchers as well as local evaluations and reporting. BIDs have been evaluated extensively. The odd thing is that Houstoun's books are a series of reports offering comparisons. What's missing in almost all the studies of BIDs is how they are managed. As a whole, these reports indicate that the greatest benefit of a BID, as opposed to a suburban type mall, appears to be that the community the BID is in is more viable, enjoyable, and functioning. For example, the 2007 Furman Study is a good example of ancillary property values rising after a BID was established:

> Our findings indicate that on average BIDs have a large, positive impact on the value of commercial property. On average, the value of commercial property within a BID increases by approximately 15 percentage points more than comparable properties in the same neighborhood but outside the BID.
> *(Furman Center for Real Estate & Urban Policy, 2007, p. 5)*

The cause is difficult to measure because an exact sense of community success is difficult to measure. Defining and measuring all the causal factors of a well-managed community is not unlike describing pornography. You know it when you see it, but it's hard to state exactly what it is (*Jacobellis v. Ohio*, 1964).

Numerous studies and reports attested to the success of BIDs, even when concerns about their function in a democratic society were raised (Stokes, 2002; Hoyt, 2008). This concern did not deny the success of BIDs but, appropriately, questioned whether the end justified the means. However, in general, these concerns were based on the speculation that a BID privatized the public process rather than the other way around. It is far different to *privatize* a public service than it is to privatize the democratic process. A first and assumed correct reaction was that privatizing the democratic process was not democratic at all. It led to autocracies and forms of corporatism that might, indeed, make things function well (be efficient) but eroded the very principles of innovation and self-expression afforded by entrepreneurship (be less effective). If BIDs and PPPs are approached in this manner, they induce this reaction. However, when the democratic process of including normally identified private capacities into the public realm, innovation and self-expression are enhanced and entrepreneurship can be viewed in an expansive manner.

This expansive perspective on entrepreneurship illustrates the import of this research question. Entrepreneurship is often referred to as BID processes (Justice, 2003), and it does not take much of a leap to consider that it is related to democratic processes. It provides an avenue of thought and deed that changes the individual from a self-interested actor (an independent entrepreneur) to an interdependent entrepreneur with community interest. In developing the research question from a public administration point of view, it was clear that the role of entrepreneurship in PPPs, like BIDs, was not solely a linear path to profit maximization but also a holistic experience that was causal in community development.

BIDs are directly in contrast to suburban malls because they operate democratically rather than autocratically, another distinction between the public and private sectors. In their business plans, suburban malls rarely state a concern regarding what their social impact is on the greater community. In fact, it is the other way around; they are concerned about the impact the community has on them. BIDs have an opposite perspective and are obsessed with their impact on the community because BIDs are the community. They are comprised of not only invested businesses but residences; invested people. An improvement in the BID is an improvement to the community. This cannot be wholly said for a suburban mall. The same can be said regarding "big boxes" such as Walmart who have great community impact, but often little interest. Therefore, the impact can be and often is not beneficial to the host community even if it is to a larger audience somewhere across the state or world.

Most people's lives are local, yet today they are bombarded by greater community and even world concerns to a degree that is unprecedented. Decentralization efforts, such as BIDs, also address this erosion of specific locality (Stokes, 2002). In the face of economic circumstances larger than ourselves and our neighborhoods, efforts to restore reasonable determination, the ability to make decisions and choices can be reconstituted by extending governance authority to the disenfranchised, marginalized, or neglected. This is exactly what BIDs accomplish, and why the BID manager is chiefly a professional public administrator and government operative (Gargan, 1997). In almost every aspect of the literature this is overlooked.

A public administrator may be inclined to be bureaucratic or entrepreneurial. Both aspects are two faces of one system that pulls public management from centralization to decentralization and back again; from unified benefit to fields of endeavor that need to be tilled; from conservation to risk taking. The BID movement is a practice of pragmatic citizenship that requires a collaborative approach to economic development. The creation of community, its spirit, values, and direction on the frontiers of social and economic change call forth a unique element in public administration: entrepreneurship. This element is a compulsion to transform a cadre of individuals (monologues) into a team (a dialogue); a functioning, organized, and recognizable entity that manages its assets effectively.

The world has changed and public management is not an exception. Using resources in the most efficient way in order to satisfy citizens, demands and take advantage of the opportunities of a competitive and globalised world, for getting societies more in agreement with collective wishes, all this requires changes, imagination and innovation.

(Janeiro, 2003)

This type of public administrator manages the human process of agreement; a process that "brings people together to solve common problems, develop agreements, and manage those agreements with commitment over time" (Grossman, 1998–2005). Agreement requires partnership, which implies cooperation, direction, and communication. Collaborative partnership development appears to be the new cornerstone of community development (Morçöl, 2006). The BID manager as public administrator, in its essential form, appears to act as an expert practitioner of economic and social community processes that maximize the potential of the community.

Conclusion

The idea of professionalism in public administration has its controversies, starting with the nagging question of accountability to democratic processes (Behn, 2001). This controversy extends to all forms of public administration, and is less an issue when the task being assigned is strictly technical such as: building inspector, postal clerk, soldier, garbage collector, police, firefighter, economic development, etc. These task positions are aptly described as being "professionals in government," and those that provide the task of managing government services are "professionals of government" (Gargan, 1997, p. 1092).

In either case, the term "professional" not only describes a recognized mastery of a particular and useful skill or technology, but ascribes to itself a sense of mission and purpose. And, both derive from the establishment of collective order and purposeful public action: government. Public administration itself may not be a profession, but its practices, both in and of government, certainly are. This is because it describes more than it prescribes a sense of humanity, of human behavior, than a set of real outcomes that are achieved by good management practices. Public administration is an outcome of a desire for collective action and communal identity that seems ontological and naturally evolving (Axelrod, 1984). The outcomes of public administration derive from this desire and the actions necessary to translate desire into real things.

Professional aspects, alive within the realm of public administration, have two components described above and are separated by the need and role of management, which implies that there is a business of government. The business of government, as opposed to the private sector, trades in the realm of public values, ethics, and interest that are simply not measurable by market forces. They cope with the interdependencies of society rather than independent aspirations of the individual. Although leadership and political identity may promote one individual over another, it is the public trust that advises the government, not simply personal interest.

The public sector professional is the focused aspirant of the community representing core values and managing those values as assets to produce a healthy economic state. Communal values are derived by a pursuit of that which promotes growth and development ... for all; essentially, an entrepreneurial drive. The paradox in public administration professionalism is the balancing of one's personal values with that of the community. An assumption that they are aligned will result in inequity. The professional public administrator's task then is to eliminate assumptive values and work to discover, reveal, and sustain agreements. The questions are: Where do we draw the line of community? What establishes context? How do we determine agreements? The nature of agreements may lead us to answer these questions and provide a better science of administration.

The BID manager is an entrepreneurial public administrator whose profession arises when "private market solutions are inadequate or infeasible and collective public action is required" (Gargan, 1997, p. 1135). In almost every case, BIDs are created by choice through community-based planning processes. They start at the bottom, the common ground, and work outward. The determining choice of a community is to take collective action (Axelrod, 1984), and this inevitably moves towards other established forms of cooperation and collective action: government, so that a PPP is brokered. The desire to sustain this partnership defines the BID management professional. Usually sustained through the provision of business development services, these services reflect the public choice to be "decentralized, participatory, pluralist, and inclusive" (Fry and Nigro, 1998, p. 1207), and to manage that choice effectively. BID managers step onto the cutting edge of new public administration as revitalizationalists; facilitators of value-based community identity and the management of the agreements that eventually sustain that identity. This describes a process of transformation from individual, rational actor, to interdependent transrational activist. The profession of BID management, therefore, steps beyond and above technical aspects of community development such as clean and safe, promotions, design, and business recruitment and retention, to the practice of governance; a purely public administration task.

The concern for comparative research on BIDs is admirable and necessary, but this is true in every aspect of economic development. Further research would be helpful to determine if a BID's economy improved using basic measurement standards such as vacancy rates, job creation, sales and property tax collection rates, private sector investment, customer satisfaction surveys, property valuation and tax assessments ratios, business success rates, and market identity.

However, what may be more important in measuring community improvement in BIDs is social investment, upgraded infrastructure, support from the community, effective PPPs, residential investment, sense of identity and purpose, established functioning community organizations, diversity, political activity, and a sense of being safe and protected; i.e. all the elements of social or community capital. It might be well said that the concern about quality of life, as a community standard that is inclusive and acts as a dialogue of the value of each of us as part of a community, is that which differentiates private administration from public administration. The differentiation is not the desire for quality of life, but the intention directed to the individual or the community. Here, the focus might reveal that we are all public beings, and yet operate as individuals. I believe this "truth" guides the public administration professional as a measure of public trust (Putnam, 1993; Fukuyama, 1995).

The public administration professional practices the art of community and partnership building, of directing his or her intention to the public good. A BID manager, as public administration professional, also does not ignore what is valuable in and about a community, and instead promotes these values. In the same argument, Dwight Waldo pointed out in 1954 that logical positivism tended to simply ignore the importance of values (Waldo, 1954, p. 86), "it is not sufficient to treat values as mere data in causal theory or simply present them to others under the guise of an academic division of labor" (Fry and Nigro, 1998, p. 1190). It would seem that public administration is as much an art as a science. And, it may now be derived as much from the public sector as well as the private. Most BID managers would attest to that statement as they attempt to garner cooperation from their Boards of Directors.

If there is an art to public administration it would be the art of community; the creation and occurrence of not only the sense, but the practice of community building that sustains the community. If there is an "art of community" then this is a strong direction for public administration research, and BIDs, as local as they are, "where the rubber hits the road," are exceptional laboratories for this research. Such research might ask the questions: Why is community growth and development an art? What is created when effective multi-sector partnerships are present? How does the public manager practice this art? What connotes success? When is a community partnership considered created, established, and sustainable? What are the measures of success? This may help distinguish the practice of public administration in the art of community development.

Some Advice on the Success and Failure of BIDs

The subject of the degree of success of BIDs is a complex question. Because BIDs are PPPs, they can and must be evaluated based on private, public, and partnership standards. Although a great deal of debate has occurred on the subject, a universal agreement as to what defines success and the standard of success is also not universally determined. This issue is true of government in general and emphasizes the dominant public side of BIDs. This is because all BIDs are conducted at the local level of government, in specialized markets, and under different forms of governmental structures. The state and federal government do not contribute to evaluation of BIDs. It is solely a local determination, which is as it should be. In the end, the BID by presenting a budget and the local government by approving an annual budget determines annually the value of the BID and its continuance. This process, which involves an ongoing and dynamic partnership process, a certified audit, an annual summary report, a political review, and future projections, is the primary determination of the success of a BID. During the year, a BID conducts various projects that support business development, but in the end it's the success of the PPP, evidenced by an approved budget, that determines the success of a BID.

In order to determine BID success, we need to know what a BID is. It is common for people to assess a BID from only one point of view or type of measurement. BIDs need to be evaluated in their entirety not unlike most public entities. BIDs are somewhat complex because they are synergistic. They function legally as both a PPP between the municipal government, the business community, and the community at large. And, they function as a special district form of sub-government (under and part of the municipality) and have special public authority and finances. And, they function as a retail-commercial cooperative (a mall). There are also a number of other public and private functions that a BID manages. Consequently, the primary reason why most BIDs that fail, fail, is because they do not manage the PPP and its aspects well.

Criteria of BIDs that Failed or Struggled: A Conversation

BIDs are a challenge for a community because they work to improve things, change things, reorganize things, focus and allocate resources, and manage assets. BIDs challenge communities because, in most cases, businesses don't deal with the same issues as residents, owners are not citizens of the municipality, and there are opposing aims. Such as: business wants more customers and tourist, residents don't. BIDs are designed to face these challenges as a PPP so that the community grows, becomes more economically competitive, and has a higher quality of life.

BIDs that struggled, or failed, all had one primary reason: they became a political football (private vs public, partisan issues, power challenges, old unresolved grievances) that does not allow the fledgling BID to mature. The BID spent all its time managing municipal politics and could not spend enough time on business development and building its financial and other resources. Some evidence suggests that only (approximately) 3 percent of BIDs in the United States had these problems to the degree that they failed. Each of these BIDs seemed to get entangled in a partisan political fight, and they lost.

There are a number of BIDs that struggled due to undercapitalization. Yet, no BID failed solely because of this issue. Other sources of funds came available, and the strength of the BID partnership prevailed. BIDs can have smaller budgets, but it's how they leverage that budget. Some leverage almost nothing. Some leverage up to four times their budget.

BIDs fail when they fail to plan. In the first years of a BID, including the process of establishing a BID, BIDs must conduct serious and professional business and infrastructure planning to include, but not be limited to, market research and a business plan, branding and identity management, and needed streetscape improvements and redevelopment.

BIDs also struggle when they communicate poorly. BIDs must communicate to their members, the government, the community at large, and customers. The best advice is to not rely on the BID manager, but to hire a professional. Communication is internal to the district stakeholders and external to customers. Newsletters are internal to members of the BID and the community. Advertising is essential and for customers.

Two basic purposes to keep in mind when managing BIDs:

1. BIDs are essentially customer service districts. It's about the customer.
2. It's the BID's job to "manage the conversation" about the district: what it is, who it is, and what it can do for people to add value to their lives.

Lastly, BIDs struggle due to poor management. The manager is the most important part of the BID. BIDs require a professional and proven manager, and then one that has strong public and private administration capability. Often Boards of Directors overshadow or interfere with the manager. This is a mistake. Choose a manager that the Board has confidence in. Look for proven managerial, planning, and partnership capability. The manager does not have to be the best or even do many of the tasks of a BID such as marketing and communications, commercial leasing, environmental work, engineering, business recruitment, mall management, or public administration. But, they should be familiar with it. Most important, they are a proven and excellent manager. That is, they are proven to produce results.

BIDs are resilient due to the strength of the PPP and the management capacity. The primary reason most BIDs fail or struggle comes down to this:

1. BIDs fail because the PPP is poorly managed, and politics takes over. BIDs cannot survive this. ADDITIONALLY, BIDs must:

    *   have professional management where the manager is the focus of success;
    *   conduct professional business development and infrastructure planning to include a business plan, design and streetscape improvements, market research, branding, customer service planning, and communications;
    *   conduct professional communications and marketing as the number one service of the BID—partnerships live and die on the quality of communications both internally and externally; and

- remain non-political at all costs.

2. BIDs must have a sufficient amount of funds and other resources. Like any other business, BIDs represent the business of business; a lack of capital is almost always the culprit of failure:

    - correctly fund the BID;
    - the BID budget should increase as it progresses;
    - spend the funds allotted; and
    - create a capital fund ASAP.

3. Manage the BID like a professional business entity, not like (professional) government, but be appropriately transparent. Be professionally communicative, in partnership with government, citizen-driven, and respectful of the community. Support the manager as a key aspect of the BID. Failure to do this will cause the BID to fail:

    - be lean and pragmatic (produce results);
    - communicate to the community; hire a true professional not an amateur—this is the second best investment a BID can make after the manager;
    - be citizen-driven—make sure your Board is not too large but also represents the businesses (landlords and renters), government, and the community; and
    - do not undermine, devalue, or demean the manager. It's all about the manager and the management of the BID. Choose a manager that is respected, capable, and supportable. The manager manages the BID management organization, not the Board. The Board reviews and provides oversight. The manager is the professional on the BID, not the Board.

4. BIDs are entrepreneurial in a way government is not. BIDs take risks, move things forward, and address the crucial issues of the town's economy. Encourage this:

    - be patient and realistic (time plus money plus management equals results); it takes time for BID plans to unfold (five–seven years);
    - the first year or two are chiefly organizational and planning years; and
    - encourage the BID to think big, manage the conversation of the town as a market, plan for the long term, and agree on items of success—"moments of truth" that tell you that you are being successful and going in the right direction.

Note

* This chapter was originally published in the December 2008 Issue of the *Public Performance & Management Review*.

References

Axelrod, R. (1984) *The evolution of cooperation.* New York: Basic Books.

Behn, R. D. (2001) *Rethinking democratic accountability.* Washington, DC: Brookings Institution Press.

Berger, P. L., & Luckman, T. (1966) *The social construction of reality: A treatise in the sociology of knowledge.* New York: Anchor Books.

Berk, E. (1976) *Downtown improvement manual.* Chicago, IL: The ASPO Press.

Briffault, R. (1999) A government for our time? Business improvement districts and urban governance. *Columbia Law Review,* 99(2): 365–477.

Brodeur, M. (2003, April). *Ten tips for designing a consumer friendly town.* Ipswich, MA: American Planning Association, EBSCO Publishing.

Denhardt, R., & Denhardt, J. V. (2000) The new public service: Serving rather than steering. *Public Administration Review,* 60(6), July/August: 549–559.

Elliott, H. (1997) *A general statement of the tragedy of the commons.* University of Florida, 1–12.

Fry, B. R., & Nigro, L. G. (1998) Five great issues in the professionalism of public administration. In RHM (eds), *Handbook of public administration* (2nd edn) (pp. 1163–1208). New York: Marcel Dekker.

Fukuyama, F. (1995) *Trust: The social virtues and the creation of prosperity.* New York: Free Press.

Furman Center for Real Estate & Urban Policy (2007) *The benefits of business improvement districts: Evidence from New York City,* July. Furman Center Policy Brief. New York: New York University.

Gargan, J. J. (1997) The public administration community and the search for professionalism. In J. M. Shafritz and A. C. Hyde, *Classics of public administration* (4th edn). Fort Worth, TX: Harcourt Brace College Publishers.

Gingrich, N. (2005) *Entrepreneurial public management as a replacement for bureaucratic public administration: Getting government to move at the speed of the information age.* Washington, DC: Gingrich Communications.

Grossman, S. A. (1998–2005) *Business improvement district information guide and handbook.* Working paper. Newark, NJ: Cooperative Professional Services.

Grossman, S. A. (2008) *The role of entrepreneurship in public-private partnerships: The case of business improvement districts,* Doctoral Dissertation. Newark, NJ: Rutgers, The State University of New Jersey, School of Public Affairs & Administration.

Hoagland, J. (1993) Prepared for non-combat, April 15, and Beware "mission creep" in Somalia, July 20, *Washington Post,* Washington, DC.

Houstoun, L., Jr. (2003) *Business improvement districts.* Washington, DC: Urban Land Institute.

Hoyt, L. (2008) From North America to Africa: The BID Model and the role of policy entrepreneurs. In G. Morçöl, L. Hoyt, J. W. Meek, & U. Zimmermann (eds), *Business improvement districts: Research, theories and controversies* (pp. 111–138). New York: CRC Press, Taylor & Francis Group.

Jacobellis v. Ohio (1964) Washington, DC, Stuart, Potter, Supreme Court Justice.

Janeiro, D. B. (2003) Training of senior managers. Conference: Public Administration: Challenges of Inequality and Exclusion, International School of Administration, Galician School of Public Administration, September.

Justice, J. B. (2003) *Business improvement districts, reasoning, and results: Collective action and downtown revitalization,* Doctoral Dissertation. Newark, NJ: Rutgers University.

Kettl, D. (1993) *Sharing power: Public governance and private markets.* Washington, DC: Brookings Institution Press.

Kettl, D. F. (2002) *The transformation of governance.* Baltimore, MD: Johns Hopkins University Press.

Lewis, E. (1984) *Public entrepreneurship: Toward a theory of bureaucratic political power.* Bloomington, IN: Indiana University Press.

Lindblom, C. E. (1959) The science of muddling through. In J. Rabin (ed.) (1988). *Handbook of public administration* (2nd edn). New York: Marcel Dekker, Inc.

MacDonald, H. (1996) BIDs really work. *City Journal,* 6, Spring: 29–42.

Mant, J. (2007) *Place management: Why it works and how to do it.* (Sydney Vision, UTS Papers in Planning No 13). Sydney, Australia: Faculty of Design, Architecture and Building, University of Technology.

Mitchell, J. (2001) Business improvement districts and innovative service delivery. *American Review of Public Administration,* 31(2), June: 201–217.

Moe, T. (1984) The new economics of organization. *American Journal of Political Science,* 28, November: 739–777.

Morçöl, G. (2006) Business improvement districts: A new organizational form in metropolitan governance. *International Journal of Public Administration,* 29(1–3): 1–4.

Morçöl, G., & Zimmerman, U. (2006) Metropolitan governance and business improvement districts. *International Journal of Public Administration,* 29: 1–29.

Newland, C. A. (1997) Realism and public administration. *Public Administration Review,* 57(2), March/April: ii–iii.

Osborne, D., & Gaebler, T. (1992) *Reinventing government.* Upper Saddle River, NJ: Addison-Wesley Publishing.

Putnam, R. D. (1993) The prosperous community: Social capital and public life. *America Prospect,* 13: 35–42.

Schaeffer, P., & Loveridge, S. (2002) Toward an understanding of public-private cooperation. *Public Performance & Management Review,* 26(2), December: 169–189.

Schumpeter, J. A. (1947) The creative response in economic history. *The Journal of Economic History,* 7(2), November: 149–159.

Scott, W. R. (1995) *Institutions and organizations.* Thousand Oaks, CA: Sage Publications.

Searle, J. R. (1995) *The construction of social reality.* New York: Free Press.

Stanford Graduate School of Business (2005) Public Management Program: Public Management Initiative, "1996–1997 Public Management Initiative Social Entrepreneurship," Stanford University, CA.

Stokes, R. J. (2002) *Business improvement districts: Their political, economic and quality of life impacts.* New Brunswick, NJ: Rutgers University.

Taylor, F. (1911) *The principles of scientific management.* New York: Norton.

Waldo, D. (1954) *The administrative state: The study of the political theory of American public administration.* Transaction Publishers; new edn (revised December 1, 2006).

PART II

4

RETAIL/COMMERCIAL COOPERATIVE MANAGEMENT AND ASSET-BASED COMMUNITY DEVELOPMENT

In Part I we identified four fundamental characteristics (pillars) of the profession of business district management: PPPs; Public Entrepreneurship (PE); Social Capital (SC); and Placemaking/Place Management (PM). These four characteristics constitute a unique management orientation. The professional business district manager must (always) balance and be attentive to a public–private mix in every activity and endeavor. Commonly, private sector notions and attributes take on social and public importance. Business district management is essentially PPP management. At its heart is interdependence and making public (bringing to the public process) private sector nomenclature.

In this part we further explore the profession of business district management as a result of a change in progressive economies (since the 1950s) from a product to a service orientation. In the modern world, service is the new product. In management terms: service is the business of business. We also discuss the management technologies in the context of the four characteristics and discuss how "place" is managed. Managed districts are also about the business of business. Therefore, the profession of business district management is about managing the business of business in a community. This correlates to shopping center and "mall" management. Maybe malls are not the enemy. Maybe they are our friends. Maybe they are our partners.

Cooperative Retail/Commercial Management (Grossman, 2006–2014)

Where Service is the Competitive Edge

Retail/Commercial Cooperative Management, employed most notably by suburban malls and shopping centers, is standard practice in successful business communities and exemplifies the service-oriented economy of modern times. This service orientation, not unlike social capital, is the glue that holds together public and private sector cooperative management practices. PPP management is generally practiced as "service management" and its technology is remarkably similar in MBDs and suburban malls. But often, in MBD development, malls, shopping centers, and big boxes are seen as the enemy rather than as part of the regional market and a partner in managing business intent on working as a team and addressing common customer service needs. In this light, we examine how the MBD movement is a technology and policy transfer from privately managed malls. One of the experts in professional business district management is your mall manager. Although traditional suburban malls are owned by one company and in a sense are autocratic, whereas MBDs have multiple public and private owners and are democratic, the attention to customer service is the same. Management is an extra cost in malls, shopping centers, and MBDs. What can we learn from malls? Why haven't we?

What are the similarities and differences (correlates) between suburban malls and MBDs? The difference begins with a suburban mall as "a mall with walls" with an emphasis on private to private sector partnerships, and then later, an MBD as "a mall without walls" requiring MBDs to be a partnership between the public and private sectors of the community. The strongest similarity is that both emphasize the management of service to customers in shaping business and commercial development. This is about managing the internal conversations customers are having about their experience in the business district or mall. For example, is it safe, clean, relevant, accessible, understandable, fun? Either you manage that conversation or it will manage you.

Management is suspect when there are no measurements in place to determine if you are successful. Most managers have "Moments of Truth" (Albrecht and Zemke, 1985, p. 31)—happenings, situations, or customer behaviors—that give them a day-to-day snap shot of the success of the district or mall. What are your "Moments of Truth" that let you know you are managing the conversation successfully? Unlike suburban malls, MBDs do not have lease agreements that determine cooperative arrangements; therefore, an MBD relies on public authority, legitimacy, and processes to determine and sustain agreements, and maintain the financial commitments necessary to support agreements as the organization's services and programs. But, MBDs, especially BIDs, have laws which define public agreements and commitments between public and private sector actors. These laws act as a contract. MBDs exist within complex and comprehensive communities with varieties of mixed uses, opinions, and often contradictory needs. The managers of MBDs must interact with a variety of professional skilled contractors, public officials, and citizens who will have a professional influence on the outputs/outcomes of the MBD. These results exist within the fluid performance of service articulation and perception. Overlooked and often inappropriately maligned, as business development entities suburban malls are an equivalent to MBDs, and where much of the private sector management technology is derived.

BIDs utilize the same "technology of management" that cooperative apartments, malls, and commercial parks use. This technology is "Cooperative Professional Management" (or Retail/Commercial Cooperative Management) and it is designed to manage communities in a comprehensive manner. The technology does not address individual property directly, but rather the community as a whole accomplishing a community purpose. For instance, malls may be owned by a sole proprietor, and town centers and co-ops may be owned by many proprietors. This may affect the management process, but it does not affect the goal of management, which is to address common concerns. In each one of these places there are multiple users renting or owning, and the users are tied to a specific environment with a specific purpose. Being clear about that purpose is fundamental to this cooperative professional management technology.

Town centers and the BIDs that manage them are not unlike malls, which have overall business growth and development as their primary and common purpose. All business areas are communities. A common purpose in itself defines a community. A clear vision of what is possible for the community and shared by all causes the purpose to grow and develop. Communities (of all kinds) thrive when a shared vision is achieved and well managed as the underlying means of addressing common concerns. The chief concern of a business district is the customer's satisfaction with the value they receive.

Value is accessed by the customer in four ways:

1. the environment;
2. media;
3. the type of shop and products offered; and
4. the professional level of management provided.

Cooperative Professional Management is comprehensive in addressing each of these four ways the customer accesses value in the community. Success is directly attributed to the clear expression and availability of the community's vision. Cooperative Professional Management is a management technology that fundamentally ensures the successful delivery of a community's vision and values.

The Active Ingredient: Cooperation

Cooperatives are a unique kind of community in which addressing common concerns and cooperation are considered the most important manner of relating, communicating, and acting. Individuality is not discouraged, but exists within the umbrella of cooperation. *Cooperation* is the "fuel" which drives interdependent processes. In many communities this is a new concept requiring a new way of thinking and speaking. Essentially, it is refocusing a community's priorities from the individual (or "me") to the community (or "we").

Many modern societies for quite some time have supported development through specialization and exclusive project orientation, referred to here as **Redevelopment**—as a desired phenomenon. Cooperatively managed communities do not address integration and inclusion, referred to here as **Revitalization**. *Revitalization* is transformational and alters the entire outlook of a community and creates a new community vision. *Redevelopment* is directed towards fixing specific problems that are eroding an already existing situation. Both have their merits and must be used appropriately. In the life of many communities, particularly business communities, Redevelopment has gone as far as it can and fixing problems have become so extreme as to have little relevance to a clear vision. The sense of community is lost in the need to fix problems.

At this extreme point, it is time for *"Revitalization."* The community may have fragmented into constituencies attached to one solution or another as the single remedy to all problems. *Revitalization* is not a step-by-step linear occurrence as is *Definition* working from project to project. It is comprehensive, moving in great strides to a profound vision of what is possible. In this way, *Revitalization* allows *Definition* to begin from a fresh start ... and a new vision.

Re-Focusing "The Customer's Conversation"

The "conversation" we are talking about is the one each person is always having with themselves about their environment and how it feels to them. Environments might be said to "speak" to us. And, what they say are things like, "you are welcome or not welcome ... you are safe or not safe ... you are important or not important ... you are wanted or not wanted ... ." These aspects about the environment become the thoughts and feelings each of us has every second and what we "talk" to ourselves about. To be successful, BIDs (and other business cooperatives using Cooperative Professional Management Technology) are very attentive to this internal conversation that people have about their environment. The goal is not only to be attentive, but also to manage this internal conversation effectively. The goal is to manage the *dialogue* between people and their experience of the business district environment. It is vital to "get over there" with the customer and understand what that conversation is and how to improve that conversation.

Managing "The Conversation"

The key to business district management is to know what you are managing. What is managed is the actual dialogue or "*conversation*" your customers are having with and about your business district. This conversation can be said to originate in four primary ways: **(1) Management**—among the business community itself that conversation is about, "Are we organized and managed well?"; **(2) Environment**—among the customers who actually come to your district that conversation is about, "Is it clean and safe and well planned? Is this designed properly?"; **(3) Communication**—among the competitors and potential customers that conversation is about, "Who are these people and do I like them? (Is our public relations and promotions effective?)"; and **(4) Economy**—among the community that conversation is about, "Is this a viable and exciting district that meets our needs?" Is our district growing and developing according to the times? The point is, if your customers do not have a positive response to those conversations then you will eventually have fewer and fewer customers. If the response is negative, it points to a lack of management, and particularly a lack of management of a community's vision. The result is deterioration, loss of customers, blight, aggression, and apathy.

A Comprehensive Approach

MBDs, like BIDs, are service districts. Their interest is in serving their customers so that the customer has an efficient and enjoyable experience—an experience of receiving value.

It goes without saying that customers need to be generated and once generated they need to be taken care of, attended to, and adjusted to. As we pointed out in the previous section, there are four ways a customer gets their perspective of your district and accesses value. For this reason, BIDs are not single project oriented, or in fact "project oriented." BIDs are service oriented with each project expanding or establishing a service that articulates the community's values inherent in a shared vision. The four ways the customer accesses your community and its values are by specific types of managed services that fit into general "service domains." These domains are required by the BID to be successful and able to manage each aspect of "the conversation." It is essential to be balanced and comprehensive with each domain. Each service domain manages an aspect of the conversations your customers have about your district. Most BIDs have the following service domains: Management, Environmental Maintenance and Design, Communications–Promotions and Public Relations, Business Recruitment and Retention, Business Practices and Performance, Planning and Development, and Volunteerism and Leadership.

BIDs as a "Tool"

BIDs are a "tool." This tool is a management structure that organizes and is responsible for community agreements to be fulfilled. These agreements, when put into action, are the services the BID provides. When the services are well managed they become "the conversations" about your district. The services and conversations are multidimensional and organic—they grow and develop.

The Goal

Town centers and other business and commercial centers are "economic generators." Their purpose is to generate the economy so that social needs are met. For this reason, town centers are designed to promote a higher volume public use and to have a "magnet" effect to draw people to the area. Consequently, town centers have unique needs and standards to meet to fulfill on public demands and desires. Traditional town centers also act as "common ground" for the community at large and are expected to not only be efficient, but enjoyable.

The key conversation going through a person's mind about your business district is usually, "Am I comfortable and am I having fun?" *Comfort* is associated with the efficiency of the environment to meet a person's requirements to access that environment effectively. *Fun* is associated with how enjoyable the environment is at meeting a number of personal and social needs. The work of a BID, mall, or co-op is to ensure that the environment is efficient/comfortable and fun/enjoyable. If it isn't, people don't want to be there. Each society and culture has different standards about comfort and fun, and often according to technology changes, these standards change. However, one thing never changes and that is that people like to mingle, feel safe, and feel that their life occurs in an exciting and quality place.

Seven Key Objectives

BIDs identify common areas of interest, usage, and the challenges required to maintain a competitive, successful, and effective environment. BIDs employ professional management to address those common issues. Management always costs an additional fee above regular rent or taxes. In itself management is a special or enhanced service. The paramount common interest **is the customers** that the business district attracts, and specifically customers' perception of that district. In a comprehensive manner, the BID works to manage customers' perception and experience of their district so that the customers feel comfortable and enthusiastic about spending their time and money there.

This technology can be called "*Managing the Conversation*" (that conversation being the internal experiences/perceptions of the customer). The conversation we are managing is the conversation about the community as a whole. We can envision seven key objectives of this technology that develop a community conversation. And, in essence, are the building blocks of a community that is aware of *Itself* (as a community) and able to act on *Its* own revitalization. These seven objectives are:

1.   **Commonalties/inclusion** rather than personalities/exclusion.
2.   **Interdependence** rather than independence.
3.   **Comprehensive** rather than one-track.
4.   **Management** rather than no management.
5.   **Professional** rather than amateur.
6.   **Focusing on the customer** rather than oneself.
7.   **Integrity**—Being our vision and values rather than trying to fix them.

Shopping centers and malls have changed consumer expectations. Those expectations—of service—must be managed. Is it possible that it is not the shopping center as product competition, but the new technology of management and service that caused downtowns, who failed to adapt to this new direction, to fail? If so, then management, and what and how we manage, is the crux of downtown revitalization.

Why is Management the Key to Success, and Service as the Competitive Edge? (Albrecht and Zemke, 1985)

Understanding the answer to this question gets to the heart of the profession of business district management. If you or your Board of Directors, government partners, and the community do not understand this, your managed district will struggle until it does. Shopping centers and malls that don't understand this also struggle. Most, however, understand this very well.

There has been a theory that malls ruined downtowns because they took away retail from the downtowns. We are going to consider another explanation. Maybe downtowns declined because they did not keep up with the most competitive management practices. And, therefore, could not keep up well with business trends. In fact, most were not and are not managed. Many of these towns think the municipal government or the COC is responsible for managing the town, but in truth neither is. These business districts are "*managed by the wind.*" If the wind blows nicely everything is okay, but if it blows, as it often does, unpredictably, then we are in crisis.

Business district management is a technology and policy transfer of suburban mall management. It simply says that business communities need to be managed in order to succeed—"*managed by professionals.*" If management, and the lack of it, determines whether or not your business district is successful, then what you manage or don't manage is crucial.

Malls and MBDs

The shopping center and mall phenomenon show us where our profession originated. Transferring the management technology to public areas, downtowns, and neighborhoods by creating PPPs is now influencing how shopping centers and malls operate. Private sector measurements like square footage costs, vacancy rates, lease terms, Net Operating Income (NOI) rate, and asset management are also important to business district managers. However, malls are not PPPs. They are private–private partnerships. They are malls with walls and operated in an autocratic manner. BIDs, for example, are PPPs and are malls without walls that operate in a democratic manner.

If you do one thing at this point, determine what the total commercial/retail square footage of your district is, and then extrapolate the rate of each service you provide. Knowing the value of your district and cost advantage of the service you provide is valuable. It may be far less than what the private sector pays. Then again, is it as effective?

COCs and MBDs

Chambers of Commerce, generally, are not business district management entities. They are advocates, and political actors, and a networking effort. They are not PPPs, and may in fact oppose, or be less interested in, such partnerships, and only see them as a form of privatization. They are not partnerships or in contractual partnerships, and act more like a club, but that club acts like a membership community. Defining the private-ness of business is fundamental to the COC. Financial capital is important to the COC. Rarely discussed, yet of high value to COCs, is social capital. The COC also supports entrepreneurship. MBDs, however, are more closely related to malls than COCs.

COCs are not guided by community development, nor do they have the same authority as an MBD, and especially a formal BID. This is because a COC operates as a club not a community, whereas a mall is a community. A COC is not a PPP. In fact, a COC is not a partnership.

COCs are more different than similar to MBDs. Malls, which are communities, even though they are private–private partnerships, are more similar than different to MBDs.

Malls and shopping centers are "communities" not clubs. MBDs, and especially BIDs, are formalized communities with real public authority, and this is why we examine them closely. A BID is not just a funding mechanism. The funding of a BID is mandatory as a public assessment created by law, and is the basis of the PPP contract because the municipality acts as reviewer and collector of the funds, while the BID organization acts as the planner and the implementer of the funds. Planning and implementation are not simply projects or programs, but the strategic development of the community at the level of the district; a sub-governmental unity; a governing device for the neighborhood.

Mbds, and particularly BIDs, are communities within the greater community. All aspects of the community's health impact the success of the community. This is why the Main Street Program and all other programs have more than one step. Communities develop holistically and comprehensively. MBD organizations act as the local governance body and specifically as the local community developer. An organization that only concentrates on business development soon fades from prominence and impact, and tends to become more political and less managerial. This may be the most significant difference between MBDs and COCs.

Asset-Based Community Development

Asset-based development, rather than needs-based assessment, has become a new paradigm in the community development field. MBDs use an asset-based rather than needs-based approach to determining the direction, network, and services it will provide to develop the community. Quality of life is a result of services managed to enhance community assets. These assets must be identified first, and agreed upon, developed, and then managed with commitment over time. The Model that determines this is: **Agreements–Management–Commitment–Accountability** (Grossman and Holzer, 2016). Asset-based approaches do not fix the past, but consciously plan for and create the future. An asset-based approach must be managed by community-based organizations and attend to functional change in a community. Asset-based development is contextual, assessing assets as parts of greater and greater wholes and the conversations that link the understanding and perception of the asset at each level. Therefore, it is a highly inclusive, participatory, and linked approach. "The whole is greater than the sum of its parts" is an explored and practiced axiom. It is comprehensive because it is contextual and each project or service fulfills an agreement to improve a quality of life as a service advantage and a larger vision/promise. Unlike needs that are often very subjective and personal, assets are most effective as shared, linked, and networked community phenomena and wither when isolated or restrained:

> **Agreements are not only the identified assets, but the vision of what the community** will be based on these assets. It sets a direction and is non-political. This is not a fix-it, or problem solving, approach to community development. It is about moving forward and harnessing all the community's assets and potential in order to do so.
>
> **Management is the key to success.** No business, organization, institution, or individual succeeds without management. The quality of management is the key indicator of success. Successful MBDs manage Agreements not Disagreements. They may disagree but they do not compromise on the community vision because this vision is a promise for a powerful and fulfilled future. Asset management also is about identifying the potential and "promise" of various assets vital to being authentic and fulfilled. Managing

agreements is a collaborative effort because the agreement is a form of consensus not persuasion. Without management nothing actually can happen. **Commitment is equal to resource and service management** and in our culture it is synonymous with "money." Commitment allows our agreements to be managed and not disappear even if people change or circumstances fluctuate. Our commitment to something indicates where our resources will go. Commitment is not less than 100 percent; it does not require knowledge; and, it is always social. It is a dialogue of the value of known and shared assets.

Accountability is a matter of trust management; therefore it is a skill by having a profound relationship to reality. We are accountable for who we say we are and to our partners. The purpose of partnerships is to be accountable for empowering the partnership as a whole and each part therein.

A simple and common way of determining community assets, especially hidden assets, is to ask the question of citizens, elected officials, community planners, and planning bodies, "*What do you love about the town? What is great about the town?*" This question is not a needs question, but an immediate assessment of what matters, what is valuable, and what defines quality. The answers are always transferable and quickly have great currency-building ownership and capital in and with others. Asset-building questions are not typical. Problem solving-oriented questions are typical. Communities are not built on problems, but on the perception of potential and real assets. Development is the management of all these assets in a comprehensive and coordinated manner. Asset building and development act as a "community option" that promotes decentralization, comprehensive community development, and long-term strategies for development.

Destination Management/Marketing

Our task is to integrate Chapter 2 within the field of destination marketing, which defines the "place" in place management. The merger of destination marketing (private) and place management (public) can be called destination management—a fundamental discipline of the profession of business district management.

The tourism field is fast becoming the destination marketing field. This is because tourism no longer is linked solely to holidays. It has expanded to include quality of life enhancers due to discretionary income as a permanent part of the budget of common people; urban areas that have revitalized their importance as a place where society occurs, social life happens, and value is added to the quality of everyone's life; and where business and entertainment are integrated. The concept of tourism has expanded to address everyday quality of life standards. "Tourism" today includes small town tourism, cultural tourism, ecological tourism, history tourism, urban tourism, and linked regional tourism that impacts MBDs.

In order to be competitive and attractive, the first thing a managed district (including malls and shopping centers) must accomplish is determining and managing itself as a value destination. Destination management is the most common of common services for an MBD, and it requires skill in the planning and implementation of destination marketing—"an integrated (comprehensive) marketing communication approach." Every service the managed district provides can be interpreted as part of a destination marketing strategy.

To master destination marketing, we need to understand what it is, how it functions, and how destination management, service management, and asset management are linked in the profession of business district management. Destination marketing for MBDs is a matter of these five management components (points):

1. **A Destination Vision and Values Determination** (A scenario of the future. The "What's So and So What" of your district).
2. **Integrated Branding and Communications** ("Marketing is an exchange process between the" (Pike, 2008, p. 26) ... supply-side (the assets of the MBD and its region) and the demand-side (the customer)).
3. **Service and Asset Management Orientation**.
4. **Societal Marketing Orientation** ("... the process of matching destination resources (assets) with environment opportunities, with the wider interests of the society in mind" (Pike, 2008, p. 27)).
5. **Integrated Marketing Communications** (a process of managing the conversations of customer perceptions that create brand value ... "by strategically controlling or influencing all messages sent to these groups and encouraging data-driven, purposeful dialogue with them" (Pike, 2008, p. 263) customers and other stakeholders).

If there is any practice you would master to become more effective as a professional business district manager, destination marketing is it. The skills of destination marketing integrate all the skills the professional business district manager utilizes as listed above.

Destination Marketing—Asset-Based Planning and Managing the (Market) Conversation

Understanding why the business district is a "destination" for the various markets and customers that utilize it brings together retail/commercial cooperative management, asset-based planning, and marketing and advertising. The district's destination capability and potential are its greatest assets, and the skill of destination management is essentially asset-based management—turning the planning and maintenance of assets into marketable resources that add value to the customer's experience of the district. Appendix C is the 2015 Annual Report of the Ironbound BID, Newark, NJ, summarizing the activities of the BID.

Tourism is a two-sided coin. Tourism creates identity and destination ability. It brings in money directly to town and supports a wider range of services and goods than would otherwise be available for the town. Indirectly, tourism supports other people when shop owners in turn employ people and buy goods and services in the area, a phenomenon called an "economic multiplier effect." Tourism supports property values by creating a ready market for stores and homes for the people that own and work in them. Tourism is also behind many efforts to preserve the historic nature of an area.

On the other hand, tourism brings traffic congestion and crowds. The crush of traffic and people may seriously affect the quality of life for the residents. Tourism often adversely affects the ability to provide municipal services like police protection. The structure of taxation in the state does not easily provide a method for capturing a portion of the money spent by tourists to use in providing services necessitated by their presence.

There are mutual interests between business and residents' interests in preserving quality of life. A town's culture, values, and history are foundations of the area as a destination. In this way, business owners also have a strong interest in controlling the impacts that come from tourism. If visiting Flemington becomes no longer enjoyable, tourists and residents will go elsewhere. Suitable limits must be established that reflect town values. The management of tourism to sustain these values is essential to the quality of life in the area.

Before you place billboards and ads, you must have your advertisement and marketing infrastructure in place. Once you get your message about the district focused and have shoppers' guides, visitors' guides, a few good advertisements, marketing partners, etc., then you can go for the more prominent billboard (or large ad) approach, which is concise and messages extremely well, pointing/directing customers to your district *as a destination.*

The point of destination marketing is to clearly *know your district as a destination—a value-added experience for your customers.* You must have effectively answered these questions to be effective in destination marketing: Why is the district a destination? Are we managing our moments of truth? Have we found our added value? Are we managing the assets that sustain these values?

If you are not good at destination marketing, hire a professional. Those districts that do not do this, or do this poorly, will be confused, strained, or eliminated. In many ways, this topic—destination marketing—is the most crucial and practical part of the profession of business district management, and is not done as well as it can be by most districts. It's about effective communication—the most important, but often most neglected skill in MBDs. If your district is a "place"—a place designed to provide value to others—then it must be a destination in the mind of your customers to be a successful market. Otherwise, it's just noise.

At the heart of these plans is a rediscovery of the significant values of the community developed through its history and interpersonal relationships. It is these values that downtown revitalization and planning intends to build on and manage. A simple and common way of determining community assets, especially hidden assets, is to ask this question of citizens, elected officials, community planners, and planning bodies: "What do you love about the town?" This question is not a needs question, but an immediate assessment of what matters, what is valuable, and what defines quality. The answers are always transferable and quickly have great currency-building ownership and capital in and with others. Asset-building questions are not typical. Problem solving-oriented questions are typical. Communities are not built on problems, but on the perception of potential and real assets. Development is the management of all these assets in a comprehensive and coordinated manner.

Examples of Assets

1. River
2. History
3. Small town feel, love having neighbors, the perfect small country town
4. Eclectic nature of the residents—a little quirkiness
5. Old Victorian homes—feeling of being back in time
6. The ease of living—everything I need is right here
7. A safe place—feels like home, a definite charm
8. It's all about the feet; you can walk everywhere—stroll through town
9. The quality of light along the river
10. Accessibility of hiking/biking/canoeing/kayaking
11. Adorable, charming, architecture, colorful paint, cheerful, sense of history, preserved sense of past
12. Location
13. Genuineness
14. Inns and restaurants
15. Alfresco dining
16. Artisans and crafts
17. Safe and clean
18. Economic potential
19. Variety of quality owner-operated destination stores.

Examples of Community Values

- Being honourable; honor your word
- Communicating effectively
- Committing to success
- Being truthful
- Being accountable

- Being informative
- Having a good relationship to the facts
- If you don't know, don't make it up, and if you do make it up, clean it up
- Having fun is important
- Being pragmatic and results oriented
- Being creative
- Doing our best
- Being fair and equitable
- Being in action.

Summed up, these attributes speak to a great sense of town life. This is present in the nature and structure of the town, and fully recognized as a valuable asset. Little wonder that an eroding of these values, real or perceived, causes anxiety in a traditional town. The challenge of the MBD is to revitalize and build on its environmental, locational, social, cultural, historic, architectural, and business assets (including the surrounding communities), and expand and maintain the community's identity and essential value. As proven in other developing areas, much of the current anxiety of the community will prove unnecessary as intrinsic value is seen to be enhanced rather than eroded by the challenges of well-planned future growth. Factually, people new to the area are attracted for exactly the value that exists and often become staunch supporters of community-based planning. They seek walkable public/community places that build a sense of community and meet real social and economic needs.

Revitalization plans are "daunting" if left to one aspect of the community such as local government. Its success relies on an integrated community approach and the sustainability of community partnerships that merge public and private interests. Asset building and development act as a "community option" that promotes decentralization, comprehensive community development, and long-term strategies for development.

ALPP/SWOT ANALYSIS: ALPP stands for: **Assets, Liabilities, Partnerships, and Problems** and is based on the SWOT analysis. **SWOT ANALYSIS** stands for **Strengths, Weaknesses, Opportunities, and Threats** (Hill and Westbrook, 1997). ALPP may be more appropriate for MBDs and other PPPs. ALPP analysis can be applied to the following areas: Administration and Management, Quality of Life and Environmental Improvements, Business Recruitment, and Public Relations and Marketing.

The *overarching agenda* of an MBD is to identify what is valuable about the district and the town and to find agreement in such a way as to communicate a plan for revitalization. Having done that, we can then look at revitalization in a destination-oriented manner. Then we can attempt to make recommendations on maximizing ideas, management, projects, and procedures that align with the development plans.

ALPP/SWOT analysis (alternately ALPP/SWOT matrix) is a *strategic planning* method used to evaluate the Assets/Strengths, Liabilities/Weaknesses,

TABLE 4.1 ALPP/SWOT Analysis is a Matrix of Positive Factors and Challenges

	Positive factors	Challenges
Internal factors	Strength/Assets	Weaknesses/Liabilities
External factors	Opportunities/Partnerships	Threats/Problems

Partnerships/Opportunities, and Problems/Threats involved in a *project*, organization, or in a *business* venture. The aim of any SWOT analysis is to identify the key internal and external factors that are important to achieving objectives (see Table 4.1).

ALPP/SWOT Analysis for Four Committees of the Board of Directors

Assets: An asset increases the value of your district and contributes to the growth and focus of the district. It is something you and your customers need and come to the district for.

Liabilities: A liability is an unfocused, distracting, or unimportant issue or item that stunts growth and devalues your community. It is something you and your customers don't need and drives customers away.

Partnerships: Partnerships solve all problems, create opportunity, promote communication and participation, and reduce risk.

Problems: Are the obstacles to partnerships, increase risk and isolation, and erode communication.

References

Albrecht, K., & Zemke, R. (1985) *Service America!* Homewood, IL: Dow Jones-Irvin.

Grossman, S. A. (2006–2014) The Business District Executive Management Certification Program. Newark, NJ: Rutgers, The State University of New Jersey, School of Public Affairs & Administration.

Grossman, Seth A., & Holzer, M. (2016) *Partnership governance in public management.* New York: Routledge.

Hill, T., & Westbrook, R. (1997) SWOT analysis: It's time for a product recall. *Long Range Planning*, 30(1): 46–52.

Pike, S. (2008) *Destination marketing.* Burlington, MA: Elsevier Inc.

5

SURVEY RESEARCH, PERFORMANCE MEASUREMENT, BUDGETING AND EVALUATION FOR MANAGED BUSINESS DISTRICTS

Performance Measurement: Managing a Relationship to Reality

Downtown business centers have changed to compete with shopping centers and key to this has been the ability of using the public–private partnerships (PPPs) of BIDs. Key to managing these PPPs is effective performance management that evaluates the partnership. The purpose of measurement is to observe objectively if the promises we have made are in fact being fulfilled. A well thought out measurement effort has the ability to demonstrate the effectiveness of the management program and build trust. Based on the work of the Rutgers University Business District Executive Management Certification Program (BDEMCP), to obtain a complete and meaningful understanding of PPP success, the partnership as a whole, not only parts and projects, must be evaluated in an integrated manner. This program describes the nature of PPPs, examines BIDs as PPPs, the profession of business district management, and concludes with an integral balanced measurement approach for practitioners of PPPs—an Integrated Balanced Scoring Approach. Each sector is evaluated, the partnership organization, and the integration of the whole. Public aspects of the partnership are assessed as quality of life (QOL). Private aspects of the partnership are assessed as a return on investment (ROI). And, the management aspects of the partnership are also assessed as organization and management capacity (OMC). A combined final score provides an assessment of the partnership's success (Grossman, 2012).

This chapter addresses the practical management concerns of MBDs that determine success and establish a measurement model that accurately evaluates the complete and comprehensive PPP-managed district.

The Power of Measurement

Understandably, each organization will have its own definition of success because you're looking for appropriate measurements (reality check points) of that success. Such a result-oriented reality is achieved in context to the organization, group, or even within a profession. The fundamental philosophy, values, principles, and actions are embedded in the context. In Chapter 4, we discussed the concept of "Managing the Conversation," the perceptions of your district that people talk about. Performance measurement is the primary tool to evaluate your effectiveness in "Managing the Conversation." As Spitzer states, measurement is not always about numbers. It is essential to acknowledge that measurement is about "perception, understanding and insight"—Managing the Conversation (Grossman, 2006–2014).

The key to success is management of the conversations of success. It allows you—your organization—to win. We cannot win if someone else manages the conversation for success (wagging the dog). We know someone else is "wagging the dog" when we are timid, incremental, poorly trusted, not communicating, stifling entrepreneurship, and not making promises.

What is Performance Measurement

Performance measurement can be understood as "evidence-based management." Evidence-based management works to assess results, determine the effectiveness of strategies, and the efficiency of operations to make adjustments and address shortfalls: To assess the level of success in delivering on our promises. "Intelligence" may well be the ability to understand reality. Success is understood by how reality is measured; therefore, what is measured lets us know what reality we are successful at. Strategic planning and management, promises, performance-budgeting, and measurements allow us to create, agree upon, and understand the reality we seek. Performance measurement (evidence) and evaluation let us know if we are fulfilling on our promises. This is the single most neglected area in the profession of business district management. As pragmatic and results oriented as MBDs are, it is common to find no systematic reality check or review of performance in most districts. This is largely due to a misunderstanding as to what to measure.

We have identified the primary purpose of an MBD to establish and maintain a functioning PPP to improve the district. In order to adequately measure such a partnership, both sides of the equation must be measured. The public side is often more qualitative and quality of life oriented. The private side is more quantitative and concerned about an ROI. Each presents part of the reality we are trying to achieve. There are three parts: the public side, the private side, and the partnership side.

In this chapter, we examine how to measure the PPP associated with MBDs. Public entrepreneurship and social capital are the essential components of PPPs.

Therefore, assessing the capability of these components will tell us about the health—the reality—of our organization and district. Customer service, cooperative retail/commercial management, asset-based management, and destination marketing are the key domains of business district management. Therefore, assessing the capability of these components will tell us a lot about our skills and the health of our organization and district. Each can be measured as to how well the QOL and ROI has been improved, as well as measurements that evaluate OMC.

Understandably each organization will have its own definition of success because you're looking for appropriate measurements (reality check points) of that success. Such a result-oriented reality is achieved in context to the organization, group, or even within a profession. The fundamental philosophy, values, principles, and actions are embedded in the context.

Trust and Performance

We can explore the fundamental notions of public management performance by examining how we arrive at an agreement on what is being performed. If we are to be accountable for performance (and perform with accountability), we must be as clear as possible regarding what it is we intend to achieve. The key to that statement is "we," which takes us to how agreements are formed and managed. How do we achieve "we" in a manner that works; in a manner that identifies a goal and maps out who is accountable for achieving the goal, particularly when that achievement requires cooperation by all stakeholders? It appears that it is not performance itself that is at issue in determining how communal processes work. It is accountability that defines a partnership in which each partner is interdependently accountable for the success of the goal. Performance capability may be overshadowed in our society by an acute performance anxiety that begins as a poorly understood notion of accountability between partners. It may well be the anxiety of being responsible, fundamental to democracy, which causes this anxiety. We might assume it does if we are not properly trained to be responsible in partnerships. It may also be the anxiety of not knowing the facts about issues affecting community needs. It may be the anxiety of distrust prevalent in rational actor theory. And lastly, it may circle back to the notion of sovereignty in a democratic society as an evolving capability of democratic citizenship.

Performance in government, in public activity, is evasive. It is particularly uncanny due to its political and managerial processes and dichotomies. But, it is less evasive than the accountabilities that underlie performance assumptions. "But to place more emphasis on accountability for performance, we need cooperation. And to evolve such cooperation, we need to create mechanisms for evolving trust" (Behn, 2001, p. 217).

There appears a variety of different aims and theories regarding performance and the accountabilities associated with successful performance in our democratic societies. The principal-agent theory (Taylor, 1912; Brownlow, Merriam, and Gulick, 1937; Barnard, 1938; Moe, 1984, Wood and Waterman, 1994), based on a market model that can be described as a distrust model; i.e. the chief thing you can trust is that you can't trust anyone. In this theory, we find a prescription of reality based on the idea that people will take advantage of circumstances to optimize their benefit over the benefit to the community leading to a potential "tragedy of the commons." Consequently, the principal must manage the agent and be watchful for the erosion of effectiveness and efficiency in a hierarchical relationship. As a policy, this is representative democracy leaning towards auto-cracy and control. The distrust model tends to achieve an emphasis on centralized government.

There is also a counterpoint, cooperative management theory (Kaufman, 1969; Kettl, 1993; Lindblom, 1988; Light, 1997; Behn, 2001) that is based on a political model and can be described as a trust model (Light, 1997) in which an innate desire to achieve social success is assumed and maintained, and reality is described in a process-oriented fashion. In this theory, planning, management, and imple-mentation are mutual between citizens and government, and a team approach is utilized that emphasizes partnership. As a policy this leans towards direct democ-racy, communitarianism, and networking. The trust model tends to achieve an emphasis on decentralized government and federalism.

Concerns regarding the nature of public sector performance and the appro-priate measurements of performance are at the crux of public administration. In a tug of war between service and political accountability, public administration, i.e. government, may be viewed as performing below par. But measurements of success and the reality of failure in the development and evolution of commu-nities is not an exact science due largely to the necessary human element of social and organizational capability which together define an individual's equity in society (Fredrickson, 1971). This capability, like many things, is developmental. Highly desired, it is not instinctual. It must be learned by each generation. At its core the key question facing each individual is whether or not, and to what degree, they can trust another to execute a mutually advantageous agreement to obtain desired life outcomes. That is, "can I trust you to perform adequately" based on our agreement? The question alone is a product of anxiety based on some degree of uncertainty regarding the partner in the agreement, and fundamentally the uncertainty of the proposed venture to achieve what is desired. We might say that ontologically, in the background of certainty and the discourses that describe reality, there is uncertainty; a bracketed or bounded rationality (Simon, 1997). The value of knowledge is a result of its limitations in what may seem like an unlimited world; therefore, it is a dialogue at minimum between what is limited and what is unlimited. Dialogue requires cooperation and accountability by each participant to perform adequately in the dialogue. We do this by learning the rules inherent in our discourses. And, discourses are networks of conversations (Foucault, 1972) that provide the rules for achieving various realities.

We can ask ourselves how discourse, dialogue, partnership, and agreement processes affect governance. Immediately we see that communication, and a sincere cooperation regarding communication, will define the parameters of whatever reality or real event we are pursuing. These parameters can be measured by the sense and degree of trust the participants express in the project and performance process. The following hypothesis emerges: Trust reduces performance anxiety and enhances accountability for performance through a mutually agreed upon description of the reality that the endeavor will function in.

A trust building public administration strategy (in a democratic society) might begin by addressing the foundations of citizenship in a manner that propels each individual and the collective force of community to achieve excellence in:

1.   sustaining high quality of life standards;
2.   conservation of the commons;
3.   renewed acknowledgment of the dignity of all people as an ongoing exploration;
4.   respect for leadership and the emergence of leadership in all endeavors, especially those that are non-economic in nature;
5.   ongoing inquiry into the accountabilities of citizen sovereignty; and
6.   instilling trust as an operating principle.

This strategy is not solely designed to perform government functions on a strictly economic and physical level of inputs and outputs, but to strive for an outcome that not only establishes citizen participation in general oversight, but infuses a practice of communal accountability in which the dual domains (politics and administration) encompassing the formal aspects of government are nested as a function within the less formal organizational power of community development. At heart is the issue of trust between these two interlocking domains. As this strategy is implemented, foremost are the basic human principles of trust that permit people to discover their impact in a communal effort. Central to this reform is having the citizen a central concern of public administration, policy, and management. Paul C. Light acknowledges that "there can be little doubt that the tides of reform rise and fall with public trust in government" (Light, 1997, p. 88). The trust strategy does not distinguish between public trust and government. They function as one and the same phenomena of the human organizational ability to broker and sustain promises as a fundamental partnership agreement.

Martha Derthick has described a world where distrust causes policy asymmetry or policy improvisation (Derthick, 1990) resulting in the erosion of the central agreements of constitutional partnership: laws. This describes a government strategy based on a distrust model emphasizing a fuzzy logic of the separation of powers where separation is apparently more important than integration. In this way, the Constitution is the contextual document intending to hold as integral the purpose of its society. Their intellectual studies of the powers within that society are not intended to create allomorphism. Trust implies an integration of purpose achieved often through the forge of new ideas in which the outcome idea is indeed literally new, greater than the sum of its parts. Trust is not a monologue, but a dialogue that must be consistently and continually renewed. The separation of powers articulated in the United States Constitution can be observed not (or not only) as a field of competing monologues, but a forum of dialogues encouraged, achieved, and sustained. Functional dialogue might be said to be the performance of trust. The encouraging and fostering of true dialogue implies a willingness to invent and reinvent the purpose of community. This is because dialogue is a process of partnering rather than imposition. Even if "at the core of confusion is trust" (Light, 1997, p. 46) and this confusion causes distrust, it is so when trust is bolstered by monologue rather than dialogue. In the former, confusion is a result of misunderstanding; a misunderstanding inherent, accepted, and provoked in principal-agent management theory (Moe, 1984), inevitable when monologues compete and do not collaborate. In the latter, confusion is a natural process of learning, inventing, and transformation achieved through cooperation and the capacity of dialogue.

At this point, the trust strategy can address the concept of social capital. It is acknowledged by most scholars that "trust" is the most direct measure of social capital (Fukuyama, 1995; Knack, 2002), but rarely is the process of dialogue-capacity explored in its relationship to the notion of social capital. As Fukuyama defined it: trust is a qualifying condition of social capital (Fukuyama, 1995) not because it can be measured very accurately, but because it evokes an essential purpose of sociability. If we consider that trust is a social mechanism arrived at through the process of true dialogue and not competing monologues, we fully understand that trust puts the social in social capital. We also begin to admire that trust is valuable and this explains why it may have "capital" and is a medium of value exchange. We can infer that the processes of dialogue, which utilize trust, are considered highly valuable.

Social capital is a term that implies this value and its possible rate of exchange. If social capital is an indicator of social competence indicating the ability to participate effectively in the public forum, it is a valuable asset if applied practically by all actors in the public forum. If social capital is a form of capital, then it is an appropriable and convertible asset even though it acts like a "collective good" (Coleman, 1998) rather than private property. No one player has exclusive ownership rights of social capital. It is not a commodity delivered as a monologue expressed solely by one individual. It is an expressed asset of sociability that defines the value of community (in the interaction of dialogue building). An individual's capability in the social realm increases by an accountability to greater and greater communal expressions as "social capital is a collective dimension of society external to the individual" (Lochner, Kawachi, and Kennedy, 1999, p. 260). This accountability may point us towards more appropriate measures of social capital. At its most fundamental level, the term social capital may best be observed as social competence, which defines an important aspect of the developmental characteristics of a mature adult human being. It represents a level of competence in a basic vein of human potential. Social competence by the citizenry, in the dialogue "sovereign" (as applied in the United States Constitution), may well be considered to be the guiding principle of public administration in a democratic society by defining its performance and accountability parameters.

Government is not a substitute for economic forces even as it helps define the role of the greater community and the values identified therein. The economy exists within the community, not the other way around. Before there is an economy and a value exchange system, there is a community identified by its constituent members. It is perfectly natural for the community to utilize economic resources to maintain, build, and sustain its assets and values. In the development of a trust strategy, the notion that public or private sectors are more or less efficient seems a mundane argument. Interdependence blurs the boundaries between the public and private sectors (Kettl, 1993). Government provides goods and services that enhance the social welfare, which is not well subjugated to the market because the value is often not as well defined or agreed upon even if acknowledged.

Value exchange is lopsided in the supply–demand market model in which there is limited supply and seemingly great demand. When government supplies, it is an accumulated response of the community, managed and delivered by government where the government is the only buyer and its reasons for buying are in flux. We must understand that in a market model there is always a third causal factor; the notion of value, which is an effect or intention of a trust dialogue. A value functions as a social identifier that expresses the discourse of a community's sense of humanity. In other words, the fundamental structure that holds a market model together is the partnership that exists. The glue is trust. "In public/private partnerships, contracts replace hierarchy" (Kettl, 1993, p. 22), and promises (trust mechanism) replace procedure. Government does not usually work effectively on the market distrust model, but must work on the political-co-operative trust model even if trust is elusive or confusing. Government cannot perform in a competitive efficient (cost–benefit ratio) manner because often as a buyer it is developing (or processing) a dialogue of trust around an emerging community asset whose value is undefined. The market approach cannot be competitive unless the buyer can define what it wants to buy (Kettl, 1993). This is often a less known fact in defining communal standards of quality of life then in defining a private sector commodity whose impact may have social implications, but whose intent is individual satisfaction.

The distrust model may be more efficient in the short term, but it assumes an effectiveness that often cannot be proven in the public sector until the dialogue of public value is concluded, which may never occur as a decisive event. As Don Kettl points out "As market imperfections increase, the tendency toward vertical integration increases. As vertical integration increases, the problems of public accountability increase" (Kettl, 1993, p. 197). This seems to indicate that privatization can cause higher levels of distrust of government. This would make perfect sense because the private sector market model is a distrust model and that distrust will infuse the public process if for no other reason than the citizen is more excluded from public deliberation by the natural inclination of private entities who compete, yes, with the citizens they are presumably serving.

What may occur to further the distrust is the fact that the private entity may perceive itself to be in a one-on-one contractual basis with the agent of government rather than the sovereign of government. Therefore, there is no avenue for extended dialogue, but a contractual and arranged dialogue between the principal and the contractor only. Performance becomes more restricted to outputs and has little basis for monitoring true outcomes, as the intention required for outcomes becomes a stilted discourse if not a monologue.

"The market is a way of managing scarcity" (Kettl, 1993, p. 206). This quote emphasizes the distinction between the influence of the distrust/control-monologue-oriented market model and the trust/cooperation-dialogue-oriented political model. It is a distinction between commitment and trust. If we associate commitment with money, funds, and eventual financial resources, we can say that commitment is a result of the effectiveness of wealth in a community. Trust, as described, is a mechanism of social value building. Trust leads to commitment. Distrust might be said to lead to compromise at best. In this way, we can see that trust must be present when finances are operative because the finances are an expression of a commitment borne through a trust dialogue. This may be because a dialogue must be renewed and nurtured or tends to devolve and disappear. We can see immediately the erosion of commitment when the dialogue of trust is neglected and subject to inertia. Scarcity may be the result of the inertia of trust, which seems to require continual infusions of dialogue to grow and develop. Scarcity is a hard fixed discourse in which economic (rational actor) theories are generated. It explains self-interest over cooperation, profit maximization over social equity, moral hazard over trust, shirking over commitment, principal-agent management over team leadership, and most tragic of all information asymmetry over education.

Robert Behn would have us re-examine the principal-agent/command-control theories of management accountability (Wood and Waterman, 1994; Moe, 1984) in which the public agent is beholding to his/her superiors, and the ultimate superior: the citizen. Behn wants us to consider the fantastic: that each citizen, operative, and agent, public and private, may have a vital accountability in some way to "everyone" (Behn, 2001, p. 199); at least everyone in their "accountability environment" (Kearns, 1996; Dubnick, 2005)—in other words, a "360 degree – accountability" (Behn, 2001, p. 199). Paul Light echoes Robert Behn's sentiments regarding 360 degree accountability by noticing that accountability built on "trust puts its faith in capacity and performance accountability; distrust in compliance and the capacity to create and enforce deterrence. Trust expresses a preference for structural reforms, distrust for procedures" (Light, 1997, p. 77).

Above we noticed that distrust is the absence of a reinforced trust mechanism in which trust is an evolving phenomenon of social capacity, and distrust is an inert factor in trust negligence. I suppose we could simply say that there are people that are optimistic and pessimistic about human nature and its potential. Trust certainly seems to require optimism. It also requires attention and an internal sense of duty whereas distrust relies on external controls. More importantly 360 degree accountability is another term for real dialogue, one that is ongoing, interactive, and evolving. It is an expression of circular social interaction, respect, and dignity. One can assume in a 360 degree dialogue we might come up with many new things. Whereas, the principal-agent form of accountability is a one-way, often predictable, monologue, from up to down, assuming the superiority of the principal over the agent. An assumption Robert Behn appears to find unqualified.

How we approach accountability/responsiveness causes different views of performance. If we operate from a model of distrust we will engender distrust even if we perform on paper by the most efficient market standards. Our performance will be measured by our ability to control events. If we operate from a trust model, we will increase social capability and provide our society with the opportunity to discover and build upon identified community assets. Our performance will be measured as an indication of leadership and community development in which the people say, "Look what we have done." A trust model may pursue things that are worth failing at. While a distrust model will play it safe and generally pursue the status quo.

The question before us is not whether a market model operating on scarcity and distrust outweighs a cooperative model operating on potential and trust building. It is whether we believe in the basic (Skelcher, 2007) principle that each citizen has the capacity for social accountability, and that the community of citizens expresses our greatest potentials and has the capacity to achieve them. If we do not believe this and we cannot trust this principle, then our performance is a matter of herding the unfortunate, the undisciplined, the unforgiving, and the unable to pastures of resignation. In the final analysis, I believe our first step is to set a policy of citizenship that reinvigorates a sense of public service as the best example of human capacity. And, this policy is a matter of management concern. 360 degree accountability is only possible if everyone is given the opportunity to make a difference and to be responsible for the difference they make, and the actions of the collective body.

The second step is to support Paul Light's idea that we must experiment, not simply for the sake of experimentation, but as an opportunity to learn and involve people in a learning process. This emphasizes public entrepreneurship (Lewis, 1984) as one of leadership and innovation rather than private entrepreneurship that simply contracts public products to private entities. Lastly, we must re-examine the concept of a separation of powers as a segregating device, and understand its integrating, overlapping, and interdependent aspects. In this way, we might understand that our approaches to performance cause a public performance anxiety; an anxiety confused by notions of distrust. The trust model causes performance anticipation. Performance anxiety in the public realm leads to control management rather than cooperative management. In the military, control management may indeed be appropriate as we certainly may not trust our enemies, or trust civilians to be militarized without severe persuasions. However, in the general work of governance, we are building and sustaining communities, which must evolve to meet new challenges and opportunities. Our best policy may be one in which we encourage, support, and nurture the potential of individuals and communities to reach their best potential.

The Context of Measurement

The "context of measurement" will largely determine its effectiveness. The context of measurement is actually more important than the measurement itself. One of the major reasons why performance measurement is seldom able to deliver on its positive potential is because it is almost never properly "socialized," that is, built in a positive way into the fabric of the organization ... too much traditional performance measurement has been seen as "the reward for the few, punishment for the many, and a search for the guilty.... . it is not about doing measurement; it is about creating an optimal environment (context) for its effective use" (Spitzer, 2007 pp. 3–4); "no organization can be any better than its measurement system" (Spitzer, 2007 pp. 14–15).

BIDs represent powerful tools in urban development. BIDs represent a form of PPP between local government and the private business sector to foster revitalization and growth of commercial districts and downtowns. It is necessarily more "relational" rather than "transactional"—hence the partnership underpinning of social capital. Special districts are established by local governments. Governance choices, such as taxation levels, the bundle of services, the level of services and management, are determined by the PPP representing stakeholders from the district. Implementation is carried out typically either by staff or organizations under contract to the BID's governance board. In this way, business and property owners can choose to supplement governmental services or receive new services in a way they cannot through voluntary associations. Government gets resources, capacity, and local management that could not be sourced through traditional government processes. This is a powerful and effective tool for urban and community development, leadership, business development, and downtown revitalization. The PPP model that BIDs represent means that "someone" is responsible for our commercial districts. This merging of both private and public capabilities encourages entrepreneurship as well as organizational strengths and is a successful form of governance due to the professional management of these factors.

BIDs are a proven tool for downtown revitalization. BIDs have been established in the United States since 1975 and internationally since 1966. As BIDs continue to be successful, the model is enjoying extraordinary growth. A survey in 1999 found 246 BIDs while a survey in 2007 found 739. It is not possible to know if the 1999 survey completely identified all of the BIDs in the country but it appears this model is experiencing extraordinary growth. At the same time, it appears somewhere around 100 BIDs have been terminated. In 2010, Rutgers-Newark's Institute of Business District Management conducted a United States BID census for the International Downtown Association (IDA); 1,001 BIDs were found (Becker, Grossman, and Dos Santos, 2011).

Despite this rapid growth of the BID model, there is no formal national database on BIDs. This may be due to BIDs being a grass-roots phenomenon. State, not federal, legislation is necessary to allow BIDs to be created, but once states act, creation and continuance are localized. As ultra-local entities, there is no national definition of what constitutes a BID, no national census like the Census of Governments, and very little national research. In most states, there is no formal tracking at a state level. In large regions like Los Angeles, New York, and Chicago, there is region-level tracking of BIDs, but even in these states there is no formal state-level tracking. No one knows exactly how many BIDs there are, how rapidly BIDs are expanding throughout the country, and where they are (and are not) geographically. This means that there is no fact-based national conversation about BIDs because there is no mechanism to have this conversation. Also, because there is no way to have a national dialogue with BIDs, there is little understanding about how BID implementation varies around the country, how the PPP varies, how connections with government vary, how management needs vary, and a plethora of other questions about how BIDs differ around the country. In addition, there is no understanding of how and why BIDs fail. Anecdotal evidence suggests that somewhere around 100 BIDs in the United States have been terminated or dissolved, but there is no national understanding of why because there is no national tracking capacity … yet.

Balanced Scorecard: Third Generation—Strategic Control

The adoption of the Third Generation Balanced Scorecard coincided with it being a tool to support strategic control. This approach supports the notion of forming consensus within a management team, which, we are told in the readings for this discourse, are consistent with thinking on leadership, articulated over many years. Further, we note that the Balanced Scorecard has evolved to be a strategic management tool that involves a wide range of managers and provides control boundaries; however, it is not prescriptive and most importantly integrates formulation and implementation.

Key components of the a Third Generation Balanced Scorecard are:

1. Destination Statement: What the organization is attempting to achieve.
2. Strategic Objectives: What needs to be done, in which timeframes to reach the destination on time.

3. Strategic Linkage Model and Perspectives: The strategic objectives are spread over four zones or perspectives. The bottom two focus on process (Internal Processes, and Learning and Growth) and the top two on desired results (External Relations and Financial).
4. Measures and Initiatives: The ability to monitor the organization's progress towards achievement of goals.

PPPs: The Emerging Role of Partnership Governance

This is a timely subject as economic trends are forcing new approaches to the delivery of public services and meeting public needs through multi-sectoral collaborations. These collaborations, although not entirely new and even as a common dialogue, tell us that public and private sectors compete, and PPPs are evolving and defining the role of partnership governance. From privitization to publicization, PPPs are redefining public service and management.

PPPs are established to merge multi-sectoral capacities and manage social and economic change. How do we correctly define, determine management, and measure PPPs in relation to government, the delivery of public services, and democratic systems?

PPPs, due to their complexity, are referred to in a number of descriptive ways, creating confusion. Though some studies exist, the literature is remarkably sparse, particularly when applied to public management and performance. Additionally, there appears to be a bias towards the private, rather than public, aspects of PPPs, which causes descriptive breakdown. Although there is a generic understanding of how public and private sectors interact as potential partners, PPPs can be viewed organizationally; as a legal contract between a public and private entity; by governance status or politically. One area of particular growth in PPPs is at the special district level.

Of the over 80,000 forms of government in the United States, over 35,000, by far the largest proportion, are special districts generally operating as forms of PPPs. They are a growing phenomenon with fiscal, service, and political impact. In general these districts are poorly understood and even more poorly evaluated to determine their performance significance. This performance evaluation deficit is due less to a lack of interest and more to the complexity of a balanced approach regarding the significance of public accountability, participation, and participation with real services and sustainability outcomes. These districts are notable and unique for four reasons. They are:

1. sub-units of government (secondary not primary);
2. supported by public financing formulas in the form of taxes or special assessments;
3. formal and contractual PPPs;
4. professionally managed.

To better understand PPP trends and their impact on government, a discussion on the nature of partnerships between public and private actors is required. Most units of government employ partnerships to provide a framework for communities to manage assets and compete in broader markets by combining private resources and expertise with governmental authority and public resources. In this symposium, we seek further understanding of the purpose and nature of PPPs in public administration—examining the public, as well as private, processes associated with PPPs. PPPs are formed, implemented, and managed through multi-sectoral collaboration. These collaborations establish new publicly oriented organizations that enhance governance and public management. In PPPs, one can expect a range of public to private participation, from chiefly private to chiefly public. Consequently, new forms of hybridization in management practices may emerge PPPs, in both policy and practice, that are shaping and redefining public management and democratic practices (Skelcher, 2007).

A uniform and comprehensive understanding of PPPs is remarkably unavailable. This is further compounded by a lack of performance data that can enhance this understanding of both public and private attributes involved in these partnerships. The dearth of process, performance, and political data on PPPs is out of step with their sheer numbers and obvious impacts on communities and government. Additionally, as government trends towards more, not less, PPPs, the requirement for accurate data is critical. These partnerships uniquely legitimize new facets of community development as well as encourage more direct investment both socially and economically in changing and competitive markets by non-traditional actors. By most accounts, PPPs are effective, but due to a lack of guidance they can appear to pose threats to the very public processes and economic objectives that they were created to enhance. Systematic and substantive assessment regarding special districts is now timely in order to realize and sustain the best practices and good opportunities that PPPs offer.

Throughout the world, PPPs are challenging and reshaping traditional assumptions of public management—its promises and performance—at all levels of government. This merger forges a distinctive form of governance (partnership governance as well as a new form of public management, PPP management—an expertise within public administration) that brings together the knowledge and skills of business, government, planning, and community development in a collaborative manner and in many cases achieves a form of citizen-driven governance. When we look worldwide, PPPs are becoming mainstream policy and a management tool for governments in collaboration with business to apply entrepreneurship and social capital, at the heart of community revitalization and development. The chapters in this book discuss how and why PPPs are defining a normative field in public administration and a distinct skill set. The symposium examines the role of partnership governance in an evolving application of PPPs that build management capacity for community and economic development.

It is clear that a uniform and comprehensive understanding of PPPs is less available due to the overarching nature of PPPs. This is further compounded by a lack of performance data that would enhance the understanding of both public and private attributes involved in these partnerships. PPPs are found in almost every aspect of governance and particularly are associated with the evolution of democracy–citizen ownership of and involvement in governance. In this regard, some see PPPs as a detraction, while others see them as an enhancement depending on which side of the public–private spectrum we are associated with. On the one hand, we can perceive PPPs as challenging democracy when the PPP moves towards the private end of the PPP spectrum (Dilger, Moffett, and Struyk, 1997); and on the other hand, PPPs are equally challenging to the free market when the PPP moves towards publicization and expanded forms of governance and community development at the public end of the spectrum. Often misunderstood is that as experiments in democratic capability, PPPs are dynamic building blocks of communities and enhance public management capacity by allowing a formal path to citizen governance. Some succeed better than others, but again, it depends from which end of the spectrum we are making our evaluation.

Clearly in government, there are ethical problems when public trust is sabotaged by private agendas, that to many look as if government processes are always tainted by congenital distrust and greed. The trust we wish to have in public process seems often misappropriated. The issues of individual and community rights complicate this process; a process central to PPP development. The rational actor, often labeled as positivist, may explain evolving individualism, but does not adequately explain the concept, implication, and practice of the more developed skills of trust involved in partnerships in which the partnership is paramount. Without distorting its explanation towards distrust and its inherent limitations, the purely rational model tends to be less satisfying in explaining PPPs. Therefore, efforts in explaining the most pressing concerns of governance—partnerships, citizen-driven participation, citizenship, and community development—have remained unanswered yet seem more successfully approached when a balanced transrational/partnership model is applied up front. Exploring this approach is the necessary subject of this book.

By combining private resources and expertise with the governmental (public) powers, PPPs provide an essential institutional framework for government to compete in a variety of evolving markets and public arenas. Competition is not solely finance oriented, but also includes asset-building value enhancement processes and management technology, and organizational prowess. It is noted that PPPs, due to their complexity, are referred to in a number of appropriate descriptive ways that retain the integrity of this complexity. In the case of PPPs, complexity across sectors of society is a good and organic thing. PPPs can be viewed organizationally (PPP management corporation); as a legal contract (special district or project) between government and a private entity; by governance status (sub-unit of government); or politically (quasi-governmental). And, we can assume a number of additional descriptions along the continuum of public–private partnering (Jackson and Vinsom, 2004). From the number of PPPs around the world there emerges one general theme—improvement through cooperation. It is discussed in this book that there is a need for those involved in PPP management to approach cooperation as a necessary skill set and become a bridge between government and business; and, not just a bridge, but a partnership, a managed partnership, a formal collaboration. This requires the managers of PPPs to walk a tightrope between the public responsibilities and accountabilities associated with the public sector, and the entrepreneurship and business agenda associated with the private sector. This points to a key finding: PPPs are created to implement what either side cannot do effectively on its own, thus lowering the risk of our societal investments.

At the heart of a PPP is the ability to use the strengths of both sectors to achieve stakeholder buy-in and apply competitive technologies. Partnerships are formed by and require not only cooperation but collaboration. Both the process of arriving at consensus-oriented agreements as a mutual qualitative imperative and the management, or implementation, of the partnership requires skillful collaboration. Collaborations establish new organizations and the functional networks of civilization (Agranoff, 2012). Partnerships are a result of a policy to collaborate—to be multilateral rather than unilateral (Grossman, 2016). In every PPP, we see this process, and in successful PPPs we see this process implemented either in the creation of a new organization that integrates existing organizations under one umbrella organization, or in the creation of a new umbrella organization. We see new leadership and existing leadership evolve to embrace and represent all parts of the partnership. Difficulty arises when the new organization erodes the partnership and is not inclusive, collaborative, and synthesizing. If that happens, either it takes on the unintended role of a sub-department of the government, or acts as a single issue business advocate competing with other self-identified agencies, thereby violating the premise of the collaboration.

As stated above, controversies surrounding PPPs tend to travel along the partnership continuum, from concerns regarding privatization and "elite" exclusion to publicization and government intrusion. There are those who are unsure of the privatized conveniences of profit seekers at the private end, and the partisan and special interest politics of government at the public end. Nonetheless, it is clear that PPPs are never strict forms of privatization. They are better understood as forms of democratic process that call for the citizens and private sector to become involved and accountable to the public and to be creative in solving immediate social and economic problems. PPPs are poorly evaluated when the aim is to diminish either aspect of the partnership. An expectation of diminishing attributes contributes to diminishing results, and the practice of mutually expanding and synthesizing attributes in these partnerships is not only intended, but functions to reduce risk and produce results. Often overlooked in evaluating

PPPs is the level of partnership incompetence from conception to implementation. Partnership management and planning are skills well suited to the public manager, but poorly identified. This may be the single most debilitating liability for a PPP. As we move towards more and more forms of partnership governance to solve social and technical problems, reduce investment risk in public projects, and provide a variety of public services, skills of PPP management are required.

The Management and Measurement of PPPs: An Integral and Balanced Approach for Practitioners

It is axiomatic that government, particularly democratic government applying the ethic of protecting both majority and minority perspectives, is a networking process, but also, and consequently, partnership-driven. Even if the process is less than rational, the desire to bring people together, solve common problems, and develop and manage those agreements with real commitments of resources is the basis of the business of government. The business of democratic government steps beyond governing, as it must, and engages its citizenry, despite its plurality and multi-sector properties, in the process of community development and management. In the 21st century, PPPs provide a unique perspective on the collaborative and network aspects of public. The advancement of PPPs, as a concept and a practice, is a consequence of the NPM of the late 20th century, globalization pressures, and the advent of a more strategic rather than bureaucratic state. Today, partnering is the new governance. The term "PPP" is ubiquitous and applicable to this phenomenon, but is prey to thinking in parts rather than the whole of the partnership. And, this devaluation of context, as it maneuvers across a continuum between both sectors, is hermeneutically abstract making it difficult to pin down a universally accepted definition of PPPs. If we do not embrace the whole partnership rather than only the parts, as a new and complete phenomenon, then our assessment of partnering in the evolution of democracies seems unsubstantial. And, that would be a mistake.

Throughout the world, PPPs have emerged at the local level of government as BIDs. They have received some careful scrutiny in the past 12 years because they provide insights about the challenges of modern government. They also reveal the complexities of PPPs. There is an effective approach to addressing the gap in performance criteria for PPPs by utilizing an Integrated Balanced Scorecard approach developed by Robert Kaplan and David Norton in 1992. This method recognizes the need to integrate various stakeholder perspectives to obtain a correct evaluation of management, investment, and service aspects of an organization. With this comprehensive approach, Kaplan and Norton have anticipated the performance measurement needs of the PPP movement, and the partnering needs of government. This chapter describes the nature of PPPs, examines BIDs as PPPs, and concludes with an integral balanced measurement approach for practitioners of PPPs—an Integrated Balanced Scoring Approach.

From Privatization to Partnership

As a result of the NPM initiatives of the late 20th century, which succeeded in enticing market considerations and strategic thinking into public management, the term "PPP" has also developed and expanded in conjunction with its increasing application. "It is noteworthy that these partnerships approaches reveal how contemporary social democratic and neoliberal policy thinking has evolved beyond nostroms celebrating either state of market ... experimenting with new government structures that crossed the public-private divide" (Bradford, 2003, p. 1028). At first the dichotomous term—public, excessive delegation, partnership—seems exotic to management. It speaks of a dangerous liaison, potential treasonous behavior with "the enemy," and political naïveté. "Partnerships are complements not substitutes for existing command and control policies" (Lubell, Schneider, Scholz, and Mete, 2002, p. 159). However, when we examine PPPs as a complete phenomenon, we immediately notice integrating, networking, and collaborating processes, which tells us that alterations, changes, and reformations are occurring and desired. PPPs do have a revolutionary tinge about them. As Stephen Linder points out, "partnerships arise as a derivative reform in areas where privitization seems less tractable" (Linder, 1999, p. 37). We can conclude that PPPs, by their multi-sectoral nature, the variety of stakeholders, and the risks associated with change, are complex and not easily defined. PPPs are organized along a continuum between public and private nodes and needs as they integrate normative, albeit separate and distinct, functions of society—the market and the commons. The questions that arise are: How do we measure PPPs in a manner that allows for these fluctuations, does not diminish either sector, and in fact reinforces the intended partnership? How do we know PPPs are successful?

There is a difference of purpose between the public and private sectors (Schumpeter, 1947; Moe, 1984; Kettl, 1993, Schaeffer and Loveridge, 2002), chiefly due to the accountability for democratic processes, and to most of us it follows that there is a difference between public vs private sector management. But, when we look at PPPs, we are compelled to notice that this differentiation is porous and possibly becoming more so (Grossman, 2008; Meek and Hubler, 2006), the distinctions of governance and business strategies less reliable, and the separation of that which is specifically private and public less discernible (Bozeman, 1987). Graham Allison addressed this issue in 1980 paraphrasing Wallace Sayre's comments at a November 1979 Public Management Research Conference in Washington, DC, "public and private management are fundamentally alike in all important aspects" (Allison, 2004, p. 34). But, there is a fundamental difference. Private management is based on a rationalist perspective whereas public management must grapple with social and transrational objectives. Management, however, is fundamentally about producing useful results, and both sectors share that objective. At the least, management in both sectors is measured by the results produced.

Virtually worldwide, the interdependencies between the public and private sectors are becoming more apparent, eroding traditional understandings of what is government and what is business, and evolving into something quite new—a practice of partnering (Lowndes and Skelcher, 1998). Lowndes and Skelcher add that, "partnerships are frequently contrasted with competitive markets and bureaucratic hierarchies" (p. 313), which trend to be autocratic. PPPs are in contrast to privitization as they represent a key aspect of democracy, private sector participation in public life—a definition of citizenship. PPPs serve a policy strategy to support moderation between extreme political views for those either less or more supportive of state action. Consequently, in a democracy, we should expect to find collaborative multi-sector partnerships that aim to resolve economic and social problems, and we should expect them to be evolutionary rather than static. "The idea of 'collaborative advantage' (Huxham, 1996) presents an attractive strategic alternative to the market, quasi-market and contractualized command and control relationships that have dominated the public management reform movement internationally in the past decade" (Lowndes and Skelcher, 1998, p. 313).

Multi-sectoral partnering is experienced on a continuum of private to public in varying degrees of implementation according to the need, time restraints, and the issue at hand. Even though these partnerships are now common, it is normal for both private and public sectors to be critical of the other's approach and methods. It is at the merger of these sectors, noticeable in BIDs, that we see how a unified partnership has immediate impact in the development of communities and the provision of public services. Carol Becker furthers our understanding of BIDs as PPPs stating, "BIDs ... are quasi-governmental entities, or organizations that have features of both government and private organizations" (Becker, 2010, p. 413) and are not only a forum of debate, but also an arena of action in the interplay of business and culture (Becker, 2010; Ruffin, 2010; MacDonald, Stokes, and Blumenthal, 2010; Ewoh and Zimmerman, 2010). Ewoh and Zimmerman add, "Globally business improvement districts have proliferated as the most influential public-private mechanisms for revitalizing business districts and promoting infrastructure improvement projects" (Ewoh and Zimmerman, 2010, p. 395). BIDs are more than a public–private interchange. They exist because of a public contact, and like all PPPs begin and end with an intention that private benefit is supported by a clear and present public benefit. This provides us with a definition of PPPs: a contractual agreement between a public agency (federal, state, or local) and a private sector entity (National Council for Public–Private Partnerships, 2010). Through this agreement, the skills and assets of each sector (public and private) are shared in delivering a service or facility for the use of the general public. In addition to the sharing of resources, each party shares the potential risks and rewards of the service and/or organization.

Too often, in the interest of partnership, the public sector will relinquish its oversight role that risks agency loss due to "information asymmetry and diverging preferences" thereby moving delegation to abdication and a shirking of public responsibility by public officials and private developers (Erie, Kogan, and MacKenzie, 2010, pp. 649, 655). This alarms public sector advocates (Skelcher, 2007). Equally, the public sector, in the interest of partisan politics, may overstate the political nature of BIDs. This can alarm private sector advocates. In either case, when the promise of interchange and teamwork, which sustain the partnership, receive less encouragement and wither, and the PPP is not equitable, it tends to fail (Roelofs, 2009). A fundamental objective of PPPs is to enhance public management capacity, and yet this is universally misunderstood and, consequently, poorly measured. Success is achieved when a comprehensive balance of public, private, and partnership interests are managed and measured. As stated above, often overlooked is the primary measure of a BID, like all PPPs, which is not simply the ROI or the QOL, but the effectiveness of OMC—how the BID functions as a PPP (Grossman, 2010). The result is an overemphasis on privatization, a undervaluing of publicization to describe and evaluate a key strategy of PPPs, and a lag in identifying pertinent evolving management technologies and practices for public administration.

At first glance, PPPs may seem more designed for the realm of economic and infrastructure development than general purpose government. Yet, when we look closer at the growth areas in government, we notice that by sheer numbers PPPs dominate, typically operating as special districts, and almost always as a form of public contract either by expanding public management or services thereby achieving a key strategic goal-enhanced management capacity. We live in a world of special governing districts (school, water, public safety, redevelopment, business, industry, military) and resultant PPPs and hardly notice it. PPPs and formal public authorities, special districts, are utilized because they resolve difficult and transitioning problems that pose risks for either sector if they act alone. Like all partnerships, they are chiefly designed to reduce private sector risk (social predictability) and public sector risk (financial) through appropriate risk delegation and skill alignment of each sector, which supports entrepreneurship. Consequently, as social and economic concerns often have similar and systemic development challenges, PPPs have become a significant part of mainstream political and commercial functions. If we count, the most numerous forms of government in the United States are special district PPPs.

A unique model of these districts receiving well-deserved recognition and attention are municipally based and established BIDs (Briffault, 1997; Grossman, 2008). BIDs offer a window into the function of PPPs and how they are changing the public management landscape (Morçöl, Hoyt, Meek & Zimmerman, 2008; Mitchell, 2008; Grossman, 2010). In the literature there is an abundance of information on what BIDs are, what they do, and how they are designed, but little information regarding how PPPs are managed, perform, and what measurements would be most useful in assessing the intended integrative purpose of PPPs. This can be attributed to the lack of performance measurements in the public sector as a whole, but equally to the misunderstanding of the mechanisms of multi-sectoral partnerships. These mechanisms are well established in BIDs, and are chiefly in three functional areas that apply to the private interests, the public interests, and the partnership as a whole and complete functioning phenomena. PPPs integrate private sector interests and can be measured as an ROI with public sector concerns measured as QOL. However, a true integration is not simply the merging of sectoral performance areas just as planning is anemic without implementation, but must also include measurements of the OMC of the PPP as a whole. ROI and QOL produce measureable outputs and outcomes. OMC measures empirical and functional processes, communication, identity, the ability to perform as a whole, and the management of the PPP.

PPPs and Lessons from BIDs

Everyday conversations about PPPs often are clouded by ideas and practices of privatization and the privatizing of public interests (Savas, 2000). Little is discussed or observed about the impacts of strategic publicization (Bozeman, 1987; Mather and Skelcher, 2007; Grossman, 2010) and of private interests even though it is a fundamental aspect of public–private partnering. Publicization describes private citizens/corporations contractually assuming public accountabilities and services. (Publicization—where private citizens/corporations assume public accountabilities and services (Grossman, 2010). Privatization—where the private sector provides public services.) Privatization describes the private sector contractually providing public services. Privatization does have influence on public processes, but publicization also has considerable influence. The "publicization" process allows private sector actors to take on public accountabilities and in this process dissolve public–private dichotomies that hamper creativity and innovation. This creates new hybrid management capacities for community and business development. This new capacity is notably entrepreneurial (Grossman, 2008) and acts as an alternative public option for achieving economic and social stability and success.

The predominate literature on PPPs leads us to believe that PPPs are created chiefly as a means of enticing private investors to invest in public projects like hospitals, transportation, and large-scale development. Success of such PPPs is often measured by the project investment and the capital raised for that project. The interest in such PPPs is chiefly to raise funds for public transportation and infrastructure without raising taxes. Since most of these projects are already built by private industry through general contracting procedures, it is this financing element that describes the partnership. This is a questionable partnership as there is no long-term shared, or hybrid management capacity, and success is primarily measured by ROI. This joint fund-build approach addresses immediate functional infrastructure problems, but is not designed to shepherd social and economic change. It also does not have a well-defined sense of strategic publicization found in most PPPs. Success is rarely looked at in terms of the joint management opportunity and strategic goals. In this scenario, at the end of the project, the partnership fades and the two participants return to their respective public or private corners. The partnership is project oriented and short-lived.

There is an argument that fund-build arrangements are PPPs, only heavily skewed on the private end of the public–private continuum. I would agree, but not use this as an elemental example of PPPs, because it tells us that partnering-government is fundamental and not new to public administration (Linder, 1999). The fund-build type of PPP is not true of most special districts, i.e. water and water treatment districts, many that skew to the public end of the public–private continuum and are sub-units of government. BIDs (BIDs, SIDS, SADs, BIAs (Business Improvement Areas)) fall almost in the middle of the continuum as they provide services as an outgrowth of ongoing publicly oriented community and economic development.

The implication that PPPs leverage efficiency because private sector share-holders are more attentive to financial success than public stakeholders (Ostrom & Ostrom, 1977; Osborne and Gaebler, 1992: Savas, 2000) has skewed research on PPPs towards privatization assessments as if PPPs solely justified private capability. However, the key interest of PPPs is not efficiency, but innovation and change management to resolve collective action problems and form cooperative ventures. Efficiencies may be obtained due to the private sector's "get it done" sensibilities, but taken as the purpose of establishing PPPs is a key reason they encounter political resistance and fail. Although research is just beginning (Becker, Gross-man, and Dos Santos, 2011) on why PPPs fail, indications are that most BIDs fail because they run into political resistance and, instead of adapting to public needs, resist the requirement to be effective as public actors. This is a prescription for failure for PPPs.

In a PPP, private sector actors soon find out that in public processes there is an uncertainty—a risk—of outcomes tied to the peculiar processes of determining a consensus of the public value of an outcome (Stokes, 2008). This is an education, communication, as well as planning issue, all of which are public rather than private concerns. "Government actors would need to think and behave like entrepreneurs, and business actors would have to embrace public interest con-siderations and expect greater public accountability" (Linder, 1999, p. 37). Often a stated planned outcome as it is pursued has unintended consequences that later shed light on the full needs, implications, and designs of the project. Adjustments are made and usually lead to higher costs to achieve the desired outcome. Costs that reflect greater quality of life standards such as safety, convenience, social connection, and historic preservation, not fully understood at the beginning of a project become insistent as the end approaches. One aspect of a PPP may be to encourage private investment, but the other is certainly to encourage public par-ticipation by private actors and assume aspects of governance (strategic pub-licization). The latter institutionalizes the outcomes of cooperation and interdependency, and the former infuses the process of institutionalization with innovation, ideas, performance, and entrepreneurship (Grossman, 2008). It must be noted that entrepreneurship is understood to be as much a public process as it is a private attribute, and its role in PPPs works to transform private sector ambitions into public accountabilities, and to foster innovation and change in public management. This attests to the strategic nature of PPPs and their role in society to advance social and economic change, provide new solutions, and enhance management aligned with these solutions by drawing "on communal traditions of cooperation" (Linder, 1999, p. 36).

Definitions of PPPs tend to stress the contractual relationship between government and the private sector to further "cooperation not competition" (Linder, 1999, p. 36) and range between management and political reform problem solving, risk reduction and innovations in public service. Erie, Kogan, and MacKenzie (2010) define PPPs as being "distinguished primarily by the pooling of public and private resources and their ostensively public objective," (p. 647). This definition implies the importance of both public and private resources, technologies, and capabilities as a strategic investment. Jurian Edelenbos and Erik-Hans Klijn (2007), identifying the social capital, trust and networking properties of PPPs that reduce risk factors, define PPPs "as a cooperation between public and private actors with a durable character in which actors develop mutual products and/or services and in which risk, cost, and benefit are shared" (p. 27). The "durable character" of PPPs implies strategy, management, institutions, and contracts, and cooperation implies usefulness of capacity and social processes. Barbara Gray (1989), in discussing how collaboration works in PPPs, may have the most essential definition of PPPs "as arrangements in which parties who see different aspects of a problem can constructively explore differences and search for solutions that go beyond their own limited vision of what is possible" (p. 5). This implies that PPPs are not normative approaches to government and collective action. They are transformative, entrepreneurial, and synthesized as new approaches to problem solving. Graeme Hodge and Carsten Greve (2009) argue that PPPs are a phenomenon of public administration, not just a technique, and define PPPs as "co-operative institutional arrangements between public and private actors" (p. 33). This implies that PPPs are not simply conversational or conceptual, but functioning aspects of society. In the definition process of PPPs, it is helpful to distinguish social definitions of partnering to the managerial aspects of partnering. Institutional arrangements are clearly contractual, not simply procedural or political. The National Council for Public–Private Partnerships (2010) defines PPPs as:

> a contractual agreement between a public agency (federal, state or local) and a private sector entity. Through this agreement, the skills and assets of each sector (public and private) are shared in delivering a service or facility for the use of the general public. In addition to the sharing of resources, each party shares in the risks and rewards potential in the delivery of the service and/or facility.

The most definitive aspect of a PPP is the requirement that the public side be willing to partner. "Governments pursuing partnerships must assess the 'fit' between their preferred paradigm and the prevailing institutional landscape" (Bradford, 2003, p. 1029). This implies a rare but realistic sentiment: that formal government may not be the whole solution and neither is the private sector, but if they are willing they can be good partners in creating more holistic and networked approaches to service provision, problem solving, and management. The challenge of partnering is not to diminish, but enhance, each partner. The partnership is based on "dividing outputs equally" (Farrell and Scotchmer, 1988, p. 279) even if inputs are unequal. Enhancement occurs within the context of the partnership and is intrinsically connected to the partnership's organization and management functions to produce results and avoid a tragedy of the commons.

In the 1970s and leading to the present day, the idea to synthesize various private capabilities, public capabilities, and eventually public and private capabilities appears first as an effort to improve retail by creating professionally managed retail cooperatives (shopping centers and malls) and later traditional downtown business centers. Additionally, from the public sector there was a strong desire to encourage entrepreneurship as well as a desire to eliminate unnecessary redundancy by managing common assets, values, and services. This required organizations built upon interdependence and cooperation. In the private sector, this became privately owned retail cooperatives such as malls, in industry it became managed industrial parks, and in traditional downtowns it became what are known as MBDs and eventually BIDs, which function as publicly endowed sub-units of government.

Consequently, the business district and downtown revitalization movement emerged. BIDs (and other downtown revitalization efforts like the Main Street Program) merge business and government in a cooperative and collaborative manner, but one that is quite different than the early 20th century industrial–company town model (in which the company was the "principal" and the community was the "agent": a hierarchical relationship). This new model is a partnering model— a more horizontal strategic model—that requires the recognition and elevation of a political/community aspect of business, particularly small retail/entertainment businesses. In the 1990s, the movement grew in leaps and bounds and eventually went worldwide with the support of organizations like the International Downtown Association (IDA).

BIDs have a distinct public sector sensibility even as private sector technology is utilized. While suburban malls have an autocratic private sector basis and behave like faux communities, BIDs are real communities. Malls and BIDs meet by utilizing a similar business development technology of the retail/commercial cooperative. They diverge because suburban malls have walls and are wholly privately owned, whereas BIDs are "malls without walls" and include a variety of public and private properties. In economic and business terms, both are set up as legal and functional retail commercial cooperatives operating (organized) much like other legal cooperatives: co-op apartments, farm cooperatives, food co-ops, health co-ops, etc.

BID Fundamentals

- A BID is a legal PPP (the ordinance acts as the contract) between business and citizens of a designated neighborhood and the municipal governing body, whose aim is to increase public involvement and accountability by the private sector, infuse public process with entrepreneurship, and provide professional management (Mitchell, 2008; Grossman, 2008; Justice and Goldsmith, 2006).
- A BID unifies businesses and community stakeholders to work towards a common goal: that of an economically revitalized community business district (Stokes, 2008).
- Economically, a BID mitigates retail sales leakage by allowing the area to compete more effectively for regional market share through the generation of greater local marketing resources and strengths (Houstoun, 2003; Gopal-Agge and Hoyt, 2008).
- A BID supports businesses in the area through commercial recruitment, retention, and promotion as well as through the sponsorship of "shop at home" and downtown image-building campaigns (Morçöl and Zimmerman, 2006; Stokes, 2008).
- A BID creates a stronger unified voice to represent community and business interests to local government agencies (Wolf, 2008).

BIDs often fund and manage services such as safe and clean programs, marketing and advertisement, holiday decorations, infrastructure and park improvements, and special events (Feehan and Feit, 2006). As stated above, research on BID management and performance, like PPPs in general, is also lacking and as Jerry Mitchell (2008) points out, it is often based on "preconceived notions and ideological formulations" (p. 109). There are few agreed upon determinants of such evaluation, and less for PPPs that must factor wholly qualitative needs such as quality of life, learning, and issues of community pride. Much of this lack of research can be attributed to the novel nature of a BID PPP vs the public-only or the private-only stance many researchers employ. On both sides of the public–private aisle, such research would benefit all in understanding the true nature of the system that is an amalgam of private and public infusions. Nonetheless, in May 2007, Ingrid Gould Ellen, Amy Ellen Schwartz, and Ioan Voicu of the Furman Center for Real Estate and Urban Policy, New York University, NY, undertook a basic economic evaluation of 55 New York City BIDs and their impact on property values. In asking the question, "Why should BIDs increase property values?" (Ellen, Schwartz, and Voicu, 2007, p. 3), the report answered with this qualitative response, "fundamentally, the answer lies in their success in improving the level and quality of local public goods provided – either by direct provision or by drawing more of the City's resources" (ibid.). Although they further state that a market or government failure caused this rather than a lack of planning and management, the point is well taken that the effect of a PPP is evident. In conclusion, the report also addresses private sector investment concerns stating that, "on average, we find that BIDs generate positive impacts on the value of commercial property, a finding that is robust to alternative in comparison areas" (ibid., p. 31). There has been plenty of anecdotal evidence that BIDs have a positive impact, and most of this (including the Furman Study) indicates that it is the PPP nature of the BID that causes the impact.

As a form of special district, BIDs are noted for their localized nature at the neighborhood level (Briffault, 1997). Special districts range from large to small. A typical large district such as the Tennessee Valley Authority set up by Congress on May 18, 1933, "a corporation clothed with the power of government but possessed of the flexibility and initiative of a private enterprise" (Roosevelt, 1933), had a mission to manage power production, navigation, flood control, malaria prevention, reforestation, or erosion control in the Tennessee River Valley throughout the state of Alabama. Another large special district is the Port Authority of New York and New Jersey established in 1921, which operates the airports, seaports, bridges, tunnels, and other regional transportation services of the New York City/New Jersey area and also acts as a developer, most notably as the developers of the World Trade Center.

Most special districts are municipal and provide the management of an important resource such as water, public sewer, economic development, and transportation (Houstoun, 2003; Caruso and Weber, 2008). Some special districts manage development areas such as industrial parks, and in the case of BIDs, areas that have special customer service needs or business revitalization concerns such as traditional downtown business centers. All special districts have seven points in common that reinforce aspects of a PPP: (1) provision of specialized services that address communal needs; (2) financed by special assessments; (3) have government oversight and accountabilities; (4) are part of the government; (5) require government action to be established; (6) are quasi-governmental; and (7) encourage the use of or transfer of private sector technology. BID management has a specific job to achieve agreement between the public and private sectors, to remain non-political but politically astute, and to keep all stakeholders motivated and engaged in a process of change that may take many years and requires vigilance.

Today, BIDs represent a worldwide evolution in the capacity of government to develop and transform local communities and their cooperative economies (Hoyt, 2008, pp. 112–113). BIDs represent a relatively new form of sub-governance that relies on a functioning partnership between the public and private sectors at the neighborhood level. As a partnership, BIDs appear to extend functional aspects of democracy that traditionally invite and permit business and private citizens into the formal processes of community development and governance. At the heart of a BID is its partnership between the business community and the local government. This PPP is encouraged by state statute and the consequent local laws that enable and describe the partnership. The controversies that surround BIDs tend to travel along the continuum of the partnership. There are those who are unsure of the motives of profit seekers at the private end, and the politics of government at the public end. It is clear that BIDs are not strict forms of privatization and may be better understood as preliminary, albeit primitive, forms of democratic process that call the private citizenry to become publicly involved and accountable as well as creative in solving immediate social and economic problems. PPPs are poorly evaluated when the aim is to diminish either party in the partnership (Schaeffer and Loveridge, 2002). It would be expected that the expectation of diminishing attributes contributes to diminishing results, and the practice of mutually expanding attributes in such partnerships are not only intended, but functional.

PPPs, like BIDs, are challenging because of a fairly sustained and understandable belief that business and government are different, possibly adversarial. They seem to exist in different realms of human achievement; they have different rules and objectives; they seem to describe the human condition differently (business: personal and individual achievement; government: communal and interpersonal cooperation). This dichotomy is fueled by an ongoing debate as to which realm functions better for society: a market system (business/private), or a cooperative system (government/public). This debate must be transcended for PPPs to succeed. The idea must be that both sectors may actually work together, may be partners, and that the merger is beneficial. At its core and to transcend an adversarial debate, this new partnership agreement must be managed on an ongoing basis.

An Integral Hypothesis for Practitioners of PPPs: A Balanced Scorecard Approach

The integral hypothesis for practitioners of PPPs is based on the concept of the Balanced Scorecard. Following prior initiatives, the Balanced Scorecard we know today was developed by Robert Kaplan and David Norton of the Harvard Business School (Kaplan and Norton, 1992) as a performance measurement tool. The Balanced Scorecard embraces both strategic planning and a futurist orientation (where are we going?) by integrating this with performance measurement (where are we at?) arriving at performance management (how are we getting there?). The balance in the Scorecard is arrived at by merging economic/private ROI and social/public measurements, and scoring the results to get a snap shot of how well the organization is doing in meeting its strategic objectives, promises, and vision of the future. This integral hypothesis creates a balance between three elements: financial and market investment labeled ROI, non-financial and social investments labeled QOL, and a third non-financial element, the partnership investment labeled OMC. As Kaplan and Norton pointed out, a meaningful and true assessment must recognize contextual as well as content-oriented criteria. In the case of PPPs, this criteria must address public, private, and partnership perspectives. For example, a business district may have more customers and a higher ROI score, but the neighborhood may experience increased air pollution due to increased traffic, lack of parking, and noise contributing to a lower QOL score, but the management or management organization communicates well its efforts to address these issues and holds open meetings, which provides a higher OMC score. The truer score is a combination of each element.

The idea of a Scorecard is an honest approach to performance measurement. It tells us that measurement is a snap shot of what is happening, not a prediction of what will happen. Of course, if we don't know what is happening, let alone where we are going, any performance passes as accomplishment. The key to the Balanced Scorecard and the Integral Performance Hypothesis for PPPs is an agreement, a promise, on where you are going. Therefore, measurements mean little without the agreement—without a promise of a strategic goal there are no meaningful measurements. Performance must be measured against a context of a known and purposeful commitment to construct a future reality. Granted, the future once arrived at may be different than envisioned, but the premise of this method is that it will be deliberately and consciously managed not guessed at.

The Kaplan–Norton Balanced Scorecard emphasizes "four perspectives." The four perspectives are:

- Financial—resources, outputs, economy, asset management (ROI);
- Customer—quality of life, safety, cleanliness, livability, destination management, entertainment (QOL);
- Internal Processes—organization, communication, development, skills (OMC); and
- Innovation and Learning—entrepreneurship, social capital, adaptation (OMC).

The Balanced Scorecard method is an integrating performance measurement process that aligns with the Agreement–Management–Commitment model of PPP development, and is well suited for assessing the management of PPPs.

Performance management is as effective as its measurements. Consequently, in most work environments the area in most dire straits is a lack of evaluation and more, the lack of effective evaluation. Correct evaluation allows us to obtain useful information so that we can determine if we are on target with our strategic outlook and project goals (Reenstra-Bryant, 2010). Reenstra-Bryant (2010) adds, "evaluation is really a set of tools to address the uncertainties associated with program models, develop greater understanding of the results that certain efforts do produce, and identification of needs for revised agendas and strategies" (p. 522). Performance measurements provide not only a baseline, but an objective look at "the truth." Managers tend to be consumed with day-to-day operations and seem to have little time to conduct survey and other evaluative research. The success and popularity of the manager and the renewal of the organization's ability to continue are often enough. PPPs feel they are judged every day by business and government providing more than enough scrutiny. This opinion has led to a field that is virtually empty of objective data on its functional aspects including management, business development and investment, public impact, customer satisfaction, quality of life, and organizational effectiveness.

A Universal PPP Survey

Return on Investment (ROI), Quality of Life (QOL), and Organizational and Management Capability (OMC)

In the fall of 2009, responding to this dearth of standardized evaluation criteria for MBDs, the Business District Management Certification Program at Rutgers University–Newark, NJ (Grossman, 2006–2014) developed a Universal Public–Private Partnership & BID Survey based on balancing public, private, and partnership criteria by including but separating three criteria areas: return on investment (ROI), quality of life (QOL), and organizational and management capability (OMC) (Grossman, 2012).

The survey begins by collecting practical and demographic information to determine the type of management, location, size, and budget of the management organization. The survey is set up in a five-point Likert scale. The scale is numbered from 1–5 going left to right. The OMC section has 20 data criterion. The ROI section has 22 data criterion. The QOL section has 22 data criterion. The score is determined by adding up each criterion according to its representative number. Scoring was based on a reasonable proportion of the total score. The total score is determined by adding together the score of each section as follows:

BOX 5.1 UNIVERSAL PPP SURVEY KEY

EACH STATEMENT HAS FIVE ANSWERS: Choose only one for each statement.
METHOD OF SCORING: Use five-point scale from left to right: a=5; b=4; c=3; d=2; and e=1.
ADD CHOICE IN EACH STATEMENT FOR A TOTAL SCORE.
INTERPRETATION KEY:

Highest score is 340—Very Successful—High performing, well established public–private partnership—regional to multi-regional impact player.
High score range is 272–339—Successful—Consistently good to excellent performance—good to excellent public–private partnership—could be better in key areas—local to regional impact player. Be wary of stagnation.

> Moderate score range is 185–271—Fair to good performance, struggles at times particularly with public–private partnership—needs improvement in key areas—stagnant in key areas—local impact player.
> Low score range is below 184—Poor to fair performance—ineffective public–private partnership—struggles, is not innovative—verging on failure—confusing regarding district to municipal impact. Danger zone is below 136—in various states of failure—confused to negative impact player.
>
> *(Grossman, 2006–2014)*

The survey is based on the following principles:

- If the management organization's PPP is unsuccessful then the managed district is less successful.
- If OMC is unsuccessful then the managed district is less successful.
- If ROI is unsuccessful then the managed district is less successful.
- If QOL improvements are unsuccessful then the managed district is less successful.
- The total of OMC, ROI, and QOL provides a more complete and accurate assessment of success.

The survey serves to assess the general state of the PPP's performance from a broad perspective touching on three key aspects of performance measurement: OMC, ROI, and QOL. The overall score relates to the overall condition of performance within the organization, however, it should also be analyzed in three separate sections to determine where improvements that will have the greatest performance impact can be made. Measuring performance personally and organizationally in a systematic manner is necessary to ensure positive progression, effectiveness, and efficiency of programs and management within PPPs. The process of regularly evaluating all the key indicators that lead to the success or failure of a given goal or mission creates an organizational atmosphere that is both proactive and responsive, traits that are paramount to success in an environment of constant social, demographic, and economic change. Further and more refined evaluation of programs and processes related to ROI and QOL are prudent in order to determine necessary actions to improve on those PPP functions. Obviously, more targeted or program-specific evaluations would have to be done in order to determine specific actions to impact improved performance as a whole. By methodically assessing a PPP's OMC, ROI related to programs and activities, and the overall QOL, as impacted by the management organization, the PPP is able to confidently determine direction, adjust resource allocation, validate actions, and engage their constituency.

Conclusion

It often seems that there is a logical assumption that the components of human endeavor, particularly public and private, are compartmentalized, and examined as self-fulfilling and functioning. It is as if any part of the performance process is set aside as the entirety of accomplishment all by itself with little regard for context, interdependency, and partnerships. This has worked to erode trust of performance evaluation. As a whole, balanced performance measures tuned to the frequency of real multi-sectoral contexts are a more complete measurement of PPPs.

When we discuss the public performance of PPPs, we are referring fundamentally to the promise of democracy as it is constituted in the building of our society. We are describing how this affects the performance of tasks through the balance of competing perspectives and the organization of the PPP as a public institution. PPPs are increasingly a significant contributor to the evolution of local governance including planning processes, the execution of projects, the implementation of policy, and the enhancement of local management capacity. We cannot forget that every performance refers to a promise, or a set of promises, that sets goals and describes an agreed upon future as a strategic objective—both publicly and privately. When we speak about performance in general, we are speaking fundamentally about measuring outputs and outcomes against inputs and implementation in relation to such promises; therefore, we are assessing management processes. It follows that performance evaluation is a series of measurements of the inherent promise(s) in every performance. Although the chief differences between private and public sector management are the degrees of inclusion and the fulfillment of public outcomes, PPPs promise that there is both value added and risk reduction in collaborating to create something neither sector can do alone very well. If we are on the high end of either of the inclusionary and public outcome aspects, we can safely presume that we are operating in a more public environment. If we are on the lesser end of these aspects then we are most likely operating in a private environment. If we are operating contractually at reasonably high levels in both aspects, we are in a PPP like a BID. The importance of this distinction is twofold:

1. inclusion underwrites democratic functions and tends to diminish autocratic functions, which provides a different perspective on performance; and
2. a greater depth and breadth of the promises between people is more imperative in public environments due to:

    a   the extent of partnering needs, which place outputs as parts of outcomes;
    b   the performance process being more non-linear so that input "A" may not directly impose upon or predict output or outcome "B," and
    c   the consequent timeline for expected results to occur and retain impact is often expanded.

The PPP organization must achieve a level of organizational competency based on the cooperation and commitment that established the PPP's purpose. As J. Smith and P. Wohlstetter (2006) point out, "public-private partnerships are motivated largely by a pursuit of the comparative advantages inherent to organizations in the other sectors" (p. 250). A pragmatic evaluation of performance, the thorough knowledge of the nature of the PPP as it is intended to function, and a balanced scoring of private perspectives regarding ROI, public perspectives regarding quality of life, and the partnership perspective regarding OMC to grow and develop the partnership is also required to assess performance effectively.

The Universal MBD Survey: Quality of Life (QOL), Return on Investment (ROI), and Organizational and Management Capability (OMC)

As individual as they are, what are the universal criteria that can be used to measure the success of MBDs? The test provides a snap shot of success of your MBD based on a criterion developed in this course. It reveals which areas of management need attention.

This is based on the following hypothesis:

- If the management organization's PPP is unsuccessful then the managed district is less successful.
- If the OMC is unsuccessful then the managed district is less successful.
- If the ROI is unsuccessful then the managed district is less successful.
- If the QOL is unsuccessful then the managed district is less successful.

References

Agranoff, R. (2012) *Collaborating to manage: A primer for the public sector.* Washington, DC: Georgetown University Press.

Allison, G. T. (2004) *Public and private management: Are they fundamentally alike in all unimportant respects?* Classics of Public Administration (5th edn). Belmont, CA: Wadsworth/Thompson Learning.

Barnard, C. (1938) Informal organizations and their relation to formal organizations. In J. M. Shafritz & A. C. Hyde (1997) *Classics of public administration* (4th edn). Fort Worth, TX: Harcourt Brace College Publishers.

Becker, C. (2010) Self-determination, accountability mechanisms, and quasi-governmental status. *Public Performance & Management Review,* 33(3), March: 413–435.

Becker, C., Grossman, S. A., & Dos Santos, B. (2011) *Business improvement districts: Census and national survey.* Washington, DC: International Downtown Association.

Behn, R. D. (2001) *Rethinking democratic accountability.* Washington, DC: Brookings Institution Press.

Bozeman, B. (1987) *All organizations are public: Comparing public and private organizations.* San Francisco, CA: Jossey-Bass.

Bradford, N. (2003, December). Public-private partnership? Shifting paradigms of economic governance in Ontario. *Canadian Journal of Political Science*, 36(5): 1005–1033.

Briffault, R. (1997) The rise of sublocal structures in urban governance. *Minnesota Law Review*, 82: 503–550.

Brownlow, L., Merriam, C., & Gulick, L. (1937) Report of the president's commission on administrative management. In J. M. Shafritz & A. C. Hyde (ed.) (1997). *Classics of public administration* (4th edn). Fort Worth, TX: Harcourt Brace College Publishers.

Caruso, G., & Weber, R. (2008) Getting the max for the tax: An examination of BID performance measures. In G. Morçöl, L. Hoyt, J. W. Meek, & U. Zimmermann (eds), *Business improvement districts: Research, theories, and controversies* (pp. 319–348). New York: CRC Press.

Coleman, J. S. (1998) Social capital in the creation of human capital. *American Journal of Sociology*, 94: 95–120.

Derthick, M. (1990) *Agency under stress*. Washington, DC: Brookings Institution Press.

Dilger, R. J., Moffett, R. R., & Struyk, L. (1997) Privatization of municipal services in America's largest cities. *Public Administration Review*, 57(1), January/February: 21–26.

Dubnick, M. (2005) Accountability and the promise of performance. *Public Performance & Management Review*, 28(3), March: 376–417.

Edelenbos, J., & Klijn, E.-H. (2007) Trust in complex decision-making networks: A theoretical and empirical exploration. *Administration and Society*, 39(1), March: 25–50.

Ellen, I. G., Schwartz, A. E., & Voicu, I. (2007) *The benefits of business improvement districts: Evidence from New York City*. New York: Furman Center for Real Estate and Urban Policy, New York University.

Erie, S. P., Kogan, V., & MacKenzie, S. A. (2010) Redevelopment, San Diego: The limits of public-private partnerships. *Urban Affairs Review*, 45(5): 644–678.

Ewoh, A. I. E., & Zimmerman, U. (2010) The case of Atlanta metro community improvement district alliance. *Public Performance & Management Review*, 33(3), March: 395–412.

Farrell, J., & Scotchmer, S. (1988) Partnerships. *The Quarterly Journal of Economics*, 103(2), May: 279–297.

Feehan, D., & Feit, M. D. (2006) *Making business districts work*. Binghamton, NY: The Haworth Press.

Foucault, M. (1972) *The archaeology of knowledge*. New York: Routledge.

Fredrickson, H. G. (1971) Toward a new public administration. In F. Marini (ed.), *Toward a new public administration* (pp. 309–331). San Francisco, CA: Chandler.

Fukuyama, F. (1995) *Trust: The social virtues and the creation of prosperity*. New York: Free Press.

Gopal-Agge, D., & Hoyt, L. (2008) The BID model in Canada and the United States: The retail-revitalization nexus. In G. Morçöl, L. Hoyt, J. W. Meek, & U. Zimmermann (eds), *Business improvement districts: Research, theories, and controversies* (pp. 139–158). New York: CRC Press.

Gray, B. (1989) *Collaborating: Finding common ground for multiparty problems*. San Francisco, CA: Jossey-Bass.

Grossman, S. A. (2006–2014) The Business District Executive Management Certification Program. Newark, NJ: Rutgers, The State University of New Jersey, School of Public Affairs & Administration.

Grossman, Seth A. (2008) *The role of entrepreneurship in public-private partnerships: The case of business improvement districts*, Doctoral Dissertation. Newark, NJ: Rutgers, The State University of New Jersey, School of Public Affairs & Administration.

Grossman, S. A. (2010) Reconceptualizing the public management and performance of business improvement districts. *Public Performance & Management Review*, 33(3), March: 361–394.

Grossman, S. A. (2012) The management and measurement of public-private partnerships: Toward an integral and balanced approach. *Public Performance & Management Review*, 35(4), June: 595–616.

Grossman, S. A. (2016) *Partnership governance*. London: Routledge.

Hodge, G., & Greve, C. (2009) PPPs: The passage of time permits a sober reflection. *Economic Affairs*, 29(1), March: 33–39.

Houstoun, L., Jr. (2003) *Business improvement districts*. Washington, DC: Urban Land Institute.

Hoyt, L. (2008) From North America to Africa: The BID model and the role of policy entrepreneurs. In G. Morçöl, L. Hoyt, J. W. Meek, & U. Zimmermann (eds), *Business improvement districts: Research, theories and controversies* (pp. 111–138). New York: CRC Press, Taylor & Francis Group.

Jackson, E. L., & Vinsom, C. (2004) *Public authorities and public corporations*. Institute of Government, University of Georgia, Athens, GA: University of Georgia Press.

Justice, J., & Goldsmith, R. (2006) Private governments or public policy tools? The law and public policy of New Jersey's special improvement districts. *International Journal of Public Administration*, 29(1–3): 107–136.

Kaplan, R. S., & Norton, D. P. (1992) The balanced scorecard – Measures that drive performance. *Harvard Business Review*, January–February, Watertown, MA, pp. 71–79.

Kaufman, H. (1969) Administrative decentralization and political power. In J. M. Shafritz & A. C. Hyde (ed.) (1997). *Classics of public administration* (4th edn). Fort Worth, TX: Harcourt Brace College Publishers.

Kearns, K. (1996) *Managing accountability: Preserving the public trust in public and nonprofit organizations*. San Francisco, CA: Jossey-Bass.

Kettl, D. (1993) *Sharing power: Public governance and private markets*. Washington, DC: Brookings Institution Press.

Knack, S. (2002) Social capital and the quality of government: Evidence from the States. *American Journal of Political Science*, 46(4), October: 772–785.

Lewis, E. (1984) *Public entrepreneurship: Toward a theory of bureaucratic political power*. Bloomington, IN: Indiana University Press.

Light, P. C. (1997) *The tides of reform: Making government work, 1945–1995*. New Haven, CT: Yale University Press.

Lindblom, C. E. (1988) The science of muddling through. In J. Rabin (ed.), *Handbook of Public Administration* (5th edn) (pp. 177–187). Belmont, CA: Thomson-Wadsworth.

Linder, S. M. (1999) Coming to terms with the public-private partnership: A grammar of multiple meanings. *American Behavioral Scientist*, 43(1), September: 35–51.

Lochner, K., Kawachi, I., & Kennedy, B. P. (1999) Social capital: A guide to its measurement. *Health and Place*, 5: 259–270.

Lowndes, V., & Skelcher, C. (1998) The dynamics of multi-organizational partnerships: An analysis of changing modes of governance. *Public Administration*, 76, Summer: 313–333.

Lubell, M., Schneider, M., Scholz, J. T., & Mete, M. (2002) Watershed partnerships and the emergence of collective action institutions. *American Journal of Political Science*, 46(1), January: 148–163.

MacDonald, J. M., Stokes, R., & Blumenthal, R. (2010) The role of community context in business district revitalization strategies. *Public Performance & Management Review*, 33(3), March: 439–458.

Mather, N., & Skelcher, C. (2007) Evaluating democratic performance: Methodologies for assessing the relationship between network governance and citizens. *Public Administration Review*, 67(2): 228–237.

Meek, J. W., & Hubler, P. (2006) Business improvement districts in Southern California: Implications for local governance. *International Journal of Public Administration*, 29: 31–52.

Mitchell, J. (2008) *Business improvement districts and the shape of American cities.* Albany, NY: State University of New York Press.

Moe, T. (1984) The new economics of organization. *American Journal of Political Science*, 28, November: 739–777.

Morçöl, G., & Zimmerman, U. (2006) Metropolitan governance and business improvement districts. *International Journal of Public Administration*, 29: 1–29.

Morçöl, G., Hoyt, L., Meek, J. W., & Zimmerman, U. (eds) (2008) *Business improvement districts: Research, theories and controversies* (pp. xv–xviii). New York: CRC Press, Taylor & Francis Group.

National Council for Public–Private Partnerships (2010) www.ncppp.org. Access date: December 7, 2010.

Osborne, D., & Gaebler, T. (1992) *Reinventing government.* Upper Saddle River, NJ: Addison-Wesley Publishing.

Ostrom, V., & Ostrom, E. (1977) Public goods and public choices. In E. S. Savas (ed.), *Alternatives for delivering public services: Toward improved performance* (pp. 7–49). Boulder, CO: Westview Press.

Reenstra-Bryant, R. (2010) Evaluations of business improvement districts. *Public Performance & Management Review*, 33(3), March: 509–523.

Roelofs, J. (2009) Networks and democracy: It ain't necessarily so. *American Behavioral Scientist*, 52(7), March: 990–1005.

Roosevelt, F. D. (1933) *Presidential Address.* Tennessee Valley Authority, TN.

Ruffin, F. A. (2010) Collaborative network management for urban revitalization. *Public Performance & Management Review*, 33(3), March: 459–487.

Savas, E. S. (2000) *Privitization and public-private partnerships.* New York: Seven Bridge Press.

Schaeffer, P., & Loveridge, S. (2002) Toward an understanding of public-private cooperation. *Public Performance & Management Review*, 26(2), December: 169–189.

Schumpeter, J. A. (1947) The creative response in economic history. *The Journal of Economic History*, 7(2), November: 149–159.

Simon, H. A. (1997) *Administrative behavior* (4th edn). New York: Free Press.

Skelcher, C. (2007) Does democracy matter? A transatlantic research design on democratic performance and special purpose governments. *Journal of Public Administration Research and Theory*, 17(1): 61–76.

Smith, J., & Wohlstetter, P. (2006) Understanding the different faces of partnering: A typology of public-private partnerships. *School Leadership and Management*, 26(3), July: 249–268.

Spitzer, D. (2007) *Transforming performance measurements: Rethinking the way we measure and drive organizational success.* New York: American Management Association.

Stokes, R., Jr. (2008) Business improvement districts and small business advocacy. In G. Morçöl, L. Hoyt, J. W. Meek, & U. Zimmermann (eds), *Business improvement districts: Research, theories, and controversies* (pp. 249–267). New York: CRC Press.

Taylor, Fr. (1912) Scientific management. In J. M. Shafritz & A. C. Hyde (eds) (1997). *Classics of public administration* (4th edn). Fort Worth, TX: Harcourt Brace College Publishers.

Wolf, J. F. (2008) Business improvement districts' approaches to working with local governments. In G. Morçöl, L. Hoyt, J. W. Meek, & U. Zimmermann (eds), *Business improvement districts: Research, theories, and controversies* (pp. 269–287). New York: CRC Press.

Wood, B. D., & Waterman, R. W. (1994) *Bureaucratic dynamics: The role of bureaucracy in a democracy*. Boulder, CO: Westview Press.

EPILOGUE

The Business District Improvement Movement and its Management: Looking Forward

The terms and applications of PPPs today have become a mainstay of governance and public service delivery throughout the world. PPPs have become a clearer practice as the NPM also became better defined in its role of merging private sectors into the public realm. This is a process that marks modern public administration since the Progressive Era beginning in the 1880s. NPM is notable for efforts to merge business administration with public administration. But, as these things go, the reverse also occurred and today we see in business education and practice an infusion of new avenues of non-profit and public management. This was possible chiefly because public administration grew and developed into a true profession after WWII. This followed the emergence of a modern, consumer-driven middle class needing unforetold "infrastructure" to sustain it, and a "class" with professional ambitions. To this extent, successful governments throughout the world understand the need to anchor themselves in the varied social/economic infrastructures required of modern civilizations now including a digital and virtual reality and unprecedented communications abilities that in themselves describe modern civilization. Infrastructure no longer refers only to physical foundations or transportation, but the backbone and sustainable agreements of any social human endeavor. *Infrastructure* is the correct province of government, and governance is our access to the management of such agreements, as they arrive, develop, and are sustained.

The modern middle-class movement is often ignored as a catalyst of public administration. This movement has its roots in the 17th century Enlightenment, but exploded during the Industrial Revolution of the 1880s, forever changing political-economics globally. Without a middle class consuming everything from ideas to automation, we would not have the modern world we know and expect. Sustaining a middle class is the measurement of a First World country for exactly this purpose. Today, the *emergence* (or, re-emergence) of China, India, and Brazil, among others, is well understood by their yearning for middle-class values. These are values that are well enunciated by the United States. Increases in population parallel the growth of the middle class simply because this "class" represents quality of life opportunities that pre-Industrial civilizations could not attain through manual labor alone. Simply put, a machine does the work of 100 people or more. That means a single person can potentially have the productivity of 100+ people. This is a "game changer" as it indicates that a person could be 100+ times wealthier. And, that's exactly what is happening. But, of course, it's relational. In light of this change, what are our social relationships? What is the new class order? Who is managing what?

Throughout the 20th century and continuing into the present era, driven by data where information is intrinsically valuable, infrastructure grew to meet demand; notable are the transportation and communications infrastructures. And with it, the use of urban areas physically and psychologically shifted at an accelerated rate, literally and physically spreading out to create integrated exurbias that include not only correlational suburban areas, but also traditionally rural areas. The key here is integration, which, however, tends to have an inevitable counter resistance. Not unlike Paul Light's descriptions of the *Tides of Reform* (Light, 1997) and well linked to those reforms, the fluctuation between integrating new social, mechanical, and economic technologies, and the opposing desires for segregation, well describe the political climate of our times. This *changes the game* and how we interact and manage our societies. Finding our way into and sustaining the middle class is a global economic driver that few would argue with. Consumption requires knowledge and expert consumption requires expert knowledge. Subsequently, innovation and particularly the generalization of entrepreneurship, in our time, now explain the ability to synthesize novel integrating capacities that refine human productivity rather than simply manipulate or manage markets. Also, the way we work together has shifted. Pre-modern class structures, which remain quite successful, have been benefiting by exercising global, therefore, supra-citizenship, and are more potent than ever. For example, information is digitally mechanized to such a degree that through instruments like Facebook, billions of people transfer enormous wealth to a few elite companies. On the other hand, post-modern structures based on meta-collaboration continue to transform and transcend traditional social structures at every level, and new markets are emerging around the need for three fundamental components: **information, education**, and **service**, thus reshaping if not redefining what I have referred to as the middle class. Today's products must have at least those three components to be considered useful and/or relevant. The point of these market components is to emphasize the intense impact of modern middle-class society. Which, although the middle class has different levels (of capability, merit, value, and purpose), it has a singular aim to establish an enlightened sense of self-worth. *Self-worth* is based chiefly on the three components listed above.

Self-worth demands equity in horizontal interchanges and this is where we find a political/economic interest (even if it is self-interest) in service. Horizontal interchanges lead to partnerships.

Both PPPs and "partnership" are not new terms. But, they take on a new application in the post-modern world described above. Partnerships remain but are less relational and are more pragmatic. PPPs drive an integration of thought **and deed** and well explain the legacy of the NPM. Excellent examples of this legacy reside at the local levels of government as BIDs. As we applied the NPM, we eventually came around to an ongoing redefinition of the self-worth of government professionals, and as citizens how we relate to each other in terms of our contribution and accountability to society, and the limitations of a sectoral society (or the opportunities of a metasectoral society). In spite of itself, the NPM also fostered the need to shift to the serious conversation of the integration of public service and public management. Consequently, the NPG arrives with new attention, theories, and practice regarding collaboration, networking, and ultimately partnering, not simply as transactions and deal making but as a management practice. That is, the management of society itself as a process of partnership formation, maintenance, and dissolution.

When we see a PPP, at the heart is a partnering modality; one that follows a distinct four-step process of **Agreement, Management, Commitment**, and **Accountability**, as described in this book. This *partnering modality* also influences public to public interaction, although such interaction, as we might expect, tends to reflect invested interests. Yet, a shift is occurring most notably among public administration professionals, as the new tools of partnership management are employed.

As mentioned above, we can look at PPPs from a purely transactional basis in the provision of a specific service or item (transportation, health, and the arts are good examples). That is reasonable as it gets to pragmatic functions of partnerships, but it is a limited use of partnering. The focus on transaction, the negotiation and contract administration, often obscures the actual partnership, and may reveal that it is only a project-provisional partnership better described as privatization, or simply contracting; two practices that are as old and, therefore, as useful as government itself. But today, partnering has a distinct governing aspect; therefore, a policy and management function that far exceeds transactional analysis. Partnering may be a uniquely useful democratic concept, but, for example, when we look at BIDs, what we see is private actors taking on, both individually and collectively, public responsibilities and authorities once reserved for government. A process called *publicization* tells us that citizens, the private sector, are *stepping up* to their inherent sovereignty (organizationally); even if it is tuned to special interests, it's an act of governance. What we have with BIDs is an example of this as partnership governance, a form of *shared governance* acknowledging a shared economy and purpose. Because, it is shared and multi-sectoral, legislation creating BIDs specifically allows for private citizens to organize and manage public services that tend to address not only business or economic concerns, but also quality of life, social, and cultural concerns as well. This looks like, sounds like, and walks like government; the management of the community. This is because it is *governance*.

As public administrators, the neglect of governance erodes confidence in government. In my experience, confidence is sensed as trust. Trust is the experience of being empowered and being able to empower others. This is the *raison d'être* of the NPG, a march towards a government that includes and empowers its citizenry in the act of governing. This is the new governance. Its skill set is partnership.

We look at BIDS not as private sector instruments surviving the public, but public tools of successful multi-sectoral community partnerships. BIDs are cautioned these days that it is inappropriate, and in fact perilous, to neglect the public side of the partnership. And, this is as it should be. Anecdotally, in virtually every case of BID failure, it appears to be generated by the public side, or better stated, a neglect of the public side. BIDs tend to fall to political persuasion rather than mismanagement. Old sectorally divided paradigms would have us segregate this partnership and essentially deny it. This appears to be a fatal mistake for BIDs. The new paradigm is integration that looks like a partnership in which each part sustains itself but is encompassed by the wholeness of the partnership. This new paradigm recognizes that a BID manager is a combination of a public and business administrator, a PPP manager, an entrepreneurial inspired executive, a community development specialist, and a co-op manager—a job not to be taken lightly. And, this type of professional/public manager informs public administration wholly. It clarifies the profession of public management and identifies an important new skill set. Lastly, it is not going away. In fact, the BID and PPP movements are growing steadily worldwide as governments seek effective ways to provide governance and services. As this time, BIDs are a growing trend in the United Kingdom and Europe, Asia, and South America, and have a strong hold in Australia and Africa. It is not a fad. It's a trend that is becoming the norm. As government struggles with adequately providing services, planning, and realizing potential based solely on traditional models, it turns to actively utilizing all components and capabilities within its communities in an entrepreneurial manner. Because governance is chiefly a mode of determining who we are and what we can be counted on for, and we understand the partnership tenets of the NPG practiced by BIDs, public administration enters a new *Age of Public Accountability*.

BIDs are remarkable examples of public administration. This is not due to multi-sectoral partnering, but also to the pragmatic management of real life community development. *Development-towards-improvement* is what most ordinary citizens experience as good government. At the local level of government, the "heroes" of local government are community development professionals. They are heroes not only because of what they accomplish, but how they do it. It is always a result of networking, collaborating, organizing, and being *at-service*.

Successful BID managers reflect these attributes, and consider them to be some of the significant measurements of success. After all, the truest measure of success in government is the well-being of society; a quality of life that reflects our commitments to meaningful, enjoyable, and productive lives—together.

Seth A. Grossman

2015

Reference

Light, P. C. (1997) *The tides of reform*. New Haven, CT: Yale University Press.

APPENDIX A

2007 Research Study on BIDs and the Role of Entrepreneurship in Public–Private Partnerships

Research Questions and Methods

The guiding research question for this study was: What is the role of entrepreneurship in PPPs? The methodology employed to answer that question was a mixed methods approach completed through conducting telephone interviews with nine BID managers, three in New Jersey and six others located throughout the United States, coupled with an email survey of 650 BID managers in the United States. The guiding research question was derived from the initial inquiry: How are BIDs successful in terms of delivering on the intention of the enabling legislations and, consequently, improving the delivery of public services, community organizing, and melding private and public sector technologies?

Research Methods

This study was conducted through nine telephone interviews with BID managers throughout the United States (three interviews in New Jersey and six telephone interviews outside of New Jersey). Those interviews established the questions for a survey of approximately 650 BID managers in the United States, employing a definitive email database of the known BIDs and MBDs. In other words, the survey was applied to the known universe of BIDs in the United States.

Business district management (BDM), a form of PPP management, was the dependent variable (DV) in a causal relationship. Public entrepreneurship (PE) was the independent variable (IV). The hypothetical research equation was BDM = PE, inferring that if there were public entrepreneurship operating as a distinct identifier at the sub-government level of BIDs, then there would be better understanding of its role in PPPs. Key sub-variables of public entrepreneurship identified in the literature and utilized in this research were: trust, innovation, organization, leadership, strategy, and asset management.

An interview is a qualitative approach that, for the purpose of this study, was designed to understand how people viewed the issue of entrepreneurship and to investigate other perspectives that would assist with compiling the survey questions. The survey is a quantitative tool that, for the purpose of this study, obtained a broad picture of the general population of BID management phenomena in the United States, which represented almost half of the BIDs in the world. Quantitative analysis offered the advantage of exploring the specific correlations of the research equation in terms of probable outcomes, measurable impactors, the importance of specific impactors on items of interest, and, by looking beyond simple relationships, addressed the correlations among variables in the hypothesized BID relationship, both positively and negatively.

As stated above, this research addressed the role of entrepreneurship in the management of PPPs. Public entrepreneurship, which addressed the public administration aspects of entrepreneurship, was operationalized as:

- building upon the assets of the community;
- identifying leadership;
- emphasizing organization and management to achieve a community vision;
- utilizing economic and community development technologies;
- building on comprehensive community development strategies;
- uniting public and private sector stakeholders; and
- emphasizing goodwill, trust, and the strength of social accountability networks.

When accurately assessing and evaluating the management behavior of BIDs as PPPs, the community building processes must be measured. Inescapable in this research were the qualitative aspects of social capital and the chief facet of trust as it was developed and maintained in the community building processes that PPPs represented as well as the qualitative aspects of innovation that were essential to entrepreneurship. Trust and trust building were a unique concern in the entrepreneurial practices of PPPs due to the differing understandings of trust in the public and private sectors. This research anticipated that entrepreneurship might be redefined by applying the principles of social capital and, most importantly, of trust building between public and private actors merged within decentralized sub-government units where pragmatic results were expected by community members.

The survey addressed the complete population, or known universe of the unit of study, and it was expected that this population would be motivated, literate, cooperative, and capable of completing the survey, which would provide a stronger response rate. The respondents were familiar with the issues and would not need to consult historic data. By emailing, geographic districts were reduced and limited by those that had available email addresses. Likely, there were more

BIDs than those represented by the sample; however, the email list contained all the known email addresses of BIDs and ensured that the participants could be located and surveyed with no intrusion other than the email itself. Demographic data was added to the survey to examine the impact of gender. The questions were not personal but of an experiential and professional nature. The survey questions could be considered as somewhat specific; therefore, they would offer a degree of difficulty for non-professionals. The interviews aided in the creation of the type and quality of questions and with the sequencing of the questions. In general, questions were short and intended to build on each other. Email surveys reduced various bias issues, such as social desirability and false respondents, since there was no face-to-face interviewing, responses were anonymous, and the emails were personalized.

Two scaling systems were reviewed to quantify the qualitative-oriented questions. A Likert (1932), or summative, scaling system used a one to five scale and captured the correlations of interview judgments (e.g. Strongly Disagree, Disagree, Agree, Strongly Agree, Undecided); and a Guttman (1950), or cumulative, scaling system measured concepts, e.g. when a number of statements about a concept are presented, each statement indicated a degree of acceptance of the concept, cumulating in a strong acceptance. The survey was conducted by electronic mail, utilizing the professional electronic surveying tool, Survey Monkey.

Pros and Cons of Research Methods

Research methods are generally defined in two categories: (1) quantitative, which utilizes statistical methods to determine specific correlations between impact variables (factual data) to determine what is occurring; it is based on numbers and is deductive; (2) qualitative, which uses direct observation, comparison, reflection, and interviewing techniques to determine how and why something is occurring; it is based on words and is exploratory and inductive. Quantitative research is based on a model that simplifies reality and extrapolates generalities applicable to the general population, while qualitative research methods work to reflect reality through direct human interaction, are case specific, and limited when making conclusions about the general population. The chief difference is in the assumptions and level of analysis in which those assumptions are made. Quantitative analysis has a broader viewpoint, while qualitative research is much more focused (Creswell, 2003; Berg, 2004).

Quantitative data is based on qualitative judgments regarding human interaction and observation. While the quantitative research tends to be prescriptive, it is also normative and less explanatory regarding causal factors and is less useful in developing theories about PPPs but more useful in proving established theories regarding these partnerships.

Surveying is one of the most important measurements in quantitative research. There are generally two types of surveying methods: questionnaires and interviewing. Questionnaires generally do not require the researcher to be present or to interact; whereas, interviewing does require direct interaction. Questionnaires are generally administered by mail or email but may be conducted by a group or presented directly by the researcher. Interviews are a more interactive form of research and imply a one-on-one exchange between the interviewer and the interviewee. Interviews may be done in person or by telephone or can be completed, to an extent, electronically through emails. The negative side of surveying is never the survey itself but in obtaining the data. Validity concerns due to interviewer and interviewee bias can undermine the survey. The survey for this study was conducted electronically based on available email addresses with no direct contact. Direct interviewing was an initial part of this research to aid in designing the survey instrument.

Surveying takes time, attention, and persistence. Various forms of survey scaling techniques help code surveys and interpret qualitative data into a quantitative format. Scaling assigns numerical values to objects according to a rule, or ruler. This ruler must be internally consistent in order for the research survey to have meaning. Three scaling techniques were:

i   Thurstone (1928), or equal-appearing interval scaling. In this case, objects are measured in an equal hierarchical manner, e.g. a scale from one to ten with one as the lowest and ten as the highest—ten is exactly nine units of measurement higher than one;

ii   Likert (1932), or summative scaling. Usually employs a one to five scale and captures the correlations of interview judgments (e.g. Strongly Disagree, Disagree, Agree, Strongly Agree, Undecided); and

iii   Guttman (1950), or cumulative scaling, which tends to measure concepts, e.g. a number of statements about a concept are presented; each statement indicates a degree of acceptance of the concept, cumulating in a strong acceptance.

Surveying techniques utilize scaling to convert qualitative data into quantitative data. The research for this study used Likert scaling and Guttman scaling only on the final question to determine the integration of management, entrepreneurship, and social capital. Thurstone scaling was considered unnecessary in addressing the survey's conceptual issues.

Quantitative analysis has the advantage of exploring specific correlations of this research in terms of probable outcomes, measurable impactors, the importance of specific impactors on items of interest, and looking beyond simple relationships to address the correlations between variables in a relationship, both positively and negatively. The data limited and shaped the analysis. This approach was well suited to determine the causes or effects of the independent variables. Cross-sectional analysis, which examines the relationships and causes of a specific occurrence in time, or longitudinal analysis, which takes place over time, were not used in this study.

Data Analysis

Nine Interviews

Prior to conducting the email survey, nine interviews were conducted with BID managers throughout the United States between January 1, 2008, and February 11, 2008. The interview data were used to inform the survey. Each interview was approximately an hour and 15 minutes in duration, was conducted by telephone, and was recorded with the permission of the interviewee. Three BID managers were from New Jersey (Maplewood, Jersey City, and Wildwood); one was from Brooklyn, New York; one was from Wausau, Wisconsin; one was from Hastings, Nebraska; one was from San Francisco, California; one was from Lititz, Pennsylvania; and one was from Raleigh, North Carolina. The BIDs ranged in size from small (a $99,000 annual budget or less) to large ($2,000,000 annual budget or above) and represented urban, small town, town centers, and exurban locals. Conversations with interviewees ranged from those about hard-nosed management to those emphasizing pragmatic entrepreneurship. Typically, BID managers engage in both almost simultaneously. One interviewee stressed, "I'm in the trenches. What makes the BID different is that I have business people in the trenches with me."

The purpose of these interviews was to investigate thematic aspects regarding the role of entrepreneurship in the PPP that BIDs represented and to ascertain the effectiveness of questions that might appear on the survey. The interviews followed the pattern of questions in a snowball effect based on those questions that allowed the interviewees to examine the questions in more depth. This effect was not unexpected because the questions were designed to examine the nature of the BID's PPP as well as the impact of entrepreneurial characteristics.

The interview method was based on the research question dependent variable, PPPs, and its independent variable, entrepreneurship. The research question assumed that the research subject was part of a PPP and the management of that partnership. Initial questions addressed this assumption by ascertaining if the interviewees, in fact, perceived BIDs as PPPs. Each interviewee accepted the premise that BIDs were bona fide PPPs with one interviewee stating, "Managing the relationship. This is our job." It was unanimously acknowledged that public and private actors were on the governing Boards of Directors as stipulated in state enabling legislations. The managers saw themselves as situated between business and government. As one interviewee stated, "If it gets out of balance, we are not considered as successful unless we strike that balance." Some saw their role as more managerial than entrepreneurial, while others were just the opposite.

One interviewee stated that "entrepreneurship was not necessary, but it made the BID more successful." From the interviews, it became evident that most BID managers might perceive themselves as a part-manager/part-entrepreneur to a higher degree than expected from traditional public administrators. In almost all circumstances, if BID managers were typical of the interviewees, they would see themselves as possessing both management and entrepreneurship characteristics and skills at fairly strong levels. The consensus among those interviewed was that BIDs were designed to harness entrepreneurship and to *challenge the public sector to think more creatively*.

The research question presented a problem in the definition of entrepreneurship, which was usually interpreted as referring to financial profit or commercial product innovation and the exploitation of markets. Such a definition excluded public forms of entrepreneurship as those involved in BIDs, which had no such direct profit motive. Nonetheless, this sentiment from one of the interviewees indicated that a broader sense of entrepreneurship was well understood, "For us to meet our goals and expectations, we need people who think outside of the box. Without these ideas we would probably stay stagnant." The remark indicated that the BID manager was not merely an advocate for business but also, in a larger sense, for organizational change. Another interviewee supported this expansive role by stating, "My job is to be a catalyst for change. I have to be the spark plug for the organization, and have to manage that change and be forward thinking." A number of interviewees noted that a definition of entrepreneurship accounting for non-profits and the public sector should be addressed up front in the survey. Thus, the survey expanded the concept of entrepreneurship to include a broader aspect of the human potential of entrepreneurship, greater than solely a financial or profit motive, which appeared to be more descriptive and to encompass the role of BIDs and the community as a whole. An up-front description of entrepreneurship, therefore, was considered unnecessary because it could add bias to the survey. Additionally, strategic thinking, which had broad social applications, was a characteristic of entrepreneurship and spoken of in terms of a community or team vision. It was generally agreed that entrepreneurship was not limited by business-only connotations. Interviewees affirmed this by stating, "We talk about the vision as a promise ... as a way to leverage creativity ... and create a new experience of the district."

The interviews established that the interviewee managed a bona fide BID or its equivalent. Questions were associated with how BIDs as PPPs were perceived by the interviewees and how entrepreneurship functioned in the PPP and the perceived role of the BID manager. When answers to these two themes brought forth discussion supporting a high correlation with networking, organizing, and trustworthiness of the BID entity, it became apparent that these were common variables of social capital. The key findings of the interviews suggested that entrepreneurship was highly descriptive of BID management behavior, that the social capital characteristics of trust and building relationships with others through membership in clubs and organizations were highly correlated to entrepreneurship in BIDs, and that it might indicate significant, if not unique, aspects of entrepreneurship in public processes. Therefore, social capital questions were added to the survey.

The interviews supported the premises of the research, that: BIDs were true PPPs, BID management was a hybrid of (public and private) management technology, and entrepreneurship was a key element that synergized the partnership. BID managers who were interviewed indicated strong association with the ideas of change and being *change agents*. This indicated that PPPs might be perceived as structured for change to offer a bridging capacity to government when change was needed through citizen action. The findings that the social capital aspects of trust building, strategic visioning and leadership, sociability and networking as integral aspects of BID management, were expected but they were initially not associated with entrepreneurship. This finding established a new hypothesis responding to the function of social capital in public entrepreneurship. The interviews indicated that entrepreneurship in PPPs like BIDs required, or was infused by, classic activities that built social capital. To get at the role of entrepreneurship correctly, it became apparent that questions regarding social capital should be present in the survey.

Survey Analysis

The survey consisted of 32 questions with the final question (Question 32) offering a series of 17 entrepreneurial/social capital and managerial attributes and aspects of BID management. The statistical analysis was descriptive and inferential, examining correlations and regressions. T-tests were conducted using the demographic variable of gender, which did not produce significant results. Filters allowed analysis of the size and type of BID.

Statistical OLS Regression Analysis

The statistical analysis and frequency data for all of the variables and regressions were applied to the four themes of the research: (1) PPPs; (2) Entrepreneurship; (3) Social Capital; and (4) Management, as follows:

a   Entrepreneurship (IV) to PPPs (DV)
b   Entrepreneurship and social capital as independent variables (IV) to PPPs (DV)
c   Social capital (IV) to entrepreneurship (DV)
d   Management (IV) to entrepreneurship (DV)

The OLS regression included gender as a dummy variable. A Cronbach Alpha test was followed by tests for assumptions for the regressions and t-tests, ANOVA, correlation, and regression analysis. Results were consistent with the ANOVA analysis. Social capital was a statistically significant predictor of entrepreneurship in PPPs.

There were positive significant correlations for the four constructs. The strongest correlation was between social capital and entrepreneurship (0.640, significant at the 0.01 level of significance). Some regressions, entrepreneurship and PPPs $p < 0.0005$, showed significance. The regression with social capital and entrepreneurship on the dependent of public/private was also significant ($p < 0.0005$) but only the independent variable of entrepreneurship was significant in the model. Social capital on the dependent variable of entrepreneurship was also significant ($p < 0.0005$) and management on the dependent variable of entrepreneurship indicated significance with $p < 0.0005$.

The t-tests for the four constructs related to gender indicated no significance. The ANOVA test for Question 6, budget, based on the four dependents indicated no significance. The ANOVA indicated no significance for Question 6. Because the variables were not normally distributed, a Kruskal–Wallis test was also applied, which also revealed no significance (Kruskal and Wallis, 1952). The ANOVA test for Question 7, type of BID management, posed a problem with unequal sample sizes. Of particular concern was the not-for-profit category with only one response. An analysis could not be done on a group of one; therefore, to conduct the test, the question was aggregated into two categories: (1) non-profit as the dominant group and (2) others. This resulted in sample sizes that were unequal but better than having one group with seven, one with 34, and one with 200. Independent samples (t-test) were conducted and no significance was found for the variable of social capital = social capital p-value = 0.013. This revealed that the non-profit group had significantly higher scores on the construct of social capital than the group of *others*. A Mann-Whitney U test was conducted and found a significant p-value of 0.022. This provided some insight into questions regarding why some people chose the non-profit over the for-profit route. Non-profits might allow for a more direct use of social capital capabilities.

The information in Table A.1 shows the cluster analysis data for the four constructs (typological groups): PPPs; entrepreneurship; social capital; and management. There were 274 original survey responses; however, 19 were deleted because they answered "no" to Question 4 (the organization I manage is a BID). Of the remaining 255 records, some items were not answered by all participants

TABLE A.1 Case Processing Summary

	Cases					
	Valid		Missing		Total	
	N	%	N	%	N	%
Public/private partnerships (PPP)	245	96.1	10	3.9	255	100
Entrepreneurship	221	86.7	34	13.3	255	100
Social capital	237	92.9	18	7.1	255	100
Management	239	93.7	16	6.3	255	100

(missing data). Pair wise deletion was used to exclude cases only if they were missing data required for a specific analysis but records will be retained for analyses in which all data were present.

Future Research: Lessons for Organizational Theory and Community Development Practice

The conclusions were drawn from a combination of the research and the literature. Chiefly, the finding that social capital was highly correlated to entrepreneurship in BIDs was something not specifically addressed before and led to some new theoretical ideas about public entrepreneurship. The public nature of BIDs (that they are units of government) was virtually ignored except in terms of policy. This policy interpretation was discussed in the literature. The strong association with social capital in the interview and survey results supported BIDs as formal PPPs and seemed designed to enhance public management. This requires further explanation. Entrepreneurship, as a public function, clearly has a different focus than private entrepreneurship. Public entrepreneurship is motivated by public service and community building. This was also clearly indicated in the interview and survey results.

Key to this discussion is the idea that entrepreneurship is a human behavior that works to transform one set of values to another set of values. In the public realm, this can be understood as transforming private sector attributes into public sector behavior. The survey results indicated that a fusion occurred in the practice of BID management typical of B. Bozeman's (1987) Multidimensional Theory of the Impact of Publicness on Organizational Behavior and the evolving relationship between entrepreneurship and management indicated by Robert Carton's (Carton, Hofer, and Meeks, 1998) Entrepreneurship Paradigm.

After over 17 years of work with BIDs, I have seen an overindulgence built on the false notion that BIDs, like some forms of PPPs, simply privatize public space. But evidence points out that BIDs make private endeavors public. An important lesson derived from this research was that business district management was a form of public administration. The privatization debate is falsely applied to these special districts, even though most BIDs are managed by a private non-profit corporation. The management entities of BIDs are so extensively guided by public rules that they are less quasi-private and may be more quasi-governmental agencies (quagos not quangos). They act as buffers between more formalized government units but, nonetheless, retain governmental characteristics. "BIDS work within an economic development policy arena encompassing the public, private, and nonprofit arenas" (Mitchell, 2008, p. 51).

BIDs are accepted as true forms of governance akin to local government; therefore, the idea of such concepts as *private governments'* lack of transparency and democratic accountability is not unique but is measured in the same vein as those understandings that inform us about local government. From this standpoint, we can begin to discern the functionality of BIDs as a form of public management where private and public attributes of society merge in our democratic processes. We are reminded that democracy has transformative origins in which we find our dignity in public accountability rather than in only personal prowess. In part, BIDs provide a window into the functionality of public and private sector mutuality as it occurs and provide a means of comprehending our sense of community in a quickly changing world.

Many public administration scholars are calling for democratic anchorage regarding BIDs with limited understanding of how BIDs actually work or the nature of governmental intervention in business development. There has been little examination of how the public nature of economic and business development defines a community in relation to BIDs. An adversarial relationship is assumed, or worse, a sense of separation. The research indicated something quite different. BIDs represent a new paradigm of cooperation. Critics applying a notion of traditional business/state segregation miss the opportunity to apply observations of a business/state partnership. This partnership works without destroying the traditional social constructs of government or free market business characteristics. There is clear synergy that allows for the evolution of freedom within evolving communities.

Management in the public realm also requires community development (community planning, organization, and leadership) and economic expertise (jobs, business development, housing, and public infrastructure) and BIDs are no exception. When BID managers are tied to local business oversight and are responsible for producing direct services with market impact, they succeed by applying an array of partnership building skills in both the private and public sectors. BIDs represent a decidedly public choice, a choice by private individuals to organize, leverage community assets, and participate in public accountability. When tied to local government contractually through an ordinance, as well as being a direct recipient of public funds, BIDs are neither purely independent nor a privatization of public service. They represent a new manner of providing public services in the form of entrepreneurial public management, translating typically governmentally centralized services to special localized needs, and applying business acumen to communal activities. Public entrepreneurship has the element of direct investment at the neighborhood level. This might explain why entities like small businesses with traditional tax aversion subscribe to the creation of BIDs.

The subject of entrepreneurship over the past four decades moved into the public realm. This was to be expected considering the tendency of private sector operatives to mold government in their image, and considering the term entrepreneurship speaks to a human capacity not only to economic behavior. In a changing and globalizing marketplace, government must be nimble in order to develop communities effectively and allow them to compete successfully. Because entrepreneurship is, to a large degree, a basic aspect of human behavior, there is little consensus on its characteristics, but where there is agreement, it is towards the ability to innovate, take risks, and organize others. Similarly, the term PPP theoretically exists on a continuum from purely public to purely private.

Unlike state or county governments, it is difficult to determine the exact number of BIDs because they are established locally with little reporting requirements to state government and they are continually being created. This is a dynamic growth field in government. Given these limitations, this study focused on the public side of these partnerships and on entrepreneurship, examining its determinant factors. The study combined public organization theory with local government capacity to conduct community development in the form of BIDs.

If the role of entrepreneurship were to transform something of little or no value into something of value, then the role of public entrepreneurship (exhibited in BIDs) is to transform private ambitions into public accountabilities. Additionally, entrepreneurship is a pragmatic process and results–driven. Its outputs can be measured by well-defined outcomes. The results of this study suggested that the role of entrepreneurship in PPPs was, in large part, garnering network assets through increased social capital and managing private investment in the delivery of public services and processes. The BID manager, not unlike the BID organization, is both public manager and public entrepreneur. The result is increased local public management and an expanded formalized economic political capacity that acts as an addition to traditional government. The findings suggested that PPPs attracted entrepreneurial types, both male and female. Additionally, PPPs required skilled public managers with strong entrepreneurial skills. BIDs, as PPPs, are specifically designed to transform private sector energy into public processes so that business development is reminiscent of traditional community development. The difference is that traditional community development seeks solutions to social problems; whereas, BIDs focus largely on future outcomes that encompass economic success.

The traditional way of addressing community development needs has been by either providing money for a project or identifying some singular need or problem and organizing an effort to meet it or resolve it. This is a fix-it model of community development, well suited when something is actually broken, but poorly suited when the problems in a community have to do with enhancing the systemic organizational aspects of the community. PPPs have arisen as another way that strengthens and broadens unity within a community. PPPs develop out of the recognition that there is greater power available in communities through their neighborhood, towns, business organizations, and corporations than the people involved often realize. This collective power resides in the relational purpose expressed and acted on as a functioning and real dialogue between community stakeholders and that works to invent and implement a positive future rather than attempting solely to fix something from the past.

PPPs are mechanisms of government and street level community development that unite communities, their sponsors, and volunteers around a shared vision of community value and an accepted direction that expresses those values. The special power of partnering provides a significant competitive advantage and breakthrough results. The combination can be nothing less than transformational. Public-oriented partnerships work by bringing people together to solve common problems, develop agreements, and manage those agreements with a commitment over time.

Transformation is not magically accomplished. It is managed, pragmatic, and results oriented. Transformation is a form of performance that stresses outcomes and sustainability of public process. Public administration and government harness the work and products of transformation, which changes private attributes into public accountability, independence into interdependence, commitment into action, and disagreement into agreement. Beyond compromise is the integral promise of partnerships that break through assumed rational limitations. When this breakthrough occurs, and without losing the ability to disagree or complain, communities improve and deliver on their promises. At the crux of this process is the entrepreneurial public administrator, exemplified by the BID manager. The BID manager forges, facilitates, and uses not only new approaches to what is valuable in a community but does this by managing a PPP that unites disparate forces in society.

In determining the successful communities, we must measure the quality, accountability, and accessibility of the partnerships they keep. Achieving the ability to be an effective and efficient partner is the result of focusing attention on the community rather than solely on oneself and seeing one's purposes as being enhanced and largely determined by the community(s). Community in this context refers to any political entity, group, organization, family, or society to which one belongs. The process of community building has entrepreneurial roots because it takes courage, action, and creativity to forge new relationships, especially those that are intended to last.

Much has been said about public entrepreneurship but little research has been conducted to examine the characteristics of public entrepreneurs. Entrepreneurs, and certainly public entrepreneurs, are moving targets, noticeable because they are always up to something, always organizing others around a venture, and always on a quest that stretches into the future. The results of this research suggested that public entrepreneurs were strongly characterized, not only by normative entrepreneurial attributes, such as being innovative and forward thinking, but especially correlated to the development and maintenance of social capital. Therefore, what seems to separate the public entrepreneur from the private entrepreneur is not a financial profit or product motive but rather social capital processes that may alter, if not transform, the way public value is constructed. This transformation is built on enhancing the definition of what is valuable about the community. It requires the ability to enroll others in the process of change. This transformational process is a networked dialogue resembling public sector activity.

Involving what is typically described as the private sector in PPPs appears as a deliberate means to address this process and to abstract and reassemble community assets necessary to be competitive. It is inescapable, particularly in regards to BIDs, that being competitive in a manner that adds value to the citizen investment has become a public concern. It is competitive by constructing value from devalued or unrecognized community assets and seizing the opportunity to exploit this resource in a manner that positively affects everyone. In other words, the community as a whole is seen as being more valuable, economically as well as aesthetically. This describes a classic public entrepreneurial skill. Networking seems chiefly to be a process of building and maintaining social capital and establishing a trust environment, one built on shared value constructs, to conduct the business of governance.

The public management entrepreneur must master the art of community, the building of dialogues of value that allow each person to act on a value exchange as an opportunity. If we look at this practically, we can see that, in deteriorated communities, there are few or no conversations of value. There is, instead, an obsession with conversations that devalue the community. An example of this is the effect of the 1964 Newark, New Jersey riots, which dominated conversations about the city over the following 40 years and consistently worked to overshadow the city's assets. The result of organizing community development around devaluing conversations is slum and blight. The great challenge of public administration and management is to create a sense of collective action to rediscover and refine what is valuable about the community and effectively manage those assets.

In highly competitive arenas that have been devalued and are interlocked with established communities, the business market, as well as its surrounding community, requires a collaborative push that is highly structured. These structures, like BIDs, are well articulated by PPPs. These partnerships are not private ventures but public actions with private participation. They are not simple privatization schemes. Their interchange redefines, transforms, and re-energizes, through entrepreneurial volition, a community improvement process that is propelled by revitalizing a sense of place that bustles with people-oriented business sensibility.

With this in mind, traditional PPPs that often address transportation, medical, water and sanitation, and redevelopment issues because of their public standing, address those problems that define communities and make them work. These are usually seen as, and often are, the privatizing of traditional public services. In some PPPs, it is not advisable that the private entity become in or of government because the political impact may be too great and its expediency impractical. When privatization is the motivator, a partnership with the public sector is conveyed to reduce perceived risk to the private actor and secure investment that is not easily obtained through public processes. Also, if the venture fails, the government must step in to ensure that the service continues, thereby, underwriting the process and further reducing risk to its constituents. Additionally, in these privatization partnerships, the government is permitted to establish a virtual monopoly for the private investor that reduces competitive risk. Government enters these arrangements because they may not have the necessary capital for investment or the kind of management capacity necessary to operate the venture.

Although an argument can be made that BIDs take on some of these aspects, it is not their chief aim. BIDs are not strictly project oriented but take on ongoing governance responsibilities as well as enhancing fundamental public services to meet market and quality of life requirements, which are often intermingled at the neighborhood level. Although this research did not obtain data on the length and sustainability of BIDs, from the interviews and observations it appeared that BIDs were not short-term ventures. Those that are rescinded appear to have suffered unsustainable and crippling political intervention. But they are anomalies and in the minority. In determining the public impact of BIDs, longevity should be a factor. The longer a BID is in existence, the more the BID behaves like a public rather than private entity. BIDs may also affect local government by encouraging more entrepreneurial characteristics and the longevity of a BID would be a factor. BIDs and their managers are expected to be entrepreneurial. This initial expectation may become a normative practice, over time, especially in governments that have professional community and economic development capacity.

BIDs create synergy and a synthesis of traditional public and private capability to unfold a hybrid new capability that borrows the best from each sector. This reveals three underlying conditions that are brought forth by the BID process:

1. urban and downtown environments that remain distressed have not figured out how to express their value to their suburban neighbors;
2. distressed business communities disguise a pent-up entrepreneurial desire; and
3. PPPs legitimize the entrepreneurial spirit by bracketing sensitive market revitalization in standard and understandable public institutions.

From this study, it could be deduced that BIDs performed a vital function in restoring the social and economic equilibrium in threatened, but viable, communities. These communities often are surrounded by vibrant suburban markets and functioning and affluent neighborhoods and municipalities. Survival and success of the distressed community is often related to bridging suburban and urban consumer expectations. This bridging capability is a form of entrepreneurial networking, which is an often-overlooked skill in public management in general.

As intriguing as BIDs' business-minded aspects are, BIDs are not just business development oriented, but also the process of comprehensive community development that borrows much of its managerial technology from residential co-ops and suburban malls (retail commercial co-ops). Cooperatives in many fields evolved at about the same time as BIDs began to emerge. On the public side, BIDs represent a localized need to cooperate in changing and competitive markets. Being able to adapt to change while sustaining community assets is a good strategy. It counters the throwaway culture associated with suburbanization and consumerism.

BIDs are distinct from suburban malls because they exist in traditional communities and these communities and the culture of the people are generally considered a key economic asset of the district. Suburban malls cannot honestly make this claim, even if they portray themselves as quasi-communities. Mall culture may be a result of malls being the de facto downtown of bedroom communities, an attribute that does not transfer over to urban malls. In their business plans, malls generally do not state that their intended impact is on the greater community. They are concerned about the impact the community has on them. They are reacting not to the demand for public space but to private goods. BIDs have an opposite perspective and are highly concerned with their impact on the community because BIDs are the community. Again, unlike the suburban mall, BIDs are comprised not only of invested businesses but also of residences of invested people. An improvement in the BID is an improvement in the community. This cannot be said for a suburban mall. The same dynamic occurs with big boxes, such as Walmart and Home Depot, that have great community impact but often little interest in that impact. Therefore, the impact can cause difficulties rather than opportunity for the host community. We would not describe suburban malls as community development projects; they are commercial redevelopment projects. Future research is needed to examine BID communities as social/economic networks.

In the case of BIDs, PPPs, which often are stigmatized as privatization efforts that derail democratic process in favor of purported efficiency, instead more accurately act as public orientation devices. An awkward term is publicization, which describes a process of and movement towards government. A more accurate description of publicization is the democratization of collective market economies.

The phenomenon of publicization progressed since the 1970s, as much from the efforts to decentralize government as to develop cooperative business management techniques to compete in every growing, mobile, and local economy that is challenged by globalization. The lack of organized management in downtowns is often overlooked as a significant culprit for the downtown's demise. By using the organized management techniques developed in suburban malls, downtown business communities can also compete in modern economies.

Traditional public administrators do not manage suburban malls and, in the past, they did not manage the downtown business community. Business people managed downtown business environments and often held public office. But this changed with suburban malls and strip shopping centers, leading to a fragmentation of business leadership not easily resolved without public intervention.

This intervention, however, appears to have caused a long-term change in public policy. Public intervention into business communities was not and still is not readily understood. Business people had other staging opportunities (malls) as they chased customers who exited urban areas for suburbia in unprecedented numbers. Business people as residents did the same thing. Many left downtowns, both commercially and residentially, further eroding management capacity and political presence.

From a public management perspective, we can deduce that the demise of downtowns is due less to the retail competition of suburbia than it is to a hesitation in adopting a new management style evidenced by the creation of shopping/entertainment/restaurant-style malls, as well as by the loss of political power in the downtown business community. Both are management disasters. Today, for example, a local COC has remarkably little or no political power compared to the pre-1960s, and to have any political power, many have become regional and big business oriented. This excludes them from supporting competitive business community strategies (like BIDs) because it pits their small business constituencies against each other in a manner that may discourage membership. Poorly examined in much of the research, BIDs act to restore a resipiscent political viability to local downtown businesses by providing an avenue for collective action, increased social capital, and public legitimization at the local level where it is needed. Simply put, BIDs bring the knowledge, expertise, and financial resources of the business community back into the community development process and significantly restore a business-led collective political package.

It is obvious that if a vital segment of the community, the local business person, was denied political access, important resources will be lost. The lesson to be learned from BIDs is that community development and revitalization must be comprehensive, not simply project oriented. And community development must be politically comprehensive in a manner that provides local businesses with real access to the political process of governance. BIDs provide some valuable proof that citizen-driven action is less effective when it is exclusionary, particularly when a vital section of the community, such as the business community, is excluded. The private sector and everyday citizens possess talents and resources that can be accessed to stimulate public processes to tackle the big issues—social and economic equity, economic survival, and innovation in communities—not as offshoots or arm's length transactions, often ascribed to privatization, but as an infusion into real governance.

The private sector counterpart of a BID manager is a suburban mall manager. The management style of the latter is, of necessity, an autocracy, while a BID manager operates within a democracy. This is the chief distinction between most public and private sector activities and it seems to be true in the revitalization of our traditional downtowns. Whereas, suburban mall technology has developed the way many modern retail businesses relate to one another, BIDs, by using a similar but more democratic cooperative management technology, are changing the way many downtown business communities operate. Malls rely on principal/agent contracts but BIDs initiate a horizontal and evolving set of agreements among area businesses, the community at large, and the local government.

Older urban and traditional localized downtown markets must compete within their regional area but without automatically sustaining and managing mutual interests. BIDs re-examine the localization of mutual interests, while adopting the retail commercial cooperative technology utilized by suburban malls to establish supportive but self-reliant service-sector economic generators.

Service-sector economies are based on convenience and area malls excel at maximizing convenience to serve a mobile society. However, this same convenience and ease can become monotonous. Suburban malls excel in standardization and, consequently, offer less variety than downtowns. Traditional downtowns excel at diversity and niche opportunities, but suffer from the neglect of creative management of urban landscapes, which gives them the appearance of being harder to access comfortably. However, there are similarities in that both urban and traditional business areas use quality of life issues to define success. Standards of safety, cleanliness, accessibility, and design are basic requirements of both suburban and urban areas with suburban areas now setting the standard. Urban and traditional downtown areas that cannot attract suburban customers either fail, reflect the worst aspects of slum and blight, or are extremely marginalized.

The Role of the BID Manager as Entrepreneurial Public Administrator: The Practice of Downtown and Community Revitalization

If we sum up the literature, we are compelled to determine a new understanding of how the private sector becomes part of the public sector without deteriorating it, and, in fact, enhances both sectors. In this chapter a theory and model of community development is discussed that addresses the synergistic concepts of public entrepreneurship and social capital as they function in the community development behavior for which PPPs strive.

No longer directly part of traditional government, as a result of a series of suburbanization, decentralization, and privatization movements since the 1950s, BIDs have ventured into the management of various economic development, educational, social, and housing needs and information dissemination. The idea that public administrators are functionaries of political structures or private entrepreneurs seeking asylum in government has changed dramatically when we consider the role of BID managers.

BIDs shift government towards a truly entrepreneurial public administrator, merging strategic community planning and policy and cooperative management services with market forces. BIDs, along with government, address the organizational problems created when traditional market approaches fail to function adequately. BIDs resurrect the local market by public intervention that rebuilds essential community partnerships. BID intervention has remarkably useful entrepreneurial characteristics, demonstrating that public administration can utilize relatively normal processes of entrepreneurship to energize social capability, reconstruct social/economic/political networks, and infuse public process with innovation and creativity. However, for public administration to capture and sustain this energy, it must establish formal public processes, resulting in the type of formal institutions that BIDs represent. We can also speculate that the demise of a BID amounts to the deterioration of the PPP, which has previously sustained the revitalization network. In both sectors, the *entrepreneurial leap* (Schumpeter, 1934) is taken when the equilibrium in society becomes unbalanced, but not disruptive (Schneider and Teske, 1992). The entrepreneur exploits the imbalance; the "disequilibrium conundrum" (Schneider and Teske, 1992, p. 739) by identifying niche opportunities that tend towards equilibrium in society (see Figure A.1).

Entrepreneurship (in general) creates ongoing innovative values systems (Weber, 1904; Mort, Weerawardena, and Carnegie, 2002) and the organizations that manage them. In a democratic system, disequilibrium is the norm with "punctuated equilibrium" (Schneider and Teske, 1992, p. 739) events, therefore, in a viable democracy, a contextual pro-entrepreneurial bias is available in both public and private sectors. Hypothetically, we find that entrepreneurship flourishes at similar rates in both public and private sectors when imbalance, but not disruption, occurs in a society. Imbalance can be understood as a shift in values or an understanding of existing values, thereby, redefining what is valuable to a society. Entrepreneurship acts to transform our understanding of what is valuable. A value construct achieves social legitimacy in this public process. The role of entrepreneurship is to transform the personal into the public (what is valuable to me into what is valuable to us), the future into the present (vision into reality), the individual into the community (child into adult), the rational into the transrational (survival into sustainability), and to exceed normative limitations (creativity). Entrepreneurship requires collective action and the entrepreneur requires a community to succeed.

Weber (1904) wrote about the influence of the Protestant work ethic on entrepreneurial spirit. This was a particularly American understanding of values but, nonetheless, illustrated that a value system could be exploited in innovative ways if the culture supported a sense of economic pragmatism. Pragmatism appears to be a key value-component of the modern middle class. This is the

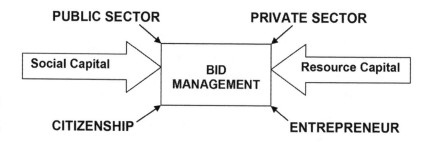

FIGURE A.1 BID Management

Calvinist concept; it is understood that hard work pays off by supplying solutions to society's needs. This is further enunciated by understanding that hard work creates a demand by inventing or recognizing a societal opportunity that can bring an even bigger payoff.

The chief difference between the private and the public entrepreneur was not the desire for risk taking (Carland, Hoy, Boulton, and Carland, 1984), since it was arguably prevalent in many non-innovative activities and true in every endeavor due to an endemic limitation of knowledge and information. The difference has to do with acting on creative desires, which insists that a creative opportunity is first recognized within the societal environment and requires societal reconfiguration to succeed.

In this way, we can see that entrepreneurship is foremost a public phenomenon that allows for individual avenues of organizational (not self-centered) leadership. A public entrepreneur was "a person who creates or profoundly elaborates a public organization" (Lewis, 1984, p. 11), and this required the compliance, if not intention, of the community at large. Entrepreneurship is a social function of groups inclined or desirous of change and new value creation. The public entrepreneur, due to circumstance and traits well documented by entrepreneurial research, becomes the leader of the change action in a community. Ironically, due to the nature of media, the individual action often appears most public, while the context that encourages entrepreneurship, as a causal discourse (Berger and Luckman, 1966; Foucault, 1972), remains in the background.

This causal discourse encourages entrepreneurship at its most fundamental to be "the creation of new organizations" (Thornton, 1999, p. 20), thereby, promoting the context-dependent and collective intention of the discourse. Entrepreneurial behavior might be better measured by examining the conditions for entrepreneurship, change, and a community's desire for new value creation. The entrepreneur as rugged individualist is often mistaken as the causal element of innovation, consequently entrepreneurship; whereas, research indicates that the desire for expanded communal value may be what is driving the need for change. An entrepreneur, both private and public, may be the individual who *pops* up in an entrepreneurial environment. Not unlike popcorn, an entrepreneur, seemingly motivated by profit, may be more encouraged to be the innovator in society and pop due to a number of trait factors that make that person the most optimal member of society to act, rather than persons expressing a purely personal impulse. This does not diminish the role of the entrepreneur but is simply a description of the conditions of entrepreneurship, which are necessary to gain a clear understanding of the entrepreneurial event and its processes, i.e. context matters (Weber, 1904; Guth and Ginsberg, 1990; Schneider and Teske, 1992; Thornton, 1999; Mort, Weerawardena, and Carnegie, 2002). Again, entrepreneurship is not purely a business or private sector characteristic, although it may be associated as an economic aspect of human potential that is initiated by a confluence of environmental factors acting on a ready and willing subject.

Due to its contextual nature, entrepreneurship can be seen as a driving force of political/economic change in society as it harnesses the charismatic aspects of strategic leadership (Mort, Weerawardena, and Carnegie, 2002) in divulging human potential. This leadership, more than any other trait, defines the individual and group entrepreneur and appears reliant on the opportunities society presents in the pursuit of collective opportunity growth and value development. Entrepreneurship is distinguished by its direction. It points to a possible future rather than simply reconciling the past. The entrepreneur as leader is forward thinking, where change is a new construct rather than only a refinement, and considered successful if the forward vision escapes the stasis of established rationality without losing the success of the past. In this way, entrepreneurship, in general, is the practice of social transformation, in which new elements of social action are created and sustained and, as a result, new products, processes, and possibilities can be achieved.

Contrary to the normative individual hero worshipping that characterizes much of economic literature, every entrepreneur must operate in a public entrepreneurial milieu. The distinction is not whether one is a public entrepreneur because all entrepreneurs must succeed in a public setting. The distinction is whether one is a private entrepreneur, which in our society may be simply another term for capitalist. This too does not diminish private entrepreneurial intention but points to its defining characteristics. The private sector offers financial capital growth opportunities, while the public sector enhances these opportunities through the collective actions of society.

To this extent, public entrepreneurship must be considered a redundant term as all entrepreneurial behavior is public in nature. In a sense, public entrepreneurship may be considered as emphasizing the obvious role of leadership in society, both financially and socially/politically. It is also an expansive term that helps illuminate the possibilities of other viable sources of capital than financial, such as: social, political, knowledge, information, culture, and spirit. In our society, entrepreneurship and leadership are mutually inclusive and synonymous. At its heart, entrepreneurship elicits a sense of adventure and competence in the pursuit of new definitions and abilities of a society and opportunities for members of that society to express themselves in a community building function. Entrepreneurship is not a separate activity from social process but a causal factor in society.

Trust and cooperation aspects of social capital (Fukuyama, 1995; Coleman, 1998), in relation to entrepreneurship (Lewis, 1975; Schneider and Teske, 1992), largely define the success of BIDs as public community and economic development organizations. This is substantiated by applying O'Connell's (2005) "field of accountability" and Dubnick's (2005) "promises of accountability" to the examination of BID legislative intentions associated with the creation of trust networks, social capital, and organizational leadership affiliated with public entrepreneurship.

Along with the level of trust, one of the measurements of social capital in this research was the number of clubs and meetings in which the BID managers and members of the BID Board of Directors participated. It was usual to expect that people who were more trustful would go to meetings and join more groups. Also, it was understandable that these people would be more willing to associate with others and be willing to work with those people. We should look at trust as not just a symptom of one's good nature but as a social skill, therefore, strong indicators of trust might indicate higher social skills. If trust were a skill, then it can be taught. Social capital is obviously more complex than other variables because it describes the complex subject of social behavior. In determining what makes an entrepreneur a public or social entrepreneur, future public administration research might look further into trust as it correlates with entrepreneurship because it seems to be one of the strongest indicators of public entrepreneurship. Social capital may be a result of other factors as well but this research suggested that it was associated with entrepreneurship in general and public/social entrepreneurship in particular. This may be because entrepreneurship works to transform and discover new and useful aspects of public value. It follows that public entrepreneurship discovers and transforms new and useful aspects of public value. As the exchangeability of value is perceived as capital, the exchange of something of public or social value would create social capital.

"The BID approach is not only about doing things differently, it is also about implementing innovative theories and concepts" (Mitchell, 2008, p. 46). Distinguishing between the processes and management of community development is a normative role for public administration practitioners. The practice of downtown revitalization in BIDs, with its strong level of entrepreneurship, reflects a new pragmatism in public administration. Rational economic theory assumes that disagreement (distrust) is at the heart of human motivation; whereas, transrational socio-economic theory begins with agreements (trust) as the basis of human motivation (Wilber, 2000). This research recommended the following model of strategic community development. The model distinguishes agreement-oriented strategic partnership governance processes from principal-agent processes that assume a disagreement-orientation. This model addresses forward thinking strategic community development processes. As an agreement-oriented process, the model relies on professional organizational skills, social capital, and the committed networks that sustain that capital, not maintain a status quo.

Partnership Model: Agreement–Management–Commitment–Accountability

1. **Agreement** (on identification, goals, values, and assets common to all). Successful collaborations work on agreements, not disagreements. (These agreements are the values and assets of the partnership.)
2. **Management** (having professional and specified management capability that manages the agreement). Agreements are maintained through professional management; therefore, management is the key to successful collaboration.

3. **Commitment** (the reliable and sufficient source of funds/resources). Success is achieved when collaborations, as partnerships, are committed to accomplishing their agreements. Commitment is an absolute and equitable contribution of resources by stakeholders in an ongoing manner; that is, over time. This enables accountability.

4. **Accountability** is based on a Promise/Performance Axiom: *What By When.* (i.e. what will be accomplished and by when it will be accomplished; both should be as articulate and exact as possible). Accountability is always a public phenomenon. As collaboration generates partnerships, accountability organizes the results of the partnership. Partnerships provide a big enough accountability for transformation. The Promise/Performance Axiom that is the dialectic of Accountability, literally what the partnership can be counted on, states that it requires a promise to accurately perform, i.e. there is no truly meaningful performance without a promise. A promise states *what* will be done (agreement) and *by when* (management): a promise, therefore, has an articulate *What By When* formula. It's a statement of integrity that provides agreed upon and measurable standards for performance and unites individuals to accomplish goals. The promise does not fix past problems, but is designed to envision a clear and real future for the partnership to act and measure success. Without it we are dealing in fantasy and magic rather than reality and understanding.

Figure A.2 suggests that the level of trust can be evaluated at each stage. Low trust provides, at best, short-term objectives, low capability, and low potential. High trust provides long-term, ongoing, high skill, and highly desired potential. Low trust at the agreement stage results in instant gratification and output orientation; high trust results in real change and an outcome orientation. Low trust at the management level results in ad hoc or by proxy management; high trust results in professionalism, sustainability, and perceived real performance.

Low trust at the commitment level results in deception, compromise, and floundering; high levels result in completion, transformation, investment, and sustainability.

The model identifies the organizational components necessary to move ahead in a comprehensive community development process. When the energy to move ahead is lost in a community, the community's attitude is often one of managing its disagreements rather than its agreements. We can expect to find little evidence of entrepreneurship because disagreements imply that a direction for the community has not been obtained or desired. On the other hand, communities that put their plans into action and achieve results have discovered something important. They discovered agreements and how to manage them with a sustainable commitment to reach a well-defined objective. A commitment is credible, not because politicians are motivated to keep it, but because institutional or structural arrangements compel their compliance.

	LOW	(TRUST)	HIGH
AGREEMENT	Instant gratification Output-only orientation Adversarial. Dichotomous		Real change Outcome orientation Partnership
MANAGEMENT	Ad hoc/proxy Manipulative Exclusive Miscommunication		Professionalism Transparent Inclusive Communication
COMMITMENT	Deception Compromise Incompletion Short-lived Disagreement Confusion		Commitment Collaboration Action Longevity Promises Clarity
ACCOUNTABLITY	Low-performance No measurement		High-performance Balanced measurement

FIGURE A.2 Agreement–Management–Commitment–Accountability Trust Matrix

Where we put our attention has a lot to do with perceptions and attitudes but also extends to an ability to get something accomplished. When attention is on disagreement, exclusionary experiences occur that, at best, result in a compromised effort rather than cooperative progress towards identified and needed goals. The *attention* of disagreements is on the individual, or better said on *me*. Disagreements are distinguished by the presence of competing monologues.

Agreements are different. As Searle (1995), discussing how social reality was constructed, pointed out, "There are portions of the real world, objective facts in the world that are only facts by human agreement" (pp. 1–2). If our attention is focused on community agreements, the community in which all the individuals or subgroups participate, an inclusionary experience occurs. Disagreements are concerned with an individual's, or a single group's, idea of self. Miller, Justice, and Illiash (2002) observed that, "the more humans agree, the more institutional facts they accept, and, therefore, the more reality humans perceive" (p. 95). Agreements broker a broader concern about how the entire community envisions itself; consequently, what it is willing to support. This vision is not arrived at by compromise, because compromise implies giving something up. The vision is arrived at through the dialogue and the building of consensus, which implies expanding, embracing, and growing capabilities aligned with transformation and entrepreneurship.

Disagreements and agreements are not accidental. They are maintained. To endure over time, each has to be maintained by a *structure* in the community that manages them. Sometimes, the structures are apparent and institutionalized and sometimes they are less visible. Nonetheless, it is not just the matter of agreeing or disagreeing or only the focus of our attitudes or attention that makes things happen or not happen. What matters is the *structure* that manages what we experience.

This still does not completely explain why something progresses or why something is accomplished or effective over time. There can be agreement and management, but there is one additional ingredient necessary to obtain positive results. That ingredient is commitment. Many people say that it is money or other capital resources. And they are correct. This is because money and commitment are inseparable concepts in our culture. Therefore, where we put our money and other resources is directly linked to the commitment we have to make things happen. This is something widely known in public administration, which implies that commitment is largely a public not private matter, furthering the public intention of PPPs.

Figure A.3 addresses BIDs as a unique accountability field that combines both economic and social aspects of community development.

The figure suggests three hypotheses:

1. If social capital and entrepreneurship were linked, then the BID will be successful.
2. If BIDs are successful when they have highly functioning social capital, then BIDs with low social capital will be considered less successful.
3. If BIDs are considered successful when they have highly functioning entrepreneurship, then they will be considered unsuccessful when they do not have highly functioning entrepreneurship.

Community organization is an evolving and motivating factor in governance. This study suggests that BID managers were motivated towards the discernment and articulation of community identification, organization, and building. This begins with trust in government. Trust begins at the community level but does not stop at participation. It continues to establish citizen-driven organizations with real authority and independent funding capacities to address the desires, needs, and future visions of the community.

The politics/administration dichotomy may be the anvil and hammer of the field of public administration. Forged from this dichotomy, the determination to distinguish private values from public values seesawed through the 20th and early 21st centuries. Within this ongoing debate, BIDs represent a third door of public administration built on PPP management. This third door is depicted by pragmatic leadership, exemplifying virtues of the state as less the product of the principal and more the actions of the agent. This allows horizontal compliance between the nodes and modes of networks with its highest aim being a working partnership.

	LOW Social Capital	HIGH Social Capital
LOW Entrepreneurship	Management of disagreements, highly unsuccessful socially and economically. **(Chaos)**	Management of agreements, successful socially, but less successful economically. **(Social Non-Profit Model)**
HIGH Entrepreneurship	Business and residential discord. Management of disagreements. Less successful socially, but more successful economically. **(Business Model)**	Business and residential affinity. Management of agreements. Successful both economically and socially. **(BID Model)**

FIGURE A.3 Agreement vs Disagreement: Social Capital and Entrepreneurship Impacts

Adversarial dichotomies are arguably the products of scientism that seeks truth in a truth/falsehood dualism. This dichotomy causes an either/or scenario, which does not devalue the uncertainty of the muddy and muddling democratic processes, nor does it serve democratic processes well. By flattening out all choice to a binary static, dualism may produce a presumptive and fixed balance but does not achieve equilibrium that is subject to organic and changing circumstances. Dualism is effective in establishing logical systems in the process of storing and retrieving data. This is a necessary capability that at best offers access to information but at its worst becomes a dictator of small truths that cannot solve important issues. A two-dimensional world often threatens to become an inescapable one-dimensional world that succeeds only by dispensing its alternative by demonizing the alternative's best attributes. In the latter part of the 20th century, the notion that government is a problem rather than a solution best exemplifies this one-dimensional limitation. Governmental inferiority to the free market has not been proven. Problems become problems through a variety of shifting and often misunderstood occurrences. Government and the private sector can, in most cases, work together to find the best solutions.

BIDs represent a new paradigm in public administration that may satisfy entrepreneurial needs. The entrepreneurial phenomenon that BIDs represent exposes a repressed need for innovative and creative social and economic expression. This paradigm is notable due to its use of sustainable partnerships and breakdown of traditional public–private dichotomies. This is conducted with some degree of courage as it operates in the multiple dimensions of a varied and deeply expressive democratic society. In this paradigm, the realm of public services is the protectorate of a professional public management entrepreneur.

Future research on entrepreneurship must address the pragmatic nature of entrepreneurship by including independent variables of production and performance. Entrepreneurs are noticeable because they do things and enroll others in a production/performance quest. The entrepreneur is causal to human production and does things that engage others, while the everyday citizen is caught up in the doing process caused by the entrepreneur. There are the entrepreneurial people who cause things to be done and a great majority who are in a doing process because of another's doing.

Achieving participation required political structures, which allowed for it, and which permitted follow-through and implementation (Pressman and Wildavsky, 1973). This participation is brought about by decentralizing governance and public services so they can be applied at community levels of management. A shift in policy from centralized to more decentralized is required, as well as a shift from vertical to more horizontal political systems. Policy defines an administrative structure to sustain not only its intent but also its application. Control of policy solely by the elected is a poor democracy, therefore a poor system, particularly in an emerging, informed, entrepreneurial, better educated populace, which presumably describes the modern world.

The conflict between modern information-based, information egalitarianism, and pre-modern, essentially feudal, information-restricted, elitist societies characterizes the social/economic relationships we have inherited. This can result in political conflict between an emerging informed entrepreneurial citizenry, today's middle class, and the older, feudal/paternalistic model. The function of a bureaucracy is related to the perceived needs of the citizenry. In each system, both old and new, the perceived needs are often very different. New systems have emerged to meet the needs that have to do with improving a newly defined quality of life. If Maslow's (1943) hierarchy of needs holds true, a shift to higher levels of need must then shift social relationships built around those needs. Consequently, government will shift to meet this new level of need, which can cause a shift in power in a society.

BID managers act on the definition and redefinition of established power norms, sourced by the interpretation of inclusion and exclusion in real community networking processes. Power transfers can occur only when established institutions facilitate and institutionalize the emerging power structure. A business improvement decentralizes a source of governmental power, affording more localized and direct participation in the planning and provision of public services. It resolves ineffective partitions within a society by redefining the community and sets up a bureaucratic system of accountabilities, responsibilities, and procedures designed to sustain the community and maintain its new authority.

BIDs, like many special districts, are an increasingly decentralized practice, merging the political will of government with a commitment to participate in a measure of governance by its business community. The purpose of a BID is to provide statutory authority for municipalities to create publicly financed PPPs *and* to designate business-led non-profit corporations or commissions as their management. Consequently, BIDs are part of continuous progressive movement in government and public administration to: (a) keep politics *per se* out of the implementation of business/government community revitalization efforts, rather than placing them in the hands of business management and community development professionals; and (b) support increased community participation and investment. BIDs provide a balance between centralized government growth (publicization) and entrepreneurial expertise (privatization) by allowing for a legal PPP.

This partnership creates a hybrid of public management that unites management with entrepreneurship and financial with social capital. Ideally, the formal power of governance that a BID offers will result in a private investment of funds and resources for entrepreneurial purposes, while legitimizing collective action. Instead of shareholders, stakeholders emerge with a real stake in achieving communal goals rather than being limited solely to risk for personal gain.

Establishment of a BID is the recognition by government that it cannot provide everything to all its constituencies, while emphasizing that there is a place for the political sphere to serve special interests. However, this comes about by establishing real political structures that promote self-sufficiency, while encouraging public accountability. In promoting self-sufficiency, the politics of the municipal government are aimed at establishing structures that are strengthened by public authority. Therefore, the goal is the emerging PPP that enhances municipal capacity and increased private investment.

According to BID managers in the survey, BIDs were designed to harness local community interests through a shared power system that directly addressed the conversion of private interests into public benefits. Community interests reflect social as well as economic capability. State BID statutes permit municipalities to create BIDs as a form of public authority. BIDs are a compelling prospect for any government as they persuade some of the leading individuals in a community to participate in an extended process of governance. A BID requires the willingness to work together and interact based on what is good for the community as a whole. It represents the *mining* of the community's knowledge, experience, goodwill, creativity, and commitment to aspire to higher degrees of excellence. This is an apt description of the foundations of community revitalization. BIDs operate by maximizing the inherent potential of a community and by providing a capable, dignified, and respectful means of tapping into and maintaining community resources required to meet current economic demands. It has been demonstrated that utilizing these community resources through a BID structure can increase economic capacity and accelerate success. Success is linked to effective networks, backed by larger governmental structures and maintained by appropriate standards.

The research suggested that a BID's community development capacity relied on the integration of four defining elements:

1. support of entrepreneurial asset-based planning and management rather than "fix-it" project-based solutions;
2. "Mining Social Capital" by providing organizational structures that encourage social investment and network competence;
3. establishing economically oriented, community-based organizations with bona fide partnership capability and legal institutionalized authority; and
4. employing an ongoing interdependent, social and team building learning and implementation process.

In light of the BID phenomenon, public administration is compelled to examine the practices of leadership development and community organizing in the articulation of PPPs that sustain communities. Research will have to step outside the doors of traditional government and discern the important connections of government to the successful development of communities. For transformation in government's relationship to business development, there must be a transrational imperative in which the individual (the independent entrepreneur) takes on the attributes of increasingly responsible public roles, rather than simply applying private sector techniques.

The call for comparative research on BIDs is desirable and necessary but this is true in every aspect of economic development. It would be helpful to determine if an economy improved by examining basic standards, such as vacancy rates, job creation, sales and property tax collection rates, private sector investment, customer satisfaction surveys, property valuation and tax assessments ratios, business success rates, and market identity. However, what may be more important in measuring community improvement is social investment, upgraded infrastructure, support from the community, effective PPP, residential investment, sense of identity and purpose, established functioning community organizations, diversity, political activity, and a sense of being safe and protected (see Figure A.4). Quantitative and qualitative research studies are able to measure quality of life standards. These standards differentiate private administration from public administration. The differentiation is not the desire for quality of life but the intention directed to the individual or the community to be inclusive. As Bozeman (1987) pointed out "all organizations are public" (p. xi). This also has us consider that all individuals are public beings. Yet, we are encouraged to operate as self-centered individuals with the premise that we are not as responsible for others as we can be, nor are our public activities profitable.

It may be time to recognize that the public administration professional practices the art of community as well as the science of politics and of directing his or her intention to the public good. Public administration might be well served if it were considered a craft as much as a discipline. A BID manager, as public

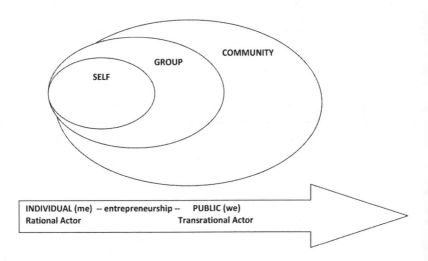

FIGURE A.4 Range of Public Sector Transformation

administration professional, does not ignore what is valuable in and about a community but promotes these assets. When we examine BIDs, it appears that public administration, not unlike entrepreneurship, is as much an art as a science. Most BID managers might attest to that statement as they attempt to garner cooperation from their Boards of Directors and municipalities. Yet, if there is an art to public administration, and entrepreneurship is part of it, it would be the art of community development. This craft is involved in the creation and occurrence of not only the sense, but the practice of community development. If there is an art of community development, then consideration of the role of BIDs suggests a direction for further public administration research. The role of BIDs may help define the practice of modern public administration as being informed as much by the art of community development as by the science of politics.

★★★

This study explores the public nature of private enterprises. However, much of our society's discourse on this subject is skewed towards concern regarding private sector intrusions into the public arena, wanted and seemingly unwanted. A shift is occurring where once business technology migrated to government, now public administration technology is migrating into the private sector.

In America, confluence of democratic and free market parables have created an unsubstantiated belief in the power of the private sector to be more effective, efficient, and less tainted by politics than government. Casual observation tells us that this is not so, certainly not in every situation. This belief rests on an improperly applied either/or dichotomy and is, for the most part, a questionable political tactic with far reaching, often damaging, consequences. This chapter strongly suggests that public and private aspects of human behavior work together in a social dance, all, not just part, of the time.

The future of public administration can no longer be contained behind the walls of formal government. In the past century, private sector business functions were meritorious in solving the emergence of global impacts. In addition, an evolving middle class defined political will marked by unprecedented consumerism (of everything from knowledge to materials), dominating political and social change. This phenomenon, in the late 20th and early 21st centuries, cannot be underestimated and has begun to shift global power to Asia, which previously lagged behind. Eventually, this movement will catch up in Africa and Latin America.

For public administration, this phenomenon indicates that government and governance processes are shifting. The acceleration of PPPs, like BIDs, is an example of informal government that is more horizontally networked and less vertically controlled. Of course, formal government will not go away and evidence points to an enhancement of civic responsibility, local management capacity, and sustainable planning by these partnerships. Centralized hierarchical government is not the progressive element in society that it once was. Also, private sector technologies (business administration) were and still are necessary in public realms. However, today the technologies of public administration are the skills required for successful private sector operations.

As markets are sustained by civil society, local and global companies must effectively participate in public processes, perceive social impacts, and generate aspects of civil society. The skill set to do this is derived from public administration. It integrates and reinterprets private sector perspectives into the management of public concerns. Consequently, we can expect to find an increasing number of public administrators working for private companies, defining and creating public solutions to real life commercial impacts. This is not a completely new phenomenon but it is a new requirement for the private sector. Therefore, public managers must be trained in capacities that identify a hybrid of public/private technologies that will be desired by private companies furthering a publicization of private sector behaviour. BIDs point to how this can be accomplished.

References

Berg, B. L. (2004) *Qualitative research methods*. Boston, MA: Pearson Education, Inc.

Berger, P. L., & Luckmann, T. (1966) *The social construction of reality: A treatise in the sociology of knowledge*. New York: Anchor Books.

Bozeman, B. (1987) *All organizations are public: Comparing public and private organizations*. San Francisco, CA: Jossey-Bass.

Carland, J. W., Hoy, F., Boulton, W. R., & Carland, J. A. C. (1984) Differentiating entrepreneurs from small business owners. *The Academy of Management Review*, 9(2), April: 354–359.

Carton, R. B., Hofer, C. W., & Meeks, M. D. (1998) *The entrepreneur and entrepreneurship: Operational definitions of their role in society.* Athens: University of Georgia, Terry School of Business.

Coleman, J. S. (1998) Social capital in the creation of human capital. *American Journal of Sociology,* 94: 95–120.

Creswell, J. W. (2003) *Research design: Qualitative, quantitative, and mixed methods approaches.* Thousand Oaks, CA: Sage Publications.

Dubnick, M. (2005) Accountability and the promise of performance. *Public Performance & Management Review,* 28(3), March: 376–417.

Foucault, M. (1972) *The archaeology of knowledge.* New York: Routledge.

Fukuyama, F. (1995) *Trust: The social virtues and the creation of prosperity.* New York: Free Press.

Guth, W. D., & Ginsberg, A. (1990) Corporate entrepreneurship. *Strategic Management Journal,* 11: 5–15.

Guttman, L. (1950) The basis for scalogram analysis. In S. A. Stouffer et al. *Measurement and prediction. The American Soldier Vol. IV.* New York: Wiley.

Kruskal, W., & Wallis, W. (1952) Use of ranks in one-criterion variance analysis. *Journal of the American Statistical Association,* 47(260): 583–621.

Lewis, E. (1984) *Public entrepreneurship: Toward a theory of bureaucratic political power.* Bloomington, IN: Indiana University Press.

Likert, R. (1932) A technique for the measurement of attitudes. *Archives of Psychology,* 140: 1–55.

Miller, G., Justice, J., & Illiash, I. (2002) Practice as interpretation. In A. Kahn & W. Hildreth (eds), *Budget theory* (pp. 89–114). Newark, NJ: Rutgers University.

Mitchell, J. (2008) *Business improvement districts and the shape of American cities.* Albany, NY: State University of New York Press.

Mort, G. S., Weerawardena, J., & Carnegie, K. (2002) Social entrepreneurship: Towards conceptualization. *International Journal of Nonprofit and Voluntary Sector Marketing,* 8(1), July: 76–88.

O'Connell, L. (2005) Program accountability as an emergent property: The role of stakeholders in a program's field. *Public Administration Review,* 65(1), January/February: 85–93.

Pressman, J. L., & Wildavsky, A. (1973) *Implementation.* Berkeley, CA: University of California Press.

Schneider, M., & Teske, P. (1992) Toward a theory of the political entrepreneur: Evidence from local government. *The American Political Science Review,* 86(3), September: 737–747.

Schumpeter, J. A. (1934) *The theory of economic development.* Cambridge, MA: Harvard Press.

Searle, J. R. (1995) *The construction of social reality.* New York: Free Press.

Thornton, P. H. (1999) The sociology of entrepreneurship. *Annual Review of Sociology,* 25: 19–46.

Thurstone, L. L. (1928) Attitudes can be measured. *American Journal of Sociology,* 33: 529–554.

Weber, M. (1904) The objectivity of the sociological and social-political knowledge, *Archiv für Sozialwissenschaft und Sozialpolitik,* 19. Bd., Heft 1, S. 22–87.

Wilber, K. (2000) *Integral psychology.* Boston, MA: Shambhala Publications.

APPENDIX B

Board of Directors Manual for BIDs

BIDs represent powerful tools in urban development. BIDs represent a form of PPP between local government and the private business sector to foster revitalization and growth of commercial districts and downtowns. Special districts are established by local governments. Governance choices such as taxation levels, the bundle of services, the level of services, and management are determined by the PPP representing stakeholders from the district. Implementation is carried out typically either by staff or organizations under contract to the BID's governance board. In this way, business and property owners can choose to supplement governmental services or receive new services in a way they cannot through voluntary associations. Government gets resource capacity and local management that it could not get through traditional government processes. This is a powerful and effective tool for urban and community development, leadership, business development, and downtown revitalization. The PPP model that BIDs represent means that "someone" is responsible for our commercial districts. This merging of both private and public capabilities encourages entrepreneurship as well as organizational strengths and is a successful form of governance due to the professional management of these factors.

BIDs are a proven tool for downtown revitalization. BIDs have been established in the United States since 1975 and internationally since 1966. As BIDs continue to be successful, the model is enjoying extraordinary growth. A national (USA) survey in 1999 found 246 BIDs while a similar survey in 2007 found 739, and later in 2010 over 1,000 BIDs were found. It is not possible to know if the 1999 survey completely identified all of the BIDs in the country but it appears this model is experiencing extraordinary growth. This is in part due to how well the model adapts to diverse local needs. New York City has over 60 BIDs and this model is promoted by the Mayor as a way of addressing needs that government struggles to provide. North Carolina has 47, and New Jersey has over 85.

Performance measurement and evaluation let us know if we are fulfilling on our promises. The primary purpose of an MBD, particularly a BID, is to establish and maintain a functioning PPP to improve the district. In order to adequately measure such a partnership, both sides of the equation must be measured. The public side is often more qualitative and quality of life oriented. The private side is more quantitative and concerned about a return on investment (ROI).

Customer service, cooperative retail/commercial management, asset-based management, and destination marketing are the key directives of business district management. Therefore, assessing the capability of these components will tell us a lot about our skills, and the health of our organization and district. Each can be measured as to how well the quality of life (QOL) and ROI has been improved, and measurements that evaluate organizational and management capability (OMC).

Below are answers to typical questions regarding BIDs

1. **HOW IS THE BID CREATED?** The BID, itself, is created by ordinance supported by a community planning process. A community-based planning process establishes the extent, purpose, mission, and initial budget of the BID.
2. **HOW IS A BID TERMINATED?** The municipal government can rescind the BID ordinance in the same manner that it was created.
3. **WHO GOVERNS THE BID?** The BID is governed by a non-profit management corporation or commission designated in the enabling ordinance. It is often required that BIDs have at least one local elected official on this board as a voting member, and that the board be comprised of a majority of business and property owners of the BID.
4. **WHO DETERMINES THE BID BUDGET AFTER THE INITIAL BUDGET?** In cooperation with local government, the BID and its Board of Directors determine the budget of the BID, although the municipal government usually must approve it annually by resolution. Without this approval the BID does not have a source of assessment funding.
5. **WHAT SPECIFIC BENEFITS WILL I GET FROM A BID?** The services and benefits of a BID are summarized in the budget. Also, the BID will produce an annual report summarizing its services and accomplishments, and future plans. The key benefit a BID provides is a voice for the business community and the ability to professionally manage advocacy and services to improve business capability for the district as a whole.
6. **WHO COLLECTS THE BID ASSESSMENT?** One of the chief partnerships of a BID is with the local government, which usually acts as collector and disperser of the BID's funds. It is their responsibility to bill and collect the funds as a special assessment and insure that 100 percent of the funds are given to the BID.

7. **WHO PAYS THE BID ASSESSMENT?** Normally the property owner designated in the BID ordinance pays the BID assessment. Some BIDs have fees that properties or business pay.

8. **CAN THE BID ASSESSMENT BE PASSED THROUGH TO A TENANT?** Yes, if the law permits. If so, it allows a landlord to pass along public assessments like property taxes and special assessments to tenants unless otherwise specifically stipulated in the lease agreement.

9. **CAN THE BID HAVE FUNDRAISERS?** Yes, the non-profit management corporation or commission of the BID can raise additional funds and seek grants from public and private sources.

10. **DOES THE BID REPLACE ANY MUNICIPAL SERVICES?** No, a BID should only "enhance" not replace public services.

11. **DOES THE BID REPLACE URBAN ENTERPRISE PROGRAMS OR REDEVELOPMENT AUTHORITIES?** No, UEZ (Urban Enterprise Zone) programs, redevelopment authorities, and BIDs are designed to complement each other with the BID acting as a business constituency focused on improvements and customer satisfaction, and the UE on business recruitment and job creation. Both are intended to revitalize activity business in commercial, retail, and industrial areas.

12. **IS THERE MUNICIPAL OVERSIGHT OF THE BID?** Yes, there are usually four primary oversights: (1) ordinance oversight by the municipal council; (2) many BID statutes require at least one elected person to be a voting member of the BID Management Corporation's Board of Trustees; (3) the municipal council must approve the annual BID budget and be presented with an annual report; and (4) the BID must conduct an annual certified audit, which must be submitted to the municipal and state government.

The Role and Functions of the District Management Corporation/Commission and Board of Trustees: Strategy and Committee Structure

Introduction

A BID enables local property owners, merchants, and residents to plan for, manage, and finance supplemental services and improvements beyond those already provided by the local government. A BID is a formal PPP governed by the enabling municipal ordinance. The BID is funded by a "special public assessment" levied against properties within the district designated in the BID ordinance. The level of assessment is determined by the BID. Although the municipality collects the special assessment, it is not commingled with other municipality funds. It is held in a special account and returned to the BID in its entirety to be used for BID purposes. A non-profit corporation, usually called a

District Management Corporation or DMC, comprised of property owners, tenants, residents, other non-profits, and public officials, is responsible for administering the BID. The establishment of the BID is the decision of the local government in conjunction with property owners, merchants, and tenants who felt that additional services, improvement, and professional management of the business environment were needed.

Four Essential Elements to Sustaining an Effective BID Partnership

- **AGREEMENTS**—BIDs manage agreements not disagreements. These agreements become the strategy and the services the BID provides.
- **MANAGEMENT**—Professional management is the key to success. Volunteers generally do not manage BIDs.
- **COMMITMENT**—BIDs are committed to accomplishing their agreements, everyone in the BID contributes equitably, and BIDs have a guaranteed source of basic funds from a mandatory public assessment. This enables the BID to be fully accountable and no nonsense about fulfilling its promises.
- **ACCOUNTABILITY**—BIDs measure three aspects of the organization's PPP to determine success: the public side using quality of life (QOL) measurements; the private side using return on investment (ROI) measurements; and the partnership as a whole using organization and management capacity (OMC) measurements.

★ —Agreements–Management–Commitment–Accountability—★

The Role of the District Management Corporation/Commission (DMC)

The BID legislation identifies a District Management Corporation (DMC) as the body responsible for carrying out the day-to-day operation of the BID. The chief job of the DMC is to manage the PPP the BID represents. The DMC is a non-profit corporation with at least four classes of general membership represented by property owners, tenants of both commercial and residential space, and municipal officials. Other classes of membership may be created to accommodate additional interested individuals or organizations. A separate non-voting class may be created for local community boards or organizations, and other representatives may also be included as non-voting members.

The Role of the District Management Corporation/Commission (DMC) Board of Trustees

A Board of Directors represents the DMC, which functions as the main policy and decision-making entity for the BID, hires the manager, and with the manager determines the BID budget. In many BIDs, an Executive Committee, comprised of the elected officers of the Board, is authorized to conduct the day-to-day business of the DMC. In this capacity, the Board is responsible for the success or failure of the BID. The originating Board is appointed by the incorporators and sometimes ceremoniously by the municipal council. Individuals elected and selected to this Board should realize the seriousness of their obligation and approach membership on the Board with a sense of duty to the community. They should also be individuals who are willing to participate in BID activities and get involved in BID oversight and decision making. Although the Board is made up of a majority of business and property owners, every Board member's opinion should be given equal consideration in all matters. This notion is embodied in the "one person one vote" rule adopted by most Boards.

Creation of By-Laws: The first task of each Board is to prepare and approve a set of by-laws. The by-laws are the procedural rules governing the Board, with which the DMC cannot legally function. They describe the purpose of the corporation, composition of the Board of Directors, elections and terms of office of each director, appointment of officers, voting procedures, designation of special committees, proper protocol at meetings, etc.

Meetings: BIDs are often required to observe "Open Public Meetings or Public Records Acts." Even if this is not required, it is recommended that the BID adopt communication and record keeping practices similar to the Acts. Inclusiveness is the intention of a BID. The Board of Directors usually meets on a monthly basis. However, the number and frequency of meetings held each year are a function of management style and the activities of the BID. Some Boards prefer "hands-on" management, holding frequent meetings to assess ongoing activities and to confer with the district manager (Executive Director) on his or her progress on different matters. Other Boards prefer a management style that grants more independence to the district manager, meeting only occasionally to vote on certain issues and to receive periodic progress reports by the district manager.

The choice should not be arbitrary. Each Board's management style should be based on an evaluation of the needs of the BID in conjunction with the capabilities and needs of the district manager. The district manager is usually not a member of the Board, but attends all Board meetings and usually presents the agenda, and may be given a vote only in the case of a tie-breaking decision.

Executive Committee: Boards can choose to form an Executive Committee composed of the officers (Chair, Vice Chairs, Treasurer, and Secretary) and others such as special or sub-committee chairs. This committee may be given authority to approve expenditures and other proposals on a regular business cycle. One advantage of this system of management is that frequent meetings of the complete Board of Directors are not needed.

The Executive Committee submits progress reports to the full Board at meetings of the full Board, and special or sub-committees can meet at their convenience. The formation of the Executive Committee and its members must be approved by the full Board in accordance with the by-laws.

Attendance of Meetings: Achieving a Quorum: A quorum always refers to voting members of the Board of Directors. Whenever the Board of Directors or the Executive Committee meets, a quorum must be achieved before a vote can be taken on any issue. A quorum can be defined as a third or a majority of bona fide Board members or Executive Committee members (the precise definition is given in the by-laws). However, *a quorum can be any number deemed sufficient to represent the corporation* and conduct business efficiently. This rule makes it important that whoever is selected to serve on the Board, or Executive Committee, be willing to attend meetings regularly. A quorum is essential for conducting BID business and voting.

Occasionally, it may be necessary to remove someone from the Board of Directors or the Executive Committee. The by-laws must contain language describing the reasons and procedures for removal. Procedures for filling vacancies caused by removal, death, sickness, or resignation must also be included in the by-laws.

Committees: Committees, or task forces, should be formed whenever the need exists, and usually address an aspect of the approved budget. A committee is formed by a group of two or more Board members who volunteer to investigate a particular issue or project, monitor program progress, and/or oversee fiscal operations. Non-Board members can participate on a committee if Board approval is given. Committees can be formed for a variety of purposes including planning, budget and financial review, program audits, capital construction, nomination of new Board members, program design and review. The committee does not usually have the authority to make financial decisions based on their own vote, although sometimes the Board may temporarily confer that authority for the sake of expediency.

Budgets, Borrowing, and Purchasing

Approval of the Budget: Although January 1 is usually the official beginning of each budgetary (fiscal) year, the yearly agenda of the Board of Trustees officially begins in the previous year when the budget is proposed for the next year to the Board for their discussion and approval. This process should begin no later than June. The submission of the final budget and report to municipal government should be no later than October 1.

There may be instances where the Board desires to switch money in the middle of the year from one area of the budget to another. This is called a budget modification. A budget modification is possible as long as it has the approval of the Board or authorized committee and does not come from areas of the budget that have already been committed to contractual agreements. You do not need municipal council approval to move money amounts from one part of the budget to another.

Borrowing Capacity: BIDs are usually permitted to borrow funds as a line of credit from private lenders equal to their assessment budget for periods from government entities for that and longer periods, but do not have the capacity to obtain bonds. However, BIDs are also often allowed to receive and pay off a government bond or loan. The BID assessment necessary to pay off the bond will remain until the bond is paid off regardless of the existence of the BID budget or services.

Non-contractual Expenditures: Every DMC should establish an internal procedure for approving non-contractual expenditures. The procedure should be based on a dollar value criterion tailored to the particular needs of the DMC. The size of the budget, expected level of expenditures, frequency of expenditures, and Board member recommendations for specific controls must be taken into consideration.

The development of internal procedures should be a two-part process. First, the Board should determine the level of authority required to approve specific purchases of services and supplies. Second, the DMC needs to determine who has the authority to sign checks and to pay for those services and supplies.

As a first step, the Board should set an upper limit on each level of purchasing authority. Table B.1 illustrates how this is done.

Next, the Board should determine check-signing authority for different levels of expenditure. As an example, all checks might, as an example, require the signature of two Board members. In general, the Executive Director should not be a signatory of checks.

Contractual Expenditures: The BID's largest expenditures will be major service and improvement programs. These programs are usually provided under contractual agreements with private firms, although sometimes they are delivered directly by the DMC. **Note:** BIDs are not required to abide by the NJ Local Public Finance Law regulations. Yet, a thorough solicitation and approval process is required for general services, although professional contracts such as lawyers, accountants, and specialists may be approved by Board discretion.

For example: The contracting (subcontracting) process consists of a solicitation phase and an approval phase. Solicitation usually takes place during the time of the Board's approval of the budget and the start of the fiscal year. At that time, potential bidders for services and improvements stipulated by the newly approved budget are solicited. Solicitation can be made through a formal Request for Proposals.

Telephone solicitations or advertisements in a newspaper or electronic media may also be utilized. It is recommended that all solicitations be issued on a competitive basis to at least three responsible bidders. All correspondence should be documented and filed for future reference.

TABLE B.1

Purchasing Authority	Budget Amount
DMC Board of Directors	over $100,000
DMC Executive Committee	up to $100,000
BID Executive Director	up to $25,000

All bids for service leading to a contract must be submitted in writing on company letterhead. Cost must be itemized sufficiently so the DMC can properly evaluate the bid. Once bids are received they are evaluated and discussed by the appropriate person or committee. This person or committee then makes a recommendation for approval to the Board of Directors.

Every DMC should establish internal procedures for the approval of sub-contracts. These procedures should be similar to the approval system for non-contractual expenditures described in the previous section.

Subcontracts should also be signed by an officer (preferably the Treasurer or Chairperson) who has been given the authority to sign by an affirmative vote of the full Board. Once authorization has been given a letter should be drafted by the Board Secretary containing a simple statement describing the nature of the authorization and reporting the results of the full Board vote.

Annual Meetings

Annual Meetings of the District Management Corporation/Commission (DMC)

Once each year the Board of Trustees must hold a meeting of the DMC membership. This is called the Annual Meeting of the Corporation. In most cases the members of the DMC are the Board of Trustees, not all of the members of the BID. The annual meeting is usually held between September and December. Letters of invitation must be sent to every member of the BID Management Corporation as defined in the by-laws. Other public officials involved in the community, i.e. the mayor and municipal council, may also be invited. *The purpose of this meeting is to elect new Trustees for the Board.* Usually a year-end summary report is also given and acknowledgments are made. Many DMCs in their by-laws allow BID members in general to make nominations to the DMC. This is a recommended practice.

Several Items Are on the Agenda

- New Board members are elected at the annual meeting whenever the term of current Board members has expired. The length of term of the Trustees is stated in the by-laws. A nomination committee may solicit and announce nominations according to class, e.g. property owners, tenants, residents, certain business designations such as arcades, hotels, or restaurants, and those representing different parts of the district. Only DMC members present may vote in the election.
- An officer of the Board or the district manager briefly describes the purpose of the BID, past accomplishments, and plans for the future.

- It is recommended that the Annual Report, which must also be submitted to the municipality with the proposed budget no later than October 1, be presented at the Annual Meeting or at an earlier meeting of the full Board. The proposed fiscal year budget (contained in the Annual Report) should be an important component of this presentation even though the existing Board of Trustees is responsible for the approval of the budget.
- If desired, a special guest speaker may be invited to provide insight and direction of the BID. This could be a state expert, or local official who has some involvement with the BID program or anyone else who the Board feels has something interesting to communicate to the members of the DMC.

Annual Meeting of the Trustees

The Annual Meeting of the Trustees is different from the Annual Meeting of the Corporation. In December, or the following January, the Board of Trustees holds their Annual Meeting. **The primary purpose is to elect officers of the Corporation**, whereas the Annual Meeting of the Board is to elect Trustees and fill vacancies on the Board. **Note**, however, vacancies filled by appointment can happen at any full Board meeting.

Financial Reports

Each year the Board of Trustees must submit a financial report and certified audit to the municipality. On May 1 of each year the Board should be able submit a certified financial audit for the previous fiscal year.

The audit must be completed by a certified public accountant.

If deemed necessary, the second report is an Annual Financial Report to the Board and is due no later than December of each year. It contains several components. Most importantly it contains an itemized breakdown of revenue and expenses for four periods: actual income and expenses for the current fiscal year January 1 through September 30; projected income and expenses for the current fiscal year October 1 through December 31; actual income and expenses for October 1 through December 31 of the previous fiscal year; and the recommended budget for the upcoming fiscal year as approved by the Board of Directors. It also contains descriptions of service and improvement programs, a list of the board of directors, and the requested special assessment for the upcoming fiscal year. This report can be assembled by the Executive Director. Both reports should be presented to the Board by the Executive Director of the BID.

The Role of the District Manager or Professional Management

The DMC should hire at least one individual (or independent contracting management firm) on a substantive part-time and preferably full-time basis to manage the daily operation of the BID. In the case of smaller BIDs without a full administrative budget: (a) a part-time professional should be hired to manage specific projects, seek funding, and guide the Board; (b) management services can be purchased from another DMC; (c) two or more BIDs can pull resources together and hire management; or (d) a committee of the Board (Executive Committee) may have this function.

The district manager is responsible for all activities related to the BID and in that regard is important for the success of the BID.

The district manager reports to the Board of Trustees except in those situations where an organization has been subcontracted for administrative duties. In that situation, the management agreement usually states that the district manager, although hired with the approval of the DMC, is not an employee of the organization. Even in this situation, however, the DMC's Board of Trustees retains complete oversight over the activities of the BID. The district manager hires staff.

In practice, the district manager is the Executive Director/CEO and should be able to operate fairly independently consulting with the President of the DMC and Executive Committee for advice or instruction as needed. This has proven to be a successful arrangement made possible by the high caliber of individuals hired to be district managers/Executive Directors.

The district manager/Executive Director/CEO is responsible for a broad spectrum of tasks requiring skill in many different areas such as program development, project management, general record keeping, public relations, liaison activities, budget formulation, vendor selection, contract compliance, writing, and public speaking. The district manager must establish a good working relationship with the community groups, municipal government, and agencies.

Comprehensive Strategy

The Steering Committee discussed how to include the community survey input, achieve the vision, and provide comprehensive services that could be built on over the years. Six general service areas were identified and a budget, which allows for furnishing those services:

1. Management and Administration
2. Promotions, Advertising, Public Relations, and Special Events
3. Quality of Life: Environmental Improvements and Maintenance
4. Business Recruitment and Retention
5. Planning and Legal
6. Business Development, Practices, and Support.

At the heart of these plans is a rediscovery of the significant value of the community developed through its history and interpersonal relationships. It is these values that the redevelopment and BID plans intend to build on. In the recent BID study, a community-wide survey collected statements citing the most valuable aspects of the community.

Six Key Coordinated Service Areas

Cooperative Business Management starts by understanding that every aspect of the business environment contributes to a successful experience by the customer. Cooperative Business Management is a comprehensive and coordinated approach. It requires the attention of an active professional management effort. Successful business districts (including malls, shopping centers, and shopping strips) manage the business environment in a comprehensive manner as a service to the customer. Service is the competitive edge. Management is the key to success. Services are grouped into the following six categories:

Management and Administration: The BID will be managed by a BID Management Corporation, a non-profit corporation, or a public commission. The DMC will hire a professional manager or consulting service and maintain a professional office.

Marketing and Public Relations: The BID will develop a destination marketing strategy; corporation design theme; provide joint advertising; conduct appropriate market surveys; support and design special events; support retail promotions; coordinate public relations; and have a customer information center.

Quality of Life: Environmental Improvements and Maintenance. The BID will support a Downtown Revitalization Plan and provide for better managed and enhanced parking sites; improved safety and clean-up efforts; enhanced street lighting, signage, and more pedestrian friendly designs. The BID will also provide for more user-friendly outdoor design for streets and sidewalks, including benches, trees, lighting, façades, etc. It will also address pedestrian access, wayfinding and signage improvements as well as traffic problems in general.

Business Recruitment and Development: The BID will develop business investment guides and financing programs; business development, support, and training programs; develop cultural, retail, and dining theme plans; develop long-range strategies; and pursue public and private funding.

Planning and Legal: The BID will develop Board training, an annual BID budget and work plan, as well as short- and long-term business plans. The management will work on redevelopment strategies and coordinate with the city's economic and redevelopment plans and projects. It will work as a team player with local banks, community organizations, and cultural organizations. The BID management will also address upgrades to local regulations and codes.

Business Practices and Performance: The BID will operate as a business community in a cooperative and planned manner necessary for effectively responding to customer demands. Common business standards and operating procedures, such as standardized times when all businesses are open, address the organizational capacity of the district, and communicate a higher level of business sense and service.

Work Strategy and Board Committee Structure

Work Strategy

The following is a set of objectives for the BID and an initial work plan for each committee:

- maintain a professional management capacity and office;
- manage the PPP;
- build synergy and partnerships throughout town for different parts of the district (highway to downtown) and between the government and business both locally and regionally;
- establish financial, funding, and program partnerships;
- develop corporation promotional design theme and public relations program;
- provide coordinated and joint advertising;
- support and design special events;
- support retail promotions;
- design and implement wayfinding signage systems;
- support the implementation of the District Revitalization Plan;
- enforce existing codes and encourage façade improvements;
- establish "pedestrian-friendly" as an environmental theme;
- better managed and enhanced parking sites;
- improved clean-up efforts;
- continue downtown and vacant property improvements and redevelopment;
- develop and coordinate business investment guide and financing programs;
- develop cultural, art, retail, and dining themes;
- coordinate with municipal redevelopment efforts;
- improve apartment quality and code compliance.

Getting Started

The BID "gets started" by creating a non-profit DMC, by-laws, election of officers, obtaining funding capability (which usually means getting a line of credit with a local bank), and hiring a professional manager/Executive Director. Having accomplished those necessary tasks the following is an initial work plan for this fiscal year. **Note**: this is a start-up plan and it will evolve as the Board, its committees, and the Executive Director design and implement the activities of the BID in the first year. It is recommended that annually the Board plan a one- or two-day weekend retreat in September after Labor Day to review its vision, benchmarks, and create a new work plan for the coming fiscal year. Additionally, it is recommended that within two years a three-, five-, and ten-year projected business plan is also developed and that it is discussed in general at this retreat. A work plan provides clear objectives, priorities, and a timetable to gauge progress and success.

Measure for Success

The BID must identify a reasonable business plan that should have three-, five-, and ten-year objectives that specifically addresses the future vision of the district at significant yearly intervals, and has specific measurable goals that provide a basis for evaluation.

It is understood that many aspects of a BID are intangible such as customer satisfaction and a sense of well-being. However, there can be reasonable "benchmarks" against similar districts and both quantifiable (crime rates, bags of trash, number of visitors, vacancy rates, property values, etc.) and quality of life measurements that are in line with the vision the BID has agreed upon. Performance management establishes measures (goals) for success based on outcomes and performance.

There are three essential questions that the Board of Trustees must ask itself when designing programs. And, each question needs to be based on the Vision and Mission Statements:

1.   What is it that we want to become?
2.   How do we get there?
3.   How do we chart our progress and success?

Answering the first question leads to developing a vision shared by all, which was accomplished in the Steering Committee process. The second question leads to the development of a strategic game plan (program). The third question requires the development of "milestones and benchmarks." Milestones and benchmarks focus attention on results, performance, and measured success. In developing short- and long-range game plans, all three questions need to be asked simultaneously. They provide focus and momentum.

Framing Performance Measurements for the BID

The committees of the Board outline the areas that have been identified as important areas of improvement for the district. Each must have goals, milestones, and results that can be evaluated and measured. An appropriate benchmark for any business community is the presence of a strong and effective organization: BID–Downtown Management Corporation. Performance measurements for business districts usually fall into four categories; however, the overall category is customer satisfaction. The three categories are:

1.   **Quality of life (QOL)**
2.   **Return on investment (ROI)**
3.   **Organizational and management capability (OMC).**

If the management organization's PPP is successful then the managed district is successful.

DATE: _____

PROMISE:_____

A) One action/project. What is it and when will it be done? BE CLEAR AND PRECISE:

<u>**PROJECT:**</u>

B) What values are achieved by these projects?

_____

1.   **2.**   **3.**
_____

C) What performance: goal, milestone (a half way check in measurement to assess that you are on target), and a specific result will be reached? Each stage measures your performance and has an actual by-when date (day and time). Follow the format:

_____ *By When:*   *(What) Performance GOAL:* _____

_____

By When: **(What) Performance MILESTONE:** _____

_____

By When: **(What) Specific Measurable RESULT:** _____

_____

FIGURE B.1 Project Performance Form

If the QOL improvements are successful then the managed district is successful. If the ROI is unsuccessful then the managed district is less successful. If the OMC is successful then the managed district is successful.

Performance measurements can be thought of as representing the "values" of the district and its commitments to the community established in the Mission Statement.

Initial Work Plan and Objectives for Board Committees

The following duties and objectives are to present in a chart form the various work schedules of the BID in its initial year. By when, targeted dates are established not as absolutes, but as guides to be a benchmark for a timely success of the work represented in the budget. The actual dates may vary in the end result.

Executive Committee

Summary: This committee will include all management and administrative functions and also include audits and official financial records, nomination sub-committee, and planning sub-committee.

Examples of Committee Plans

1. Objective: *Establish financial, funding, and program partnerships*

Priorities	Timetable
Develop (minimum) three-year business plan with Manager	
Develop funding relationship with local banks	
Meet with municipal government and interface budgets and program	
Investigate BID administration of specific municipal programs such as: special events, parking, sidewalk and garbage clean-up, street improvements, and redevelopment	
Meet with corporate sponsors	
Determine auditor	

2. Objective: *Maintain a professional BID office location and/or welcome center*

Priorities	Timetable
Obtain and furnish office	
Hire management	

Communications and Promotions Committee

Summary: This committee is responsible for all activities that communicate the activities and perspective of the BID, and bring customers to the district for special events, activities, and opportunities. Including, but not limited to, newsletters, visitors, holiday, users guides and advertising, retail promotions, cultural events, parades, parties, and competitions.

1. Objective: *Develop corporation promotional design theme and public relations*. Be professional about communications. Hire a professional. Stay in touch with your membership.

Priorities	Timetable
Website	
Develop BID newsletter for members and customers	
Develop a public relations campaign to keep BID in the public eye	
Conduct appropriate market, customer, and business surveys	

2. Objective: *Provide coordinated and joint advertising*

Priorities	Timetable
Determine advertising needs	
Revise by:	

3. Objective: *Support and design special events*

Priorities	Timetable
Coordinate with municipal, Bus. Assoc.	
Design Christmas Holiday Event	
Seek long-term corporate support	
Develop 2 theme events	

4. Objective: *Develop Tourism model*

Quality of Life Committee

Summary: This committee is responsible for managing and implementing a Revitalization Plan, and all environmental design, plans, services, and upgrades including public facilities like cleanliness, streetscapes, signage, parking, development, façades, and building codes and designs. The committee's goal is to upgrade customer accessibility and satisfaction with the district's physical environment.

5. Objective: *Create and implement Revitalization Plan—hire a professional for Board Retreat*

Priorities	Timetable
Act with the municipality to seek funds	
Hire grants professional	
Street lighting plan	

Priorities	Timetable
Design **unified and linked** signage system to identify access, businesses, government services, parking and banner system on integrating the business communities in town	
Coordinate with promotional theme	

6. Objective: *Enforce existing codes and encourage façade improvements*

Priorities	Timetable
Façade improvement program	
Include code reinforcement efforts	

7. Objective: *Establish "pedestrian-friendly" as an environmental theme—priorities to be developed*

8. Objective: *Better managed and enhanced parking sites*

9. Objective: *Improved clean-up efforts and trash receptacles design and system*

Priorities	Timetable
Trash, graffiti, and debris study: removal in entrance and accessibility routes	

10. Objective: *Improve apartment quality and code compliance—priorities to be established*

Business Development Committee

Summary: This committee is focused on upgrading business investment, financing, training, and retail mix plan for the district. Its priority is business vitality, growth, and development.

1. Objective: *Develop and coordinate business investment guide and financing programs*

Priorities	Timetable
Identify expertise to assist business	
Create database of existing vacancies	
Further define business zones to establish target list of businesses to recruit	
Develop demographic marketing guide and recruitment package	
Need funding	
Contact Small Business Development Centers in the County	
Join appropriate business associations such as: Business and Industry Association, Chamber of Commerce, and go to appropriate conferences	
Work on improved relations between businesses, residents, and local government	

2. Objective: *Develop cultural, retail, and dining theme*

Priorities	Timetable
Research and develop niche strategy as retail, cultural, and dining area	

3. Objective: *Recruit new businesses—hire professional*

4. Objective: *Business friendly environment—research municipal ordinances and practices, recommend necessary changes*

FIGURE B.2 BID Organizational Chart

Authority of BIDs

A significant aspect of BID public accountability occurs at the opposite end of the fiscal year, when the DMC proposes the budget for the DMC and SID. Once the corporation proposes its budget to the municipal governing body, the municipal governing body must approve the budget by resolution. This approval is equivalent to a first reading of the budget, not adoption. A public hearing on the budget is held for approval. The hearing must be advertised prior to the hearing. This hearing is an opportunity for both those paying assessments and any member of the public to either support or oppose the operation of the BID by commenting on the effectiveness of its use of funds.

The budget is adopted by the municipal governing body only after the approval, advertising, hearing process is complete. In some instances, the process can be prolonged by an amendment to the budget that exceeds limits within the statute, thereby requiring another hearing. A budget not being approved effectively means that the DMC and the BID it oversees cannot operate in the coming year.

PPP, BID & Managed Business District Performance Survey

DATE OF TEST: _____

SECTION ONE: BASIC INFORMATION

1. Official name of the Public–Private Partnership (PPP)/Managed Business District (MBD) (in the enabling ordinance):

_____

1.a. Ordinance Identification Number: _____

2. Registered Name and Address of the PPP's/ MBD's Management Organization:

_____

Name

_____

Address

    2.a. Is the Management Organization of the PPP legally a: (Circle one)

Government	Private Non-Profit	For-Profit	Municipal
Office	Corp.	Corp.	Commission

    2.b. If a Corporation: Federal tax status identification number {Ex. 501 (c) (6)}: _____

    2.c. Is the management corporation or commission designated in the enabling BID ordinance? (Circle one)
    Yes   No

3. Management Corp. Telephone and Email Address:

_____   _____

Telephone   Email Address

4. Name of the designated Chief Executive Officer/Manager:

_____

    4.a. The CEO/Manager is: (Circle one) (FT=Full Time; PT=Part Time)

FT	PT	Independent	Government
Employee	Employee	Contractor	Employee Volunteer

    4.b. The CEO/Manager is: (Circle all that apply)

Business District Management Certification	Degree in Public Administration
Main Street Certified Manager	Degree in Business Administration
Certified Business Administrator	Certified Public Manager
Certified Economic Development Director	OTHER:_____

5. Person completing this questionnaire (print clearly):

_____

Name   Title   Affiliation

6. CEO/Manager: (Circle one)
Male   Female

7.a. The Organization's current publicly funded-only budget is: (Circle one)
a. $99,000 or below   b. $100,000 to $250,000   c. $251,000 to $1,000,000
d. $1,000,001 to $2,000,000   e. over $2,000,000

7.b. The Organization's current privately funded-only budget is: (Circle one)
a. $99,000 or below   b. $100,000 to $250,000   c. $251,000 to $1,000,000
d. $1,000,001 to $2,000,000   e. over $2,000,000

8.a. The Organization's total budget is: (Circle one)
a. $99,000 or below   b. $100,000 to $250,000   c. $251,000 to $1,000,000
d. $1,000,001 to $2,000,000   e. $2,000,000 to $3,000,000   f. over $3,000,000

8.b. Last fiscal year total budget: $

_____

9. Does government levy a mandatory tax, assessment, or fee on your behalf? (Circle one)

Yes, government levies and   No, we bill it and collect   Not applicable, no
collects it on our behalf   ourselves   mandatory public
                                                              assessment

10. Are you required by ordinance and/or statute to have an elected official on your Board of Directors or Commission? (Circle one)
Yes   No

11. Are you required by ordinance and/statute or by laws to have an elected official on your Board of Directors or Commission as a voting member? (Circle one)
Yes   No

SECTION TWO: ORGANIZATION AND MANAGEMENT CAPABILITY

1. Determine the percentage increase from the previous year's _publicly funded-only_ budget in relation to the current year's budget (divide previous year's budget by the current budget): (Circle one)
a. More than 10%   b. 5%–10%   c. 1%–4%   d. No change   e. Decrease

2. Determine the percentage increase from the previous year's _total_ budget (assessment and other funds) in relation to the current year's total budget (divide previous year's budget by current budget): (Circle one)
a. More than 10%   b. 5%–10% c. 1%–4%   d. No change/   e. Don't know
                                             decrease

3.a. The average CEO/Manager has been in the job position: (Circle one)
a. Over 10   b. 7–10   c. 5–7   d. 3–4   e. 1–2   f. less than 1
years   years   years   years   years   year

3.b. The Organization has had how many CEOs/managers to date? _____

4. The number of members of the Board of Directors, or Commission, of the management organization is equal to the following percentage of businesses in the district: (Circle one)
a. 5% or more   b. 4%–4.9%   c. 3%–3.9%   d. 2%–2.9%   e. 1%–1.9%

5. The District's Management Organization's meetings are open to the public: (Circle one)
a. Always   b. Almost always   c. Sometimes   d. Rarely   e. Don't know

6. The Management Organization encourages partnering between government, community, and business to achieve revitalization of the community: (Circle one)
a. A great deal   b. A fair amount   c. Somewhat   d. Only a little   e. Not at all

7. How involved, on average, are the people on the BID Board of Directors in other social, community, or professional organizations? (Circle one)
a. A great deal   b. A fair amount   c. Somewhat   d. Only a little   e. Don't know

8. The Management Organization is trusted by:

8.a. The Local Government: (Circle one)
a. A great deal   b. A fair amount   c. Somewhat   d. Only a little   e. Not at all

8.b. The Business Community: (Circle one)
a. A great deal   b. A fair amount   c. Somewhat   d. Only a little   e. Not at all

8.c. Other local Community and Economic Development Organizations: (Circle one)
a. A great deal   b. A fair amount   c. Somewhat   d. Only a little   e. Not at all

8.d. The Local Chamber of Commerce: (Circle one)
a. A great deal   b. A fair amount   c. Somewhat   d. Only a little   e. Not at all

8.e. The Community at-large: (Circle one)
a. A great deal   b. A fair amount   c. Somewhat   d. Only a little   e. Not at all

9. The BID's PPP between government and the business community works productively: (Circle one)
a. A great deal   b. A fair amount   c. Somewhat   d. Only a little   e. Not at all

10. People help each other learn in this organization: (Circle one)
a. A great deal   b. A fair amount   c. Somewhat   d. Only a little   e. Not at all

11. There is consistency between words and behavior in this organization: (Circle one)
a. A great deal   b. A fair amount   c. Somewhat   d. Only a little   e. Not at all

12. There are clear expectations established in this organization: (Circle one)
a. A great deal   b. A fair amount   c. Somewhat   d. Only a little   e. Not at all

13. The Management Organization can implement changes in its services quickly: (Circle one)
a. A great deal   b. A fair amount   c. Somewhat   d. Only a little   e. Not at all

14.a. There is a high degree of collaboration in this organization with other organizations: (Circle one)
a. A great deal   b. A fair amount   c. Somewhat   d. Only a little   e. Not at all

14.b. There is a high degree of collaboration in this organization within the organization: (Circle one)
a. A great deal   b. A fair amount   c. Somewhat   d. Only a little   e. Not at all

15. In this organization, scenarios and guidelines are used more often than rules: (Circle one)
a. A great deal   b. A fair amount   c. Somewhat   d. Only a little   e. Not at all

16. This organization is designed around collaboration rather than compromise: (Circle one)
a. A great deal   b. A fair amount   c. Somewhat   d. Only a little   e. Not at all

17. Government has determined a different level of funding than the one originally requested by the District Management Organization: (Circle one)
a. Not at all   b. Only a little   c. Somewhat   d. A fair amount   e. A great deal

18. Report performance information to a governmental organization: (Circle one)
a. Monthly   b. Quarterly   c. Biannually   d. Annually   e. Not at all

19. At a minimum, report performance information to the public: (Circle one)
a. Monthly   b. Quarterly   c. Biannually   d. Annually   e. Not at all

20. Publish an annual financial and performance report (paper or electronically): (Circle one)
a. Monthly   b. Quarterly   c. Biannually   d. Annually   e. Not at all

21. Time of passage of annual budget by local government (or, appropriate authority) after the Management Organization has approved a budget: (Circle one)
a. 1–3 months   b. 4–5 months   c. 5–6 months   d. 6–8 months   e. 9 months or more

22. Board of Director's Attendance at Board Meetings—averaged annually: (Circle one)
a. more than 80%   b. 60%–79%   c. 40%–59%   d. 25%–39%   e. less than 20%

SECTION THREE: RETURN ON INVESTMENT

1. The District's Management Organization is considered an innovative organization: (Circle one)
a. A great deal   b. A fair amount   c. Somewhat   d. Only a little   e. Don't know

2. The Management Organization is an agent for change in the community: (Circle one)
a. A great deal   b. A fair amount   c. Somewhat   d. Only a little   e. Don't know

3.a. The Management Organization takes risks to improve the community: (Circle one)
a. A great deal   b. A fair amount   c. Somewhat   d. Only a little   e. Don't know

3.b. The Management Organization is a PPP: (Circle one)
a. A great deal   b. A fair amount   c. Somewhat   d. Only a little   e. Don't know

3.c. The Management Organization enters into partnerships in the public and private organizations: (Circle one)
a. A great deal   b. A fair amount   c. Somewhat   d. Only a little   e. Don't know

4. The Management Organization identifies resources and leverages assets: (Circle one)
a. A great deal   b. A fair amount   c. Somewhat   d. Only a little   e. Don't know

5. In this organization, work is designed to permit experimentation: (Circle one)
a. A great deal   b. A fair amount   c. Somewhat   d. Only a little   e. Don't know

6. The organization is quick to respond to market opportunities and threats: (Circle one)
a. A great deal   b. A fair amount   c. Somewhat   d. Only a little   e. Don't know

7. The current vacancy rate in the service district is: (Circle one)
a. Less than 3%   b. 3.1%–6%   c. 6.1%–10%   d. 10%–15%   e. Don't know

8. The vacancy rate in the service district compared to last year is: (Circle one)
a. Less than 3%   b. 3.1%–6%   c. 6.1%–10%   d. 10%–15%   e. Don't know

9. The value of commercial property in the district has risen in three years by: (Circle one)
a. 15%–25%   b. 5%–14.9%   c. 0%–4.9%   d. Lost value   e. Don't know

10. The total failure rate for commercial businesses is: (Circle one)
a. 3% or less   b. 4%–7%   c. 8%–10%   d. 10% or more   e. Don't know

11. Number of new restaurants in the district in the last complete calendar year: (Circle one)
a. 6 or more   b. 4–5   c. 3–4   d. 2–0   e. Don't know

12. Number of new retail establishments in the district in the last complete calendar year: (Circle one)
a. 6 or more   b. 4–5   c. 3–4   d. 2–0   e. Don't know

13. Since its inception, <u>compared to the total public funds budgeted received so far (total years)</u>, the Management Organization has caused what dollar ratio of hard, physical, capital improvements to the District? – <u>Round off</u> (Circle one)
a. 1:5 or more   b. 1:4   c. 1:3 times   d. 1:2 or less   e. Don't know.

14. Amount of the total current budget directed to advertising and marketing is: (Circle one)
a. 25% or more   b. 15%–24%   c. 10%–14%   d. 9% or less   e. Don't know

15. Visits to the Management Organization's website increased in the last complete calendar year by: (Circle one)
a. 35% or more   b. 25%–34%   c. 15%–24%   d. 1%–14%   e. Don't know

16. Number of documented overall complaints in the last calendar year as compared to the previous calendar year about the Management Organization decreased by: (Circle one)
a. 50% or more   b. 25%–49%   c. 10%–24%   d. $10% or less   e. Increased

17. How many outdoor billboard-type advertisements where placed in the last calendar year? (Circle one)
a. 20 or more   b. 15–19   c. 6–14   d. 1–5   e. None.

18. Number of documented formal tours of the service district in the last calendar year: (Circle one)
a. 50 or more   b. 25–49   c. 6–24   d. 1–5   e. Don't know

20. Data: Total square footage of commercial property in the service district is collected: (Circle one)
a. Annually   b. Ever two years   c. Every three years   d. Every four years
e. Don't know

21. Cost per square foot of commercial space in the most recent complete calendar year increased from the previous year by: (Circle one)
a. 10% or more   b. 5%–9%   c. 2%–4%   d. 1% or below   e. Don't know

22.a. Website is updated: (Circle one)
a. Daily b. Weekly c. More than Monthly d. Monthly e. Don't know, or don't have a website

22.b. Facebook (or social media site) is updated: (Circle one)
a. Daily b. Weekly c. More than Monthly d. Monthly e. Don't know, or don't have a social media site

SECTION FOUR: QUALITY OF LIFE

1. The District's Management Organization is guided by an agreed upon Vision Statement as a Promise to the community: (Circle one)
a. A great deal   b. A fair amount   c. Somewhat   d. Only a little   e. Don't know

2. The District's Management Organization has improved the quality of life in the community: (Circle one)
a. A great deal   b. A fair amount   c. Somewhat   d. Only a little   e. Don't know

3. What best describes your perception of the cleanliness of the service district compared to last year? (Circle one)
a. Much cleaner   b. Somewhat   c. The same   d. Somewhat   e. Dirtier
                      cleaner   dirtier

4. What best describes your perception of safety in the service district? (Circle one)
a. Much safer   b. Somewhat safer   c. The same   d. Somewhat less safe
e. Unsafe

5. Generally speaking, how professional is the Management Organization? (Circle one)
a. Excellent   b. Very good   c. Good   d. Fair   e. Poor

6. Attendance to Board meetings by the Board is: (Circle one)
a. Excellent   b. Very good   c. Good   d. Fair   e. Poor

7. The Management Organization conducts customer satisfaction surveys: (Circle one)
a. Monthly   b. Quarterly   c. Biannually   d. Annually   e. Not at all

8. The Management Organization's collaborations with the local government increased by: (Circle one)
a. 26% or more   b. 16%–25%   c. 6%–15%   d. 5% or less   e. Decreased

9. Collaborations with other Community Development Corporations increased by: (Circle one)
a. 26% or more   b. 16%–25%   c. 6%–15%   d. 5% or less   e. Decreased

10. Number of Community Festivals/ Promotions held in the current year: (Circle one)
a. More than 20   b. 11 to 20   c. 3 to 10   d. 1 to 2   e. Don't know

11. Number of bank robberies decreased/increased in the last complete calendar year compared to the previous calendar year by: (Circle one)
a. decreased more than 50%   b. decreased 1% to 49%   c. stayed the same
d. increased   e. Don't know

12. Number of assaults decreased/increased in the last complete calendar year compared to the previous calendar year by: (Circle one)
a. decreased more than 50%   b. decreased 1% to 49%   c. stayed the same
d. increased   e. Don't know

13. Number of commercial robberies decreased/increased in the last complete calendar year compared to the previous calendar year by: (Circle one)
a. decreased more than 50%   b. decreased 1% to 49%   c. stayed the same
d. increased   e. Don't know

14. The percentage of money in the Management Organization's total budget spent on cleanliness and safety: (Circle one)
a. less than 10%   b. 11%–25%   c. 26%–35%   d. 35%–40%
e. more than 40%

15. Number of documented compliments about the BID organization's performance increased by: (Circle one)
a. 50% or more   b. 25%–49%   c. 10%–24%   d. 10% or less   e. Decreased

16. Number of years since a comprehensive streetscape improvement project was conducted on the major thoroughfare: (Circle one)
a. less than 5 years   b. 6–10 years   c. 11–20 years   d. 21–30 years
e. Don't know

17. Collection of District-wide customer email contact data: (Circle one)
a. Annually   b. Biannually   c. Quarterly   d. Monthly   e. Not at all

18. Number of public meeting places, parks, plazas, etc. created or rebuilt since the District was formed: (Circle one)
a. 20 or more   b. 15–19   c. 10–14   d. 1–10   e. None

19. Upkeep and maintenance of private property buildings and business signage has improved: (Circle one)
a. A great deal   b. A fair amount   c. Somewhat   d. Only a little   e. Not at all

20. Rate the service district's advertising branding: (Circle one)
a. Excellent   b. Very good   c. Good   d. Fair   e. Poor

21. The service district boundaries have expanded: (Circle one)
a. Three times   b. Two times   c. One time   d. Never   e. Decreased in size

22. The Management Organization assists in and/or sponsors the creation of other PPPs or managed business districts: (Circle one)
a. A great deal   b. A fair amount   c. Somewhat   d. Only a little   e. Don't know

Scoring

Only Sections 2–4 are scored.

Each statement has five answers: Choose only one for each statement.

Method of scoring: Use five point scale from left to right a=5; b=4; c=3; d=2; and, e=1.

Add choice in each statement for a total score.

Interpretation key:

Highest score is 370—Very Successful—High performing, well-established public–private partnership- regional to multi-regional impact player.

High score range is 300–370: Successful—Consistently good to excellent performance- good to excellent public-private partnership—could be better in key areas-local to regional impact player. Be wary of stagnation.

Moderate score range is 222–300: Fair to good performance, struggles at times particularly with public–private partnership—needs improvement in key areas—stagnant in key areas—local impact player.

Low score range is below 221: Poor to fair performance—ineffective public–private partnership—struggles, is not innovative—verging on failure—confused regarding district to municipal impact.

Danger zone is below 150: in various states of failure—confused to negative impact player.

APPENDIX C: ANNUAL REPORT OF THE IRONBOUND BUSINESS IMPROVEMENT DISTRICT

Newark, NJ, March 16, 2015

Seth Grossman
Executive Director

IBID Board of Directors

Steven T. Yglesias, President
Renato Baptista, 1st Vice President
Victor Matos, 2nd Vice President
Manuel Lopes, Secretary
Brian Morgado, Treasurer
Licinio Cruz, President Emeritus

Jack Guerra
María A. Henríquez
Hal Laessig
Ellen LaMotta
Manuel Lopes
Víctor Matos
Snezana Opacic
John Peneda
Zelia Prata
Chris Silva
Betty Spiropoulos
Helena Vinhas
Ausgusto Amador
Ras J. Baraka

IBID Staff

Seth A. Grossman, Executive Director
Vince Baglivo, Associate Director Communications
Christopher Bernardo, Director of Operations
Leysly Roldan, Administrative Assistant
Francisco Pereira, Program Support
Pereira & Azevedo, Accountants
Richard Allen, Corporate Counsel

Introduction

2014 was an election year in Newark, Ras J. Baraka won the mayoralship and a new administration began. Baye Adolfo-Wilson became the new Deputy Mayor of Community & Economic Development, and work began on the redevelopment of the Prudential Area. The mayor's office immediately established a new Office of Cultural, the Arts & Tourism, which we believe will help focus the City as a destination. The Prudential project on Broad St. in downtown Newark is moving along as is the old Haynes building, which is slated for Whole Foods. The IBID furthered discussions on obtaining 55 Prospect St. – Prospect Fire House as a Community Arts & Cultural Center as well as leasing Peter Francisco Park to better manage the area and rebuild the park. A First Block Task Force was established to address growing crime issues around Penn Station and Peter Francisco Park. This effort met with great success as the Newark Police Department quickly became an effective partner. The NewarkBound Magazine, which has already changed the Newark's perception as a positive and exciting City continued to move the City forward, and has become the most anticipated media coming out of Newark. The Ironbound is looking at having its first hotel as the downtown Marriot and Indigo hotels came on line.

Our cleaning crews have been active and the IBID looks great, tunnels between the downtown and the Ironbound continue to be painted and maintained against graffiti, and new IBID banners/poles are still planned for (East) Ferry Street and planters on East Ferry St. and Wilson Avenue in spring 2015. The Ironbound has many Portuguese, Spanish and Latin American populations, and the largest Brazilian population on the East Coast. Our events such as: the Portugal Day Festival, Gooches Garlic Run, & the Ecuadoran Festival, Halloween and holiday celebrations are great draws for Newark and the Ironbound. The bottom line is that the Ironbound is one of the region's top tourist destinations and is poised to grow. This year, we should have our first 95-room boutique hotel at Madison St. and Lafayette St.

In 2014, it became clear that the economy is no longer in recession, but it is far from robust in New Jersey. This makes for a tenuous retail environment, and once again has softened Newark's ability to grow residentially. Efforts by the City are underway to begin improving municipal finances, but this will require that hard choices regarding employment and services will have to made, and this will need to occur over a number of years. As the city's fiscal help improves so will investment in the city. Fueled by stronger consumer spending, we expect the Ironbound economy to grow at a modest 3% this year – up from 2.4% in 2014. Much of this is due to fairly strong local trends but poor global trends such as a tightening labor market, low inflation, low energy prices, a need for new housing, a strong dollar, and a very modest rise in interest rates. The downside is that globally, the economy is not as good and challenges in Europe will affect tourism. World economies are entering their slowest growth period since 2009. The unifying theme is that the global economy is taking longer than expected to recuperate from the bursting of the debt bubble during the last decade. We expect the economy to grow for the Ironbound in 2015, but not by much. Nonetheless, the future looks bright. In addition to improved unemployment numbers and the increase in the availability of capital, small business owners should benefit from lower energy costs and an increase in consumer confidence. It could very well be the beginning of the economic boon we all have been waiting for. And for small businesses, that would be welcome news in 2015.

The Ironbound Business Improvement District (IBID) is a certified Special Improvement District established in December 2000 by local ordinance. As stated above, first and foremost, the IBID is a unique public-private partnership between the Ferry Street business community, the municipal government, and the neighborhood. The IBID works with the City to improve business and community development services, rebuild our infrastructure, and market the Ironbound as a reliable and exciting destination. Administrative funding is created through an annual assessment on commercial property in the district, collected by the City, but transferred and managed by the IBID. In January 2015, the IBID celebrated its 15th Anniversary, and we have much to proud of. We continue to have the most stable property values in the area, the lowest vacancy rate, and a growing market.

The IBID has built partnerships with the important Newark entertainment, arts, government, education, and cultural institutions. After last year and this year's success with the Ironbound Unbound gallery and the Newark's Arts Council, we are vigorously exploring a lease of the Prospect St. Fire building as an Ironbound Arts and Cultural Center. This is chiefly a partnership between the IBID, Councilman Amador, the Newark Fire Department, Sumei Multicultural Arts Center, and the Newark Arts Council. By working together, we have successfully addressed shared goals for the future of the Ironbound and the City of Newark.

Promise of the IBID

The Ironbound Business Improvement District is a diverse and vibrant community with deep ethnic roots, rich in culture and tradition. We are a bustling retail and restaurant destination easily accessible to the world. Our proud and friendly people welcome visitors to explore our international flair and ambiance and live a true Portuguese, Spanish, Brazilian, and South & Latin American experience.

We are committed to providing a friendly "neighborhood", one that will include a safe and clean environment that gives our customers a feeling of being wanted and appreciated. It will be so unique that those who come to enjoy what so many of us have taken for granted will undoubtedly come back for more.

IBID Strategy

As stated above, first and foremost, the IBID is a unique public-private partnership between the Ferry Street/Wilson Avenue business community, the municipal government, and the neighborhood. The IBID works with the City to improve business and community development services to the district and provides additional enhancements and focus. Administrative funding is created through an annual assessment on commercial property in the district, collected by the City, but transferred and managed by the IBID. The Ironbound business area has the most stable property values in the area, the lowest vacancy rate, and a growing market. Much of that growth is due to the establishment of the nearby Prudential Center and Red Bull Arena. However, a decade+ long commitment to marketing the Ironbound brand by the IBID has helped keep the district become top-of-mind with longtime customers while encouraging and recruiting new customers.

The business community of the Ironbound-Ferry Street/Wilson Avenue area is basically strong and vibrant, and the City of Newark appears to be on a long-awaited economic upswing and renaissance. Although Newark can be said to be going through revitalization, it has been a long incremental process that has translated a disjointed manner to its neighborhoods. The Ironbound, a historically immigrant community is celebrated as a unique ethnic enclave, but at the same time struggles with urban issues that plague New Jersey. Community-based organizations like the Ironbound Business Improvement District (IBID) and the Ironbound Community Corporation (ICC) face these challenges by addressing a comprehensive integration of services that tackle social, housing and economic issues comprehensively.

Ferry Street and Wilson Avenue are the most active business area in the Ironbound, but not the only one. Lafayette Street as well as Market Street and Elm Street, are very active, but it is noticeable that these streets are actually parallel and/or divergent from Ferry Street. Ferry Street and Wilson Avenue are unmistakably the hub of the Ironbound, and a key commercial corridor for the City of Newark. There are over 640 businesses in the Ferry Street business area and over 800 in the entire Ironbound neighborhood. Restaurants and professional business as well as industrial operations are scattered throughout the area. Although heavy industry tends to be located along the Passaic River to the east and north, to the southeast are Newark Airport and a regional Budweiser complex. Over 720 trains pass through Newark's Penn Station each day, which also houses the Greyhound Bus Terminal and the PATH Light rail trains to Jersey City-Hoboken and New York City. Summary of IBID advantages:

- *A Strategic Gateway:* Ferry St. and Wilson Avenue Business Area are strategic gateways to the East Ward from Downtown and Penn Station.
- *Cultural Identity:* Ferry Street & Wilson Avenue form the heart of the historically Portuguese Ironbound neighborhood. The corridor is dominated by Portuguese and Brazilian businesses, with some Spanish establishments as well. Ferry Street area is famous for its Portuguese, South and Latin American, and Spanish restaurants, which draw visitors from across the region.
- *Retail Potential:* Ferry Street and Wilson Avenue are probably the most thriving commercial district in the City, with its renown Spanish and Portuguese retail and restaurants, vibrant Brazilian retail, banks, offices, chain retail including one of Newark's only full-service supermarkets, and the Ferry Street/Wilson Avenue business corridor is at the center of a transportation and entertainment nexus and is New Jersey's premier restaurant district.
- *A Transit-Rich Corridor:* Ferry St. & Wilson Avenue are served by NJT bus line and within walking distance of Penn Station. Strong pedestrian-oriented commercial presence mostly in the form of traditional storefronts.

The IBID has been a leader in the Ironbound assuring that business people and their customers will only continue to grow in a special part of Newark.

First Block Task Force

Ironbound District's First Block Task Force Unites Community to Fight Crime & Increase Safety

A coalition of Ironbound business and commercial property owners, local residents and representatives of the Ironbound Business Improvement District (IBID), the City of Newark, Newark Police Department (NPD) and NJ Transit has been working cooperatively to address issues of crime and public safety in the area around Newark Penn Station, gateway to the Ironbound.

In April 2014, the IBID organized the First Block Task Force in response to concerns expressed by merchants, property owners, and businesses in the first block of Ferry and Market Streets near Penn Station regarding increased crime and quality of life deterioration. The Task Force serves as an Advisory Committee for the community to help address their concerns and work on solutions. While the area has struggled with issues related to the significant homeless population in the area, in recent months incidents of panhandling, illegal drug use and distribution, robbery and car break-ins have increased dramatically. The issue is persistent and exacerbated in the evenings, early mornings, and weekends.

"We appreciate the concern and participation of so many Ironbound stakeholders who have helped identify the many different factors contributing to the problem," noted Seth A. Grossman, the IBID's Executive Director. "Those factors include increased displacement of the homeless as well as individuals who are now contributing to the growing problem of panhandling and illegal drug use in the Ironbound."

"Out of town feeding programs for the homeless in the area, while well intended, are generating considerable trash and debris and further attracting criminal activity. The growing number of smoke shops selling herbal drugs, plus a lack of maintenance, lighting and security on area buildings are also factors contributing to illegal drug transactions and other crimes," he added. The Task Force is working with East Ward Councilman Augusto Amador to identify funding for additional police patrols and the creation of a new Mini-Station on Ferry Street to better serve the blocks near Penn Station as well as an extended area that includes Bruen and McWhorter Streets and Railroad Avenue. Working with the former Third Precinct, a 3:00 p.m. to 11:00 p.m. police patrol has been added to Ferry Street as a mandatory post, along with mounted police patrols. A police task force, ten Metro Police that previously served only the downtown district side of Penn Station and Rt. 21, has also been extended to cover the Ironbound area of concern identified by the First Block group.

Additionally, the Newark Police Department installed a police command station at Peter Francisco Park to help monitor and direct increased enforcement efforts. "The Newark Police Department really stepped up and addressed this issue," Grossman pointed out. Two police officers have also been stationed in the area, greeting and speaking with pedestrians as they move through the Park. The Newark PD's "eye-in the-sky" is stationed at the eastern tip of the park. A similar unit has also been installed by NJ Transit Police facing Raymond Plaza East and Penn Station.

Other solutions being pursued by the First Block Task Force include expanded police patrols between 8:30 a.m. and 9:30 a.m., and the possibility of the IBID leasing Peter Francisco Park from the County of Essex, managing permits for its use and supervising programming and activities similar to the changes at Military Park in Newark's downtown. The Task Force is exploring locations and associated costs for a Mini Police Station, considering the purchase of a Segway personal transport to enhance security patrols, addressing smoke shop owners regarding compliance and cooperation, encouraging the installation of lights and security cameras and educating customers not to support panhandlers. The IBID is also working with the City of Newark regarding a more comprehensive panhandling ordinance and one to regulate feeding programs.

Peter Francisco Park Operating Proposal

More commonly described as the surface and that portion of the subsurface of the Peter Francisco Park identified on the City's Tax Map as Block 181, Lot 45, consisting of real property and improvements on approximately 3 acres.

Peter Francisco Park is located in the Ironbound community within the IBID boundaries just east and slightly south of Penn Station in Newark, New Jersey in a triangular park, named for Peter Francisco. The Park is at a primary gateway to

Newark's Ferry Street, the most successful commercial retail corridor in Newark. The Park is located at the intersection of Ferry Street and Edison Place, on the right when traveling south on Ferry Street. The Park was built in 1966 by the Municipal Council of Newark. Later on June 27, 1976, coinciding with the Bicentennial of the United States, a 12-foot obelisk was placed in the park in honor of Peter Francisco. The Park is named In honor of Peter Francisco, the Hercules of the American Independence. Peter Francisco (c. 1760/61–January 16, 1831), known variously as the "Virginia Giant" or the "Giant of the Revolution" (and occasionally as the "Virginia Hercules" or some variant thereof), was a hero of the American Revolution. The cover page of a 2006 issue of Military History asked a rhetorical question which suggested he may have been the greatest soldier in American History. George Washington once said that Francisco's prowess directly enabled American victories in two battles. Washington went on to state the war may have even been lost without Francisco's participation.

1 Park Management and Security: Ensure that Park Management Implements Adopted Policies, Preserves the Park's Resources, and Operates and Maintains the Park Efficiently

A – Landscape design oversight

Expertise and training in park planning and landscape design will be established with the responsibility and authority, in conference with the City's Department of Parks & Recreation to review and/or recommend for approval all landscape and architectural designs, modifications, structures, features, and maintenance procedures, as well as prepare landscape design plans, to ensure continuity of the park design and implementation of adopted policy.

B – Park amenities

Improve and maintain park amenities and ensure adequate visitor service.

1 Address restrooms, drinking fountains, trash receptacles, benches, secure bicycle parking, and telephones should be provided at convenient locations throughout the park and properly maintained. Amenities must meet all applicable accessibility codes and regulations.
2 These amenities should be consistent with the intensity of activity of the particular area and should not detract visually or physically from the character of the park.

C – Visitor information

Information should be provided to visitors to enrich their park experience, to direct visitors to park features, and to communicate park regulations.

1 Historic, environmental, educational, safety and general information about the park, the Ironbound, and the City of Newark will be made available to residents and visitors through programs, tours, literature and exhibits.

2 A park visitor center will be examined to provide information and exhibits to educate visitors about the the City of Newark, the Ironbound and the park's uses, history, and resources, to serve as a staging area for interpretive activities, and to provide an opportunity for the sale of park-related merchandise. Visitor center will require a new building/structure. A small visitor information kiosk may be considered to provide more limited services at a strategic location.

3 Outdoor advertisements of future or current events in the park will be strictly regulated as defined by the Park Code and the City regulations. Agencies other than the IBID, which desire to conduct events should confine such activities to public media announcements, or to an area within an existing building.

4 Visitor information must be available to persons with disabilities and meet the requirements of all applicable codes and regulations.

D Policy Designs

Signs to communicate information about the park and regulations regarding its use will be used effectively and efficiently. The number of signs will be minimized.

1 A park sign plan setting forth guidelines and standards will be prepared, adopted, and implemented, and included in any Construction Plan.

2 Informational, directional, and interpretive signs and maps will be standardized to optimize communication and should be sited effectively to avoid visual clutter and degradation of the park experience.

3 General park information signs will be placed at all park entries with information about park uses, regulations, and restrictions.

E – Special events

Events that attract large numbers of participants or spectators will continue to be regulated under the municipal code. All events must be prior approved by the IBID, and all IBID powers, authorities and compliances will be applied. City policies for permit and reservation issuance to prevent degradation of the park's landscape and reduce impacts on adjoining neighborhoods. Large gatherings may well be accommodated in other Newark parks, balancing the citywide recreational program and alleviating wear and tear on Peter Francisco Park. Ongoing use of park will be carefully monitored so that measures may be taken to allow adequate turf and landscape recovery time.

1 Proposed events will be reviewed to determine that they meet a standard of appropriateness, in accordance with the City and IBID interests and regulations.

2 Locations of events within the park will be reviewed to ensure that the event is appropriate for that location. Factors to consider will include the area's existing land use and potential damage. Carrying capacity will be determined for each area based on size, security and environmental sensitivity.

3 Fees, deposits, insurance and performance bonds paid by events to the City of Newark will be made adequate to cover additional maintenance costs and repairs of any potential damage.

F – Concessions

Concessions are a cost effective way to provide some visitor services in Peter Francisco Park. Concession services will be consistent with adopted policies, the purposes and environment of the park, the IBID and the City of Newark, and will continue to be regulated and closely supervised.

1 It is desirable for merchandising concessions that provide service on a long-term and continuous basis to be located within a building.

2 Mobile cart food concessions will meet visual design standards, vendor regulations, and permits will be reviewed by the IBID to ensure compliance with policy and design standards.

3 All vendors will establish effective litter control and permanent concession facilities will provide an enclosed garbage disposal area.

4 Lease agreements permitting the sale of merchandise will specifically include the sale of items that relate to the park, its landscape, features, historic buildings, and recreational activities.

G – Gifts and donations

Ensure that gifts accepted for placement in Peter Francisco Park will contribute to the historic and use character of the park and are compatible with the park environment.

1 Additional features tendered to the park will be carefully reviewed prior to acceptance to assure that they will not diminish the integrity of the basic design.

2 An endowment fund may be created to allow prospective donors to contribute to the restoration and maintenance of the park.

3 The City of Newark and the IBID will work closely with neighborhood associations to develop additional funding opportunities.

4 All gift proposals for Peter Francisco Park will be in accordance with existing municipal and IBID "Guidelines for Acceptance of Major Gifts" and the policies of the Peter Francisco Park plans.

H – Recycling

Recyclable material generated within the park will be recycled within a designated area. Professional and volunteer programs to remove litter from the park and to increase public awareness about recycling and the impact of litter on the park will be addressed. Recycled materials will be considered for all appropriate uses within Peter Francisco Park.

I – Park security

A sense of security is essential for park users to enjoy their park experience. The park will be, to the greatest extent possible, free of the problems of panhandling, crime, vagrancy, public feeding, abuse, noise, car traffic. Providing a secure park environment will be the highest priority.

1 Security systems and park patrols in concert with the City of Newark, the Newark Police Department, and NJ Transit may be employed throughout the park. Mounted, bicycle and motorized patrols, and other high-visibility security measures will be continued and expanded to protect park visitors and property.
2 Night lighting may be installed in areas receiving nighttime use. Adequate roadway and pathway lighting may be provided to improve safety for pedestrians, joggers, and bicyclists. Park lighting will not detract visually or physically from the character of the park.
3 Illegal activities including drug use and sales, and camping shall not be allowed in Peter Francisco Park. Efforts will be made to eliminate illegal activities through cooperation with community groups, the Newark Police Department, NJ Transit, the Department of Social Services, the Health Department, and the Department of Public Works and Neighborhood Services. Camping in the park damages the park landscape, creates litter and fire hazards, and reduces the perception of the park as a safe place to visit.

K – Adjacent urban development

Urban development adjacent to Peter Francisco Park should be consistent with the unique qualities of the park. Development or design modifications within Peter Francisco Park should not adversely affect the adjacent neighborhoods. As the intensity of development outside of the park increases, it should not visually intrude upon the park. The City of Newark and the IBID will work cooperatively with the Planning Department and other municipal and County departments to review potential impacts of proposed projects to the park. The IBID is supportive of extending the viaduct bridge across the rail lines and into Peter Francisco Park to connect the IBID to the downtown.

L – Pets

Dogs and other pets must be under the control of owners at all times. Leash laws and animal waste regulations will be enforced as defined in the City Code and Health Code.

2 Objective II–Buildings, Structures, and Monuments: Minimize the Impacts that Buildings and Monuments have on the Park Landscape, and Preserve the Open Space of Peter Francisco Park. Mantain and Preserve Historic Structures

A—New construction

Restrict construction of additional buildings, structures or monuments in Peter Francisco Park. It should be recognized that additional structures in the park might alter the balance that presently exists between open space for general park use and special uses requiring buildings.

1 New special use facilities such as a Visitors/Police Center, museums, recreation centers, and stadiums that are not essential to the mission of Peter Francisco Park and/or the IBID will not be sited in the park.
2 Installation of new statues or monuments in the park will not be discouraged, as they may add to the park's design intent, and may be compatible with naturalistic urban nature of the park.
3 Construction of a new structure in the park will only be considered when:

    a There is a clearly demonstrated need for a defined service to the public that cannot be met by existing conditions.
    b Sufficient, detailed information is available that alternative sites outside the park have been studied and that the proposed structure can be located only in the area in question.
    c The effects on the park of the proposed structure have been fully assessed to ensure that the structure will not have deleterious effect on the park landscape.
    d Sufficient effort will be expended to assure the very best architectural quality.
    e Design plans for any proposed structure will include measures and mitigations that minimize negative impacts upon the park environment.

4 Viaduct bridge to Triangle/Unity Park Redevelopment area.

B – Historic structures

Preservation of notable park structures that have historic, architectural and aesthetic value will be encouraged as well as restoration or reconstruction of other features that provide continuity with the past.

1 An historic resources survey will be conducted to inventory and evaluate the historic values of buildings, structures, monuments, and landscapes in accordance with established city, state and federal criteria.

2 Special and immediate effort will be made to identify, organize, and preserve existing plans and plan documents related to the design and construction of all significant park features.

E – Park maintenance structures

Maintenance structures will be designed and sited to minimize visual and other impacts on the park.

1 Wherever feasible, maintenance structures will be consolidated within existing buildings or be held off site.

2 Maintenance structures will be visually screened to the greatest extent possible. Where utilitarian structures such as storage containers are employed and visible to park users, screen fences or planting will be used to mitigate their visual impacts on the park environment.

F – Energy and resource conservation

Encourage energy and resource conservation and recycling systems that would contribute to efficient management and operation of Peter Francisco Park. New structures, or substantially remodeled existing structures, should, where feasible, incorporate energy and resource conservation systems.

3 Visitors/Mini Police Center

A need has been identified for better visitor information and security for both resident users and tourists. Visitor centers and information kiosks provide visitor information and serve as staging areas for tours and other services. Visitor centers will serve an educational purpose, with information and exhibits on the City of Newark, the Ironbound, the park features, history, and natural resources. These may also provide opportunities for generating revenue through retailing, fees for services such as tours, and fundraising appeals.

Visitor/security center

There is one visitor center proposed in the park. This would be a destination point that attracts visitors and provides additional security and community organization. Due to limited department funds, a park partner organization (such as the Friends of Peter Francisco Park) should play a role in the development and operation of the visitor center. The visitor center could also provide an important visible presence for the IBID and the City of Newark. The visitor center will have the potential for generating revenue through the sale of park-related merchandise. This revenue may be important for funding operation of the visitor information services. Selection of a visitor center location may be influenced by many factors including redevelopment of the park.

4 Park Concessions

Concessions can play an important role in providing visitor services in Peter Francisco Park. It is generally more cost effective for the IBID to contract out for some services than to provide them. Food vendors, rentals, tickets are examples of services that may be provided by concessions. The IBID would receive a percentage of revenue, or a flat fee, from concessions. Concession contracts are awarded on the basis of competitive bids. The revenue generated from concessions can play an increasing role in supplementing the park budget.

Issues

It is important to balance concessions and the need to generate revenue with preservation of the park landscape and experience. Concessions should provide services that are informational, educational, or recreation serving, and that enhance the visitor's experience. Most people are pleased to have the services provided by the concessions, but there is a limit to commercialization and its appropriateness in the park setting. There have been concerns expressed about concessions that cater primarily to tourists and offer typical souvenir sales without much relevance to the park. The location and appearance of some food concessions can also be an issue. A balance is needed between the need to increase revenue and what is determined to be appropriate for Peter Francisco Park.

Considerations

- New opportunities for concessions should be explored. New or expanded concessions should meet a standard of appropriateness and be recreational or recreation serving.
- Concessions should be consistent with municipal and state regulations (recreational purpose) and the Objectives and Policies for Peter Francisco Park.
- Concessions should be appropriate to the park landscape.
- Retail concessions should include merchandise related to the City of Newark and the Ironbound, information, recreational activities, landscape, horticulture, history, and natural resources.
- Food concessions should meet appearance standards. Carts can be supplied with IBID and/or Peter Francisco Park umbrellas.

- Food concessions should be coordinated with existing food services in the Ironbound.

Proposed new concessions:

- Coffee Cafe, snacks, park-related merchandise
- Sale of park-related merchandise
- Gift shop
- Skate/bike rental or other concession
- South windmill area – pavilion structure (approximately 2,500 sq. ft.)
- Carriage rides

Park security

- Coordinate efforts with other City departments to address "camping," drug abuse, and other social problems in the park. Establish a regular ongoing program with the NPD to clear camps. This program will require a regular commitment of maintenance staff to clean and restore the park.
- Involve community groups in park security issues so they see the park as an extension of their neighborhoods. Establish a park neighborhood security committee as a working group to focus on park and neighborhood safety and security issues. Have an ongoing forum with community groups, Police Department, the Department of Social Services, and the Health Department to discuss park and neighborhood security and enforcement issues.
- Support community groups that are proactive in area security issues.
- Seek legislation to assist security efforts in Peter Francisco Park such as a Safety Zone.
- Implement a "Park Watch" program: install signs at all entries asking park users to report suspicious activities; install emergency phones at each park entrance and other locations (direct connection to police dispatch).

Peter Francisco Park must be a safe park, but as important as statistics are, the perception of safety is just as important. A sense of security is essential for park users to enjoy their park experience. Proper maintenance is one of the best deterrents to crime. A park that is well tended shows a commitment to make the park a secure place. Successful parks with high visitation are self patrolling. Visible maintenance staff also provide a deterrent.

5 Park Budget and Funding

Park operating budget

The estimated operating and construction needs of Peter Francisco Park will be determined annually. The total annual budget for the park is estimated at $50,000. This will be further determined by estimating the portion of the City budget that is spent on the park Golden Gate and additional service, security, and recreational needs of the park.

Existing expenditures do not cover all of Peter Francisco Park's needs. Current budget constraints prevent addressing the full maintenance needs in the park, maintenance has been curtailed. Additional maintenance and security staffing needs must be further identified.

Revenue generation

The park can supplement its budget by generating revenue within its facilities. Ongoing revenue can be generated from concessions, events, and permit and user fees for special events. A balance is needed between raising revenue and keeping the park accessible to users of all income groups.

Ironbound Arts & Community Center proposal

Executive Summary

In developing a Community Arts & Cultural Center, partners from public, private, non-profit, and community sectors strategically shape the physical and social character of a neighborhood, town, city, or region around arts and cultural activities. A Community Arts & Cultural Center rejuvenates structures and streetscapes, improves local business viability and public safety, and brings diverse people together to celebrate, inspire, and be inspired. In turn, the community fosters entrepreneurs and cultural industries that generate jobs and income, spin off new products and services, and attract and retain unrelated businesses and skilled workers. Together, a Community Arts & Cultural Center's livability and economic development outcomes have the potential to substantially improve the future of the Ironbound and the City of Newark.

As part of its strategic planning and economic development efforts, in 2011–12 the Ironbound Business Improvement District (IBID) and Sumei Multidisciplinary Arts Center with support of the Newark Arts Council undertook a project to assess the Ironbound Fire Station, **56 Prospect St., Ironbound, Newark, NJ** as a community and cultural asset. The station sits at a primary gateway to the Ironbound community, three blocks from Penn Station and Downtown Newark. The IBID engaged Newark Metametrics, to conduct a usage, space usage, and schematic review study and to recommend strategies to improve this 105-year-old cultural landmark. The existence of the Ironbound Community Arts & Cultural Center will show the community's dedication to investing in arts and culture, and to providing an educational service to inspire the public. This type of commitment has placed the City of Newark and the Ironbound as one of the top destinations in our region.

The long existence of the arts in Newark has shown that the City of Newark values its educational and cultural significance. The Ironbound Community Arts & Cultural Center provides an opportunity for the preservation of an historically significant building and provides a cultural experience for visitors and residents. To give this project the multi-disciplined approach that it required, the IBID assembled a team of community advocates and experts who drew on their experience to analyze a wide range of data, opinions and best practices.

The Ironbound Business Improvement District (IBID) is a certified Special Improvement District established in December 2000 by local ordinance. As stated above, first and foremost, the IBID is a unique public-private partnership between the Ferry Street business community, the municipal government, and the neighborhood. The IBID works with the City to improve business and community development services, rebuild our infrastructure, and market the Ironbound as a reliable and exciting destination. Administrative funding is created through an annual assessment on commercial property in the district, collected by the City, but transferred and managed by the IBID. On January 11, 2013, the IBID celebrated its 11th Anniversary. We have stable property values in the area, a low vacancy rate, and a growing market.

Sumei Multidisciplinary Arts Center, is a non-profit organization, located in the Ironbound at 85 Hamilton St., Newark, NJ, whose mission is to provide a space for artists of diverse backgrounds and disciplines to interact through the arts and humanities with the local and statewide community, utilizing performance, exhibition, and education to create an exchange of cultural ideas and practices. The Center is a venue for artists from around the world to share their art, grow with their artistic abilities, and share their knowledge and skills. Sumei was founded by a collective of musicians, architects, poets, graphic designers, visual, and fine artists interested in broadening their reach. Based in Newark, New Jersey, Sumei reaches out beyond borders to bring African, American, Asian, Caribbean, and European art to the American public, and to support emerging artists in many disciplines.

The Newark Arts Council, located at 17 Academy Street, Suite 1104, Newark, NJ was created to advance and expand the artistic and cultural resources of the City of Newark, New Jersey. The agency provides leadership, direction, and technical assistance through partnerships with Newark's many artists, arts administrators, community organizations, community development corporations, planning groups, economic development agencies, and the general public. The goal of the Council is to share resources, promote advocacy efforts, assist in audience development and public awareness of arts and culture, and to serve as a cultural resource to the community.

The proposed Ironbound Community Arts & Cultural Center can be a valuable public asset governed by a cooperative association. For the art center to be established, a long-term lease purchase agreement needs to be established between the City of Newark and the Ironbound Business Improvement District. Arts and culture at a historic juncture are economic and social catalysts. Through smart collaborations with other sectors – government, private business, foundations – they create opportunities for rejuvenation and economic development, anchored in and tailored to diverse communities like the Ironbound. It is the partnerships forged that are central to a successful outcome. Partnering can be challenging. But, it is a crucial component of making this project work.

Key Issues & Strategies

The table below identifies key issues and strategies identified within this study to address them. Specific recommendations are highlighted at the end of each section of the report.

To justify its presence in this location, the Ironbound Community Arts & Cultural Center must be a vibrant visitor attraction and provide more cultural and economic benefits for the City of Newark, the community, and its tenants.

- In collaboration with the work of the IBID, Sumei Multidisciplinary Arts Center, and the Newark Arts Council, the City can invest in a lease/purchase partnership with the IBID with lease terms that allow for phased-in occupation of the Fire Station, its tenants, and the orderly departure of the Fire Department.
- The building's interior must be rebuilt and brought up to code and reconfigured to improve the visitor experience and convert more of the second and third floors into rentable and useful areas. Features to revitalize the Community Arts & Cultural Center will include a central gallery and secondary galleries, theatre, classrooms, and administrative offices.
- The Ironbound Community Arts & Cultural Center will evolve to increase its economic self-sufficiency over a phased-in process.
- The use of space, internal policies and house rules should allow tenants to be commercially successful, and self-sustaining.
- The project will explore collaboration and sharing of resources with the arts, music, theatre, and museum communities.

The Ironbound Community Arts & Cultural Center will serve as an "art incubator" to nurture and grow artistic talent, and outreach programs will be targeted to attract a diversity of artists, encourage dialogue and participation by community stakeholders to ensure management continuity and continuous improvement.

Acknowledgment

The Ironbound Community Arts & Cultural Center Team understands that this is a primary and significant project that will require sustained partners and dedicated funding to maximize the intended benefits for creation of the Ironbound Community Arts & Cultural Center. If this proposal is accepted for implementation, the City of Newark and the Newark Fire Department, and its leaders in policy making, planning, economic development, arts and cultural development have and will continue to play a supportive and ongoing role in providing guidance, technical assistance and funding for capital improvements. The Ironbound Community Arts & Cultural Center Team expresses our sincere appreciation to the City of Newark, the Steering Committee for the Ironbound Arts & Community Center, the Newark Fire Department, and numerous community organizations and individuals for their cooperation and assistance with this project. Without their support, this project would not have been possible.

 # PROSPECT FIRESTATION

The Fire station was built in 1909 as a training stable for fire department horses. It was said to be "the finest and most substantial building of its kind in the country, as every convenience for the caring of sick horses, and training of new ones … has been carefully provided for." The architects were the father and son team of John H. and Wilson C. Ely, better known as the designers of Newark City Hall and the National Newark Building at 744 Broad St. Since then it has primarily been used for Fire Department equipment storage and repair.

The current Gallery at the Firestation is the first step in the discovery of the Fire Station as an Arts & Community Center, and is a community-based and supported gallery dedicated to exhibiting a variety of artists, from emerging to established, with a special focus on local artists. It is a place for people to come together to talk, see films, performances and lectures – a place to learn from both professionals and peers, to be creative & to get inspired and a place where opportunities for new ideas and new ventures can be developed and supported. The station also aims to serve the younger generation through functioning as an educational space for young adults and children, offering classes in arts and technology.

An overall observation is that the materials stored in the various places throughout the building seem to be somewhat mixed between new or actively useful materials, and old stuff just laying around. One goal is to clear the back areas of the first floor for use by the art gallery. This could be achieved, by relocating the hoses stored in room 110 to the large storage room on the second floor, room 205, or to the large back workroom #210 on the plans. Consolidation of the materials on the 2nd floor would be needed, and is very possible. The same could be done with the equipment in the back workshop #114. Not sure if the stuff in room 114 is even still used.

A second goal is to make an office for the IBID, possibly the Newark Arts Council, and/or other organizations. The best place for this would be the existing office in the front of the 2nd floor, room 219, and the adjacent storage room 218. For this you would need to relocate the steel shelving and cabinets with uniforms – perhaps to room 205. 205 would have to be totally re-organized – but it could be used in its present state of disarray. An alternate for the IBID office could be the whole south side of the third floor.

The Ironbound Community Arts & Cultural Center

Here are some possible program items that should be considered for the Ironbound Community Arts & Cultural Center:

Visual

- Workspaces for artist studios – non-residential – ala the Torpedo Factory in Alexandria, and the Silk Mill in Union City
- Spaces set up for artists to sell their work from their studios – ala the Torpedo Factory
- Artist in Residence Program – limited duration live/work studios for visiting artists – ala gallery Aferro in Newark
- Live/work artist spaces – rental units for artists – ala Artspace's PS109, Harlem
- Gallery exhibition space – ala City Without Walls or Aljira, a Center for Contemporary Art, Newark
- Art workshop space – classroom space for children and adults
- Video and photography workshop
- Film screening theatre/auditorium
- Ceramics and glass blowing workshops ala Glass Roots or Manchester Craftsman Guild, Pittsburgh

Music and Performing Arts

- Rehearsal space for musical groups
- Rehearsal space for dance and theatre groups
- Auditorium
- Video and recording studio/facility
- Individual rehearsal spaces for hourly rental

Cultural Center

- Lecture hall
- Education classrooms including school & college prep., languages, Capoeira and Martial arts, cooking, etc.
- Museum space for the history and culture of Newark, the Ironbound, Newark Chinatown, Fire Fighters, etc. ala Newark Public Library, or NJ Historical Society
- Roof Garden with playground and learning center – ala ICC's proposed new facility on NY Ave.
- Community Information and Tourism Center

Community Center

- Facility for young people to go after school for recreation and study – ala Silk Road Café, NYC
- Summer education programs
- Computer lab for homework and training
- Meeting room for community groups
- Day care center
- Drop-in assistance program, ala ICC, Newark
- Jobs training program – ala Manchester Craftsman Guild, Pittsburgh

Administrative offices

- Consolidate arts organizations
- Offices for the IBID
- Coordinated office for the Newark Arts Alliance

Auxiliary

- Kitchen/catering
- Satellite showplace or booth for other community organizations – Newark Museum, ICC, Prudential Center, etc. – potential income
- Large open space suitable for public events and rental for events – ala the Newark Museum's Engelhard Court, or the Torpedo Factory first floor – potential income
- Coffee shop or other concessions – potential income
- Accommodations/services for people with disabilities – Braille, assistive listening, housing, jobs, etc.
- Art supply store – potential income
- Art shop for members to sell their work – potential income
- Traveling exhibitions

- Community outreach programs at other venues
- Entrepreneur-based Community Information Center (CIC) see attached

Virtual

- The bricks and mortar site would very naturally call for a virtual site for arts- and community-based information: Ironbound and Newark activities, history, study help, social assistance, etc.

Marketing/comunications synopsis

Marketing/Communications

Ironbound Update Newsletter. Fall newsletter was reviewed and approved at Nov. Exec. Committee meeting and is currently in production. A review and updating of the mailing list was completed in association with recent update of directories on website. Upon completion and delivery, newsletter will be disseminated in early December through mail house and through personal distribution in district, at City Hall and other locations in Newark, and to other Newark stakeholders.

Pedestrian Safety Campaign. In support of City and statewide campaign, produced and distributed a feature story promoting an Ironbound Open House so local community members could contribute to the citywide Pedestrian & Bicycle Safety Plan currently in development. The meeting was the first held in the city and more than 30 people participated. The meeting was also promoted through website and Facebook page.

This followed earlier press release announcing IBID support for the Newark program and its importance in Ironbound District. Both efforts resulted in multiple news placements in local media outlets. Campaign has also been promoted through website and Facebook page and is highlighted in feature story in the fall newsletter.

New Ironbound Creative Campaign. New ads including updated images and an updated tagline – "Let's Meet in the Ironbound." – was developed and implemented across all marketing channels including billboards and other "out-of-home" displays such as those in Gateway Center, in online banner ads and in print publications. Update was completed in conjunction with upcoming holiday season and start of the New Year.

NewarkBound Magazine. Participating in editorial planning sessions for next issue of magazine that will follow release of current edition of magazine in December. Current edition in production includes features on artisanal food producers in the Ironbound and top Newark area diners including Ironbound locations. The magazine will also include a full page advertorial highlighting the award-winning Ironbound video produced in 2014, and a full page ad promoting the Ironbound District as Newark's top destination for dining, shopping, entertainment, etc.

Comcast Spotlight Campaign. Holiday season advertising campaigns with Comcast, FiOS and Xfinity are delivering good results in terms of clicks and visits from both cable ads and online banner ads with embedded video, email collection opportunities. Campaign started in October and results continue to show high click rates and viewership. Goals of the second phase of the campaign – increase awareness outside of Newark of the amenities that are provided in the Ironbound and Newark with particular focus during holiday shopping/dining season. The first phase focused on informing the public of Endless Arts, Dodge Poetry Festival and other local arts opportunities at the Prospect Street Fire Station Arts Center to combine with shopping/dining/community development in the Ironbound.

AAA/IBID Event. Attendance/participation in event at Portuguese Sports Club was underwhelming. While representatives from AAA were available (many who *speak* Portuguese and Spanish) to meet with interested business owners about opportunities to reach their more than 3.5 million members, including options with no out-of-pocket costs, and several great prizes were being raffled, only a handful of district business owners took part. The event was widely publicized in paid newspaper ads, through IBID newsletter, flyers distributed in the district, on IBID website, through social media and through a personalized "meet and greet" effort by AAA representatives. AAA will continue to follow up on an individualized basis with business owners. Packets are also available to interested business owners at IBID office.

Comcast Spotlight Holiday Message. Coordinated logistics, drafted script for holiday message on behalf of Ironbound District recorded by IBID President Steve Yglesias. Comcast will complete all edits in November and schedule spots to air in December throughout Essex County. A copy of the spot will be provided to IBID upon completion.

Ironbound Explorers Guide. Completed edits to current edition of guide including coordinating new images from the Devils organization, collecting and adding new partner logos and updating restaurant directory. Goal is to reprint in first quarter of 2015 when current supply is expected to run out.

TravelHost Magazine. Developed updated editorial and images for issue that will be published during holiday season to promote shopping and dining in the Ironbound as part of holiday visits to the district.

Ironbound Short Film. The film has won several new awards in international competitions marking the completion of 2014. Coordinating follow-up publicity to showcase awards won with photo of trophies on Ferry Street. Press release will promote the film as well as the partnership between IBID, GNCVB and BCDC working together to make the Ironbound the City's top travel/tourism destination.

Syndicated TV Show Sponsorship. IBID has joined with a group of Newark stakeholders to support production of an Emmy Award-winning syndicated television program called Aqua Kids to film/produce segments in Newark, including one featuring RiverBank Park's boat tours, highlighting the City's connection to the Passaic River and beyond. IBID will get 60 second advertising spots (using edited Ironbound video) on segment that will air three times across North American syndicated network of channels. IBID will be reimbursed for upfront expenditures as other sponsors come online and through trade for support of NewarkBound Magazine, one of the other backers of this initiative along with GNCVB.

TAP Information Portal – Newark Penn Station. Participated in and supported ribbon-cutting event for new Tourist Assistance Portal (TAP) at Newark Penn Station. IBID supported development of TAP touch-screen which provides information about the Ironbound and other Newark destinations, accommodations, services, etc. Participants included IBID representatives S. Yglesias and R. Baptista, along with Mayor Quintana and representatives of GNCVB, Newark business organizations, NJ Transit and other supporters. TAP introduction was highlighted on IBID website and Facebook page.

GNCVB. Attended second monthly meeting as representative of Ironbound District regarding promotional activities for the City. Also participated in a meeting of city stakeholders in response to request from Mayor's office to develop events that can help Newark reach destination marketing goals.

Newark Marketing Partnerships. Continue to meet with marketing representatives at Prudential Center, NJPAC and from Seton Hall University to discuss mutually beneficial marketing efforts. This outreach will continue including planned meetings in the weeks ahead with NJ Transit representatives and other Newark stakeholders.

Newark "Hyper Local" Online Media. Online ad campaign continues to deliver above industry average returns in terms of clicks and interaction with hyper-local audiences. Continue to disseminate news about what's happening in the Ironbound District through hyper-local online media outlets as a "star blogger" for the Patch organization and in collaboration with editor of NewarkPulse. com, BrickCityLive.com and other online news outlets.

Storefronts Newark Program. Program launch has been pushed back to spring of 2015 to coordinate with program launch in Newark's downtown district for greater impact. Worked with IBID staff member L. Roldan to identify potential locations (open storefronts in district) for participation in this program that will connect Ironbound District property owners with arts community to present pop-up galleries displaying the work of local artists to "activate" their currently dormant commercial space. No charge to the IBID or participating property owners, liability issues covered, the program is a collaboration between Newark's Solo(s) Project House and NYC's Project for Empty Space. Contact with property owners has been difficult.

Greater Newark "Fam" Tour Committee. Continue to participate in committee meetings that bring together representatives from GNCVB, greater-Newark area hotels, as well as other marketing participants like Newark Museum, NJPAC, etc. to plan and execute a "fam" tour, short for familiarization, for representatives of travel agencies and tour travel operators. The goal is to introduce more potential visitors to Newark and the Ironbound District. Event in planning stages for either fall 2014 or spring 2015.

Rutgers Graduation – Prudential Center. Worked with staff to transport Ironbound Information Booth and significant quantities of Ironbound Explorers Guide and NewarkBound Magazine to Prudential Center for distribution at recent Rutgers University graduation ceremony. Baglivo/Grossman personally handed out several thousand copies of each publication and served as ambassadors for people looking for information about Newark and the Ironbound District. IBID and GNCVB were the only local organizations represented at the event with nearly 17,000 attendees.

Ironbound Community Service Awards. Press release featuring 2014 award winners was disseminated with photos taken at event, translating into multiple media placements in community news outlets. Feature and photos were also posted on goironbound.com and will be included in spring newsletter.

UEZ Program – Ferry Street Optical. Feature story highlighting completion of work that included grant funding from Newark UEZ Façade Improvement Program at Ferry Street Optical will be included in spring newsletter. Photos from event featured through social media on Go Ironbound Facebook page.

MeetIronbound.com. A micro-website, www.meetironbound.com, was created to expose more viewers to the newly produced short film. It also provides a vehicle to note and thank the many Ironbound businesses and other Newark individuals and organizations that contributed to the production as locations, performers, etc. The site is linked back to goironbound.com and newarkhappening. com, to connect viewers with additional information and resources about the Ironbound and the City of Newark.

Online Marketing Management

Ironbound Facebook Page. Total likes continue to grow, now approaching 3,100 in total, maintaining the Ironbound District's page as one of the most popular social media sites in Newark. Continued focus on Ironbound business news and Newark-related information focusing on activities, events and opportunities to spur concurrent visitation to the Ironbound's restaurants and stores is driving interest.

GoIronbound.com. District Connect continues to feature upcoming events, news bulletins and updates and other information of interest and importance to Ironbound District stakeholders. IBID businesses and restaurants are encouraged to contribute to data collection so more local events and consumer opportunities can be presented. Posts continue to be made to website featuring events, activities and initiatives of the IBID and other Newark stakeholders. Website analytics show that our number of site visitors continues to increase and pages visited, duration of time on site, etc. continue to be consistent, bounce rate remains low, with spikes associated with specific events on the timeline.

NewarkBound Magazine

Other than the IBID's award-winning Explorers Guide, the Newark-Ironbound market does not have a designated destination marketing device. This magazine addresses this issue, expands as is built on the shoulders of the Explorers Guide, and provides focus to urban tourism capacities of the area, which are built on travel, entertainment, culture, business, and dining. The Ironbound is unique on the east coast of the USA. It is a remarkable transportation nexus including I-95/NJ Turnpike, I-280, I-78, Rts. 1 & 9, and the Garden State Parkway; it has a major international airport, and is situated on the Northeast railroad corridor at Penn Station Newark. No other neighborhood in New Jersey is so specifically situated and 20 miles from New York City, and so directly connected. The Ironbound is New Jersey's top urban tourist destination.

The glossy, 80-page, full color publication, "is packed with information, stunning photography and articles that promote the city and beyond," publisher Victor Nichols said. It features stories on food, architecture, arts and culture, family fun, places to stay and things to do in Newark and its neighboring communities." A letter signed by the CEOs of six of Newark's leading civic and economic development organizations, including Newark Alliance, Newark Regional Business Partnership, Newark Downtown District, Greater Newark Convention and Visitors Center, Brick City Development Corporation and the Ironbound Business Improvement District, praised NewarkBound as a welcomed addition to the "assets that already exist in our great city. This life style magazine is designed to inform both the local and surrounding communities and visitors about the happenings in Newark," the executives wrote.

The IBID has pursued and accomplished a successful advertising and marketing program since 2002 built upon the Newark's Ironbound Explorers Guide, a

Shopping Guide, and various ad campaigns rooted in IBID brand assets. Our annual budget in 2013 and 2014 for marketing, public relations, and promotions is $181,100. The IBID has been promoted through a multi-media approach that has included print, out-of-home and online channels in addition to an "Ironbound Update" newsletter and extensive editorial coverage. The IBID is extending its promotional efforts through the creation of a print and digital magazine (hereinafter "Magazine") that is intended to be a destination marketing vehicle to promote the interests of the IBID, the Ironbound Business Improvement District of Newark, NJ, the Ironbound Business District Management Corp., and Newark's Ironbound neighborhood in general as a premier cultural, dining, and entertainment destination and tourist venue, and that shall explore, define and communicate the Ironbound neighborhood as a key value to the City of Newark's downtown, universities, cultural assets, and the region as a whole (collectively the "Mission of the Magazine").

As stated above, the Ironbound Business Improvement District has pursued and accomplished a successful advertising and marketing program since 2002 built upon the Explorer Guide (over 300,000 published), a Shopping Guide (over 30,000 published), and various ad campaigns such as "Meet Me in The Ironbound," billboards and editorials. The Ironbound Magazine – "NewarkBound: The Ironbound & Beyond," is the next logical step in promoting the Ironbound as the City of Newark's premier cultural, entertainment and dining destination. The magazine examines and promotes the value added capacity of the Ironbound to Newark area assets as Newark's essential mode of access to these assets.

Mission of the Magazine

The Magazine is a destination marketing vehicle that promotes Newark's Ironbound neighborhood as a premier cultural, dining, and entertainment destination and tourist venue. The magazine explores, defines, and communicates the Ironbound neighborhood of Newark, NJ as a key value to the City of Newark's downtown, universities, cultural assets, and the region as a whole. Centered in a transportation nexus that connects us to the world, the Ironbound is a strong, established positive attraction and valuable asset that defines urban tourism. The magazine captures this vitality and connects this message to the world.

Partnerships

1. DMC Publishing of Florham Park, NJ will develop and publish a periodic magazine on behalf of IBID, and will comply with guidelines provided by IBID regarding the use of the IBID logo and trademarks, and editorial content, magazine layout, and cover designs.

2.   Brick City Development Corporation, Newark, NJ will assist in distribution of the magazine in support of the Newark Visitors and Convention Bureau.
3.   The following hotels will be magazine distribution partners:
4.   Kings Super Markets will be magazine distribution partners
5.   Rutgers University-Newark, Essex County Community College, and NJIT will be magazine distribution partners.
6.   The Prudential Center will provide partnership web linkages.
7.   The Red Bulls (Arena) will provide partnership web linkages.
8.   The Newark Museum will provide partnership web linkages.
9.   The following restaurants and bakeries are distribution partners:

Outline of Marketing Plan for the Magazine

1.1 The Magazine shall be a collaborative publishing effort of the IBID and DMC.
1.2 The content of the Magazine must appeal to a broad and diverse readership over an extended period of time and will consist of editorial material and topics selected by the parties for that purpose as well as IBID-supplied content to promote IBID and to inform IBID's readership of information and resources that IBID wishes to publicize.
1.3 The content of the Magazine shall be consistent with the Mission of the Magazine.
1.4 The IBID will cooperate and consult with partners to solicit advertisers for the purchase of paid advertising in the Magazine. In this regard, IBID agrees to actively assist partners through the efforts of the IBID's staff, volunteers, donors and Board members and agrees to introduce partners to the IBID's corporate/ organizational donors.
1.5 The IBID will use its own website or other platform or channel unrelated to the other party to commercialize the Magazine.
1.6 It is intended that in calendar year 2013, one edition of the Magazine will be produced and printed and distribution of the Magazine will begin in March 2013. Thereafter, it is contemplated that the Magazine will be produced and distributed twice a year.
1.7 The Magazine will be distributed at no charge to its readership.
1.8 No less than 100,000 copies of the magazine will be published and distributed throughout the Newark region, and will be supported by IBID placement ads and billboards.

Marketing Plan

While the Ironbound is a popular tourism destination based chiefly on culture, dining and entertainment, the tourism sector in Newark is challenged in terms of both urban-suburban issues, politics, and issues of urban revival. Although a number of entertainment/cultural/tourism entities, including the Prudential

Center Arena, the Newark Museum, the NJPAC, Symphony Hall, as well as area Universities, the Brick City Development Corp., business and other business improvement districts and advocacy groups such as the Newark Regional Business Partnership, have marketing budgets to fund substantial intrastate and interstate advertising and promotional activities in a sustained and systematic fashion, there is little coordinated tourism management. This is largely due to the innovation of urban tourism. This magazine works to remedy the lack of focus and cooperation through the auspices of Newark's strongest destination – The Ironbound.

Cooperative Advertising & Marketing

Cooperative advertising and promotion is a powerful method of increasing the exposure of tourism businesses by bringing together the marketing power of the Ironbound and the City's tourism businesses to achieve a much greater impact and return from advertising and promotion budgets. By focusing on destination advantages and resources, individual business's advertisements can be placed in better publications and can have a stronger visual impact through location branding. Advertisements and editorial branding available in a magazine both hard copy and electronic can also make a destination more appealing by packaging together a range of tourism products and experiences. Promotional activities can likewise have a stronger impact.

While individual advertisements are often lost in the advertising clutter, a well-designed cooperative advertisement significantly increases the likelihood of the consumer seeing a business advertisement. As well as being larger and more likely to attract consumer attention, a cooperative advertisement has the benefit of combining the branding that attracts people to Newark and the Ironbound, alongside individual tourism businesses.

Destination Target Domestic & International

Short break (1–3 days)
Events (@ Pru-Ctr, NJPAC, etc.)
Day trippers
Conferences
Business events in Newark
Events (NCAA, Super Bowl)
Conferences
Trade

Although a number of entertainment/cultural/tourism entities, including the Prudential Center Arena, the Newark Museum, the NJPAC, Symphony Hall, as well as area Universities, the Brick City Development Corp., business and other business improvement districts and advocacy groups such as the Newark Regional Business Partnership, have marketing budgets to fund substantial intrastate and interstate advertising and promotional activities in a sustained and systematic fashion, there is little coordinated tourism management. This is largely due to the innovation of urban tourism. This magazine works to remedy the lack of focus and cooperation through the auspices of Newark's strongest destination – The Ironbound.

Cooperative advertising and promotion is a powerful method of increasing the exposure of tourism businesses by bringing together the marketing power of the Ironbound and the City's tourism businesses to achieve a much greater impact and return from advertising and promotion budgets.

By focusing on destination advantages and resources, individual business's advertisements can be placed in better publications and can have a stronger visual impact through location branding. Advertisements and editorial branding available in a magazine both hard copy and electronic can also make a destination more appealing by packaging together a range of tourism products and experiences. Promotional activities can likewise have a stronger impact.

While individual advertisements are often lost in the advertising clutter, a well-designed cooperative advertisement significantly increases the likelihood of the consumer seeing a business advertisement. As well as being larger and more likely to attract consumer attention, a cooperative advertisement has the benefit of combining the branding that attracts people to Newark and the Ironbound, alongside individual tourism businesses.

TABLE C.1 SWOT Analysis (*)

STRENGTHS	WEAKNESSES
• Strong interest, ownership and love of Ironbound across many target markets	• Perception that customers have of Newark as challenged urban area – e.g.
• Variety and range of unique attractions in Newark	• Segregated operators and planners
• Proximity to New York City	• Limited cross promotion between business
• Well established and experienced professional operators already taking a targeted approach to destination marketing	• Lack of detailed data about visitors to Ironbound – why, how, where
• Strong advertising presence from major operators	• Lack of cohesive marketing and digital/online campaigns
• Existing festivals and events	• Timed, paid parking culture (day trippers)
• A unique transportation nexus.	

OPPORTUNITIES	THREATS
• New targeted approach to marketing and promotion	• Low cost deals attracting domestic and intrastate visitors out of the country
• Cooperative advertising approach	• Growth of other tourism areas including New York and Philadelphia
• Interest in history	• Limited financial resources available
• Rich environment for developing new product	• Safety and security
• Experience Ironbound campaigns	• Infrastructure renewal
• Potential to develop online marketing	• Urban–suburban political issues
• Proximity to New York region	
• Rail transport	
• High international student population in Newark	
• Urban tourism refining target market focus	
• Superbowl 2014	

(*) Humphrey, Albert (December 2005). "SWOT Analysis for Management Consulting" (PDF). SRI Alumni Newsletter (SRI International).

Marketing Objectives

1. Move to a cooperative advertising approach to increase Ironbound's representation in major tourism campaigns and publications eg. **NewarkBound; The Ironbound and beyond.**
2. Increase across the selected target markets, the

    a   number of visitors to Ironbound by 10% over two years
    b   dollar spend by visitors to Ironbound by 10% over two years
    c   number of overnight stays in Newark area by 10% over two years

3. Increase the number of visitors that come to Ironbound during off-peak periods (summer months) of the year.

Marketing Strategy

1. Work to complement and leverage Ironbound's marketing campaigns and promotions.
2. Encourage advertising by Ironbound tourism and entertainment businesses in premium private sector publication under the "Meet Me in the Ironbound" brand.
3. Develop a series of campaigns over the financial year to supplement campaigns run by the Brick City Development Corp. and the Newark Downtown District.
4. Publish **NewarkBound** Magazine. Minimum 100,000 copies. Twice a year.
5. Sell buy-in to the tourism businesses in Newark area.
6. Conduct the campaigns that achieved sufficient buy-in; and provide feedback to participating businesses and to the industry on the result of each campaign.
7. Distribute through area hotels, Kings Supermarket, Pru-Center, Red Bulls Arena, Rutgers University, area restaurants and targeted stores.

The IBID's advertising and promotional activities program will focus on facilitating cooperative advertising and promotion Newark and Ironbound product and brand strengths, using the *"Meet Me in the Ironbound"* brand.

The approach will take quality tourism products that are recognized as Newark-Ironbound's strengths, to proven markets under the umbrella of a well-branded campaign that targets specific market segments. The IBID's advertising and promotional effort will package together a range of compatible tourism products as distinct tourism "experiences" which will have high levels of appeal and more effectively come to the attention of the market segment being targeted. In developing these packages, existing and newly developed distribution channels, including the IBID's tourism website (www.goironbound.com), which includes links to area venues, will be utilized, and the advertising and promotional campaigns will complement and leverage off Newark area marketing campaigns.

These tourism experience packages will be developed, branded and then promoted to appropriate market segments by a range of means.

Positioning Strategy

- Meet Me In The IRONBOUND – *entertainment city*
- Meet Me In The IRONBOUND – *festival city*
- Meet Me In The IRONBOUND – *cultural arts city*
- Meet Me In The IRONBOUND – *historic city*
- Meet Me In The IRONBOUND – *university city*
- Meet Me In The IRONBOUND – *shopping city*

Target Markets

The Ironbound BID will work in partnership with area hotels, restaurants, BCDC, Pru-Center, NJMPAC, Newark Museum, Rutgers University, NJ Tourism, and Newark businesses to access specific target markets and segments. The table below summarizes these markets.

TABLE C.2 Target Markters

TARGET MARKETS AND SEGMENTS	PARTNERS	ACTIONS
Domestic leisure (intrastate and interstate)	Visiting friends or relatives (interstate and international visitors)	1. Magazine – motivational electronic itinerary based visitors' guides. 2. Promotions based around festivals & events. 3. Media – cooperative advertising in appropriate media.

Additional Initiatives

In addition to these marketing actions and in order to assist growth of the Ironbound tourism industry the IBID will facilitate or establish the following initiatives:

1. Strengthen relationships with BCDC – Convention and Visitors Bureau.
2. Establish an image library that is accessible to Ironbound tourism businesses.
3. Develop video ads.
4. Explore, in association with Regional Business Partnership, the opportunity to incorporate tourism categories in the annual Newark business awards initiative.
5. Support a Newark festival and events strategy.
6. Work collaboratively with partners to maximize traffic to goironbound.com and assist the ongoing development of the website through Facebook.
7. Enhance the role of the Ironbound Guides.

Evaluation

1. Results from visitor surveys.
2. Number of tourism products in Ironbound.
3. Estimated number of domestic visitors to the Ironbound.
4. Estimated number of international visitors to Ironbound.
5. Average length of stay (estimated nights) in Newark area hotels for intrastate, interstate and international visitors.★
6. Dollar spend by visitors to the Ironbound.
7. Magazine evaluations:

    • Industry buy-in
    • Responses to calls to action (feedback from participating businesses)
    • Web traffic from www.goironbound.com.

DMC Publishing develop and publish a periodic magazine on behalf of IBID, designed to support and promote IBID's interests, efforts and activities, to be distributed by DMC within IBID's service area and beyond. DMC shall provide all labor and materials necessary to publish and distribute said magazine. The magazine will appeal to a broad and diverse readership over an extended period of time and will consist of editorial material and topics selected for that purpose as well as IBID supplied content to promote the Ironbound and Newark, and to inform its readership of information and resources that IBID wishes to publicize.

Outdoor Maintenance and Quality of Life

Outdoor Maintenance and Quality of Life Management

The Ironbound BID Clean Team has completed another successful year in providing supplemental sanitation, maintenance and quality of life services to the Ironbound BID stakeholders. We're pleased to provide the following report which illustrates some of the highlights from this year's operations.

2014 quick stats:

Number of trash bags removed from the district: 29,400
Number of graffiti/sticker tags removed: 525
Number of illegal posters removed: 412
Number of QOL engagements: 425
Illegal dumping incidents: 220

IBID Ambassadors, Bernard Sims and Mark Blue clear curb cuts and crosswalks during the recent snow storm.

Snow Removal Action – February 11, 2014

The crew deployed from the Path Mark parking lot at 10:50 p.m. with the following machinery:

Two 20 cubic yard roll-off dump trucks
Two Bobcat S70 Skid-steer Loaders

The service period was **10:50 p.m. – 5:35 a.m. (6.5 hrs).** The focus of the Snow Removal Team was to have the biggest impact possible, while touching on all three of the main streets: Ferry Street, East Ferry Street and Wilson Avenue.
Snow was cleared from the following blocks:

East Ferry Street – Five Corners to mid-block between Wall St. and Niagara St. – Total of 1,500 linear ft. – 3 hrs.
Ferry Street – Prospect Street to Jefferson St. – Total of 900 linear ft. – 2 hrs.
Wilson Avenue – Five Corners to mid-block to Paterson St. – Total of 600 linear ft. – 1.5 hrs.

Total trips to the dump – 8
Roundtrip time to dump – 24 minutes
Total time spent dumping snow – 192 minutes or 3.2 hrs.
Total Weight/Tons Removed
Overflowing 20 cubic yard container = 25 cubic yards
Total cubic yards removed = 200 (25 cubic yards x 8 loads)
1 cubic ft. of snow = 5 lbs.
1 cubic yard = 27 cubic ft.
27 cubic ft. x 5 lbs = 135 lbs.
200 cubic yards x 135 lbs = 27,000 lbs or 13.5 tons of snow removed from the district in 6.5 hrs or 2 tons per hour.

E-waste Collection Event – April 2014

In April, the IBID Clean Team helped to coordinate a very successful e-waste collection event. Dozens of televisions, computer monitors, keyboards, CPUs and small electronics were collected from Newark residents and businesses. Many of the items that were collected were removed directly from the street.

The Following Report was Issued by the IBID Operations Team and Presented to the First Block Task Force on May 19, 2014.

In the past 2 weeks the Ironbound BID has worked closely with the Newark Police Department to increase visibility in and around the First Block Task Force focus area, which includes the triangular block bounded by Ferry Street on the south, Raymond Plaza East on the west and Market Street on the north. The area also includes Peter Francisco Park to the south.

The group illustrated below is an example of the type of loitering that takes place in front of 2 Ferry Street, 30 Ferry Street and the corner of Union Street and Ferry Street. This specific illustration is in front of 2 Ferry Street. The 5 individuals below are part of a larger group of about 15 individuals that spend a good portion of their day moving between the area of Penn Station and Union Street. During the past 2 weeks the Newark Police Department has increased their focus in the area with directed patrols from 11 a.m.–7 p.m. and the monitoring of the area by plainclothes detectives. Those investigations are ongoing and will continue. The main focus of the plainclothes investigations is to detect the sale of "K2" a synthetic drug that mimics the effects of marijuana … also known as "spice." All forms of synthetic marijuana were outlawed in the State of New Jersey last year. The concern is that the Smoke Shops in the area, including those within the First Block area, are serving as attractive trading posts for this drug due to the paraphernalia that is sold inside. In addition to synthetic marijuana the other major concern in this area is the trading of prescription pills, which coincides with the prostitution trade. Many of those who participate in "street life" are able to receive powerful prescription drugs like oxycodone through Medicare … they in turn sell the drug to others or trade it for sex.

On May 14th at 12:04 p.m. NYP and IBID Operations Manager, were conducting a tour of the First Block Area when they spotted an individual acting strangely near the corner Union Street and Ferry Street. The actor was trailed for about a half block and was observed panhandling in front of 42 Ferry Street where Ferry Smoke Shop is located. The actor was questioned and continued to act in an erratic manner. After a brief identification and warrants check, it was discovered that the individual had 3 outstanding warrants recorded. NYP executed an arrest following the discovery of the warrants.

Peter Francisco Park

Homeless activity in Peter Francisco Park has increased significantly in the last 6 months, after a relative dip in activity last year. In the past two weeks we have had an average of **4 homeless engagements per day**, during all hours of the day. Those who sleep in the park are not the same individuals who ply their pill selling trade across the street … in most cases, those who are homeless are the buyers … so in that way, there is a consistent supply and demand relationship. IBID Operations Manager and his staff monitor the park all day, however, there is a consistent flow of activity, with a significant bump in the afternoon hours. More likely than not, the individuals illustrated below, made an illicit prescription pill purchase and combined it with alcohol. All three individuals were advised and escorted out of the park by IBID staff.

The Newark Police Department's immediate response to the issues conveyed to them last week during the joint meeting between the Newark Police Department, New Jersey Transit Police and the IBID. The "eye-in-the-sky" which was stationed at the eastern tip of the park provided strong visual symbol of the presence of the Police Department. Additionally, two officers were stationed in the middle of the park, greeting and speaking with pedestrians as they moved through the park.

Illegal dumping

The IBID Clean Team continues to assist stakeholders by supplementing the City's efforts to remove illegal dumping and items left out for pick-up on bulk days. In July and August the IBID Clean Team averaged 6 illegal dumping incidents per week, removing large piles of debris like the ones illustrated here. These piles include large items such as dressers, desks, toilets and bed frames, box springs and mattresses. Piles are at their largest following the bulk pick-up days on the first Wednesday of each month.

Wilson Avenue Beautification

Throughout the summer of 2014 the IBID Clean Team focused on the finer details along Wilson Avenue. In addition to cleaning the sidewalks and removing graffiti, The clean team cleared weeds from every tree well from the 5 corners to Stockton Street and installed dark brown mulch. The Clean Team will continue to monitor these tree wells and will perform another round of mulching during the fall.

Anti-Litter – Poster Contest

One of IBID's primary services is to keep the area clean, but we are faced with a daunting littering problem. We realized that community involvement with a strong educational component is necessary. We are sponsoring our Annual Anti-Litter Poster Contest in the area's elementary/middle schools, and invite your school to participate. The IBID works with the Newark Public Schools, Newark Councilman Augusto Amador, and Investors Bank. The IBID conducts its public relations through Baglivo Strategic Communications and will produce 20,000 copies of the posters to be distributed throughout the participating schools. The area has four local newspapers and a regional newspaper. The IBID communicated the contest on its website and Facebook sites.

Funds will be spent on publishing 20,000 posters, awards, and public relations. Posters and poster flyers are sent to every home in the Ironbound neighborhood through direct placement with students in the elementary school system, and distribution through local media.

Over thirty (3) posters were received and 100s of students participated. Posters were provided to each school for distribution to all the students, 5,000 were distributed as inserts in the Luso-Americano newspaper, and 1,000s were distributed on the street, and at various businesses.

Goal

To raise awareness of what we can do about litter and, ultimately to have Ironbound be a litter-free community.

Why We Need It?

Litter harms the environment, water quality and wildlife, poses health risks, creates an ugly and disheartening environment, is associated with increased crime, and costs a lot of time and energy to clear away that could be used for something more positive. Litter is a serious problem that worsens when we do not pay attention and let it go unchecked. It's a problem we can solve if we work together.

Objective

"Let's Work Together to Keep the Ironbound Clean"

This is the IBID Anti-Litter slogan. Education and public awareness are long-term solutions to addressing our litter problem. The best hope for keeping our community clean is in changing behaviors and establishing good habits, especially among our young people. This contest is designed to teach our children ways to eliminate litter by becoming aware of the problem of littering, instilling a sense of pride, and building an appreciation for our community.

To involve youth in anti-litter awareness and support Earth Day, we challenge each Ironbound elementary school (both public and private) to create a unique poster with a positive anti-litter message. Each school may submit up to 4 posters in two grade groups: Group A will be first through fourth and, Group B will be fifth through eighth grade). The winners will receive awards and get their posters professionally printed and distributed throughout the community by the Ironbound Business Improvement District (IBID) Management Corporation.

Schools Who Are Participating

Lafayette Street School
Oliver Street School
Ann Street School

Hawkins Street School
South Street School
St. Casmir Academy
Wilson Avenue School

Poster Teams/Participants

- Each school organized their best poster teams with two teams from grades, first through fourth, and two teams from fifth through eighth.
- Each post identified the school; grade group; and included the student or students information on the back of the poster.

Posters Eere Judged on:

1 Artistic layout
2 Effectiveness in conveying a positive anti-litter message
3 Creativity
4 Poster-like quality
5 Advertising appeal

IBID Board of Directors Were Judges.

- Each grade group had one poster judged best of group.
- Posters were judged on effectiveness of anti-littering message, creativity, and best expression of the Ironbound neighborhood.
- Two first place winners (one from first through fourth grade, and another from fifth through eighth grade).

The winning teams' posters are the IBID's official anti-litter poster for one year. Both winning posters will be on the information poster.

The winning teams received recognition by having their poster professionally printed and displayed throughout the neighborhood.

The winning teams received the IBID good citizens award cup.

All students received awards certificates from the IBID.

Winners of the Contest

Ann Street School students Louis Fernandes, Andrew Valente and Luana Chociai won first place – Karina Barrios, a student at the Ironbound's Oliver Street School won first place among fifth to eighth grade students and Hawkins Street School student Arianna Alves won first place for first to fourth graders in the Ironbound Business Improvement District's (IBID) 12th annual Anti-Litter Art Contest. Barrios was supported in her contest entry by Principal

Douglas Petty and Art Teacher Rosalie Nascimento. Alves had the support of Principal Sandra C. Marques, Vice Principal Cristina DiTaranto and Teacher Filipa Silva.

The students accepted shining trophies on behalf of their schools that signify their success in drawing attention to the IBID's "Let's Work Together to Keep the Ironbound Clean" quality of life initiative. More than 50 entries were received from students at five Ironbound schools including Ann Street School, Ironbound Catholic Academy and Wilson Avenue School in addition to Hawkins and Oliver Street Schools.

Ann Street School & Oliver Street School named winners of 12th Annual anti-litter art contest.

All of the students who participated received commemorative certificates from the IBID. The contest was sponsored this year by Covanta Energy, the operator of the Essex County Resource Recovery Facility in Newark, Commercial District Services, the company that provides cleaning services to the IBID, and Councilman Augusto Amador.

The IBID is printing thousands of postcards featuring the artwork of the winning students plus information about the Ironbound District's trash pick-up and recycling schedules as well as rules and regulations regarding waste disposal. The postcards will be distributed through the Ironbound's schools, and to district business and commercial property owners, as well as other community members.

IBID Office Manager Leysly Roldan coordinated all details of the contest, working with the principals and art teachers from the Ironbound's schools regarding the contest rules and submissions and also supervised the judging by the IBID's Board of Directors. The IBID has printed 20,000 postcards featuring the artwork of the winning students plus information about the Ironbound District's trash pick-up and recycling schedules as well as rules and regulations regarding waste disposal. The postcards will be distributed through the Ironbound's schools, and to district business and commercial property owners, as well as other community members. IBID Office Manager Leysly Roldan coordinated all details of the contest, working with the principals and art teachers from the Ironbound's schools regarding the contest rules and submissions and also supervised the judging by the IBID's Board of Directors.

Summary

2014 was one of those pivotal years for Newark, a new Mayor was elected with a number of new Council people, a great sports event will be played that is important to our neighborhood (not the Superbowl, the Soccer World Cup), and a new hotel is being built in the Ironbound and another downtown. These are signs that we are moving ahead, and we have done so when we work together.

On May 14, AAA, the automobile club, chose the Ironbound as a key regional destination, and is holding an all-day open house at the Portuguese Sports Club on Prospect St. This means, we have succeeded in putting the Ironbound on the map as a reliable, family-oriented, and fun destination. Not many urban areas can say that. The fact is, our community specifically, and Newark as a whole, has a number of world class attractions at less than a third of the price of NYC. Our number one concern at the IBID is our customers and making sure we surpass their expectations. And, we do that not only with clean and safe teams, our outstanding marketing and advertising, our partnership with the City, and our pro-active planning, we do that with each every business in our community. You make people feel welcome and appreciated, and we thank you for that.

In 2014, we are working particularly closely with the Greater Newark Convention and Visitors Center, which has an office downtown, and a Transportation Assistance Portal, a kiosk, at Penn Station. A prominent feature of that (TAP) kiosk is the IBID's feature video of the Ironbound. If you haven't seen it, check it out. No one has a video that good and that well done about the Ironbound or Newark. Don't miss the fourth issue of the award winning Newark-Bound Magazine, which is coming out in June, and the fifth issue comes out in September/October. The IBID helped launch that magazine and today it is the most sought after publication about the Newark region available. And, the Ironbound is front and center.

An important part of Newark is the arts community. It is crucial to not only our business success, but the quality of our community. We have a vibrant, outstanding arts community and the Newark Arts Council and various arts galleries and studios are top notch. We have an opportunity to turn the Prospect Street Fire House into a Community Arts & Cultural Center with studio and office space, galleries, teaching, multimedia, dance and theatre space. This Center will take the entire community to bring to fruition. It is an big investment, but it has a big and real payoff. It is worth going for. Sumei Arts Center, Augusto Amador, and the IBID have led the way so far, but we will need a bigger coalition. The IBID will dedicate itself to this until we reach a satisfactory conclusion. It's all about managing the right partnerships, having a good plan, and sticking to it.

2015 will be a growing year for the City of Newark. We have a new Mayor that is working diligently with Newark's communities including the Ironbound. We also have a seasoned and capable Councilman, one of the elder statesman on City Council who reaches across political differences and forges working relationships. Make no mistake about it, this is key to our success. We cannot exist as an island in this City. Nor, can any other part of the City be an island. Prudently, the City budget was approved and began steps towards taking an honest and long-term approach to resolving Newark's fiscal issues. A foundation of responsibility, one that addresses everyday needs of safety, cleanliness, infrastructure improvement and planning is the cornerstone of success. We all must embrace, encourage and support each other in these tasks as partners. These are the standards that all business improvement districts are also built on. These are the standards of the IBID.

In the IBID, with the City, we have begun improving roads, water and the 100-year-old sewer system. Yes, it will cause some short-term inconvenience. But, it also will cause long-term capability that our vibrant community can build upon. In addition, the IBID continues to seek funds to improve sidewalks, rebuild parks and community areas, market our incredible cultural assets, and rebuild our streets. Of note, is the area at Penn Station, the first block into the Ferry Street business area. This is the number one area in the City where a multitude of different people and vehicles clash as they go to and from the station. Earlier this year, we formed a First Block Task Force, spearheaded by Dr. Omar Suarez, to address vandalism, vagrancy, drug abuse, pedestrian safety, and unsafe conditions. People were becoming discouraged and things were not getting better. With the Newark Police Department, we shifted police patrol, added surveillance, extended the downtown Metro police force to include that area, bring in police on horses and undercover agents, and we are working with Councilman Amador to lease Peter Francisco Park from the City, similar to what has happened in the downtown's Military Park, and rebuild it as a welcome center. Today, we are back on track and the area is much better.

We are also eagerly pursuing, with the Newark & Ironbound Arts Community (and particularly the Sumei Arts Center), the opportunity to own the Prospect Street Fire House and convert it into a Community Arts & Cultural Center housing the best in arts and culture. For two years, we have succeeded in converting one of the large garages at the Fire Station into an excellent arts space, poetry room, and gallery. We know the Arts are part of our business.

The IBID is known as an excellent partner in business, community and cultural development. This did not happen overnight and it took a solid and ongoing investment in our infrastructure. Today, we are the envy of many as a vibrant and exciting urban community. Our interest is to keep moving forward and work with all of Newark to exceed our visitors', workers', families' and customers' expectations.

INDEX

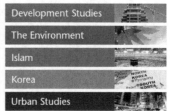